GREEK MYTHS
AND
CHRISTIAN MYSTERY

Dante, Homer and another Poet
From a Raphael drawing in the Windsor Royal Collection

GREEK MYTHS
AND
CHRISTIAN MYSTERY.

by

Hugo Rahner, S.J.

With a Foreword by
E. O. James, D.Litt., D.D., F.S.A.
*Professor Emeritus of the History of Religion
in the University of London*

HARPER & ROW, PUBLISHERS
NEW YORK AND EVANSTON

This *translation of* Griechische Mythen in christlicher Deutung
(Rhein–Verlag AG, Zurich, 1957) was made by

BRIAN BATTERSHAW

German text © Rhein-Verlag AG 1957

English translation © Burns & Oates Ltd 1963

PRINTED IN GREAT BRITAIN FOR
HARPER AND ROW, PUBLISHERS, INCORPORATED

FOREWORD

by

E. O. James, D.Litt., D.D., F.S.A.

Professor Emeritus of the History of Religion in the University of London
Chaplain of All Souls College, Oxford

The English translation of the essays collected in this volume, previously published in various journals, will be widely welcomed by those interested in the subject as they are not readily accessible to readers in this country. Throughout there is a unity of theme expounded and illuminated by a scholar whose great learning is matched by a penetrating and independent judgment, firmly grounded and rooted in Christian humanism. Taking his stand on Christ as the turning-point of civilization he seeks to show how Greek piety was sanctified by the Church, "God having spoken His revelation into the world by the Greek spirit and the Roman *imperium*, and the Church guarding this truth framed in the Greek speech of her sacred Book and in the inherited doctrine, which she has received from Latin Rome."

Since the lectures printed in the first part of the volume were delivered at Eranos congresses in Ascona under the hospitable roof of Frau Froebe-Kapteyn in her delightful home on Lake Maggiore, stress is laid on the Jungian interpretation of images in Greek mythology and the Hellenic mysteries brought into relation with the Patristic conception of the Christian mystery. The pagan cults representing the most profound expression of Greek piety are shown to have been the starting-point from which the psyche is led upwards to the heights of Christian illumination, the legacy of Greece continuing to live on within the Church.

The "mysticizing" of Hellenistic piety, it is pointed out, was by no means complete at the beginning of the new era. In the "mystery atmosphere" that then prevailed both continual birth and renewal of life were predominant, and it was the emotional rather than the dogmatic and intellectual element that characterized the cults.

v

This becomes particularly apparent in the symbolization of the processes of vegetation and their life-begetting qualities which were extended beyond the temporal order, carrying assurance of a blissful immortality. In the Christian mystery this acquired a new and unique significance in which the Cross occupied the central position in its cosmic aspects embracing the entire universe and giving expression to the fundamental laws that govern everything that happens in the world. In this context the biblical archetypes "remoulded by the artistry of folklore" are examined in great detail with illuminating results.

Set against this background, Holy Baptism, as the basic and consummating mystery of Christianity, and its liturgical imagery, are differentiated from the magical efficacy of the initiation rites in the Hellenic cults, resting as does the Christian sacrament upon the regenerative power of the death of Christ effecting a rebirth into eternal life. Similarly, in the review of the mystery of the sun and moon the dethronement of Helios and Lune by the transformation of the ancient symbolism in the liturgical year is made abundantly clear with a great wealth of learning.

In the two essays in the second part of the book, originally contributed to a collection in honour of Jung published in the *Eranos Jahrbuch*, the discussion is carried a stage further in an erudite investigation of the imagery of the soul-healing herb of Hermes, Moly, and its antetype the Mandragora or mandrake, the magic aphrodisiac plant. In the Christian symbolization and the bewildering medieval allegorization their magical properties are shown to have acquired a new significance in the therapy of souls. Applied to the human race and its spiritual problems, such were the ramifications of the lore surrounding these ancient charms, as is demonstrated by a searching examination of the complex data, that at length they emerged as sources of health freeing man from his entanglement with the sinister demonic powers, and eventually typifying the overthrow of Antichrist and the apocalyptic triumph of Christ as the head of the human race, freeing it from death and corruption.

The symbolism is brought to its ultimate conclusion in the third part in Homer's myth of the poplars and willows growing at the

gates of Hades on the borderline between death and life. As unfruitful trees throwing off their blossoms before the fruit appears,
willows readily became magic plants to prevent procreation and
so were regarded as emblems of sexual continence. Virginity in
this world being interpreted in Patristic imagery as fruitfulness
hereafter, chastity becomes a dying unto self and the attainment of
heavenly fruitfulness. This theme is followed in the concluding
essay by an examination of the voyage of Odysseus to his father's
home in Ithaca as a portrayal of the longing of the soul to return
to the port of eternity after the long and painful journey of life,
beset by the Sirens of sensuality and deadly knowledge, but safe in
the bark of the Church. Bound to its mast, typifying the wood of
the Cross with all its mystic power, the immortal seafarer at
length reaches harbour in the attainment of the Beatific Vision.

Within the limits of a short foreword it is impossible to describe
at all adequately the contents of a volume containing such a vast
quantity of complex material and its interpretation. Enough,
however, has been said to give some idea of its nature, scope and
purpose. It only remains to congratulate Fr Rahner and his translator on making accessible to English-speaking readers this remarkable compendium in a highly specialized field of knowledge
which cannot fail to be of particular interest and value for those
engaged in Hellenic and Patristic studies and of theological and
psychological symbolism. From the standpoint of the comparative
study of religion it constitutes an outstanding exposition and
vindication of the uniqueness of the Christian mystery fulfilling
all that was of most permanent value and significance in the piety
of Hellas.

CONTENTS

ix

ILLUSTRATIONS

PREFACE

This is, in some ways, a remote sort of book, for it speaks of the myths of the Hellenes and the mystery of Christianity. It leads us away from the busy streets of our day into the quiet temple grounds where Hellas and the Church encountered one another. All that it contains is apparently out-dated, antiquarian and distant, and every word in it is directed, to quote Pythagoras, to the few who learn along with us, not to the multitude who just listen: "Let but little be said; let the rest remain cloaked in secrecy."[1]

But for those who thus learn, let me hint at the nature of the call that drove me to the writing of this book. What is here contained is a gift to that living round-table, made up of men who believe that our Western civilization has broken down only in order that it may be born anew, to the *Eranos* of those who dimly perceive the truth, as did Plato in his immortal seventh letter, and can behold the kingdom of eternity through the ruins. These are the men who know the comforting law of the spirit, that the demon in man is only permitted to tear down so that the angel in man with faltering hand may trace out the sources of new life. Palaces only collapse so that treasures may be laid bare; idols begin to rock, but only so that altars may be freed upon which a purified spirit may sacrifice.

We have become Barbarians and wish once again to be Hellenes. Many are concerned for this our return, and whosoever feels a vocation to assist in this work can be certain of our reverent thanks, for what all seek is man, and all are filled by the belief that by deliberately harking back to the world of Greek antiquity, both at its upper and lower levels, either in the ether of Olympus or among the river reeds of the Cabiri, they will rediscover the whole man, the *homo humanus*. Can he ever be found this way?

At this point that spirit seeks to make itself heard which inspired

[1] Porphyry, *Vita Pythagorae*, 37.

xiii

the essays in this book; for he who stands tongue-tied before God must of necessity be bold before men. It is my aim to point a way towards that Christian humanism, towards the immense possibilities of that "new man" of whom St Paul wrote in Colossians[1] and in whom Greek and Barbarian are united in Christ, the God who became man, who is all in all.

Only he who knows by faith that there once was a man who is God has the valid yardstick for determining the true nature of man. Only such a one as this knows just why we cannot discover true man and what pertains to him, if we seek for man alone. It is only when we hold before our minds the fact that God himself became man that the painful experience of history becomes transparent in its meaning, it is only then that we understand that a mere monologue with itself, however beautiful and however sublime, can only cause the human spirit to wither. For man is the incarnate dialogue with God, the dialogue of which the first words are—and here is the original authority for every kind of humanism—: "Let us create man after our own image and likeness." In that moment man was given the power to answer God, but only in him who is both *anthropos* and Logos, for man can only address God in the manner in which God himself has spoken to him. All else is no more than a monologue with gods that are mere reflexions of himself. God hears only his own Word.

Yet the very fact that it is the flesh of the Logos become man that ultimately defines the limits of Christian humanism contains the possibility of almost explosively extending those limits to what is really a limitless degree. Now we may dare—indeed dare we must—to take up with an all-embracing gesture into this pattern of the Christian man whatever in the long perspectives of history or in the depths of the soul is true and noble in thought or deed. All that is good and true has proceeded from the Logos and has its homing-point in the incarnate God, even though this be hidden from us, even though human thought and human goodwill may not have perceived it. Every great and noble deed flows from a power which the revealing Logos has shown us to be his own special grace. Because it is aware of this, Christian humanism

[1] Col. 3. 11.

rises superior to all purely historical or psychological interest in the development of human ideals. For the humanist Christian there is only one possible attitude that he can take towards the world: he must love. Yet one can only love a person, and that is why the Christian humanist loves the human in every shape and form but only in him of whom St Paul says "*πάντα εἰς αὐτὸν ἔκτισται*– all things were created in him".[1] Here is the meaning of those words written by an ancient Christian, to the truth of which this book is a witness: "Christ is the Logos, in whom the whole human race has a portion, and all who have lived according to this Logos are Christians, even though, like Socrates and Heraclitus among the Greeks, they are accounted godless."[2]

This, however, leads us to a more exact definition of what I understand by Christian humanism. In Christ we stand at the turning-point of human civilization; God spoke his revelation into the world of the Greek spirit and the Roman *imperium*, and the Church guards this truth framed in the Greek speech of her sacred Book and in the inherited doctrine which she has received from Latin Rome. That is why the Church will continue to speak Greek even if, in a world that is dead to the things of the mind, Hellas descend into the abyss of utter oblivion, and why she will continue to pray in Latin, even if, some time in the future, the barbarian hordes shall forget the speech of Rome. To the very end of our human story there will always be good bread and noble wine, pure water and oil of olives for the sake of the Christian mystery. In like manner the heritage of Greece and Rome, now gathered back into the bosom of the Church, is ever ready to issue forth from thence in a new birth and in radiant youth.

The humanism of the Christian is therefore a love of God's own speech, and, in the contingencies of the history of civilization which prepared human speech for a revealing God, the Christian sees the finger of the spirit pointing towards Christ. The light that in the midst of human darkness blazed forth in Hellas was only borrowed sunlight, but Christ is the sun itself. And all that discourse of the finer spirits of Greece, all that talk, now whispered, now loud and eager, all that talk that argues such longing for the

---

[1] Col. 1. 16.   [2] Justin, *Apologia*, I, 46.

beautiful and the good, is no more than a wandering echo of a sound from out that mighty power of word and wisdom that rushes downward from the Logos. It is a μαντεία εὔστοχος,[1] a gift of inner sight directed towards the truth but incapable as yet of its clear perception. The Christian, however, standing as he does in the full light of the sun, can look backward with a love that has in it something nearly akin to penitence, and see how the lamps of antiquity seem almost like mirrors reflecting the first faint beams of the Sun of Righteousness that is to come. This then is the humanism of the Christian: it is to see Hellas in Christ, it is to make the Greek speech eternal by removing it from its historic particularity, to release it from the insignificance that marks it when measured by human history as a whole, by giving it a final dwelling-place in his dialogue with God; for even the most exquisite humanism would of necessity wither away, if, in a monologue, it only expressed itself on Hellenism *per se* or on the situations, arbitrarily identified with what is Greek, of some *pura humanitas* or other. The heritage of the Greek spirit only attains immortality when it is secure within the shrine of the Logos whose words are recorded in the tongue of Hellas.

It is in line with the above that this book should seek to show by a number of thoughtfully collated illustrations how Greek piety was sanctified by the Church. It is, of course, in no sense my intention to obliterate the distinction between mere human striving and the free giving by God. Yet still less is it my wish to suggest that there is an abyss between God and man over which there can never be a bridge. Hellas has returned home and we see that the dim light with which her lamps illumined the darkness was the light of the sun after all. It is as necessary today to make this plain to the lovers of humanism as it was when Hellas and Christianity first encountered each other. On the latter occasion Clement of Alexandria wrote certain words which have placed this book heavily in his debt:

"Pythagoras and his disciples, and also Plato, followed that inward vision of theirs which was aimed at the truth, and this they

---

[1] Clement of Alexandria, *Stromata*, V, 14, 116, 1.

did, not without the help of God; and so in certain things they
were in agreement with the words of the prophets. They searched
through truth in part and in whole and honoured it by the formulations of their thought which were in clear harmony with the
intelligible nature of things; for they had received an intimation
of that which is related to truth itself. Thus the Greek love of
wisdom is like unto a lamp whose wick has been lit by men 'skil-
fully borrowing light from the rays of the sun'.[1]

"Yet it was only when the Logos of God had been proclaimed
that the full holy light blazed forth. From this we see that the
borrowed light is useful in the night, but when it is day all flames
are outshone; for the night itself has been made day by the mighty
sun of spiritual light."[2]

This describes the attitude of mind evident in this book and
this is the sense in which it will, I hope, be understood. Let me now
say a few brief words concerning its different parts.

First as to outer form. The essays collected here are of varied
origin. Those gathered together in the first part are lectures given
at the Eranos congresses of 1943 and 1944 in Ascona. They appeared for the first time in the *Eranos Jahrbuch*, X and XI. In the
second part I reproduce two essays included in a collection in
honour of Jung (*Eranos Jahrbuch*, XII). In the third part I have
gathered together certain studies previously published in the *Zeitschrift für katholische Theologie*[3] and also included a considerably
enlarged version of a lecture given before the *Historisch-antiqua-
rische Gesellschaft* in Basle in 1941. I draw the reader's attention to
these things in advance to justify the preservation of the original
form in which the various parts of this book first appeared.

Nevertheless, the selection has been neither arbitrary nor for-
tuitous, and this makes it desirable for me to say something about
the internal form of the book which gives a unity to its different
parts. In its totality this work professes to be a kind of essay on

[1] Fragments of Attic Comic writers, III, p. 483, No. 395.

[2] *Stromata*, V, 5, 29, 4-6.

[3] "Die Weide als Symbol der Keuschheit in der Antike und in Christentum" (The
Willow as the Symbol of Chastity in Antiquity and in Christian Times), in *Zeitschrift für
katholische Theologie*, 56 (1932), pp. 231-53; "Odysseus am Mastbaum" (Odysseus at the
Mast), *ibid.*, 65 (1941), pp. 123-52.

ancient Christian psychagogy. Behind the concealing images of Greek mythology I seek to trace a way of ascent to the heights of Christian illumination. Hence the book's title *Greek Myths and Christian Mystery*. For all their wisdom, the Greeks could only express the goals towards which they were seeking to lead the soul in the form of myths. What they could not find words to convey was their intimation that a way existed. Only Christian interpretation would be bold enough to make its direction plainer and show that it led to Christ.

Those Church Fathers and theologians who still preserved a feeling for the power of classical imagery have here provided my source material. "The ancients taught their wisdom by means of suggestive symbolism," says Clement of Alexandria, "and I am thinking when I say this of Orpheus, of Linus, Musaeus, Homer and Hesiod and of all other such men as were possessors of wisdom. For the great multitude their poetic psychagogy was like a concealing curtain."[1] It was this veil that the Christian Greeks tore away. The myth was changed to a mystery.

It is thus the Greek mystery which is the starting-point from which the psyche is led upward to the heights of Christian illumination, and this heading has been superscribed over the first part of the book. Whatever may be said about the history and meaning of the Greek mysteries, they are the profoundest expression of piety, the most significant factor in the shaping of life that the yearning spirit of Greece produced. The myths on which the mysteries are founded, or which they developed from out themselves, may be as fanciful and bodiless as any before them; the thing that in the highest forms of the Greek mystery forced itself into the light can be recognized in the words of Plato's *Phaedrus*, which the Christian Clement interpreted anew as a prefiguring of that fulfilment which is given us in the Logos: " 'When the soul has become wholly solitary and has returned wholly to herself, then it is that she has attained the true wisdom that surpasses all human faculties, then, when longing carries her away as upon wings to heaven.' By this Plato means that the soul, when she has attained the goal of her hopes through love of wisdom, reaches the begin-

[1] *Stromata*, V, 4, 24, 1, 2.

ning of another life that is eternal."[1] For the Christian guidance of souls the mystery is as elsewhere the supporting foundation and the primal transforming element, and it was no mere chance that the ancient Fathers of the Church called their instructions in the Christian faith: *Mystagogic Catecheses*.

My immediate intention therefore in the first part of this book is to lay bare with all the sharpness and precision I can attain the true relation between the Greek mysteries and the Christian μυστήριον. Having taken that as my starting-point and having there attained firm ground, it will then be possible for me to show with what gay freedom of spirit the Greek Christian, in the forming and interpretation of his own mysteries, laid hands upon the treasures of the past so that he might lay them upon his own altar. All the lamps of Greece, so he boldly believed, burn for the sun which is Christ. I illustrate this in the case of the mystery of the cross, in that of baptism, and of the ecclesiastical year that circles with Helios and Selene. These are, of course, no more than a few sketches, however detailed their execution, for a comprehensive picture that shows forth the manner in which the legacy of Greece continued to live on within the Church.

Already at this stage, however, it should become apparent to what manner of thing I refer when I speak of Christian humanism, of that wonderfully bold and widely ranging gesture of the Hellenic Christian, that gesture whereby he fetches everything home to Christ, the spring of water and the stars, his sea and his swift ships, Homer and Plato and the mystical numbers of the Pythagoreans. All was but a preparation—and so all can serve to make meanings plain.

From the dark womb of the mysteries it now behoves us to ascend to the heights, undergoing the irksome and difficult process of maturing. The second part of my book will tell of this and I hope that the imagery of ancient myths will yet once again have significance for the Christian interpreter and give him the chance to observe how Hellenic intimations attained fullness and perfection in the psychagogy of the Church. I have given to this part of the book the title "The Healing of the Soul".

[1] *Phaedrus*, 249 CD; Clement, *Stromata*, V, 2, 14, 2.

The eighteenth century was guilty of a disastrous misunder-
standing of the nature of Greek piety when it projected its own
"enlightenment" into the Greek soul. Such *illuminati*, for whom
every kind of mysticism, everything that is dark and sinful, everything that expresses a yearning for redemption, is "an alien drop
in the Greek blood", are even today not wholly out of supply. Yet
if they were right how could we explain the hidden longing in
myth and mystery? How could we even grasp the secret meanings
behind the *Odyssey*? No, the Greek had rather more knowledge
than most concerning the powers of heaven and those of the abyss,
powers between which man felt himself to be wrestling with his
fate. Man for him was indeed the eternal Odysseus, who, after
doing battle with storms and monsters, journeys victorious
towards his home, in perils immense and continuous, yet sure of
a safe landfall because it is God who guides him. The Christian
sees this, the most psychological of all Greek intimations, with a
new clarity of vision, recalling what he has learned from the
Logos, of heaven and hell, of original sin and of redemption by
grace.

Of the myths which such intimation helped to form and which
attained full clarity of meaning in Christian antiquity, I have
chosen two: the Homeric myth of moly, the soul-healing plant,
which bright Hermes gave to Odysseus when he was in danger
from Circe of the dark cave; and those very ancient folk-tales of
the human root of the mandrake. From these myths we shall be
able to discern once again just what is meant by Christian humanism, that knowledge which was dimly apprehended by the Greeks
but which the Church made explicit, that our upward ascent, the
overcoming of the things of darkness, and the healing of the hidden wound in man, are only possible when we have faith and give
ourselves wholly to God, thus bursting asunder the suffocating
bond of our attempted self-redemption. Man only becomes
human in God. This is what constitutes the healing of his soul.

Finally, this ascent out of the darkness, this transformation of the
dark human root into light and fair flower is something that has
an ultimate clear aim. Odysseus must return home and the Christian strives towards heaven. This is the subject of the third part of

the book and completes the account of Greek and Christian psychagogy, which is the theme that gives its hidden unity to the
whole. Our guide towards these the ultimate heights of our ascent
will be Homer whom an ancient Christian once called "σοφώτατος
μάρτυρ – wisest of witnesses".[1] I have chosen "Holy Homer" as
the title of the third part of my book.

In the mysterious *nekyia* of the *Odyssey* in which the hero
journeys northward towards the entrance to the nether world,
there is a description of this landscape of the dead. There we learn
of the "fruit-destroying willow" which is the starting-point of a
whole great system of imagery concerning the next world. The
willow is the ancient symbol of chastity, of chastity that dies
unto itself; it is also the symbol of life that eternally begets itself.
This led Christian antiquity to a marvellous final elaboration of
the ideas involved. Now the willow puts on its leaves, no longer
upon the shores of the kingdom of the dead, but by the living
waters of eternal life, and with its chaste life-giving branches
adorns the perfected soul.

Or take that other image, also conceived by holy Homer:
Odysseus, the homeward-faring wanderer has successfully over-
come all perils, but only because he has been bound to the mast.
The Christian version of this has been given us by Clement:
"Bound to the wood of the cross, thou art freed from all danger
of destruction. God's Logos will steer thy ship and the Holy
Pneuma will give thee a safe return to heaven's harbour."[2]

Thus beginning and end are united. What began in the darkness
of mystery celebrations and led us upward during the painful process of spiritual healing, is perfected in the light of everlasting life.
In the Christian interpretation of Greek myths we can discern a task
for true humanism that is fair indeed. Has not the Church here
claimed the greatest heritage of Greece as her own, correcting its
errors in a fashion both firm and kindly, and has she not thus safeguarded eternal riches amidst the ruins of the temples—doing so
for us who, late born as we are, desire to be both Christians and
Greeks? The Church alone is in her own person an antiquity that

---

[1] Isidore of Pelusium, *Epistula*, II, 228 (PG, 78, 665 A).
[2] *Protrepticus*, XII, 118, 4.

still lives on with the full life of youth, an antiquity that will never be merely antiquarian. For she alone, through the light of the Logos, knows the measure of the heights and depths of the human soul. That is why she can discern the clear lineaments of truth which the Greeks could only faintly apprehend.

Friedrich Wolters once said of St Augustine: "A century before the Platonic Academy had been closed by Justinian, he had, in his *Civitas Dei*, salvaged all the treasures of the Greek spirit and safeguarded them till the time should come for a fairer birth. And so today we can find the way back across the bridges spanning the circling current, on our standards the flaming motto 'Hellas, ever our love'."[1] Let his master, Stefan George, have the final word and so give expression to what should be the highest meaning to be found, amongst other places, in the present book.

Aus diesen Trümmern hob die Kirche dann ihr Haupt,
die freien nackten Leiber hat sie streng gestaupt,
doch erbte sie die Prächte, die nur starrend schliefen
und übergab das Mass der Höhen und der Tiefen
dem Sinn, der beim Hosiannah über Wolken blieb
und dann zerknirscht sich an den Gräberplatten rieb.[2]

HUGO RAHNER

[1] *Lobgesänge und Psalmen* (Translations into German of Greek Catholic poets from the first to the fifth century), Berlin, 1923, Introduction, p. 20.

[2] *Siebenter Ring* (1st edition), p. 128. It is quite impossible to translate these lines without complete loss of all quality, but the meaning is roughly as follows:

From these ruins the Church then lifted her head. She sternly chastised the free naked bodies, but she inherited the splendours which slept with wide open eyes and to that sense which remained above the clouds with the Hosannas surrendered up the measure of the heights and depths, then, in utter contrition, flattened herself close to the gravestones—*Translator's note.*

Part One

MYSTERION

I

CHRISTIAN MYSTERIES
AND PAGAN MYSTERIES

"Come, I will show you the Word and the mysteries of the Word, and I will give you understanding of them by means of images familiar to you."[1]

THESE words are from the *Protrepticus* of Clement of Alexandria and I have placed them at the head of this section of my book because they concisely summarize what I have to say in it. As we all know, the term "mystery" was thoroughly familiar to the ancient world and its application to the Logos no doubt seemed natural enough. Certainly St Paul had no qualms about thus using the word. He speaks of "the mystery which hath been hidden from ages and generations, but is now manifested to his saints" (Col. 1. 26). For all that, however, we are confronted by a question. Is it really legitimate from a historical, let alone from a religious, point of view to compare the Christian mystery with the mystery cults that surrounded Christianity at the time of its emergence? And to what extent, if any, may we apply the verbal figures and general terminology of the Hellenistic mystery cults to the *mysterium* of Christianity?

Yet this immediately raises a second and related question. Did not—from the second to the fifth century at any rate—a broad stream of Greek piety force its way into the Church, transforming Christianity's pristine biblical simplicity into the mystic sacramental form that lives on in the worship of the Russo-Byzantine Churches and to a more limited extent in Latin Christianity? If so, may not an apparent affinity between Christianity and the cults have been rather more marked at the end of this period than at its beginning? These are problems with which religious historians have for half a century sought to come to terms, problems which

---

[1] *Protrepticus*, XII, 119, 1 (GCS, I, p. 84, ll. 6f.).

3

they have studied with impassioned dedication; yet even now there is no end to the process of question and answer. In the circumstances I cannot make a better beginning than by giving you a sketch of the present state of enquiry in this particular field. I am still admittedly dealing with what are largely matters of theory. Yet such a review will at least assist us to attain our purpose, which is to ascertain in a spirit of detached and objective enquiry where lie the boundary-lines between the Christian mystery and the mysteries of the ancient world, and where their points of contact. We can then examine in somewhat greater detail, yet always adhering to this method of strictly objective enquiry, two aspects of the Christian mystery—the mystery of the cross and the mystery of baptism, two things which show very clearly indeed both the differences between the two entities under comparison and their reciprocal influence upon each other. Yet we must remember that although we carry out this enquiry—as it is proper that we should—in a strictly scientific spirit, there will come a point when we know we are treading on holy ground. Then our feelings will surely be very like those expressed by that great Christian Greek, Gregory of Nazianzus, in his glorious homily on the feast of Lights,[1] the sermon in which, after letting the confused pomp of the pagan mysteries pass before his hearers' minds, he began to discourse on the mystery of the Christians "with trembling tongue and with quaking of heart and spirit, as is my wont whenever I speak of God".

The importance of the Hellenistic mysteries by which emergent Christianity was surrounded cannot be exaggerated. One writer calls them "the principal factor in the spiritual life of the ancient world",[2] another, "the last word of the pagan religions",[3] and such expressions are surely not too strong. It is therefore not surprising that in the modern age, already keenly interested in all that concerns the history of religion and religious origins, a com-

---

[1] *Oratio* 39, 11 (PG, 36, 345 C).

[2] G. Lafaye, *Histoire du culte des divinités d'Alexandrie*, Paris, 1884, p. 108.

[3] P. Bratke, "Die Stellung des Clemens Alexandrinus zum antiken Mysterienwesen" (The Attitude of Clement of Alexandria towards the Ancient Mysteries), *Theologische Studien und Kritiken*, 1887, p. 654.

parison between the mystery cults and Christianity should have repeatedly been attempted.

Actually, of course, a vast quantity of religious sentiment and religious ideas is grouped together under the term "mystery". From the pristine ethnological beginnings of the mother-goddess cults that preceded the classical age, to the sublime spirituality to be found in the Hermetic literary mysteries and in Plotinus: from thence to the Islamic and Eastern Christian mystery of prayer: from the Cabiri to the Ka'ba: from the morass of Shaktism and the Barbelo-Gnostics—what a panorama it is! And how some of these things make us shudder! For fundamentally we are still Greeks at heart—to the august, rarefied dignity of the nocturnal mysteries of Eleusis. What a world of contrasts, what a monstrous mixture of moon-motherly darkness and of that clarity of perception and thought that belongs to the sunlight! And all expressed by that one word "mystery".

This alone should make us cautious and hesitant when we ourselves attempt a comparison between the things we lump together as mystery cults on the one hand and, on the other, that Christianity of Graeco-Roman times which blossomed forth from out this jumbled world. Indeed, like all living things, Christianity has its own variegated history of development.

The first thing I have to do then is to give you a very brief history of the findings of scholarship in this department, but I must again stress that this whole business of comparison is a task of immense difficulty, a task so arduous that something like downright rashness might well be imputed to anyone that attempts it, so vast are the problems that arise when we seek to find a common denominator of thought—let alone a genetic connexion—between the two entities in question.

Next I will seek to demonstrate the highly differentiated character of each of the two subjects of this comparison; this will make it easier to show in which of their varied stages of historical development they can be shown, on the evidence of specific and quotable source material, to have been in contact with one another. It is only then that—assuming that our historical instinct is reasonably good—we shall be able to say what are the essential points of difference between the Christian religion and the ancient mystery cults and where there has been reciprocal influence between the two.

I

When we survey the eventful story of these attempts to compare the mysteries of antiquity with the ancient Church, one thing becomes obvious: it was precisely this urge to make comparisons that moved scholars to subject these cults to new and intensive research; for the mystery cults of later antiquity were a territory that had remained buried and forgotten so far as the Middle Ages and even so far as the humanists were concerned. Indeed the first work that can claim to have attempted a really serious study of the Greek mystery religions is the *Exercitationes de Rebus Sacris* of Isaac Casaubon.

Unfortunately the chief purpose of this book, which was written by a Calvinist and published in Geneva in 1655, seems to have been to represent the sacramental system of the Catholic Church as the genetic product of the ancient mysteries, or at least of their general influence, and when Christian Lobeck's famous *Aglaophamus* finally put the peculiar Greek enthusiasms of the eighteenth century out of court—enthusiasms based not so much on archaeological fact as on that century's own rather shallow philosophy of enlightenment—the new emphasis on the mysteries once more caused numbers of writers to discern in them the *fons et origo* of essential parts of the Catholic faith.

In one way or another a great deal of nonsense was undoubtedly talked, so much so that there was a reaction, and classical philologists, guided by an instinct that may not have been altogether unsound—though it certainly tended once more to distort the picture—revolted against this new type of scholarship—and pseudo-scholarship—which seemed to have the mysteries on the brain, and disdained all further acquaintance with this subject. The most celebrated among the victims of this new state of affairs was Bachofen who certainly deserved a better fate. Unfortunately, to Bachofen's critics not only the mysteries but any kind of mysticism or metaphysics appears to have been profoundly distasteful.

They held that any emphasis on such matters—so Bachofen himself relates—"completely misconceives the classical way of looking at things with its peculiar freshness and light, qualities that sometimes persisted even at the graveside of friends".[1]

It was left to our own century to lay a foundation of really solid research into these matters, and here one thinks immediately of such names as Cumont, Hepding, Frazer, Wilamowitz, Kern, though the choice here is only made at random from among the most important. Simultaneously with this, however, there occurred another development: there came into being the science of comparative religion, whose practitioners with a truly astonishing zeal set themselves to the tracking down of all the discoverable relationships between the Christian and pagan mysteries. In this way, it was hoped, the precise nature of the contribution made by the mystery cults to the genesis of Christianity, or at any rate to the form of its ultimate development, could be finally discovered. Here too the first fine frenzies of enthusiasm were gradually followed by sober research and we can in fact conveniently distinguish three groups of scholars who, one after another, have concerned themselves with this business of comparison, the last group being still engaged upon the matter today.

The representatives of the first of these groups claimed to have proved the existence of an actual relation of dependence between the mystery cults and emergent Christianity, and there was particular reference here to the theology of Paul. From the very beginning of this trend the element common to both the respective entities was felt to be the concept of "rebirth". Usener was the doyen of this school in which Dieterich and Reitzenstein attained particular pre-eminence. The latter's great work, *Die hellenistischen Mysterien nach ihren Grundgedanken und Wirkungen* (The Hellenistic Mysteries in the Light of their Basic Ideas and Influence) in 1910, came to be widely regarded as the most authoritative work in this field. At first it was Reitzenstein's belief that he had found the original source material of Christian doctrine in the so-called Iranian redemption mystery, then somewhat later in the

---

[1] J. J. Bachofen, *Die Unsterblichkeitslehre der orphischen Theologie* (The Doctrine of Immortality in Orphic Theology), Basle, 1867, p. 47.

supposedly pre-Christian cult of the Mandaeans.[1] Since then serious scholarship has passed its sober and, in the main, annihilating judgement on both theories.

Even before we had settled the business of the Iranian and Mandaean theories, however, Clemen was already expressing reasoned doubts in a book which is still worth reading, namely his *Der Einfluss der Mysterienreligionen auf das älteste Christentum* (The Influence of the Mystery Religions on the Oldest Forms of Christianity). In it he pronounces a verdict which is not rendered less just by its severity. Incidentally he demolished in a single sentence one of the weakest points in the enemy's position. "To assume without proof", he says, "that almost all the mysteries were already in existence in the first Christian century is scientifically dishonest." That was in 1913.

Then yet another discovery was made: it was the concept of the "imitation of the cult hero"—and this seemed to offer even more promising possibilities. All the mystery cults of later antiquity, it was argued, had one feature in common. In their mystical and liturgical action they sought to imitate the dying and rising cult god and so partake in the power he could effectively exercise in the next world, and this was also the fundamental character of the Christian doctrine of sacrament and redemption.

Bousset became the leading authority of this school of thought thanks to his *Kyrios Christos*.[2] Cautious and thoughtful as are his various deductions, it still remains a fact that Bousset saw in the cultic imitation of the dying and rising god that is common to all the mysteries, the "spiritual atmosphere that surrounds Paul's dying and rising with Christ". But this, he maintains, is something other than mere crude appropriation; it is more in the nature of an unconscious surrender to a very powerful and basic form of religious thinking that was common to antiquity as a whole. Anyone wishing to understand how deep and wide was the influence of Bousset's conception should also read Leipoldt's otherwise most erudite book *Sterbende und auferstehende Götter* (Dying and Rising Gods).[3]

[1] R. Reitzenstein, *Das iranische Erlösungsmysterium* (The Iranian Redemption Mystery), Leipzig, 1921; *Die Vorgeschichte der christlichen Taufe* (The Prehistory of Christian Baptism), Leipzig-Berlin, 1929.   [2] (2nd edition), Göttingen, 1921.   [3] Leipzig, 1923.

Most radical of all, however, is Loisy in his excellently written book *Les Mystères païens et le mystère chrétien*.[1] For Loisy the essence both of the Greek mysteries and of Christianity (as shaped by St Paul) is the cultic and liturgical solemnization of the death and resurrection of the cult hero; *mythe et rite* correspond to each other. The "myth" of Christianity is the great drama of world redemption through Christ, which Paul, under the influence of the god-man myths of his time, read into the simple Gospel story of Jesus. The "rite" of Christianity, however, is the smaller drama of the mystical initiation of the individual.[2] "Paul's conviction of the rebirth of the Christian through baptism and faith", he writes, "contains neither more nor fewer contradictions than that of the initiates in Eleusis for whom the pledge of their blessed immortality was their participation in the fear and joy of Demeter, no more and no fewer contradictions than that of Lucius who received a similar reassurance from taking part in the death, burial and resurrection of Osiris; no more and no fewer than that of the devotees of Cybele whose faith brought about their eternal rebirth through the bloody *taurobolium* which united them with the dead and resurrected god."

More cautious in matters of detail, though the author's basic position is identical with the above, are the arguments of Angus in his *The Mystery-Religions and Christianity*.[3] Even today the possibility, nay the supposedly proven certainty that ancient Christianity is no more than a genetic derivative of the mystery cults is for many scholars the basic assumption from which their research into matters of detail proceeds.

Here and there, however, we can already see the beginnings of a more exact understanding of the problem, and there can no longer be any doubt of the result if this trend continues. Theories which postulate a genetic relationship or one of historical causality between the Hellenistic mystery cults and the essentials of Christian belief can no longer be taken seriously. One has only to read such a writer as Clemen on the results of his researches; and

---

[1] Paris, 1930.
[2] I am following the excellent summary in K. Prümm's, *Der christliche Glaube und die altheidnische Welt* (The Christian Faith and the World of Ancient Paganism), Leipzig, 1935, II, p. 472.   [3] (3rd edition), London, 1928.

rather more recently a number of works by Prümm have shown the utter invalidity of all attempts to explain Christianity in terms of a certain conventional type of the history of religion.[1] All this, of course, in no way detracts from the value of much of the research on points of detail, undertaken by scholars of all shades of opinion, by which our knowledge of the mystery cults has undoubtedly been increased.

I can only give a general indication of the nature of the second group. A more detailed account of its ideas—and the attitude of qualified rejection which is often assumed towards them—belong rather to the inner realm of Catholic theology. The reference is here to the so-called "Mystery Doctrine" (*Mysterienlehre*), which under the leadership of Dom Odo Casel owes its development primarily to the monks of Maria Laach.[2] Distinguished by a great wealth of historical learning, it unequivocally rejects all the above-mentioned theories of genetic derivation, yet it does see a kind of common ground in the "cult *eidos*" of the mystery which served as a kind of imperfect and shadowy prefiguration of the reality which was brought by God to its final fulfilment in the mystery of Christ. This *eidos*, in which—it is hoped—both terms are embraced, in a single perspective and compared in truth, is the "cultic presence of the redemptive act" constantly renewed in mystery. Each time the mystic rite is accomplished, the redeeming action of God dead and risen again is ever effectively renewed for the worshipping community, independently of any considerations of time and space. G. Söhngen in his book *Symbol und*

---

[1] See p. 9, note 2 for the main two-volume work. To this I should add *Das Christentum als Neuheitserlebnis: Durchblick durch die christlich-antike Begegnung* (Christianity as a New Experience. A Review of the Encounter between Christianity and Antiquity), Freiburg, 1939. I should also mention a third work: *Das antike Heidentum nach seinen Grundströmungen* (The Basic Tendencies of Ancient Paganism), Munich, 1942. Comparable with this are B. Heigl, *Mysterienreligionen und Urchristentum* (Mystery Religions and Primitive Christianity), Münster, 1932, and what is even today a most illuminating work by G. Anrich, *Das antike Mysterienwesen in seinem Einfluss auf das Christentum* (The Ancient Mystery Cults and their Influence on Christianity), Göttingen, 1894.

[2] The principal work to which reference can be made—among a host of others—is *Das christliche Kultmysterium* (The Christian Cult Mystery) (2nd edition), Regensburg, 1935. Also "Antike und christliche Mysterien" (The Mysteries of Antiquity and Christianity) in *Bayrische Blätter für das Gymnasialschulwesen*, 53 (1927), p. 329. See also "Mysterium" in *Gesammelte Arbeiten Laacher Mönche*, Münster, 1926.

Wirklichkeit im Kultmysterium (Bonn, 1937) has made an attempt at elucidating the theological problems arising from this view of things.

It is impossible here to enter into a detailed discussion as to how far such a theory will prove valid in regard to the later sacramental developments of the Christian mystery—say those of the fourth and fifth centuries. So far as Christianity at the time of its origin and the Pauline mystery theology are concerned, the latest findings of etymology in regard to the word μυστήριον[1] and the mental images which it served to evoke, make its ultimate rejection rather probable, though the debate is still proceeding.

This brings me to the third school of thought. Methodologically speaking its work is unimpeachable. It draws a much sharper line of division than the other two groups between the development, on the one hand, of the fundamental Christian attitudes which we find in St Paul and the earliest Christian writers and, on the other, the stand taken by the later and fully developed Christian Church in regard to the mystery cults of late antiquity. These last—as the followers of this school have clearly grasped—had also begun to attain their final and fully developed form at a later date —to be exact, from the second century A.D. onward.

These scholars further distinguish—and that very sharply—between genetic derivation and the kind of relationship that arises when a process of assimilation and adaptation has set in—particularly when that process is set in motion for a specific tactical purpose. When St Paul and even the Church Fathers of the third and fourth centuries who further developed the Christian liturgy, took over words, images and gestures from the world of the mystery religions, they did so not as seekers after treasure but as possessors thereof; they did not value these things for their own sake

---

[1] The latest and most detailed survey of the meaning of the word μυστήριον in paganism, in the New Testament and in early Christian times is to be found in G. Kittel's *Theologisches Wörterbuch zum Neuen Testament* (Theological Dictionary of the New Testament), IV, Stuttgart, 1942, pp. 809-34. The work has been revised by Bornkamm. See also E. Marsh, "The Use of Μυστήριον in the Writings of Clement of Alexandria", *Journal of Theological Studies*, 37 (1936), pp. 64-80; also Prümm, "Mysterion von Paulus bis Origenes" (The Mysterium from Paul to Origen), *Zeitschrift für katholische Theologie*, 61 (1937), pp. 391-425, and J. De Ghellinck, *Pour l'histoire du mot* sacramentum, Louvain, 1924.

but merely because they furnished material for the fashioning of a garment that would put the stranger at his ease. Clement of Alexandria, in the words which I have set at the head of this chapter, shows us the process at work: "I will give you understanding of the mysteries of the Logos by means of images with which you are familiar."

Thanks to their grasp of these things, this third group of scholars can estimate the real character of both the entities under comparison with a far greater degree of accuracy. It avoids the danger of merely levelling down Christianity in order to show it as the genetic, or at any rate the phenomenological product of the mystery cults, but it also keeps clear of the danger, which is all too often a very real one, of tacitly christianizing the mystery cults themselves. This last was something of which even the Church Fathers at times were guilty. Their aim being to stress the extent of the "devilish" borrowings of the mystery cults from Christianity, and to hold this up as an example of their iniquity, it was natural enough for them to represent the cults as rather more Christian than they actually were. In even more numerous instances modern scholars have committed the same offence; all too often in their works, the picture of these cults is—as Prümm says—"painted in Christian colours".[1]

The confusion inherent in this concept of genetic derivation was denounced by none other than Harnack, and this in no uncertain terms. We must seek to prevail, he insists, against

"this comparative mythology which endeavours to connect everything causally with everything else, which tears down solid fences, playfully bridges separating chasms and spins combinations out of superficial similarities. In this way [he continues], it is possible in the twinkling of an eye to turn Christ into a sun god and the twelve Apostles into the twelve months of the calendar, to recall, when thinking of the nativity, all the other stories of divine births, to let the dove of Jesus' baptism set us chasing all the other doves of mythology, to join all other famous asses to the ass on which Jesus entered Jerusalem and so with the magic wand of

[1] Prümm, *Das antike Heidentum*, p. 308.

'comparative religion' to eliminate every original and spontaneous feature that a story may contain."[1]

It would indeed appear that a new and most felicitous discretion can today be observed among scholars, and, thanks to this, it is the differences between the two forms of religion that tend to be stressed rather than their superficial similarities—a circumstance that, so far from obscuring the nature of their very real interdependence, actually makes it a great deal easier to discern. Fr J. Dölger and his circle are among those particularly distinguished by this growing habit of conscientious discrimination with all the painstaking study of detail that it involves. Prümm deserves special mention in this latter respect; his collation of all the material scattered about in various learned publications has been invaluable. The results of his industry are to be found in his *Das antike Heidentum nach seinen Grundströmungen: Ein Handbuch zur biblischen und altchristlichen Umweltkunde* (Ancient Paganism and its Fundamental Tendencies: A Handbook for the Study of Biblical and Ancient Christian Environment).

Actually, thanks to the prevailing reaction against the liberal-historical school with its blurring of identities, there is today a tendency to overshoot the mark, and many are positively denying the existence of any possibility of comparison between the two entities concerned. Fortunately our "third group" does not go to such extremes. On the contrary, they are ready enough to make comparisons, since they are quite prepared to admit similarities. Indeed, though they draw the lines that mark essential differences sharply enough, they do not hesitate to declare that in certain unessential matters Christianity and the cults may quite possibly have exercised a reciprocal influence on each other—and that in certain instances such influence is nothing less than a matter of historical fact.

Nor is that difficult to believe. The Church was not fashioned in a vacuum; it is the continuation of God's becoming man; it must therefore turn to man with the revelation that Christ entrusted to it—and that means that, at the time, it had to turn to the

---

[1] From *Wissenschaft und Leben* (Science and Life), II, Giessen, 1911, p. 191.

men of the Graeco-Roman world with their distinctive speech and culture. These were the media through which it had to work, the flesh in which its spirit had to be clothed; for the history of the Church is essentially the putting on of a body by the Word of revelation. The soul inhabiting that body—we call it the Church —is from heaven, but the blood thereof is Greek and its speech the speech of Rome. Is it surprising that these things should have left their characteristic marks?

Yet if the fusion was to be complete, if certain secondary assumptions, conventions and images were to be painlessly absorbed, and if, in this way, Christianity was in some slight measure influenced by the cults—though the essentially disparate nature of the two things must never for a moment be minimized—then there must have been certain special points of contact, a certain common ground of inward and outward experience. In point of fact it is possible to discern such common ground at three distinct levels.

First, to approach the problem from below, if I may so express myself. The Christian revelation is directed at man, at a being, that is to say, consisting of soul and body which can only express the truths of the other world by means of the sense-bound media of word, gesture and image, and which must for that very reason use symbols in the domain of religion rather more than anywhere else. Such symbols are not an artefact of the human mind but are indeed something anterior to any agency of the latter. They are, therefore, in their basic forms, operative in every religion and their use must be reckoned as part of the archetypal pattern of man's search after God.

This shows, incidentally, that there are good theological grounds for asserting that Jung's work is not, as has occasionally been supposed, a mere throw-back to the old liberal theory of religious origins with its thoroughly unscientific habit of explaining one thing in terms of another, but penetrates to a much deeper stratum of the human personality, a territory that is common ground to all religious experience, the mysterious world of primitive human archetypes. Catholic theology would here speak of our common human nature which is directed towards God. It would declare that it is this "religiosity"—which always expresses itself in the same basic forms—that renders this human nature accessible to a possible revelation by the speaking God, for God must needs speak in "human" terms if he is to be understood by man. Though, therefore, the evidence for their existence is in many cases debatable, the attempted identification of these archetypes and their use in other religions besides the Christian, does not imply that nature and revelation are thereby being reduced to a common level—or, for that matter, that a vague and purely human religious emotion is being identified with supernatural faith.

Secondly, there is the possibility—referred to in my introductory remarks—of contact in what may be termed the middle region, in the area, that is to say, of purely historical influence, and this is something which we shall have to discuss later in considerable detail. We shall see, however, in so far as we have grasped the character of the Christian revelation beyond any possibility of confusion, that the scholars of the third group are undoubtedly right and that this kind of borrowing has only occurred in matters of quite secondary importance.

Thirdly and finally, Catholic theologians in their study of the religious development of mankind, have never lost sight of the fact that there is also a contact directed from above: a divinely fashioned plan is discernible in human religious evolution, especially among the peoples of later antiquity. The story of that evolution is not merely one of crisis in the sense of the Epistle to the Romans, it is also the story of a pedagogy towards Christ. "Nevertheless God left not himself without testimony," says that same Paul (Acts 14. 16). The ancient mystery cults are the altar bearing the inscription: "To the Unknown God".

2

If we are to examine in greater detail the various phases of the relationship between Christianity and the mystery cults—and in telling that story I shall, as I have already indicated, largely enlist the aid of the third of the aforementioned groups and base myself on their general lines of thought—, then a comprehensive review of the nature and history of the mystery cults themselves is indispensable; for it is only by keeping before our mind the richly variegated character of this phenomenon that we can compare it with the equally sharply defined phenomenon of Christianity. Though their basic character remains unchanged throughout the ages, the "mysteries" are something quite different in the early days of Eleusis and the Cabiri, and again something quite different in the third century A.D.

It is the same with Christianity—despite the divine and continuing uniformity of its basic pattern. The Christianity of the apostolic age with its simple baptismal rites is one thing, that of the Pseudo-Areopagite's day, with all its gorgeous ceremonial, is quite another. Yet the light-hearted neglect of all such differences was the very hallmark of all this comparative-religion-mongering. With the inspired dexterity of a juggler, pieces of evidence, separated by centuries in date, were collated and compared, while the same happy synthesis was effected between phenomena belonging to the most exalted and most depraved manifestations of religious experience.

Our first enquiry, therefore, will be concerned with the historic development of the mystery cults. This will help us to fix more accurately the precise point of time in the latter's evolution when they impinged on Christianity.

The ethnologists who have played so important a part in this department of knowledge,[1] have shown us that these cults which rose up in Greece like some emanation out of the depths and gained an ever-increasing hold over men, were originally a legacy from that "world in which the Greeks set foot"—the phrase is Kern's[2]—, they were in fact an afterbirth of the pre-Aryan

[1] Cf. especially E. de Jong, *Das antike Mysterienwesen in religionsgeschichtlicher, ethnologischer and psychologischer Beleuchtung* (The Mysteries of Antiquity in the Light of Ethnology, of the History of Religion and of Psychology) (2nd edition), Leiden, 1919; K. Prümm, "Materialnachweise zur völkerkundlichen Beleuchtung des antiken Mysterienwesens" (Source Material Relating to the Ethnological Aspects of the Mystery Cults), *Anthropos*, 28 (1933), pp. 759ff., and *Das antike Heidentum*, p. 219.

[2] F. Kern, "Die Welt worein die Griechen traten" (The World in which the Greeks set foot), *Anthropos*, 24 (1929), pp. 167–219, 25 (1930), pp. 195ff., pp. 793ff.; M. P. Nilsson, *The Minoan-Mycenean Religion and its Survival in Greek Religion*, Lund-Oxford, 1927; K. Prümm, "Neue Wege einer Ursprungsdeutung antiker Mysterien" (New Approaches to the Interpretation of the Origin of the Ancient Mysteries), *Zeitschrift für katholische Theologie*, 57 (1933), pp. 89ff., pp. 254ff., and K. Prümm, "An Quellen griechiscnen Glaubens", *Biblica*, 11 (1930), pp. 266ff.

mother-goddess cults, illuminated, it is true, by the Greek spirit but having still about them a quality of pre-Hellenic darkness.

We can best assess their unique and almost anomalous quality as historical phenomena by contrasting them with the spirit of Homer and with that poet's essentially Ionic preoccupation with the things of the present world. This last was a spirit that did not easily succumb. Even as late as the fifth century the religion which it informed was to produce the Apollonian brilliance of Greek sculpture, yet it was never able to overcome the "Orphic fears" that filled the souls of pious men with dark unease, for, as Prümm has said, "the fair fashioning of the gods of death does not resolve their riddle or make them weigh more lightly upon men",[1] and the more the acids of Attic comedy, and later the rationalism of the Stoa, dissolved the traditional beliefs in gods and goddesses, the greater the disquiet that led the Greek increasingly to seek refuge in the eerie realm of the cults. The temperature of piety began to rise—indeed piety became overheated, and to express these new feelings man began to reach back to supposedly ancient things, to Orpheus and Pythagoras. Latte describes the change in religious feeling that took place between classical and Hellenistic times in these words: "A new vital rhythm, a clamorous enhancement of the ego, replaced that self-effacement in thought and word that till then had been accounted the distinguishing mark of a civilized human being. What man now seeks among the gods is the bizarre, the note of over-charged pathos, as against the Olympian calm of classical times."[2]

Meanwhile the boundary-walls of the Greek spirit, breached since Alexander's day, were falling into ruin, and across them flooded the un-Greek mystery cults of the East. Even the black fetish stone of the *Magna Mater* travels from Pessinus to Rome: it is followed by the mild Isis of the Ptolemies, and everywhere pious women bewail the dead Adonis. Thoughtful Greece and sober Republican Rome seek to guard against the thing, but in vain; for all these foreign cults—though we should not always lightly

[1] K. Prümm, *Das antike Heidentum*, p. 300, n.1. Cf. U. von Wilamowitz, *Der Glaube der Hellenen* (The Religion of the Greeks), II, Berlin, 1932, p. 260.

[2] K. Latte, "Religiöse Strömungen in der Frühzeit des Hellenismus" (Religious Tendencies in the Early Age of Hellenism), *Die Antike*, 1 (1925), pp. 153 ff.

equate them with the actual mystery cults themselves—give better expression to the religious needs of men than the official cult of the national gods. Cumont is certainly right when he says: "Even though the triumph of the Oriental cults sometimes creates the impression of a reawakening of aboriginal barbarism, they nevertheless represent a more advanced type of piety than that of the national religion. They are less primitive, less simple and better equipped with organs than the old Graeco-Italic idolatry."[1]

It is, however, a fact which we can accept as a datum of our problem—since it is being substantiated by a cumulative volume of evidence—that this "mysticizing" of Hellenistic piety was by no means complete at the beginning of the Christian era; indeed by that time the process could not really be considered to have got going at all. What in fact we find prevailing in the first century is something that I should like to call a "mystery atmosphere". The expression may not be exactly felicitous but it does describe the facts. One has only to think of the various systems of philosophy branching out from Posidonius, which all tend to be in the nature of substitutes for religion.

The wares on offer at this time were nothing if not varied. They promised comfort for this world and reassurance regarding the next; there were theosophy, Pythagorean mumbo-jumbo and the *Somnium Scipionis*. As against this, actual initiation into the mysteries seems to have been pretty well confined to certain areas and indeed to certain special places with which the cult was particularly associated.

It is only from the second century A.D. onwards that we can observe a change. Then, as philosophy condenses into a rather nebulous henotheism with a Neoplatonic colouring, pious sentiment begins to gravitate around a kind of solar pantheism, at the heart of which lay the belief in the soul's ascent by lunar paths to a blessed other world. This last is now no longer conceived under the form of a subterranean Hades, but as an astral-heavenly beyond.

Given this state of mind, it was natural that men should seek to

---

[1] F. Cumont, *Die orientalischen Religionen im römischen Heidentum* (Oriental Religions in Roman Paganism) (3rd edition), Berlin-Leipzig, 1931, p. 24.

remould the content of the varied, but still unassuming, forms of
the mystery cults. This movement affected not only the cory-
bantic frenzy of the Eastern types in an effort to ennoble their un-
Greek savagery with theosophical symbolism, but also the sober
Eleusinian rites. They were in fact searching for what Cicero
sought and described in a famous saying: "In these sacred offices
we become aware of the very basis of life and learn not only to
live happily, but to die with greater hope."[1]

Although, however, their popularity grew till it embraced the
whole Empire, closer study shows quite clearly that the individual
cults were gradually melted away into something different and
lost their original character; astonishing mongrel formations appeared catering for the most varied appetites and proclivities,
and anyone could now have a taste of the mystery dish, or at any
rate take a nibble at it.

There now came into being what Festugière has aptly termed
the "literary mysteries";[2] classical examples of this are to be found
in the collections of Hermetic writings, in the so-called "Mithras
Liturgy" as reconstructed by Dieterich or in the *Royal Road* of
Philo.[3] This, then, is the form which the system of mystery cults
of late antiquity had assumed in the third century and which it
did not assume till then; this is the picture which we can reconstruct from a mass of evidence dating from that period—and
not from any earlier one—and deriving from both Christian
and pagan accounts: and anyone undertaking the delicate
task of separating the original core of primitive ancient and
native mysteries embedded in this world-wide system of cults,
must never be misled by the kind of literary descriptions left us
by a number of writers, ranging from Plutarch right down to
Iamblichus.

We must, however, examine this phenomenon of the later
mystery cults in rather greater detail, since the Christianity of
that day had to live alongside, interact and argue with it. Let me

---

[1] *De Legibus*, II, 14, 36.

[2] A. J. Festugière, *L'idéal religieux des Grecs et l'Evangile*, Paris, 1932. Excursus on the
"Philosophical Mysteries".

[3] J. Pascher, *Der Königsweg zur Wiedergeburt und Vergottung bei Philon von Alexandreia*
(The Royal Way to Rebirth and Deification in Philo of Alexandria), Paderborn, 1931.

therefore try to trace the basic pattern that underlies the whole wide range of its various manifestations.

One feature has continued to mark the mysteries from the very earliest times: they are all cults of a "mother-religion" of which the divine woman and her male consort are the centre.[1] Old agricultural custom gradually built up into a cult legend and this in its turn into rites, the performance of which enabled the initiate to partake of the powers of the god concerned. These mysteries start off essentially as vegetation and fertility cults, the Great Mother being the embodiment of the powers of nature, the powers of continual birth and renewal.

Now, the special quality, the "mystical" element in these mysteries lies in one special thing. It lies in that something which these devotees of the mysteries see behind and beyond the visible phenomena of nature, behind the growth, begetting and withering away. The "symbol" of natural processes was for them only half of the σύμβολον; the other half, which fitted the first, reaches out beyond death into the next world. It is quite clear that at a very early stage certain dim hopes of an after-life came to be attached to these vegetation cults; the gods of growth were generally also the gods of the dead. Thus the ancient mystery, once the Greek spirit had purified it, really centred on the riddle of life itself.

As I point out later, it would be quite wrong to associate the mysteries, at any rate in their early form, with any clear intellectual belief, and even the hope of a life after death, such as it was, was probably not clearly distinguishable from a kind of sanctification of the chain of ancestors that is ever begetting new life—something that Jung has called the apocatastasis of ancestral life; this in its turn is linked with the sanctification of sex, perceived and experienced under the simple symbol of dying and reviving nature and of the earth, the mother and begetter of all things—"Ἅπαντα τίκτει χθών, πάλιν τε λαμβάνει," says a fragment of Euripides, "All living things spring from the earth and then return to it"—; then

---

[1] Cf. K. Prümm, Der christliche Glaube und die altheidnische Welt, I, pp. 290ff.: "Die Vorstufe griechischer mütterlicher Gottgestalten" (The Preliminary Stage of Greek Mother-Goddess Figures), and the same author's "Die Endgestalt des orientalischen Vegetationsheros in der hellenistisch-römischen Zeit" (The Final Form of the Oriental Vegetation Hero in Hellenistic-Roman Times), Zeitschrift für katholische Theologie, 58 (1934), p. 463.

once more the grave becomes the protecting womb of new life. In the *Choephoroe* Aeschylus has preserved a childish stumbling little prayer that is nevertheless filled with deep religious awe: "Μᾶ γᾶ, μᾶ γᾶ, βοὰν φοβερὸν ἀπότρεπε – Earth, earth, turn away my frightened cry" (i.e. let me not call in vain to thee in my fear).[1] That may well be an echo of these ancient rites.

I must note yet another point about the mysteries: it is that they were essentially a religion of emotion. As I have already indicated, they did not address themselves to the thinking, let alone the enquiring and reflective mind. They proclaim no doctrine or dogma and the fact that the cult legend takes a thousand forms in no way affects the quality of the act of piety itself.

Hepding has made this clear in the case of the Attis mysteries. This particular cult, he says, is "free from all dogma", and the same holds good for nearly all the other ancient cults which "consist essentially in the performance of certain ancient traditional rites. It is this that forms the fixed and permanent element; whoever honours the gods with the exact performance of these ritual prescriptions is 'εὐσεβής', according to the ancient conception."[2] Thus the mystery cults are directed at the instinct for sombre awe in the devotee; indeed in some forms they may be said to be directed at his very nerves.

"All mysteries have in common a ritual that uses powerful physical means, such as harsh sound- and light-effects, to work on the feelings, and also a system of symbols with highly diversified meanings that exalts these simple basic proceedings into reflexions of super-sensory secrets. The nearness of the divinity is thus rendered much more immediate than in cults whose vitality has already paled. . . . All is calculated to enforce a state of inward concentration for which the bustle of life ordinarily leaves no place. . . . This also explains the preference for ecstatic cults, for whose uninhibited rioting the Greek soul had, in other circumstances, experienced nothing but horror."[3]

[1] Both quotations from A. Dieterich, *Mutter Erde* (Mother Earth) (2nd edition), Leipzig, 1913, pp. 37ff.
[2] H. Hepding, *Attis: Seine Mythen und sein Kult* (Attis: His Myths and His Cult), Giessen, 1903, p. 98.   [3] Thus K. Latte, "Religiöse Strömungen", pp. 154ff.

Now, it is perfectly true that we must accept descriptions of the wild excitement accompanying these mystery cults with considerable caution; the fact is that we are probably too much influenced by classical accounts which contain a great deal of refined dressing-up and should really be reckoned among the "literary mysteries". The stock example here is Apuleius' description of the rites of Isis; into the same category we should also place Plutarch's impression of the celebration of a mystery cult. "At first abortive and wearisome wandering about, a number of dangerous journeys into the dark that lead nowhere, then just before the celebration all manner of fears, shuddering and trembling, or silence and anxious wonder. Then a wondrous light breaks in on everything, pleasant landscapes and meadowland receive us and we become aware of voices and dances and of the glory of sacred songs."[1] Yet even caution will not prevent us from still saying that the piety of the mystery cults was a matter of the emotions. The devotees "are not to learn but to suffer and be made worthy by suffering".[2] So says a fragment of Aristotle; οὐ μαθεῖν ἀλλὰ παθεῖν is the aim of the initiate.

May I briefly describe yet a third and final characteristic? It is one that is particularly evident during their final stage when the mystery cults have so greatly multiplied and are already in decay. I am tempted to describe the mood that marks this piety of late antiquity, the mood from which the cults derived their strange lingering vitality, as "nervous uncertainty of salvation", and it gave to the cults that last flicker of life that is like the last spasmodic pulses, now weak, now for a moment strong, of a dying organism. For the cults were dying. They were losing even the vigour to maintain their identity, and in the weariness of their decay were assimilating all that they encountered—including a number of Christian things; and while this was going on, something very strange began to happen. The decomposing elements of the dying thing began to be received into a new blood-stream and to course through new veins; they did this in Byzantium, among the Arabs and in Christianity.

[1] Stobaeus, *Flor.*, IV, 107 (cf. N. Turchi, *Fontes historiae mysteriorum aevi hellenistici*, Rome, 1923, No. 118).
[2] Preserved in Synesius, *Dion*, c. 7 (PG, 66, 1136 A).

Yet though dying, the cults were not yet dead. There was still a spiritual hunger which they appeared to satisfy. Indeed, apart from Christianity, there were but two things by which that hunger could obtain at least the semblance of being assuaged—an escapist philosophy that was as weary as everything else—oh, how weary—and a plethora of cults among which the would-be devotee could take his choice.

In such matters as these, however, the pious were clearly reluctant to leave anything to chance and funerary and other inscriptions often record whole catalogues of initiations. On the marble altar dedicated to the Great Mother and her consort Attis in A.D. 376 the Roman Sextilius Agesilaus Aedesius records the various mysteries which had promised him "everlasting rebirth". The inscription reads: "*Pater patrum dei Solis invicti Mithrae, hierofanta Hecatarum, dei Liberi archibucolus, taurobolio criobolioque in aeternum renatus*",[1] while the noble Roman lady Paulina was, according to the inscription on her grave, "*sacrata apud Eleusinam deo Baccho, Cereri et Corae, sacrata apud Laernam deo Libero et Cereri et Corae, sacrata apud Aegynam deabus, taurobolita, Isiaca, hierophantria deae Hecatae.*"[2]

I think I have been right to go into some detail about this final phase of the mystery cults when they were really already in decay. As I have already pointed out, the cults underwent considerable evolutionary change, and, in assessing the nature and extent of their influence on Christianity, it simply will not do to mix up one stage of this process with another. But what changes had Christianity itself undergone in the corresponding period?

Now, it is quite true that over the first five centuries the strictest unity of doctrine was imposed on Christianity by the grip of the apostolic tradition; it is equally true, however, that during the same period there were enormous changes in the outward forms of the Church, changes in the manner in which its doctrine was actually expressed, changes in ritual and the ideals of spiritual life. Any comparison between Christianity and the mystery cults must,

[1] *Corpus Inscriptionum Latinarum*, VI, No. 510; H. Hepding, *Attis*, p. 89.
[2] *Corpus*, VI, 1779; Hepding, p. 205. Other evidence of this accumulation of initiations to mysteries is to be found in G. Anrich, *Das antike Mysterienwesen*, p. 55.

therefore, take careful note of the time of these changes. Examine in turn the theology of St Paul, of Origen, of Augustine: how vast is the variety of forms assumed by that living unity of truth that is everlastingly the same! The Lord's Supper of the primitive Church as we see it in Corinth—and the mystery of the Byzantine rite hidden by a gilded screen: what a transformation within the living unity of the changeless faith! Obviously we must be very careful here, for we must, so to speak, leave the centuries in their places. Take for instance—to quote but one example—the mystical character attributed to the imitation in baptism of Christ, dead and resurrected. The doctrine as set forth clearly enough in Paul's Epistle to the Romans, must not be proved by adducing the words of Cyril of Jerusalem. By the same token we should not tacitly reseat the Pseudo-Areopagite with his late Greek mystery language on the Areopagus of Paul.

There are, then, certain well-established lines of division to be drawn in the story of the development of the early Church, and to these we must adhere. There is the period of the primitive Church (first and second centuries), and that is followed by the period in which ritual and theology are built up (third century), and from this there comes organically into being that final form of the Church, the form which the genius of antiquity finally stamped upon it (fourth and fifth centuries). Corresponding with the above are the three periods of the mystery cults of late antiquity, and it is only when we have got this picture clear that we can correctly assess the process of simultaneous attraction and repulsion by which these two religious entities contrapuntally influenced each other.

Let me, nevertheless, attempt a brief preliminary sketch of that process. Primitive Christianity, formed, as it chiefly was, by Pauline theology, found itself in a world permeated, as we have seen, by this "mystery atmosphere". It would, however, be inept to the point of monstrosity if we sought dogmatically to determine against which particular "mystery" St Paul was writing in Colossians or which mystery is the ultimate "source" for the teaching in Romans or the First Epistle of Peter. Such identification is quite impossible since the battle was not yet closely enough engaged for such specific attack. Indeed—and this is the hub of the matter—the two opposing forces were too palpably dissimilar for this kind of controversial in-fighting; there just was not the necessary common ground. The whole matter has been admirably summarized by Clemen: "Christianity", he writes, "is distinguished from the mystery religions both by its historical character and by the wholly different significance ascribed to the appearance and death of the Christian redeemer . . . and so one could well say with Henrici, 'If we seek to describe the general character of primitive Christianity, we would do much better to call it an anti-mystery religion than a mystery religion'."[1] For all that, however, there is in Paul, and even in Ignatius and other early Christian writers, a quite undeniable tendency to adapt to their own uses a kind of subdued mystery language.

The second period presents a wholly different picture. The third century is the age of the "mysterization" of all the thought of late antiquity—the process being carried to the uttermost limits to which it could go. It is the age in which the mysteries are embodied in Neoplatonic theosophy and mysticism; it is, however, also the age in which the cult and theology of the Church assume a clearly defined shape. It is now—and only now—that the actual debate between Christianity and the mysteries begins. The apologetic writers—especially Tertullian—denounce the mysteries as "diabolical apings of Christian truth", while for other writers, grappling with the luxuriances of Gnosticism, we can observe a parallel phase of the process and learn something of the strange admixture of mystery and myth with which the protagonists of that heresy spiced their Christian professions. Meanwhile the theologians, and above all Clement of Alexandria, proclaimed to the world of Greek culture the mystery of the Logos and in doing so did not hesitate to make use of verbal images with which that world was already at home.

It is from the theological language of these men that Greek Christianity derived the form that it has ever since preserved. No less than fifty years ago Anrich[2] produced a careful and scholarly

[1] C. Clemen, *Der Einfluss der Mysterienreligionen auf das älteste Christentum* (The Influence of the Mystery Religions on the Oldest Forms of Christianity), Giessen, 1913, pp. 81f.

[2] *Das antike Mysterienwesen*, pp. 130–54.

analysis in which he showed how this process worked its way from
Alexandria and how at the same time a certain "mystery terminology" got introduced into the verbal usages of the Church. Today
the latest research into the semantics of the words μυστήριον
and *sacramentum*[1] has made it even clearer than before how, as
a result of a process of what might be called acquisitive adaptation, a process that took place both in the language of theology
and the forms of Church ritual, much of the stock of ideas and
verbal images that belonged to the mystery cults found its way
into Christianity.

Naturally enough, as the ancient religion began to come to an
end and the now world-wide system of the cults fell into decay,
there was a further shift in the balance of forces. Despite Julian's
apostasy, despite a certain amount of crying up of his literary
work in Alexandria as "a mighty Hellenic fortress set against the
glory of Christ",[2] the cults could no longer be reckoned as a living
foe, and this holds true even though among certain circles there
was something in the nature of an organized Neoplatonic opposition to Christ—Porphyry has something to say on this subject—
for, strangely enough, it was among such aristocratic coteries,
among people who had largely cut themselves off from the
generality of men, that the mystery cults found their final and
restricted refuge.

Yet, as we have seen, this dying foe begins to have a kind of
counterpart of itself in the very ranks of victorious Christianity;
it is a kind of mannered mystery vocabulary, if one may call it
that, in which a whole mass of expressions—and also a discipline
of secrecy—and a certain amount of liturgical practice is almost
light-heartedly taken over. One need only think of what is really
the stock example here, the Pseudo-Areopagite, whose whole cast
of thought and verbal usage had such a profound effect on future
Byzantine developments. Yet even before that, we can hear Chry-

[1] Cf. my note on p. 11 and see also H. von Soden, "Mysterion und Sacramentum in den
ersten zwei Jahrhunderten der Kirche" (Mystery and Sacrament in the First Two Centuries of the Church), *Zeitschrift für die neutestamentliche Wissenschaft*, 12 (1911), pp. 188–
227.
[2] Cyril of Alexandria, *Contra Iulianum*, introductory epistle addressed to the Emperor
Theodosius (PG, 76, 508 D).

sostom preach about "the dread and awful mysteries"—language which would certainly not have been used in an earlier age; we can observe in the so-called *Apostolic Constitutions* and in Basil the signs of a significant change in liturgical forms and watch Hellenism slowly change into Byzantinism—and it is precisely this process that causes the last heirlooms that have been appropriated out of the treasury of the mysteries to pass into full Christian possession, there to acquire a wholly different significance and with it a wholly new glory.

There are then, I repeat, three distinct phases in the story of the development and reciprocal influence of the two entities under comparison, and like the layers of a palimpsest, they must be separated one from the other with the greatest possible care. It is only then that we may venture to define and evaluate the differences and similarities between Christianity and the cults. This is the task before us, and I will endeavour to show that Christianity, being the truth revealed by God in Christ, is in all but inessentials a thing wholly unconnected with the mystery cults either in its origins or its later development; I will, in fact, try to define the differences that separate the two things as precisely as I can.

The more firmly we recognize these very real and essential differences, however, the less we need to hesitate in admitting that in the third century the Church adapted herself to her Greek surroundings and exploited the Greek passion for the mystery cults by interpreting her own mysteries by means of words and images to which their devotees were already accustomed. Clement of Alexandria is the principal witness to this and I quote once more that famous chapter on the mysteries in the *Protrepticus* in which he addresses the following words to his Greek reader:

"Oh, come, thou bemused dupe! lean no more upon the thyrsus and cast away the ivy wreath. Remove the fillets from thy brow, throw off the deer-skin; come, be sober! I will show thee the Logos and the mysteries of the Logos, and I will give thee understanding of them by means of images that are familiar to thee. Here is the mountain beloved of God, not, like Cithaeron, a place where tragedies befall, but sanctified to the dramas of truth. . . . Oh, how truly holy are these mysteries and how pure this light! These are indeed the mysteries which by initiation make me holy. The Lord reveals the holy signs, for he himself is the hierophant. And with the angels thou shalt dance about the one true God, the uncreated and imperishable one, as the Logos of God joins in our songs of praise."[1]

3

Christianity is a thing that is wholly *sui generis*. It is something unique and not a derivative from any cult or other human institution, nor has its essential character been changed or touched by any such influence. As against this, Christianity is not a thing inhumanly apart, an entity that has no common scale of values with any of the works of man.

In the pages that follow I propose to explore very briefly those areas of common ground between Christianity and the cults where superficial similarities suggest that the one has been influenced by the other. Before doing so, however, let me re-emphasize the profoundly heterogeneous character of the two and show you how utterly different a thing was that Christian "mystery which hath been hidden from eternity" (Eph. 3. 9.) from the μυστήρια, the "mysteries" of Hellenism, and how wide a gulf separates the *mystère naturel* which lay behind the symbolism of the mystery cults from the *mystère surnaturel* of the salvation which the New Testament proclaims.

The character of the "mystery" of New Testament revelation, as we encounter it in St Paul (Rom. 16. 25 ff., I Cor. 2. 7–10, Col. 1. 26 ff., Eph. 1. 8–10 and 3. 3–12), can be summarized as follows. The "mystery" is the decision to save man when man had become separated from God by sin, a decision made since all eternity in the depth of the Godhead's being and hidden from all eternity. This hidden resolve is made manifest in the God-man Christ, who through his death brings the gift of "life" to all men; he calls them, that is to say, to partake in his own divine life, of which, by a morally valid act of personal acceptance, we take hold

<hr />

[1] *Protrepticus*, XII, 119, 1–120, 2 (GCS, I, p. 84, ll. 4–29).

in sacrament and in faith, and which, after our earthly death, attains its ultimate fullness in the beatific vision and complete union with God.

"Mystery" therefore connotes, at any rate for St Paul, the inner reality of this divine decision and all that flows therefrom.[1] It means the gigantic drama of human redemption that proceeds from the depths of God, is made manifest in Christ and the Church, and returns once more to the depths of God from whence it came—the "drama of truth", as Clement of Alexandria was later to call it.[2] "Mystery" in fact means at one and the same time the hidden quality of God's redeeming act and the revelation of that act; it is revealed in the true message proclaimed by Christ; it remains hidden, in so far as, even after such divine proclamation, its truth remains beyond human comprehension and can only be laid hold of by faith.

For this mystery is the drama of the supernatural life, of man's being raised up to be a child of God, and that condition is wholly beyond our human nature and beyond any human understanding. The Christian mystery is always a "hidden revelation", hidden because in this life it addresses itself only to faith, and only in the course of its acceptance by faith finds its way by slow stages until it attains to understanding, or holy *gnosis*. And yet it is truly a revelation, for it is "preached from the housetops" and is wholly free from any esoteric or secret doctrine.

From this alone it is clear that in the fashioning of his doctrine and in his choice of words concerning the Christian mystery, St Paul has in mind something radically different from the Hellenistic conception of μυστήρια. The difference is further accentuated if we see the matter in the context of semantic development. From where did St Paul get his terminology? Granted the possibility— which, it will be remembered, was one of the starting-points of our discussion—that Paul deliberately made use of certain expressions in order to combat the thing we have called "mystery atmosphere"—the thing he encountered in Ephesus, in Corinth and in Colossae—, there are still certain facts to be considered along with

---

[1] Cf. D. Deden, "Le Mystère paulinien", in *Ephemerides Theologicae Lovanienses*, 13 (1936), pp. 405–42.

[2] *Protrepticus*, XII, 119, 1 (GCS, I, p. 84, ll. 8 ff.).

any such hypothesis. It is clear that before Paul's day the word "mystery" and related terms were already in common use with a certain fairly wide penumbra of significance. Christ himself brought the message of the "mysteries of the kingdom of Heaven" (Mat. 13. 11, Mark 4. 11, Luke 8. 10) and even if we cannot identify the exact term used in the original Aramaic, the fact remains that Mark and Matthew record the use of the word which they render as μυστήριον before it was employed by Paul. And what is the sense in which Christ uses it? The mysteries of the kingdom are Jesus' "hidden revelation", his royal and sovereign communications which are nevertheless concealed within the cloak of the parables, so that "seeing they see not and hearing they hear not" (Mat. 13. 13). Christ gives the interpretation of his mystery himself.

To attribute such a meaning to the word carries us back even further, right into the ideology of the Old Testament in fact, and particularly into that of the so-called deutero-canonical books. Here the concept akin to "mystery" is the *sacramentum regis* (Tob. 12. 7), the secret decision of the king communicated only to those who are in his confidence, the plan of campaign which the supreme ruler has devised in his heart and which he deigns to communicate to his council (Judith 2. 2), the ruse of war which the traitor betrays to the enemy. This is the meaning which the translators of the Septuagint associated with the word μυστήριον. Jesus, and after him Paul, applied this meaning to the divine decision, which was also a hidden one but "now is manifested to his saints" (Col. 1. 26). How far removed is this from the meaning which the Hellenistic mind attached to the word μυστήρια, the mysteries, a word always used in the plural form. It is to the special credit of recent scholarship that it has shown the word "mystery" in the New Testament to be quite incapable of the cultic interpretation which it was made to bear in the religions of antiquity.

Till well into the second century, in the writings of Justin and Irenaeus and even in those of Clement of Alexandria, the word "mystery" continues to carry the meaning that St Paul stamped upon it and not the one that was peculiar to the mystery cults.[1] "Mystery" was the word used to describe the great redeeming drama of God's salvation, and particularly—for it is part of that drama—the unfolding of the story of that salvation in the Old Testament—a single great parable this last which finds its meaning and consummation in Christ. It was used to describe Christ's own saving works, and especially his death upon the cross. It was used to describe the Church, and, within the Church, the sacraments and the truths contained in the creeds, the formulations of the faith. All these things were called "mystery" because they are deeds, rites and words that proceed out of the unfathomable riches of God's resolve and form the visible garment, often poor and humble in itself, that conceals those same unfathomable riches and, at the same time, in however veiled a fashion, declares them the "drama of truth" indeed. An anonymous Greek of the fourth century has expressed the nature of the Christian mystery in these words: "What we declare of Christ is more than a mere telling in words, it is a mystery of piety; for the whole of Christ's scheme of salvation is called a mystery, for it manifests itself not in a mere letter but in deeds – ἐν τῷ πράγματι κηρύττεται."[2]

Now we shall have to make a rather more detailed comparison between this Christian mystery and the mystery cults in order to make clear the difference between the two, and we can summarize this last from three points of view: Christianity is a mystery of revelation, a mystery of ethical demands, and a mystery of redemption. It is these three aspects that bring it into such sharp contrast with the piety of the Hellenistic mystery cults.

It is a *mystery of revelation* of the one true God in the historic person of Christ. It is built upon the strictest monotheism and accepts on faith a sharply circumscribed form of dogmatic teaching, proclaimed by this same Jesus Christ who was crucified under Pilate. Set against this the character of the ancient mysteries as they existed at the beginning of the Christian era. There is at the beginning of that era no trace of anything in the nature of monotheism. It is only from the third century on that we begin to see something

[1] Cf. K. Prümm, "Mysterium und Verwandtes bei Hippolyt und bei Athanasius" (Mystery and Related Matters in Hippolytus and Athanasius), *Zeitschrift für katholische Theologie*, 63 (1939), pp. 270ff., pp. 350ff.

[2] Pseudo-Chrysostom, *Christmas Homily* (PG, 59, 687).

of the kind in the contrived, the painfully contrived henotheism of the solar cult with its theosophical symbol-mongering. Till then there is only the wildly proliferating irrelevance of the different cult legends, and there is—a purely emotional phenomenon —a wild yearning for salvation, conceived in purely naturalistic terms. How, in those now distant days when speculation on the origins of religion was so engagingly uninhibited, people managed to derive the basic doctrines of Christianity from the mystery cults, remains a riddle to which no answer appears to be forthcoming. "It implies no claim to prophetic gifts," says Prümm, "if we say that coming generations will utterly fail to understand how people could ever have been entirely serious when they attempted to trace an inner connexion between the fundamental ideas of Christianity and those of the mystery cults."[1]

Christian revelation is not myth but history and its precipitate is the visible Church; its character is to be seen in the clear and concrete quality of what is written in the New Testament, in the unambiguous and definable content of the apostolic tradition, in the fixedness of the essential pattern imposed upon the sacraments. The God of the Christian mystery is not a thing fashioned out of the thoughts and longings, however sublime, of pious and searching Hellenistic souls, nor is he the God of learned men or even of the mystics; rather is he the God of whom Pascal wrote in his famous confession: "The God of Abraham, of Isaac and of Jacob, not the God of the philosophers and the learned, the God who can only be found in the ways taught in the Gospel." That is why for any Greek the Christian mystery is "foolishness" (I Cor. 1. 23), for it is the mystery of God's becoming man and dying a human death.

"The Gospel of Christ crucified is wholly unmythical [said Kittel in his lectures at the University of Uppsala]; it is not a song, nor a sound, nor a thought, nor a myth, nor a symbol. It does not tell of some dim legend but of a completely realistic, completely brutal, shameful, frightful event in history, that took place within the

<hr>

[1] K. Prümm, *Das antike Heidentum*, p. 308.

immediate experience of living men. . . . The frightful realism of
the cross is not made more bearable by any patina of age or any
sublimating aesthetic quality. One can well understand why the
preaching of such a thing should be foolishness and a stumbling-
block. For all that, we are dealing here with things that cannot be
separated: in this same realism, in this naked historical fact is con-
centrated all that makes Christianity offensive and contemptible,
yet it is precisely here that lies the ultimate deep root of its power.
. . . Profound and beautiful thoughts, an air of mystery and
enchantment—in all this other religions could do as well as
Christianity, nay they could often do better. When the faithful
hearkened to the Gospel of Christ, they did so because it claimed
to be a perfectly realistic gospel of fact."[1]

And, that is why, once the Christian had ascended out of the
soft magic of the mystery atmosphere into the liberating faith in
Christ, the whole substance of the mystery cults vanished at one
stroke like an evil dream.

The mystery of ethical demands. If we are really to grasp the fundamental difference between Christianity and the cults in this particular, we must first ask ourselves to what extent the piety of the
ancient cults entailed anything like genuine devotion to a moral
ideal at all. The ancient mysteries were originally vegetation cults
and, among other things, were markedly charged with sex. Their
nature was thus hardly one to make them morally formative or
exacting.

Yet we need not be quite so sceptical as was Rhode,[2] or, more
recently, Kittel;[3] rather should we follow that most erudite and
perceptive writer Leipoldt and draw a clear distinction between
the moral demands of the ancient Greek mystery cults and the
complete amorality of the cults imported from the East. We must
further distinguish between the moral condition of the cults at the
beginning of the Christian era and their condition from the third
century onwards when an attempt was made to raise them to a

---

[1] *Die Religionsgeschichte und das Urchristentum* (The History of Religion and Primitive
Christianity), Gütersloh, 1932, pp. 124 ff.

[2] *Psyche*, I (6th edition), 1910, p. 312.

[3] *Die Religionsgeschichte und das Urchristentum*, pp. 116 ff.

higher moral plane; this later development was contemporaneous with their general transformation into a source of spiritual comfort in keeping with the solar henotheism of the day.

Yet set the ethical product of the cults, even under a favourable assessment, against the standards set by the New Testament, standards actually realized in primitive Christianity; the levels attained in each case are simply incapable of comparison—nor is this a mere assertion of biased apologetics; it is the sober and unequivocal result of an examination of the source material.[1] No, apply the test of ethical demands, and Christianity and the cults confront one another like two separate worlds through which there flows no common stream of power. Finally, the piety of the cults is at best only the tragic and earth-bound effort towards moral, and often only towards ritual, purification: it is the effort of the soul to mount upward by its own power. There is no such upward mounting in Christianity, there is only the descent of God and the outpouring of divine grace which brings about our transformation in the love of Christ.

All this is closely connected with our third point of difference: *Christianity is a mystery of the redemption by grace.* A great deal has been written—much of it fictional rather than scientific—about Hellenistic "redemption religions" and it is here that we may well see the supreme example of what happens when people get bitten with the mania for painting the picture of the mystery cults in Christian colours. Here too, however,—and this holds good in regard to every school of thought—the most recent scholarship has reached what are essentially sobering conclusions. There was, we know, at the beginning of the Christian era a general vague, though lively, longing for a healing god and a golden age of peace. Nobody should think of denying that. Yet it is equally clear that the salvation proclaimed by all the cults was a salvation essentially conceived in terms of the natural order and in that form transposed into the other world. In the words of Boulanger: "The idea that God should die and rise again in order to lead his

---

[1] Cf. also K. Latte, "Schuld und Sünde in der griechischen Religion" (Guilt and Sin in Greek Religion), *Archiv für Religionswissenschaft*, 20 (1920–1), pp. 254 ff.

faithful to everlasting life is unrepresented in any Hellenistic religion."[1]

The salvation proclaimed by Christ was on an altogether different level. It assumes the existence of sin, and is by that very token a redemption from guilt, from moral and theological evil; it is in no sense a release from the flesh, nor is the flesh, because it is matter, regarded in some way as a negation of the divine and evil in itself. There is only one thing that is evil and that is sin, and Christian redemption is the forgiveness of sins through Christ's death upon the cross—and even a scholar as convinced as Reitzenstein of Christianity's genetic derivation from the cults, recognizes a unique element here which turns the one thing into the very opposite of the other. "What is new here," he writes, "is the conception of redemption as the forgiveness of sin. The frightening earnestness of the preaching of guilt and atonement is something wholly lacking in Hellenism."[2]

And as with sin, so, in the Christian mystery, the newly granted life lies wholly outside the natural order; it is "life everlasting", "a new birth" and "a seeing of God", and there is not a shred of evidence to suggest that the piety of the cults knew of anything of the kind. Oepke summarizes this fundamental difference in these words: "On the one side, a wholly individualistic rebirth conceived in essentially naturalistic terms and without regard to the element of time (*zeitloser, naturalistischer Wiedergeburtsindividualismus*), on the other side, a linking of the spiritual with actual history, an eschatologically conceived re-creation of all things."[3]

Festugière, one of the most illuminating students of the Hellenistic spirit, writes as follows: "The union with the god in the mystery cults is always confined to the sense-bound sphere, while the purely spiritual *pneuma* of the Christian mystery is something on an entirely different level where no connexion with the senses could possibly be affirmed of it",[4] and Dölger says: "With the

---

[1] A. Boulanger, *Orphée: Rapports de l'orphisme et du christianisme*, Paris, 1925, p. 102; K. Prümm, *Christentum als Neuheitserlebnis* (Christianity as an Experience of Renewal), pp. 142 ff.   [2] *Poimandres*, Leipzig, 1904, p. 180, note 1.

[3] In his dissertation, "Die Heilsbedeutung der Taufe auf Christus" (The Saving Significance of Baptism in Christ), in G. Kittel, *Theologisches Wörterbuch zum Neuen Testament* (Theological Dictionary of the New Testament), I, Stuttgart, 1933, p. 539.

[4] *L'Idéal religieux des Grecs*, p. 219.

divinities of the mystery cults the god is always put on an equality with nature. The celebration of their resurrection is therefore . . . not the occasion for recalling an actual historical event, but a mere reminder of a process that is annually repeated."[1]

Not only is the Christian conception of redemption different in kind from that of the cults, it proceeds from a wholly different basis of assumption, for the Christian mystery of the redemption only begins to have meaning for us if we conceive of ourselves as children of God, enjoying a relationship that was lost to us through original sin and won back for us by the cross; and the mystery of grace only begins to have meaning if we think of it in eschatological terms and in relation to the perfect vision of God which the next world will afford. These, however, are the fundamental doctrines of Christianity as they were proclaimed by Jesus and given their ultimate shape by Paul, and it is the content of these doctrines that makes of the Christian mystery something new and something totally different from the ancient mystery cults. This should make it clear that in no circumstances whatever could any findings of the serious study of comparative religion do other than reaffirm, with ever-deepening conviction, the uniqueness of Christianity.

In concluding this exposition of the essentially heterogeneous character of the Christian and Hellenic mysteries, I once more make so bold as to quote some words that the Protestant theologian Kittel set at the end of his Swedish lectures: "The confession of primitive Christianity was this: 'Now we are justified through faith, and have made peace with God through our Lord Jesus Christ. I am sure that neither death nor life nor any creature can separate us from the love of God which is in Jesus Christ our Lord.' Whoever has understood these verses knows wherein lay the unique character, the 'otherness' of primitive Christianity; by reason of this he also knows where lay the real depth of its power against all other religions and philosophies of life."[2]

The palpably heterogeneous and disparate nature of Christianity

---

[1] *Ichthys*, I, Münster (new impression), 1928, p. 7*. Cf. also Dölger's basic studies, "Mysterienwesen und Urchristentum" (The Nature of the Mysteries and Primitive Christianity) and "Zur Methode der Forschung" (On Method in Research) in *Theologische Revue*, 15 (1916), pp. 385 ff. and pp. 433 ff.

[2] *Die Religionsgeschichte und das Urchristentum*, p. 132.

and the cults should, I think, now be clear. We are, therefore, now in a position to proceed to the other part of our enquiry and may seek to determine how, where, and to what extent Christianity and the cults were able to exercise an influence on each other. In doing so let us especially examine those cases where such influence has been incorrectly inferred from a purely adventitious similarity which in point of fact is capable of some quite other explanation.

A whole mass of words, rites and ideas came into being within the life of the ancient Church which were once light-heartedly designated as "borrowings" by Christianity from the cults. Yet though they stem from a common root, there is here no question of a historical or genetic relationship. Rather should we look to that which all men have in common in the depths of their souls, to that human nature, consisting of body and spirit, which is the same both in Christian and in Greek. I designated this the contact "from below". Every religion creates sensible images of spiritual truths: we call such things symbols. Even the revelation of the God-man could only reach men by means of images which they could understand: "and without parable he did not speak unto them" (Mark 4. 34); and when he speaks of matters no longer pertaining to this world, his message is wrapped in terms of fundamental human experience; he speaks of a father, of a king, of light and darkness, of living water and of burning fire, of a pearl and of a seed. The same is true of the rites he institutes as signs and channels of grace—washing, eating, anointing and judging. If after a careful investigation of the source material we come across similar usages in the mystery religions, this simply means that we have encountered what Prümm[1] calls the law of correspondence between object and form (*das Gesetz des Zusammenhangs von Sache und Form*) according to which a religious human being must always make use of certain primitive symbols with which nature has provided him whenever he seeks to express something that is no longer of this world but exists on a higher plane. The common element here is the symbolism that is built into our nature and uses the things that are common to all human life.

This brings us close to what I have described as the points of

[1] *Das antike Heidentum*, p. 331.

contact in the middle region, the region where the processes of history and cultural evolution are visibly at work. Many things which at one time were regarded as direct borrowings by Christianity from the cults merely reflect the possession by both Christian and Greek of a common cultural apparatus, a common system of social custom and convention and a common stock of ideas and practices in civil and domestic life. If the "mystagogue" kisses the altar and the Christian priest does the same, if both cross the threshold of the sanctuary with the right foot, if in the cultic initiation ceremony milk and honey is handed to the candidate and the same thing is done in the baptismal rite of the primitive Church, this provides no reason at all for supposing that Christianity has been under the influence of the cults. All that has happened is that certain things of common use in ordinary life have here and there—and with one group acting quite independently of the other—been made into symbols the content and significance of which was in either case entirely different.

At this point we may usefully consider yet another phenomenon which to the superficial observer might suggest that there had been borrowing from the cults but which in reality is simply due to the essentially universal character of religious psychology. I refer to the tendency to make a secret of matters of religion, a tendency that amounts not merely to a psychological but to some extent to a sociological law.

The deeper and more moving the religious perception of a pious man becomes, the more such experience inclines him chastely to guard it from the non-initiate, and his anxiety to do this increases if there is any danger of the profane multitude breaking in on this holy ground. We have learned from Casel's treatise on the subject something of the history among the Greeks of this "mystical silence",[1] and this is in evidence throughout Greek life. There was an old Orphic saying that touched the hearts of all Greeks if they were religiously inclined: "φθέγξομαι οἷς θέμις ἐστί, αὔρας ἐπίθεσθε βέβηλοι – I will speak to those to whom it is lawful. Ye profane, set doors [to your ears]."[2] And there is a sentence in the

---

[1] *De Veterum Philosophorum Silentio Mystico*, Giessen, 1919.
[2] Preserved by Eusebius, *Praeparatio Evangelica*, III, 7 (PG, 21, 180 B).

Hermetica which runs: "To betray to the many the knowledge in this treatise, which is full of the majesty of God, would be the sign of a godless mind."[1] The same thing is to be found in the late Pythagorean wisdom: "Of the goods of knowledge nothing should be communicated to him whose soul has not been purified; for it is not permissible to deliver that which has been won with so much travail to every passer-by, nor may we reveal the mysteries of the Eleusinian goddesses to the profane."[2]

Now this psychological law begins to operate actively within Christianity as soon as the appropriate external circumstances have come into being. However public the Christian message may be, however much it may be "a mystery preached from the housetops" and addressed to all mankind, yet from the third century onwards, as Christianity became more widespread and popular, a need is felt for safeguarding it against the breaking-in of the mass. That is why it is now—and only now—that the so-called *disciplina arcani* is born and indeed it was not till the fourth century that it became fully developed. It is, indeed, not surprising that the Church Fathers who came to Christianity from Neoplatonism should have used a manner of speaking of these things that was certainly formed within the religious world of the moribund cults. The mysteries of baptism and of the altar of sacrifice were wrapped about with awful, reverent and concealing rites, and soon the iconostasis was to make the merest glance into the holy of holies impossible for the non-initiate. They turn into φρικτὰ καὶ φοβερὰ μυστήρια-the dread and awful mysteries.[3] "This is known to the initiates" is a phrase to be found in all Greek[4] sermons and even the Pseudo-Areopagite warns the initiated Christian who has passed through the *mystagogia* against careless talk: "See that thou be not a babbler concerning the most holy things, guard the mysteries of the hidden God so that none who is not initiated may partake therein, and to make this sure, speak of the holy only to holy men and speak in holy illumination."[5]

---

[1] *Corpus Hermeticum*, II, 1; II, 11. Cf. G. Anrich, *Das antike Mysterienwesen*, p. 70.
[2] Iamblichus, *Vita Pythagorae*, 17, 35 (cf. Anrich, p. 69).
[3] To be found in a number of texts (cf. Anrich, p. 157).   [4] Cf. Anrich, p. 158.
[5] *Ecclesiastica Hierarchia*, I, 1 (PG, 3, 372 A). Cf. also H. Koch, *Pseudo-Dionysius Areopagita in seinen Beziehungen zum Neuplatonismus und Mysterienwesen* (Pseudo-Dionysius

I had something to say just now on the subject of symbols and before leaving that subject, should like to touch on yet another instance of a certain similarity of mental attitude which might suggest that the cults had influenced Christianity. The fact is that the Greek mind had an excellent understanding of the nature and purpose of symbols and that such an understanding was native to the culture in which Christianity developed.

Symbols and symbolic acts are invariably marked by a hidden limitation. Whatever acts by and through the senses can never convey—let alone exhaust—the spiritual truth it is seeking to express. The symbol always retains a hidden background; it is like a garment which at one and the same time both indicates and conceals the shape of the body beneath. Actually this sense-character of the symbol is a necessity, for it serves to hide the glory of the other world, so that it is revealed only to those who have been given eyes to see it.

Now the symbol theology of Hellenistic antiquity understood this very well, and it was this understanding that provided the magic key by means of which it achieved a sublime reinterpretation of the cultic rites of the various mysteries. Unveiled, the divine truths cannot be looked upon by any human eye, says Macrobius in his commentary on the *Somnium Scipionis*, and the initiate knows that the truth will bear no naked representation of itself; and for this reason the mysteries are as things wrapped in swaddling clothes by the protective covering of the symbol: *ipsa mysteria figurarum cuniculis opperiuntur*.[1] Clement of Alexandria shows a thoroughly Hellenic wisdom when he writes: "That is why all dreams and signs are indistinct for us men, and this is not because God is envious—for it would be wrong to imagine that God could be moved by such a feeling—but in order that our search should seek to penetrate into the meaning of the mystery and so rise upward towards the finding of truth."[2] And in this sense he quotes the profound saying of Sophocles:

the Areopagite in Relation to Neoplatonism and the Mystery Cults), Mayence, 1900, pp. 108 ff.

[1] *Somnium Scipionis*, I, 2, 17; *Saturnalia*, V, 13, 40.
[2] *Stromata*, V, 4, 24, 2 (GCS, II, p. 341, ll. 1–4).

Of such a kind is God; that know I well.
His holy word is ever full of riddles
For wise men, yet 'tis simple for the weak;
It teaches much with little.[1]

Paul knew that too, he claims, when he wrote, "But we speak the wisdom of God in a mystery" (I Cor. 2. 7).

Actually this Greek mysticism of the symbol and particularly of the verbal symbol was the hidden root from which there came into being the allegorical exegesis that received its full development in Alexandria. The divine word of Scripture is a mystery and behind the immediate sense of the words and images, nay, behind the whole historical account of our salvation, there are hidden the unimaginable riches of the Spirit and possibilities, wholly beyond our conception, of ascending to that truth of which we can form no picture at all. If a man has been granted the power to behold the truth, then all that his senses perceive is for him nothing more than the ultimate extremity, jutting into this dark world, of another world infinitely more real than this. It is but a petty reflexion, a mere imprint of what, in the vastnesses of the mind of God, is the ultimate ground and ultimate end of all things.

The man who has been granted such power of sight is the true "gnostic", for he has been initiated into the mystery of the divine word. Yet, despite the similarity of their mystery terminology, a terminology that almost irresistibly invades Christian thinking when it moves along such lines as these, it is precisely at this point that the Christian and non-Christian gnostics part company. Christian gnosticism—we might really already say Christian mysticism—always remains within the limits of the faith, within the limits of the historical sense of the word of God and of the visible *Ecclesia*. Non-Christian Gnosis seeks redemption in knowledge, breaks free of the written word and separates itself off into solitude or conventicle.

We are, therefore, wholly justified in distinguishing between object and form here also, in this innermost domain of ancient

---

[1] Sophocles, *Fragmentum incertum*, 704 (GCS, II, p. 341, ll. 6–8).

spirituality in which Christian thought and Greek speech give birth to mysticism. This distinction enables us to recognize at once that all that was best in the cults did indeed flood into Christianity. Chrysostom, for example, gave a penetrating description of the essence of this mystical theology of symbols: "This is certainly a mystery, even though it is proclaimed everywhere, for it remains incomprehensible for those who have no understanding for such things. In any case, it is no human wisdom that reveals it, but the Holy Ghost does so in the measure of our capacity to take up the Spirit into ourselves."[1]

That is absolutely typical of the ancient world's sense of mystery, only put into Christian terms: no longer is the veil drawn aside by σοφία; it is Πνεῦμα ἅγιον. For the Latin Peter Chrysologus that is the reason why Christ shrouded his teaching in parables: "*Hinc est quod doctrinam suam Christus parabolis velat, tegit figuris, sacramentis opperit, reddit obscuram mysteriis.*"[2] So Christianity is never only the religion of the naked word, of pure reason and of moral imperatives. It is at the same time the religion of the veiled word, of loving wisdom, of grace hidden in sacramental symbols. That is why it is the religion of mysticism in which, through the simplicity of word and ritual, the infinity of God opens up. The decisively Christian thing is that God alone is the mystagogue and hierophant. Only when his Spirit gives the power of spiritual sight can man become an *epoptes* of the Christian mysteries. As Clement puts it:

"Whosoever is still blind, deaf, bereft of understanding and the sharp daring sight of a soul enamoured of contemplation, sight that only the Redeemer gives, must stand aside. Like the uninitiate at a mystery celebration or like a bystander who does not know the steps, he must remain outside the divine dance, for he is not yet pure, not yet worthy of the holy truth."[3]

And now for the final cause of similarity between Christianity and the cults. That cause is nothing less than the growing influence

[1] *Homilia in Ep. I ad Corinthios*, VII, 2 (PG, 61, 56 C).
[2] *Sermo 96*, 1 (PL, 52, 469 D).
[3] *Stromata*, V, 4, 19, 2 (GCS, II, p. 338, ll. 22–6).

1. The Cross and the Tree of Life
From a Salzburg Miniature of 1481 (Munich)

2. The Church as the Woman of the Apocalypse
From Herrad of Landsberg, *Hortus Deliciarum*

of Christianity to which in late antiquity the cults themselves began to be subject, a development to which recent scholarship has
become increasingly alive. The careful analysis which I tried earlier
to present to you, has perhaps made it clear how greatly by this
time the relationship between Christianity and the cults had
changed, as compared with the centuries of Paul and Clement. The
world of the cults is still a rich one, but it is in decay, and it is a
victorious Christianity that confronts it. Yet it is precisely this
period of the fourth century that is documented better than any
other in regard to the mystery cults, a fact which is itself evidence
of their very wide diffusion.

It is therefore surely not unreasonable to suppose that—given
the growing authority of the Christian Church—Christian practice should have had some sort of influence on what was still a
popular institution and that it should have had an effect on the
form the disintegrating cults began to assume. Such influence has
indeed almost certainly been at work in much of the evidence that
the source material has revealed to us, and that we have accepted
without a full appreciation of its significance. Naturally we should
proceed here with the utmost caution. The fact remains, however,
that so competent a scholar as Cumont has not hesitated to write
about the matter in these terms: "Christianity influenced even its
enemies. The Phrygian priests of the Great Mother compared their
feast of the vernal equinox to the Christian Easter and ascribed to
the blood shed in the *taurobolium* the redeeming power possessed
by that of the Lamb of God."[1]

As against this, we know that the ministers of this same cult
complained that it was the Christians and not themselves who
were the imitators in the matter of the atoning power of the blood
shed on the *Dies sanguinis* (March 24),[2] but this only shows—at
least by implication—that an accusation of plagiarism had in all
probability already been made against the pagans, and such charges
may not have been unusual. Certainly it is typical of the prevailing state of affairs that Augustine should have expressed his

---

[1] *Die orientalischen Religionen im römischen Heidentum* (The Oriental Religions in Roman
Paganism), Preface, p. xi.
[2] F. Cumont, *op. cit.*, p. 65.

indignation because a certain server of Attis was declaring that the God in the Phrygian cap was also a Christian.[1]

It is plain from all this that the moribund cult system was quite prepared to accept Christian influences, and Hepding remarks in his work on Attis that "in the later period the allegorical interpretation of myths and the theosophical speculations that characterized the prevailing philosophy, and occasionally, no doubt, a thought deriving from Christian influence, served to deepen and spiritualize the religious content of the mystery cults".[2] Indeed, when dealing with the *taurobolium* in the Attis mysteries he writes: "It is by no means impossible that the Christian doctrine of redemption through the blood of Christ, and of the washing away of sin through the blood of the Lamb, may have contributed to the development of this baptism of blood."[3]

It seems even more reasonable to assume such influence when we remember the strong effect of Jewish monotheism on the cults, and in particular on the mystery practices of the magic papyri.[4] Even Augustine finds it necessary to warn the faithful against those adepts of the mysteries who mingle the name of Christ with the texts of their magic formulae.[5]

If in the light of all this we take a fresh look at that inscription of the year A.D. 376 to which reference has already been made, the inscription in which the Roman aristocrat Aedesius boasts of the great number of his initiations and claims on this account to have been *"in aeternum renatus* – born again to eternal life", we shall surely be tempted to make something of a re-evaluation. Scholars have been eager on the strength of this piece of evidence —and on the strength of absolutely nothing else—to ascribe to the mystery cults a doctrine of rebirth. In view of the considerations adduced above, however, the cogency of this particular piece of evidence appears somewhat evanescent.

Actually Aedesius' inscription is an argument in my favour, for it dates from a time when the Church in Rome had public recognition and was already shining forth in its full glory. The basilica

---

[1] *Tractatus in Ioannem*, VII, 6 (PL, 35, 1440 C).
[2] *Attis: Seine Mythen und sein Kult*, p. 179.   [3] *Ibid.*, p. 200, n. 7.
[4] The relevant sources are quoted by Cumont, *op. cit.*, pp. 58–60; p. 231, n. 60.
[5] "Miscent praecantationibus suis nomen Christi" (PL, 35, 1440 B).

of Peter, which Constantine had built, stood over the cave of the Phrygian mysteries on the Vatican hill, the Christian mystery of everlasting rebirth from out the water of baptism was truly being preached from the house-tops, and it was not the dead pinewood of the Phrygian mysteries that was now carried through the streets but the wood of the cross of that new mystery of which Firmicus Maternus sang.

Of these two mysteries, that of the cross and that of baptism, I shall shortly have to speak, and it was in these two that the victory of Christianity over the ancient mystery cults was finally consummated. The Church had summoned the Greek to his true home, inviting him in the words which Clement of Alexandria addressed to Tiresias, for it was the whole world of Hellas that Clement seemed to see before him in the person of the aged seer:

"Come thou also to me, old man. Throw aside the service of Bacchus and let thyself be guided into the truth. See, I give thee the wood of the cross that thou mayest lean upon it. Hasten, Tiresias, and come to the faith and thou shalt see. Christ, through whom the eyes of the blind regained their sight, shines forth brighter than the sun and thou shalt behold Heaven, old man, thou who couldst not see Thebes."[1]

[1] *Protrepticus*, XII, 119, 3 (GCS, I, p. 84, ll. 17ff.).

II

THE MYSTERY OF THE CROSS

Fulget crucis mysterium

THE wood on which Tiresias is to lean is the cross, the mystery of light which will open his eyes is of course baptism. On both of these mysteries I have something to say.

Earlier in this book the Christian mystery was referred to as "the drama of truth". It is the manifestation in Christ of the resolve to save us that is hidden deep in the mind of God, Christ's human life being the veil behind which that unfathomable "μυστήριον τῆς εὐσεβείας–mystery of godliness" (I Tim. 3. 16) lies concealed.

Once we have grasped this we shall surely understand why everything that happens in the historical unfolding of the work of redemption, everything, that is to say, that happens within the Church, partakes of the dual character of this mystery, everything is at one and the same time both hidden and manifest, and the immeasurable wisdom of God that will not be revealed till the end of days, the "σοφία ἐν μυστηρίῳ–wisdom [spoken] in a mystery" (I Cor. 2. 7) is hidden in the integument of simple, visible things. Thus the Church herself is a "μυστήριον μέγα–a great mystery" (Eph. 5. 32), because her essence, now made manifest, is the revelation of what was only dimly hinted at in the union of Adam and Eve (Gen. 2. 24). Yet by the same token the historically concrete character of the Church conceals a hidden thing which can only be revealed in the light of eschatology, namely her intimate union with Christ (cf. Col. 1. 27), from which there will one day break forth the "δόξα–glory" that now already works in secret.

The nature of this Christian mystery can be discerned above all else in the decisive saving event which is the death of God upon the cross. In that death from Paul's day onwards the ancient

Christian saw *the* mystery of all creation. For, though we must never seek to detract from its harsh and uncompromising historicity, it is a mystery precisely in this: that, being both retroactive and predetermining, it embraces everything that has happened or will happen in the world.

To quote the words of a profound scholar which represent the latest utterance on the subject, the Christian mystery is

"the resolve of God, made before all worlds, hidden from the world but disclosed to the 'pneumatic', which was finally carried out on the cross by the 'Lord of Glory' and in which all the faithful themselves are glorified. If it is thus formulated, we can see the dependence of this concept on the apocalyptic thinking of later Judaism and its distinctness from the ideas of Gnosticism and the mystery cults. As the '$\mu\nu\sigma\tau\acute{\eta}\varrho\iota o\nu$ $\tauo\tilde{\nu}$ $\vartheta\varepsilon o\tilde{\nu}$ –the mystery of God', the historical crucifixion and glorification of Christ are removed beyond the grasp of human wisdom, and are shown to be an event prepared and brought to completion in God's own sphere.... Since the 'mystery of God' is fulfilled in Christ, creation and consummation, the beginning and the end of the world are taken up in him and removed from the sphere with which they would be normally and properly identified (*werden aus ihrem Verfügungs- und Erkenntnisbereich genommen*). In the making known to us of the mystery of God's will the times are fulfilled (Eph. 1. 10).

"We have just seen that the concept 'mystery' connotes a history removed out of the sphere where the laws governing this world's happenings have relevance and the modes of worldly knowledge apply; it is the story of the hidden resolve of God moving to its ultimate fulfilment. It is, however, also of the essence of this concept that the story should unfold itself in the world. In the mystery a heavenly reality breaks in on the old aeon; the 'Lord of Glory' dies upon the cross erected by the rulers of this world. In the cross the radical contrast is made manifest between the wisdom of God, concealed until now, and the wisdom of the worldly powers, bringing disaster for the latter, but for those who believe the kerygma, salvation."[1]

[1] Thus Bornkamm in G. Kittel, *Theologisches Wörterbuch zum Neuen Testament*, IV, Stuttgart, 1942, p. 826.

Now it is of supreme importance for the understanding of the mystery of the cross that we should once again revert to the consideration of the fundamental structure of every mystery—and even in the case of the "natural mysteries" that were the object of ancient piety this seems to me more necessary than to dwell on their purely cultic and ritual aspects. "Does not the real secret of every mystery lie in its simplicity?"[1] Kerényi asks, and surely his question goes to the root of the matter. It is always the simple primitive human things that are used as symbols: ears of grain, a blossoming tree, washing, the life-giving union of the sexes, light, darkness, the moon and the sun, and there is in their very simplicity a quality of the self-explanatory and self-sufficient which actually makes them more, and not less, apt vehicles for expressing the inexpressible (ἄρρητον), the unspeakable nature (ἀνεκλάλητον) of that which their use in the mystery is seeking to convey.

Now this fundamental character is repeated in the mystery of the cross, though at a very different level and though divine action has made the actual content of this mystery into something entirely new—the human death, the blood, the wound, the primitively simple shape of the crossed pieces of wood, all the humble simplicity of the historic narrative of our Lord's death and resurrection. All these are the small things, the stumbling-block, the foolishness, the diminutive and weak things (I Cor. 1. 23, 25) in the death of the Lord of Glory (I Cor. 2. 8). Yet these are the things in which the mystery hides itself, so that through the slight thing which is the visible symbol we behold the glory that embraces the world. Justin, the philosopher, once said that the pagans imputed folly to the Christians because they dared to set a crucified human being beside the Creator of the universe. Yet, he declared, they only spoke like this "because they do not understand the mystery that dwells within this human being".[2]

One of the oldest hymns of Christianity, preserved for us by Melito of Sardis, runs thus:

[1] *Einführung in das Wesen der Mythologie* (Introduction to Mythology), p. 248.
[2] *Apologia*, I, 13 (Otto, I, p. 42).

Nature shuddered and spoke in fear:
What manner of new mystery is this?
The invisible is seen and is unashamed,
The incomprehensible is grasped and is not wroth,
The unsuffering suffers and takes no vengeance
The immortal dies and makes no refusal.
What manner of new mystery is this?[1]

I have chosen the mystery of the cross for my subject, because the discussion of it entails an attempt, however cautious, at penetrating the sublime regions of ancient Christian thought; for that thought, when contemplating the stumbling-block, the foolishness of the cross and all the meanness thereof, could at the same time discern the glory that was hidden within it, the glory which from the cross could gather together all the aeons and could concentrate within it not only all creation, but the whole redemptive work of God as a burning-glass gathers together the rays of the sun.

We can arrange the abundant material that comes from Christian sources and has something to say on this subject, under two heads: (1) the cross as a cosmic mystery; and (2) the cross as a biblical mystery.

I

Illuminated by faith, the eye of the Christian initiate passes from the cross on which the Logos and Creator of the worlds died, up to the starry heavens where circle Helios and Selene; it passes on to the nethermost foundations on which the universe was fashioned, delves into the laws governing the formation of the human body, and even contemplates the shape of common things in daily use. Everywhere the Christian sees the imprint of the cross. The cross of his Lord has put his whole world under a spell.

God, who from the beginning of time has secretly looked upon the coming cross of his Son, has stamped the pattern of that cross on the foundations of the world, has made it the ground-plan in the building of the universe. The two great circles of the heavens, the equator and the ecliptic which, by intersecting each other,

---

[1] Melito of Sardis, *Fragment* 13 (Otto, IX, p. 419).

form a sort of recumbent chi and about which the whole dome of the starry heavens swings in a wondrous rhythm, become for the Christian eye a heavenly cross. Plato, basing himself on the ancient wisdom of Pythagoras, has spoken in the *Timaeus*[1] of the world-soul manifesting itself in the heavenly chi. The ancient Christians read into this an intimation granted even to the pagans, of the world-creating Logos, who, hanging from the cross, gathers the whole cosmos together and makes the mystery of that cross the pivot of the entire world. Bousset has told us of such speculations in his essay "Plato's World Soul and the Cross of Christ".[2]

So early a writer as Justin applies Plato's words to the Son of God, and though his observations are brief, there can be no doubt that behind them was the idea, with which he was certainly familiar, of the heavenly chi being the prefiguring symbol of the cross.[3] Irenaeus works the same conception into his theological speculations about the recapitulation in the cross of all cosmic and biblical events. He writes:

"He who through his obedience on the cross wiped out the former disobedience concerning the tree, is himself the Logos of Almighty God whose unseen presence permeates us all. Since that is so, he has the whole world in his grasp in its length and breadth, its height and its depth. For by the Logos all things are guided in orderly fashion, and God's Son is crucified in them, in so far as he stamps upon them the form of the cross. It was right and fitting that, by becoming visible himself, he should impress on all visible things, this community in the cross with them, for thus by means of these visible things he was to show forth his power and to do so in visible form, making it plain that it is he who illuminates the high places—heaven, that is to say—that it is he whose grasp extends to the depths, even to the last foundations of the world, that it is he who spreads out the flat land from East to West and stretches forth the wide spaces from North to South, that it is

---

[1] *Timaeus*, 36 BC. Cf. O. Appelt's commentary, *Platons Dialoge Timaios und Kritias*, Leipzig, 1922, pp. 159f.

[2] "Platons Weltseele und des Kreuz Christi", in *Zeitschrift für die neutestamentliche Wissenschaft*, 14 (1913), pp. 273–85.

[3] *Apologia*, I, 60, 1 (Otto, I, p. 160).

he who gathers together all that is scattered, that all may know the Father."[1]

For the study of the mystery of the cross this is indeed one of the most pertinent and classical passages in ancient Christian literature. The humble sign of the cross here contains within itself and makes visible all cosmic events, for the nature of all things must be drawn into the drama of redemption through the cross. Boldly developing the thought of Paul (Eph. 3. 18), this early Christian saw in the four wooden arms of the cross a mystical symbol indicating the four dimensions of the world. The cross is the "recapitulation" of the work of creation, i.e. the ground-plan, the easily read sign, the meaningful symbol of something that is beyond all understanding and description—in a word, it is a mystery.

Irenaeus has briefly summarized all this in his work against the Gnostics in the following words: "The true Creator of the world is the Logos of God who is our Lord and who in these latter days became man. Although he is in the world, his power invisibly embraces all created things, and his mark has been set upon the whole of creation since he is the Word of God, who guides and orders all things. And that is why he came in visible form to that which was his own and became flesh and hung upon the wood, so that he might recapitulate the universe in himself."[2]

From that point onwards there goes through the whole of ancient Christian literature an unceasing hymn to the cosmic mystery of the cross and to the outstretched hands of the Logos, who from the cross embraces the entire world and brings it home to his Father. It is impossible here to quote even the most beautiful passages in these marvellous songs of praise.[3] Golgotha becomes the centre of the universe, about which by divine ordination the whole cosmos turns. "God stretched forth his hands upon the cross in order to embrace the utmost limits of the earth and this makes this hill of Golgotha the pivot of the world." So runs a sermon of

---

[1] *Epideixis*, I, 34.   [2] *Adversus Haereses*, V, 18, 3 (Harvey, II, pp. 374f.).

[3] They are nearly all collected in the three folios, inexhaustible even today, of J. Gretser, *De Sancta Cruce*, Regensburg, 1734. Cf. also O. Zöckler, *Das Kreuz Christi: Religionshistorische und kirchlich-archäologische Untersuchungen* (The Cross of Christ: Studies in the History of Religions and Ecclesiastical Archaeology), Gütersloh, 1875.

Cyril of Jerusalem, preached to his catechumens at the actual spot where Christ was crucified.[1] Gregory of Nyssa praises the cross as the seal which is impressed both on heaven and on the depths of the earth.[2]

It is particularly in Byzantine devotion that this cosmic inter-pretation of the mystery of the cross lives on. "O Cross, thou atonement of the universe," runs one of these panegyrics, "thou boundary round the wide spaces of the earth, thou height of heaven and depth of the earth, thou binding bond of creation, thou that art the width of all that is visible and the breadth of the whole world."[3] Yet the same thing is also a very ancient theolo-gical heirloom of the Latin Christians of Rome and Africa.

At the beginning of the third century, at the very time, that is to say, when the mysteries were being spread over the West by the Syrian emperors, Hippolytus of Rome praised the cosmic mys-tery of the cross in words that seem almost drunken in their ecstasy, words which I shall quote at the end of this chapter.[4] Lac-tantius, the "Christian Cicero", has this to say: "So God in his suffering spread out his arms and so embraced the whole circle of the earth, as a sign to us that from the rising of the sun to the going down thereof a people that was to come would gather itself under his wings,"[5] while Firmicus Maternus in a famous chapter contrasts the symbolic wood of the cults with that of the cross and sees in the latter the great cosmic mystery: "The sign of a wooden cross holds the machine of the firmament together, strengthens the foundations of the earth, and leads those that cling to it towards life."[6] In Latin mysticism too this praise of the cosmic cross echoed on right into the Middle Ages.[7]

Seen from this angle, a whole mass of ideas and images becomes intelligible which further develop this cosmic mystery of the

---

[1] *Catechesis*, 13, 28 (PG, 33, 805 B).

[2] *Oratio de Resurrectione* (PG, 46, 621–5); *Catechesis Magna*, 32 (PG, 45, 81 C).

[3] Andrew of Crete, *In sanctam Crucem* (PG, 97, 1021 C).

[4] Cf. also *De Antichristo*, 61 (GCS, I, 2, p. 42, ll. 14–16).

[5] *Divinae Institutiones*, IV, 26, 36 (CSEL, 19, p. 383, ll. 7–11).

[6] *De Errore Profanarum Religionum*, 27 (CSEL, 2, p. 121, ll. 6–8).

[7] Under the leadership of Augustine who often spoke of the cosmic dimensions of the cross (cf. PL, 35, 1949f.; PL, 38, 371f.; 903f.). Cf. Richard of St Victor (PL, 196, 524f.); Honorius Aug. (PL, 172, 946); Thiofrid of Echternach (PL, 157, 385ff.).

cross. The cross is the epitome of the laws on which the world is founded, and by much the same token it will appear in the heavens when the visible world comes to an end as a great sign of light preceding the coming of the transfigured Christ. Already in the *Didache*[1] a saying that has been the subject of much controversy may well be held to bear this interpretation. In the end of days there will appear "the signs of truth: first the sign of 'spreading out' in heaven, then the sign of the trumpet call, then the resurrection of the dead". This σημεῖον ἐκπετάσεως ἐν οὐρανῷ, this sign of "spreading out" in heaven, is almost certainly the cross, the cross upon which Christ has stretched out his arms that embrace the world.

There is a similar reference in the song of the Syrian Ephraem: "When Christ appears from the East, his cross will appear before him like a standard before the king."[2] And even today in the Latin liturgy on the feast of the Exaltation of the Cross, its eschatological world secret is exalted in the words: "*Hoc signum crucis erit in caelo cum Dominus ad iudicandum venerit* – This sign of the cross shall be in the sky when the Lord comes to judgment"; for it is only by the glory of the last day when time comes to an end that the mystery of the cross will be wholly revealed. "*In te universa perficis mysteria* – In thyself thou dost accomplish all mysteries",[3] is said of the cross by Leo the Great.

But that is not all, the eschatological mystery of the transfigured cross is here and now at work in this aeon conditioned by time, for the Christian of the past gave form and shape to the paradox of the "joy of the cross" and the "victory in death", in this feast of the Exaltation. The subject of this liturgical mystery is the anticipated triumph in the final victory of the cross[4] and that is what gives the feast its authentically Greek note, still in our day, "car tout μυστήριον pour le Grec c'est l'éternité dans le

[1] *Didache*, 16, 6 (Funk, I, p. 36, l. 12).

[2] T. J. Lamy, *S. Ephraem Syri Hymni et Sermones*, II, Malines, 1886, p. 407, ll. 3–6; Cyril Jer., *Catechesis*, 13, 41 (PG, 33, 821 A): "With Jesus the cross will come again from heaven, for the 'tropaion' will precede the king." Cf. also W. Bousset, *Der Antichrist in der Tradition der alten Kirche* (Antichrist in the Tradition of the Ancient Church), Göttingen, 1895, pp. 154ff.

[3] *Sermo*, 59, 7 (PL, 54, 341 C).

[4] Cf. O. Casel, *Das christliche Festmysterium*, Paderborn, 1941, pp. 102–8; 206–14.

temps," says a Russian writer.[1] The mystery of the cross blazes forth, and through both the Roman and Byzantine liturgies we detect a note which reminds us of the verses of the Christian Sibyl:

> O blessed Wood on which God was stretched out,
> The earth will not keep thee.
> No, thou shalt see the house of heaven
> When thine eye, O God, shall flash forth.[2]

In the cross then the primal beginnings of the world's foundation and the end of all worldly happenings are united, and the mystery of the cross is reflected in all the things pertaining to this world. In the apocryphal *Acts of Andrew*, the apostle, as he goes towards his cross, praises the cosmic mystery that is hidden within that cross in words that have all the exaltation of a mighty hymn:

"I know thy mystery, O Cross, for the sake of which thou wert set up. Thou art made fast in the world to make secure all that is not firm, and thou reachest unto heaven that thou mayest point towards the Logos who will come from above. Thou art stretched out to the right and the left so that thou mayest put the fearful forces of the enemy to flight and gather together the whole world. Thou art made fast in the depths of the earth so that thou mayest unite with heaven all that which is upon the earth and all that is beneath it. O Cross, thou the All-highest's instrument of salvation! O Cross, token of Christ's victory over his enemies! O Cross, that art planted in the earth but bearest fruit in heaven! O name of the Cross, that containest within thyself the whole world! Hail to thee, O Cross, thou that holdest the cosmos together up to the utmost boundaries thereof. O Cross, that hast formed thy unformed outer form into a form full of understanding!"[3]

In the so-called *Actus Vercellenses*, an account of the martyrdom of Peter which is written very much under Gnostic influence,

---

[1] M. Lot-Borodine, "La Grâce déifiante des sacrements d'après Nicolas Cabasilas", in *Revue des sciences philologiques et théologiques*, 25 (1936), p. 315.

[2] *Oracula Sibyllina*, VI, 26–8 (GCS, p. 132).

[3] *Martyrium Andreae*, 19 (Lipsius-Bonnet, *Acta Apostolorum Apocrypha*, II, 1, Leipzig, 1898, p. 54, ll. 23 ff.).

a special significance is attributed to the manner of the crucified apostle's death. The fact that Peter was nailed to the wood head downwards is for the martyrologist a symbol of the fall of the first man before the creation of the world, for he fell into sin head-long, which means, according to the Gnostic belief, that he fell into physical existence. There is a mixture here of Platonic stuff with some of the myths about human origins which we find in the *Poimandres* and Hippolytus' Naassene sermon.[1] Yet through it all we catch a gleam of the Christian belief concerning the sin of Adam which was wiped out by the cross—and indeed the mystery of the cross consists precisely in this, that by means of it mankind is given a new heavenward direction and that its fall is arrested. This is evident enough in the prayer which these *Actus Vercellenses* put into the apostle's mouth, whilst he hangs on the cross:

"O name of the Cross! O hidden mystery! O inexpressible grace that is expressed with the name of the Cross! O nature of man that can no longer be separated from God! . . . Now ye see the mystery of all creation and the beginning of all things even as it was; for the first man, of whose breed I received the form I bear, fell head downwards."[2]

For the entire cosmos then the cross is the μηχανή or "engine"—that is what Ignatius of Antioch once called it[3]—of re-ascent into heaven, and the whole cosmos is everywhere marked with its mystical sign. The seeking and enumeration of the instances where the sign of the cross can be discerned is one of the first elements of Christian symbolism. It is seen in lifeless nature, in the patterning of man and even in the tools and instruments of daily toil—and all this can only be understood in the light of the basic idea of the mystery which the cross contains. The cross is everywhere—it is in the shape of the human form when we stretch out our hands in prayer, it is in the flight of birds, in the instruments of husbandry, it is in the form of the ship's mast when it is crossed by a spar.

[1] Cf. R. Reitzenstein, *Poimandres*, pp. 242 ff.
[2] *Actus Vercellenses*, 37, 38 (Lipsius, *Acta Apost. Apocr.*, I, pp. 92–4).
[3] *Ad Ephesios*, 9, 1 (Funk, I, p. 220, l. 12).

Already in the second century we find this mystical symbolism fully developed in Justin:

"Look upon anything in the world, and ask yourself whether it could be used or even go on existing without this figure of the cross. We could not cross the sea if the sailyard did not remain intact upon the ship. The earth is not ploughed without the cross. Men could not dig or do any other work upon it without tools that bear this shape. The human form is distinguished by nothing else from that of the unreasoning beasts save that it is upright and can stretch out its hands. . . . Yes, even the symbols used by you pagans show the power of this sign. You have but to look at your standards and the *tropaia* which always accompany your marches."[1]

How common this symbolism was in the early Church we can see from similar passages in Tertullian[2] and Minucius Felix.[3] Even in the fifth century, we find Maximus of Turin, when preaching to his faithful, using a whole multitude of these images:

"Wonderful is this mystery of the cross, for by this sign the whole round world is saved. A symbol of this mystery is the sail that hangs on the mast of a ship like Christ upon the cross; and when the good husbandman sets to to plough his land, lo, he too can only accomplish his task with something figured according to the shape of the cross. Even the arch of heaven is formed in the shape of a cross, and when man strides forth, when he raises his arms, he also describes a cross. That is why we should always pray with outstretched arms, so that with the posture of our limbs we may imitate the sufferings of the Lord."[4]

It is plain from this how in their seeing, in their thinking and in their praying, the hearts of the ancient Christians were wholly filled by their beloved mystery of the cross, and indeed this fact is cardinal if we are to understand early Christian art and early

---

[1] *Apologia,* I, 55 (Otto, I, pp. 150f.).
[2] *Apologeticum,* 16, 6–8 (CSEL, 69, pp. 42f.).
[3] *Octavius,* 29, 6, 7 (CSEL, 2, p. 43).
[4] *Homilia* 50, "De Cruce Domini" (PL, 57, 341f.).

Christian symbolism. The apparently clumsy simplicity of the painted and scribbled crosses in the catacombs, the primitive character of the figures in prayer—all this is, precisely because of its simplicity, a mystery. The man of antiquity had a very lively feeling for the well-nigh dialectical contradiction between the almost contemptible humility of the symbol—the drawing, the gesture or whatever it was—and the immensity of its content. There was here a sort of tension, the "mystery tension" if I may call it that, to which he was quite peculiarly responsive, and it was inevitable that this tension should have been perceptible in the symbols—and symbolic phrases—chosen to express the inner meaning of the cross. The cross is "that tiny piece of wood to which men entrust their souls" (Wisdom 14. 5), the weak vessel which traverses the wild ocean alone, the tiny wooden rudder that nevertheless guides whole vessels. "Saving the world with pitiful wood" is a phrase coined by Gregory of Nazianzus,[1] and Gregory of Nyssa, with his truly Greek feeling for the divine paradox of the mystery of salvation, expresses the same thought, showing yet again how essential it is in the basic structure of the ancient Christian mystery, when he points out that what should most astonish us is that such a great mystery was accomplished "in the tiny space" of three days.[2] The mystery of the cross is none other than the greatness of God's wisdom visible in the foolishness of the insignificant symbol.

It was this very meanness that never ceased to fill the Christians with exaltation and gave them an added sense of triumph as the power of the cults waned before their eyes. The cross was a common piece of wood, yet it was a wood to which, in the words of Firmicus Maternus, "a man should fasten his life, for he would so surround himself with the framework of immortality".[3] An anonymous Greek of the fourth century contrasts the cross with Helios, who towards the end became the supreme cult god of all mysteries. Now, he joyfully declares, Helios is conquered by the cross, "and man who could learn nothing from the created sun, lo, now the sunlight of the cross surrounds him with its rays and

[1] *Oratio* 4, 18 (PG, 35, 545 C); *Oratio*, 43, 70 (PG, 36, 592 B).
[2] *Catechesis Magna*, 36 (PG, 45, 92 D).
[3] *De Errore Prof. Rel.*, 27, 1 (CSEL, 2, p. 120, ll. 12f.).

he is illuminated".[1] Then the author bursts into a lofty hymn of praise exalting the mystery of the cross. "O this truly divine wisdom! O engine of heaven (μηχανὴ οὐράνιος). The cross was thrust into the earth, and lo, idolatry was destroyed. This is no common wood, but wood of which God made use to bring about his victory. Wood and spear and nails and dying; these are the cradle-clothes of everlasting life, from these there came the birth of the Second Man. Oh, paradox and wonder!"

As the pagan mysteries begin to faint and fail, the paean grows louder. No longer do the lamentations over the dead Adonis fill the cities, nor the rejoicings over the resurrected lover of Venus—Origen[2] and Cyril of Alexandria[3] tell us something of this—, but the mourning at the cross and the Easter joy of the new mystery. "Under the sign of the cross", says Athansius,[4] "the spells of the Cabiri have come to an end, and by the power of this simple, humble word that has gone forth over the entire world men have despised death and have begun to think everlasting things."

For the cross is the shame of Christ and also his glory and his power. Christ crucified is "the true Orpheus" who brought home his bride, mankind, out of the depths of dark Hades; he is Orpheus Bacchicus and is so described on a well-known early Christian representation of the cross upon an iron cylinder.[5] The Middle Ages still had an intimation of this and a hymn on the mystery of the cross runs as follows:

> Brazen serpent on a pole—
> Serpent once did make men whole,
>   Cured the poisoned sting.
> Orpheus of the latter day
> Dauntlessly his bride away
>   Out of Hell did bring.[6]

[1] Pseudo-Athanasius, *De Passione Domini* (PG, 28, 1056 B).

[2] *Selecta in Ezechiel* (PG, 13, 800 A).   [3] *Comment. in Isaiam*, 2 (PG, 70, 441 B).

[4] Thus, somewhat abbreviated by myself, in the *Oratio de Incarnatione Verbi*, 47 (PG, 25, 180f.).

[5] Cf. *Dictionnaire d'archéologie chrétienne*, XII, Paris, 1936, col. 2735-55, where also see illustration of the Orpheus cross, Fig. 9249; A. Boulanger, *Orphée, Rapports de l'orphisme et du christianisme*, Paris, 1925, p. 7.

[6] Anonymous author (twelfth century) of the Easter sequence, *Morte Christi Celebrata*. Text in A. Mai, *Nova Patrum Bibliotheca*, I, 2, Rome, 1852, p. 208.

2

This cosmic mystery of the cross in itself provides the key to the whole early Christian attitude on the subject of mystery. The cross is a mystery because it gives expression to the fundamental laws that govern all that happens in the world, yet does so in so simple a manner, with such well-nigh contemptuous brevity and on so contemptuously petty a scale, that a huge paradox is created, a gigantic and incredible contrast between word and meaning, between the thing seen and what remains unseen. It is in the scale of that incredible paradox that the mystery resides.

The same quality of obedience to an operative law or plan is discernible if we regard the cross as the centre of the whole narrative of our salvation, as the climax in the drama, enacted by God since the beginning of man, in which the manner of that salvation is revealed. For the cross is also a biblical mystery, in so far as the plan of God's hidden will for our redemption finds its ultimate expression in it, though it does so, in the words of an early Christian, in a "poor and shameful mystery".[1]

It is among the fundamental principles of the early Christian theology of symbolism that everything revealed by God in the Old Testament, from the "Tree of Life" (Gen. 2. 9) to the personal Wisdom of God (Prov. 3. 18) in which this tree of life was embodied, is only made known to us because of its relevance to the coming event of our salvation through the death on the cross of the divine Wisdom made man. It is from this that the Old Testament derives its character of a single vast parable in which the future hides itself but is at the same time made known to those who have understanding. The Old Covenant contains all the "mysteries of the Logos";[2] to be more precise, it contains, as Justin says,[3] "the mystery of the cross", and in Justin's dialogue with Trypho the Jew we can see how superbly developed, even in the first decades of the second century, was this theology of the biblical mystery of the cross. This is also apparent in the so-called *Epistle of Barnabas*,[4] in which the author, who devotes a special

[1] Justin, *Dialogus*, 114 (Otto, II, p. 466).
[2] Hippolytus, *De Antichristo*, 2 (GCS, I, 2, p. 4, l. 17).
[3] *Dialogus*, 91 (Otto, II, p. 330).　　[4] *Epistola Barnabae*, 12 (Funk, I, pp. 74–8).

chapter to the matter, gathers together—in what is perhaps a rather laboured piece of exegesis—all the various prefigurations of the cross.

We may smile today at these rather childish methods of interpretation in which we can already discern the first traces of the art of the Alexandrian exegetes, but the basic belief from which all this proceeds is simply Paul's theology: "Now all these things were done in a figure for us upon whom the ends of the world are come" (I Cor. 10. 6, 11). So deeply was the ancient Christian permeated by his mystical and unquestioning conviction of the significance of the cross that, as by a single stroke of magic, the whole cosmos seemed to him to stand revealed by it and the Old Testament along with the rest. The veil of the temple was rent and the mystery of God was declared, only to be hidden once more by the bloody veil of Christ's death, a veil that will only be removed when the end of days is come "in the sign of spreading out in heaven".

Thus the interpretation of the Bible itself becomes a mystery drama that keeps the soul in continual tension. Augustine in particular underwent this experience and showed in it all the peculiar genius with which his classical and Christian mind was endowed. "In the mystery of the cross all that was hidden in the Old Testament was to be revealed—and that is why the veil in the temple was rent", runs a passage in one of his sermons.[1] Tertullian had already expressed the same feeling in a more dialectical fashion. "Yes," he says, "when it was proclaimed of old, this mystery of the cross had to be hidden by the use of images. Had it been proclaimed without them and presented to us naked, it would have been an even greater stumbling-block. And the more superb the mystery, the more it had to remain under the shadow of imagery, so that its very hardness for our understanding should impel us ever anew to seek the grace of God."[2]

It is impossible within the compass of this book to give you even an inkling of the dogmatic profundity or of the wealth of lyrically enchanting conceits and images which the theologians of this time developed out of this mystery. Wherever wood is men-

---

[1] *Sermo* 300, 4 (PL, 38, 1138 D).
[2] *Adversus Marcionem*, III, 18 (CSEL, 47, p. 406, ll. 7-11).

tioned in the Old Testament it becomes a sign for the mystic of the New (Heb. 9. 23). In all such cases he perceives "the power that God has placed in the mystery of the cross".[1] One need but think of the saving wood of Noah's ark, the wooden staff of Moses which caused the water to flow, the wooden frame from which hung the brazen serpent, the blossoming tree that grew by the waterbrook. I have discussed elsewhere how the idea of the "mystery of the wood" was developed under the image of Noah's ark sailing over the flood,[2] and one could write an account of every one of these symbols of the cross which would be of great importance not only to the student of mysticism but also for the art historian; for, alas, I doubt whether contemporary scholarship is even now alive to the real inwardness of that deep feeling for what we call "mystery" that characterized the ancient Christians and in this instance found such eloquent expression among them, though it was something that remained alive right into the days of Romanesque art and Gothic mysticism. Unfortunately I cannot range too far and so I will only speak of a single symbol in which a biblical archetype is seen in the light of the cross. The Latins referred to it as *sacramentum ligni vitae*, the Greeks as μυστήριον τοῦ ξύλου. It is the wood of the tree of life in Paradise, and I will say something about its relevance, as these men understood it, to the cross of Christ.[3]

Already in Jewish prophecy the tree of life with the four-fold stream of water around it (Gen. 2. 9, 10) was an image representing Messianic salvation (cf. Ezech. 47. 12).[4] Indeed the divine Wisdom was itself this tree of life (Prov. 3. 18) and the author of the New Testament Apocalypse sees the fulfilment of redemption under the same image (Apoc. 2. 7; 22. 2). But here there enters a new

[1] Justin, *Dialogus*, 91, 1 (Otto, II, p. 330).

[2] H. Rahner, "Das Schiff aus Holz" (The Ship Made of Wood), in *Zeitschrift für katholische Theologie*, 67 (1943), pp. 1–21.

[3] Cf. F. Piper, *Der Baum des Lebens* (The Tree of Life), Berlin, 1863; A. Wünsche, *Die Sagen vom Lebensbaum und Lebenswasser: Altorientalische Mythen* (Myths of the Tree of Life and of the Living Water: Myths of the Ancient East) (Ex Oriente Lux, I, 2), Leipzig, 1905; F. Kampers, *Mittelalterliche Sagen vom Paradiese und vom Holze des Kreuzes Christi* (Medieval Myths concerning Paradise and the Wood of the Cross of Christ), Cologne, 1897; L. von Sybel, "ὕλον Εζωῆς", in *Zeitschrift für die neutestamentliche Wissenschaft*, 19 (1920), pp. 85–91; 20 (1921), pp. 93 ff.; R. Bauerreiss, *Arbor Vitae: Der Lebensbaum und seine Verwendung in Liturgie, Kunst und Brauchtum des Abendlandes* (The Tree of Life and its Use in the Liturgy, Art and Custom of the West), Munich, 1938.

[4] Cf. also the *Book of Enoch*, 24, 3–6; 25, 1–7.

element which makes all the difference. "A right to the tree of life" (Apoc. 22. 14) is reserved to those who have washed their robes in the blood of the Lamb. Between the tree of life in Paradise and the tree of life of the New Heaven the ancient Christian saw towering up yet another tree of life on which the fate of the children of Adam is decided—the cross—, and with his mystic's eye he saw these trees all within the framework of a single image. The tree of Paradise is only a prefiguration of the cross and this cross is the centre of the world and of the drama of man's salvation. It towers from Golgotha to heaven, gathering the whole world together, and was set up in the same place where Adam was created, where he lies buried and where at the same hour of the same day the second Adam was to die; and at its foot there stream the four rivers of Paradise. These are the rivers of the mystery of baptism by means of which Adam's posterity obtains a new right to the ever green tree of life.[1] A Christian poem of the third century begins with the words:

> *Est locus ex omni medius quem credimus orbe*
> *Golgotha Iudaei patrio cognomine dicunt.*[2]
> (There is a place which we believe to be the centre
> of the world
> The Jews give it the native name of Golgotha.)

Then the poet describes how this cross – tree of life grows to an immense height, how it stretches out its arms, gathering the whole round world in its grasp, how at its foot the baptismal spring bubbles forth and how all nations hurry to the spot to drink everlasting life. The poem closes with the lines:

> *Inde iter ad caelum per ramos arboris altae,*
> *Hoc lignum vitae cunctis credentibus.   Amen.*
> (Thence we go to heaven by way of the
> branches of the high tree.
> This is the wood of life to all that believe.   Amen.)

[1] Cf. R. E. Schlee, *Ikonographie der Paradiesesflüsse* (Iconography of the Rivers of Paradise), Leipzig, 1937; W. von Reybekiel, "Der Fons Vitae in der christlichen Kunst" (The Fountain of Life in Christian Art), in *Niederdeutsche Zeitschrift für Volkskunde*, 12 (1934), pp. 87–136.
[2] Pseudo-Cyprian, *Carmen de Pascha vel de Ligno Vitae* (CSEL, 3, pp. 305–8).

The words about the bubbling spring, of course, embody the ancient Christian mystery of "the cross in the spring of water"— and who here could fail to call to mind the wonderful mosaics with which Christian antiquity in Rome decorated its baptismal chapels?[1]

We must, however, delve a little deeper. An old Hebrew tradition which has been reinterpreted by Christianity connects the tree of Paradise and the creation of Adam with the Messianic redemption. This idea finds particularly clear expression in the so-called *Syrian Treasure Cave*, a work produced by the circle of Ephraem the Syrian.[2] This work tells of the creation of the first man. God is described as making him out of the world's four elements and fashioning him into a sun man, a magnificent creature:

> And God made Adam with his holy hands
> In his own image and likeness,
> And as the angels saw the wondrous sight
> They were moved by the loveliness of Adam's face,
> And when they looked upon that face
> They saw it surrounded by flames of glory like the
>   orb of the sun.
> The light of his eyes was like the light of the sun
> The light of his body was like the sparkling of
>   crystal;
> And Adam stretched himself and stood in the middle
>   of the earth,
> And set his feet upon the spot
> Where the cross of our Redeemer was set up.[3]

This spot, however, was at the foot of the tree of life in the midst of Paradise, and later the poet says, "This tree of life in the midst of Paradise is a prefiguration of the redeeming cross which is the true tree of life, and this cross was set up in the centre of the earth."[4] A similar prefiguring mystery takes place at

[1] J. Wilpert, *Die römischen Mosaiken und Malereien* (Roman Mosaics and Paintings), Freiburg, 1916, vol. I, pp. 193, 223, 227.
[2] C. Bezold, *Die Schatzhöhle*, published in Syriac and German, 2 vols., Leipzig, 1883, 1888.
[3] *Schatzhöhle*, II, 12–16. [4] *Ibid.*, IV, 3.

Adam's death when Adam has lost his sunlike quality through sin, a quality he is only to regain through the death of the redeemer who is to come:

> And Adam departed from this world
> On the fourteenth of Nisan at the ninth hour
> Upon a Friday.
> At the same hour at which the Son of Man
> Upon the cross asked his Father to receive his spirit.[1]

Admittedly we have now entered the domain of poetic religious fancy; but the ultimate source of all these legends of the tree of life, legends often made delightful by true poetic artistry, is simply the theological mystery of the cross. Without some knowledge of this ancient symbolism, moreover, it would be quite impossible to understand much of the art either of late antiquity or the Middle Ages.

In the Ethiopic version of the so-called *Book of Adam*[2] the account of Adam's death has even more explicit references to the mystery of the cross. The dying man bids his son Seth to bury his body in the earth after the flood which is to come, "for the place where my body will be laid is the centre of the earth and from there God will come to redeem all our race".[3] And when after the flood Adam's coffin was carried out of the ark, the voice of the dead man was heard to say, "Into the land whither we go the Logos of God will descend, and he will live there, and in the place where my body lies he will be crucified, so that he will sprinkle my head with his blood."[4]

We are all familiar with the practice of medieval art which depicted the skull of Adam at the foot of the cross. We can now discern the ancient Christian source from which these pictorial symbols drew their inspiration. For a thousand years the power of this *sacramentum ligni vitae* expressed itself in word, colour and line,

[1] *Schatzhöhle*, VI, 17, 18.
[2] Text of the Ethiopic version in E. Trumpp, "Der Kampf Adams oder das christliche Adambuch des Morgenlandes" (The Battle of Adam or the Eastern Christian Book of Adam), in *Abhandlungen der Bayrischen Akademie der Wissenschaften*, Hist.-Phil. Klasse, XV, 3 (1880). Extracts in Kampers, *Mittelalterliche Sagen*, pp. 16–25. Cf. also F. Piper, "Adams Grab auf Golgotha" (Adam's Grave on Golgotha), in *Evangelischer Kalender*, Berlin, 1861, pp. 17ff.   [3] Kampers, p. 23.   [4] Kampers, p. 24.

but the works thus created no longer contain their old significance for us, because we no longer have that understanding of the mystery of the cross which the ancient Christians once possessed.

It still remains for me to say a word on the garland of legend that twines round the wood of the tree of life. There is, for instance, the story of Adam, as he lay sick unto death, sending his son Seth to Paradise to fetch from the tree of life the fruit of immortality. But the angel who guards Paradise will only give him three kernels and from these there grow the cedar, the cypress, and the pine, springing up from dead Adam's mouth; and as the strange story winds its way through all the events of the Old Testament, the wood continues to be preserved until the day when the servants of the worldly power fashion it into the cross of Christ.

All through the Middle Ages these legends were further embroidered. Yet they are nothing more than what we have called the ancient Christian mystery of the cross that has here been naïvely remoulded by the artistry of folklore[1] and so made vivid to men's minds. At the back of this proliferation of tales is the purely theological conviction that Christ and Adam, the pneumatic and the fleshly man, are intimately linked together (cf. I Cor. 15. 45–9), and while these legends are passed on by whispered word-of-mouth and by pictorial imagery, the clear, sharply defined formulations of ancient theology continue down the centuries. Thus the classical antithesis is kept alive by which the wood of Paradise is brought into relation with the wood of the cross.

All this belongs to the very substance of primitive theological thought and we can already come across it in Irenaeus as a tradition handed down by the presbyters of Asia Minor: "Because we lost the Logos through wood, therefore it was by wood that he was revealed to all men, and it was through wood that he showed the height and the length and the breadth and the depth, for—as one of the presbyters has said—in the stretching out of his hands he united both nations in a single God."[2] The two nations are the

---

[1] Cf. also A. Mussafia, "Sulla legenda del legno della Croce" (The Legend of the Wood of the Cross), in *Sitzungsberichte der Wiener Akademie der Wissenschaften*, 1869, pp. 165–216; H. Rahner, "Das Schiff aus Holz" (The Ship Made of Wood), *Zeitschrift für katholische Theologie*, 67 (1943), pp. 10f.

[2] *Adv. Haer.*, V, 17, 4 (Harvey, II, p. 372).

Jews and the Greeks who are now united by the wood of the cross
(cf. Eph. 2. 13–14). In the mystery of the cross the cosmos of the
Greeks and the Bible of the Jews converge upon each other. It is
this that makes Ephraem the Syrian say: "All mysteries were consummated by the Lord of all men in his crucifixion, and he
embraced the two worlds of the two people when he embraced
his cross."[1]

Greek and Byzantine theology have thought their way through
the profundities of these things and clothed them in the wonderful
garment of their panegyrics on the life-giving wood of the cross.
We need only read Gregory of Nyssa's teaching on the tree of
life[2] or the rapturous hymn on the biblical mystery of the wood
by the Byzantine Theophanes Kerameus.[3] Or again take those
words of an anonymous Greek on the mystery of Good Friday.
He praises God for consummating and restoring on this day his
first creation of Adam and says, "Today on the sixth day of the
week Adam was fashioned, today he received the form that made
him a partaker in the divine nature. Today he was set as a small
cosmos in the great one. . . . O the diversity of this day! O day of
grief and day of grief dispelled! O thou morning [of creation] that
didst bring forth sorrow! O thou evening [of death on the cross]
that didst bring us joy!"[4] What this Greek has uttered here in the
idiom of hymnology has become a never to be forgotten enrich-
ment of our dogmatic theological teaching thanks to the limpid
wisdom of John of Damascus.[5]

In the West the mystery of the cross developed on exactly the
same lines. Augustine in particular endowed it with the characteristic thought-forms and the beauty of his native speech. The *sacramentum ligni* touched the most profound regions of his thought.[6]
His spiritual heirs continued to be nourished by it and the Roman
liturgy resounds with this mystery as do the hymns of Venantius
Fortunatus. "*Per arborem mortui, per arborem vivificati*–By the

[1] *Sermo 6: in Hebdomadam Sanctam*, 17 (Lamy, I, p. 502).
[2] *Oratio 4: in Resurrectionem Domini* (PG, 46, 684 AB).
[3] *Homilia 4: in Exaltationem Crucis* (PG, 132, 183–204).
[4] Pseudo-Chrysostomus, *In Magnam Parasceven* (PG, 50, 812).
[5] *De Fide Orthodoxa*, IV, 11 (PG, 94, 1132f.).
[6] *De Genesi ad Litteram*, VIII, 4, 5 (PL, 34, 375f.); *De Genesi contra Manichaeos*, II, 22
(PL, 34, 213f.); *De Cathechizandis Rudibus*, 20 (PL, 40, 335f.).

tree brought to death, by the tree given life", are the words of a post-Augustinian sermon, and the preacher bursts into the cry, "*O sacramentorum immane mysterium*–O awful mystery of the secret dealings of God."[1]

Thomas Aquinas[2] is wholly dependent on the thought of Augustine in this matter, nor, without the kind of ideas that I have tried to describe here concerning the Christian mystery of the cross, could we conceivably understand Dante's *Purgatorio* (XXIII, 73–5), or the lofty discourse with "Old Father Adam" in the *Paradiso* (Canto XXVI). The charming Salzburg miniature by Berthold Furtmayr[3] (dating from 1481) might well be called the last word about the mystery of the tree of life: Eve in her grace-forsaken nakedness hands out the food of death from the tree of Paradise, but on the same tree there hangs the Crucified One, and from it the Church is plucking the physic of everlasting life.

In an Easter sermon dating from the beginning of the third century by Hippolytus of Rome there occurs a wonderful passage exalting the cosmic and the biblical mystery of the wood of the cross.[4] I should like to conclude these observations of mine by quoting it to you:

"This tree, wide as the heavens itself, has grown up into heaven from the earth. It is an immortal growth and towers twixt heaven and earth. It is the fulcrum of all things and the place where they are at rest. It is the foundation of the round world, the centre of the cosmos. In it all the diversities in our human nature are formed into a unity. It is held together by invisible nails of the Spirit so that it may not break loose from the divine. It touches the highest summits of heaven and makes the earth firm beneath its foot, and it grasps the middle regions between them with its immeasurable arms. . . .

"O Crucified One, thou leader of the mystical dances! O this

---

[1] Pseudo-Augustinus, *Sermo de Adam et Eva et Sancta Maria* (A. Mai, *Nova Patrum Bibliotheca*, I, 1, Rome, 1852, p. 3).

[2] *Summa Theologica*, III, q. 46, a. 4.

[3] Coloured reproduction in G. Leidinger, *Meisterwerke der Buchmalerei aus Handschriften der bayrischen Staatsbibliothek München* (Masterpieces of Book Illumination in Manuscripts of the Bavarian State Library in Munich), Munich, 1921, Plate 38.

[4] *De Pascha Homilia*, 6 (PG, 59, 743–5).

spiritual wedding feast! O this divine Pasch that passes from heaven to earth and rises up again to heaven! O this new feast of all things! O cosmic festal gathering! O joy of the universe, honour, ecstasy, exquisite delight by which dark death is destroyed, life returns to all and the gates of heaven are opened. God appeared as a man and man rose up as God when he shattered the gates of Hell and burst the iron bolts thereof. And the people that were in the depths arise from the dead and announce to all the hosts of heaven: 'The thronging choir from earth is coming home'."

III

THE MYSTERY OF BAPTISM

Felix sacramentum aquae nostrae

O HAPPY mystery of this water of ours!" These are the words with which Tertullian begins his work on baptism,[1] and they are almost identical with those used a century earlier in the joyous outburst of the *Epistle of Barnabas*: "Blessed are they who, hoping on the cross, descend into the water."[2] The mystery of baptism can only be understood in the light of the mystery of the cross; the water of life gushes forth at the foot of the tree of life, and life was only given to that water through God's atoning death upon the cross, "so that he might sanctify the water through his sufferings". Thus said Ignatius of Antioch.[3]

The practice of looking at the two mysteries together goes right back to the theology of Paul. "Know you not that all we who are baptized in Christ Jesus are baptized into his death? For we are buried together with him by baptism into death: that, as Christ is risen from the dead by the glory of the Father, so we also may walk in newness of life" (Rom. 6. 3–4). The bath of baptism therefore achieves two things: it redeems us from our sins and it gives us a new Christ-like life, and the only thing that enables it to do this is Christ's death upon the cross.

Thus baptism is the basic mystery of Christianity, the real initiation into our sharing in the divine life of Christ, dead and risen again; it is also the consummating mystery, the μυστήριον τῆς τελειώσεως, as it was later called.[4] It is not surprising that comparative religion should have concerned itself so energetically with

---

[1] *De Baptismo*, I (CSEL, 20, p. 201, l. 3).
[2] *Epist. Barnabae*, 11, 8 (Funk I, p. 72, ll. 24 f.).
[3] *Ad Ephesios*, 18, 2 (Funk, I, p. 228, l. 1).
[4] Gregory of Nazianzus, *Oratio* 40, 28 (PG, 36, 400 B).

this particular mystery,[1] for it seemed to the practitioners of that science that in no other point could proof be so clearly established that the original purification rites which had been taken over from Judaism had turned into the "syncretistic mystery of baptism",[2] having first got themselves overlaid with vague Hellenistic deification hopes. The task seemed particularly easy since a respectable quantity of material was available on the lustral rites of the ancient cults. We know something of such a rite, for instance, in the ritual of Eleusis, and from Demosthenes' *De Corona* we know something of the cleansing ablutions of the Sabazios mystery; the Attis cult had its *taurobolium*, there was a sanctifying bath in the Isis mystery and the same applies to the cults of Mithras and Dionysus.[3]

Unfortunately the most recent scholarship is quite remarkably firm in rejecting the whole notion of any such influences, and this both in regard to the general teaching of the New Testament on the subject of baptism and more particularly in regard to that of the Epistle to the Romans. Yet the only result of this seems to be that people of the type in question insist even more light-heartedly than before in tracing an alleged "hellenization" of the sacrament of baptism, that is supposed to have begun in the second century, and continue as of old in their efforts to demonstrate that this "primitive Catholic" mystery had no longer anything in common

---

[1] Cf. P. Gennrich, *Die Lehre von der Wiedergeburt in dogmengeschichtlicher und religions-geschichtlicher Beleuchtung* (The Doctrine of Rebirth in its Relation to the History of Dogma and the History of Religion), Berlin, 1907; R. Perdelwitz, *Die Mysterienreligion und das Problem des ersten Petrusbriefs* (Mystery Religion and the Problem of the First Epistle of Peter), Giessen, 1911; J. Leipoldt, *Die urchristliche Taufe im Licht der Religions-geschichte* (Primitive Christian Baptism in the Light of the History of Religion), Leipzig, 1928; R. Reitzenstein, *Die Vorgeschichte der christlichen Taufe* (The Prehistory of Christian Baptism), Berlin–Leipzig, 1929. In criticism: J. Dey, Παλιγγενεσία, Münster, 1937; K. Prümm, *Der christliche Glaube und die altheidnische Welt* (Christian Belief and the World of Ancient Paganism), II, pp. 273 ff., which discuss the Pauline teaching concerning baptism and the mystery of Christ in their relation to the Hellenistic mystery cults.

[2] Thus A. Oepke writing in Kittel, *Theologisches Wörterbuch zum Neuen Testament*, I, Stuttgart, 1933, pp. 541–3: "Die Taufe als synkretistisches Mysterium" (Baptism as a Syncretistic Mystery).

[3] Cf. J. Steinbeck, "Kultische Waschungen und Bäder im Heidentum und Judentum und ihr Verhältnis zur christlichen Taufe" (Cultic Washing and Bathing among the Pagans and the Jews and their Relation to Christian Baptism), *Neue kirchliche Zeitschrift*, 21 (1910), pp. 778 ff. A complete collation of all the material by Oepke (Kittel, I, pp. 528–33).

with the teaching of Jesus or its admittedly correct interpretation by Paul.

The essence of such attempts is the obsessive conviction that a so-called "magical" element is to be found in the sacrament. Even Oepke is not blameless. Usually he makes a most telling distinction between Christian baptism and "the lustrations and revivifications" of Hellenistic baptismal practice "which were wholly without moral significance and were interpreted in a purely ritual, magical and fundamentally naturalistic sense". Yet he jumps to conclusions like the rest and talks of a "forced conception of the sacrament resulting from the influence of magical ideas" (*magisch übersteigerter Sakramentsbegriff*) which is alleged to have imposed itself on Pauline thought: needless to say this was due to the influence of the magical mystery cults to which primitive Christianity is supposed to have succumbed.

It would go beyond the scope of this book to refute all this by reference to the source material, especially when scholarship has already so largely completed the task. There are, however, two points I should like to stress. First, I should like to repeat the sharp distinction I drew earlier between the enduring Christian essence of these mysteries and the mystery terminology which gradually developed alongside it. Secondly, I should like to stress the fact of a fundamental belief, continuing through all this time, that in the sacrament with its basic form fashioned by Christ—in baptism it is a simple bath accompanied by the speaking of certain words (Mat. 28. 19)—it is Christ himself, Christ crucified and glorified, who is at work. It is because its power derives in the last resort solely from the free personal will to save of the God-man that all talk of the "magical efficacy" of the sacrament remains unworthy of serious consideration—at least it does so for as long as we restrict the word magic to the clearly circumscribed meaning it bears in religious psychology.[1] As to the rites, images and words that in the course of time have attached themselves to the sacramental core, exorcisms, unctions, signings with the cross, white robe and burning light—these things are certainly something more than a

[1] Cf. Prümm, *Der christlicher Glaube und die altheidnische Welt*, II, pp. 270ff: "Christliche Taufe und Zauberhandlung" (Christian Baptism and Magic).

kind of residuum from the mystery cults. For all that, however, we are wholly within our rights in examining them to see whether at the deeper levels some connexion with the cults cannot be traced—provided always, of course, that we proceed in the spirit of our previous analysis and continue the same scrupulous scrutiny of the source material.

We should now be clear in our minds—in theory at any rate—about what we mean by the mystery of baptism. If in what follows I lay before you some of the more exquisite pieces from this ancient Christian treasury, you will see it in the form which over four centuries it assumed as the result of its organic growth, as the result of the vital principle within it. Yet despite all the dazzling riches displayed, it will remain in essence the simple sign of water and the word (Eph. 5. 26) that draws its life-generating power out of Christ's death upon the cross. This is the basic conception, this is the root from which all subsequent growth was derived. Here was, so to speak, the soul which endowed the ancient Christian with such intellectual, imaginative and creative power that in giving the baptismal mystery a characteristic outward shape, he could not only impress into his service the cosmic and biblical mysteries of the cross but could even turn to the mystery cults and utilize whatever thoughts and words he found there that, at least on the ordinary human level, were truly pure and profound.

But we can surely put the matter thus: that this ancient Christian mystery should have developed in all its richness out of the simple baptismal rites of the New Testament is due to one fact and one fact only—the character of the sacramental system itself, the fact that Christ has made an apparently trifling and insignificant action with water accompanied by a few spoken words the signal for such immense and incredible consequences. It is here that we begin to discern the effect of that feeling for the true nature of a mystery that marked the man of antiquity; I mean that awareness of a tension that arises whenever a symbol is used. It is a tension between word and meaning, between the slightness of the visible and the awful power of the invisible.

Tertullian shows a marvellous feeling for this in his book on baptism when he contrasts these two polarities with one another: "*simplicitas divinorum operum quae in actu videtur et magnificentia quae in effectu promittitur*–the simplicity of God's works which is seen in the action, their magnificence which is promised for the result of the action".[1] Here indeed you have a description of a mystery marked by all Tertullian's characteristic pregnancy; and if the Church in the course of centuries surrounded the simple rite of baptism with a wealth of mystery ritual, this only means that she was attempting to make visible to the human eye something of the divine glory of that reality of which this simple sign is the token and which it actually calls into being.

Gregory of Nyssa displays the same sensitive instinct for the nature of a mystery when he says that baptism is "a slight thing but the source of great possessions".[2] The baptismal chapel is, in the words of the Gallican liturgy, "a humble place yet full of graces",[3] and Ambrose in his poem on the baptismal church, a poem on which I shall shortly have more to say, coined a phrase which could well be set out as a kind of headline describing the whole mystery of baptism, the phrase in which he marvels at the paradox of contrast between the "minute point" of the visible and the divine effects that proceed from it:

nam quid divinius isto
ut puncto exiguo culpa cadat populi?[4]

(What greater proof can ye ask of the power of God who Acting at one small point loosens the guilt of the world?)

I am, then, going to draw your attention to certain aspects of this ancient Christian mystery of baptism. They will give some idea of how the mystery of the cross works itself out in it. They will also show you that, while the Christian of antiquity was giving visible form to this mystery which had always been so peculiarly his own, all that was precious in the world around him seemed to place itself at his disposal.

---

[1] *De Baptismo*, 2 (CSEL, 20, p. 201, ll. 20f.).
[2] *Catechesis Magna*, 36 (PG, 45, 92 D).
[3] *Missale Gothicum: Collectio ad Fontes Benedicendos* (PL, 72, 274 B).
[4] *Carmina Latina Epigraphica*, II, p. 420, No. 908 (Bücheler).

I

First and foremost baptism is "the mystery of eternal life". What is here described as eternal life is precisely that which distinguishes in its essence the Christian mystery from anything pertaining to the mystery cults. It is something utterly alien to the latter's vague longings for a rebirth, a rebirth that was always conceived of within the framework of the natural order. John calls it ζωὴ αἰώνιος, Paul conceives it as a partaking in the glorified life of his risen Lord, as that "partaking of the divine nature" (II Peter 1. 4) which has its final consummation in the direct beholding of God but already has a living root in baptism.[1]

In order to give expression to the redemptive reality of baptism which so far surpassed all the imperfectly articulate aspirations of the ancient world, in order to indicate his belief—which he shared with Paul—in this ever-increasing identity with the glorified life of the resurrected Christ, and in order to do this "by means of images that are familiar", the Christian of antiquity selected one symbol in particular from the pious and mystical usages of his surrounding world. It was one which in its transformed Christian aspect was to have a colourful history. It was "the mystery of the ogdoad"—of the number eight.[2]

It was on the eighth day that Christ rose from the dead, the day of Helios which for Christians now became the first day of the week, even as it had been the first day of creation. Now, in ancient Pythagorean thought the number eight was the symbol of perfection, the symbol denoting that which is everlasting and at rest. Eight is the number of the cube, a solid extending equally in all directions. Eight is the number of the spheres which move around the earth and there is an old saying, "πάντα ὀκτώ – all things are eight".[3]

The Christian of antiquity was familiar with all this. Advancing

[1] Cf. Prümm, *Das Christentum als Neuheitserlebnis*, pp. 167 ff.: "Das Mysterium der christlichen Taufe" (The Mystery of Christian Baptism).

[2] What follows is based on F. J. Dölger, "Zur Symbolik des altchristlichen Taufhauses: Das Oktogon und die Symbolik der Achtzahl (The Symbolism of the Ancient Christian Baptistry: The Octagon and the Symbolism of the Figure Eight), in *Antike und Christentum*, 4 (1934), pp. 153–87.

[3] Theon of Smyrna, *Expositio Rerum Mathematicarum* (ed. Hiller, p. 105, l. 12).

Lib. X, v. 304.

3. Odysseus with Sword and Moly
Gem from Ingbirami

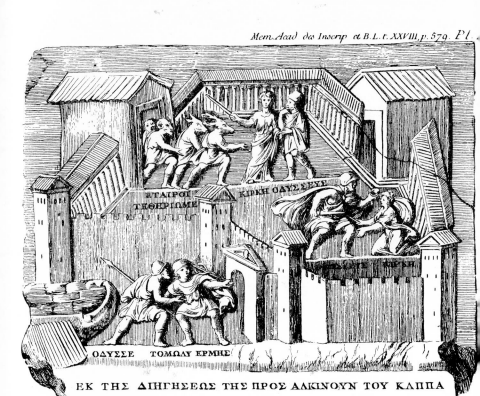

4. Hermes gives Odysseus the Moly

From the *Tabula Rondanini*

from the basic convictions of his faith to a consideration of the way
in which baptism works, he discovered the number eight at every
turn and gave it a Christian interpretation. On the eighth day the
Lord arose; the Christian himself will have received baptism on
an Easter day, which is the liturgical eighth day, and this is also the
day on which the Spirit brooded over the waters. Eight persons
passed over the water in the ark, and the saving wood is a symbol
of the cross. Already in the Second Epistle of Peter (2. 5) we are
told that God "spared not the original world, but preserved the
eighth person Noe, the preacher of justice", a fact which is clearly
regarded by the First Epistle of Peter as a prefiguration of baptism
(3. 20–21), the ark "wherein a few, that is eight souls, were saved
by water. Whereunto baptism being of the like form (ἀντίτυπον),
now saveth you also . . . by the resurrection of Jesus Christ."
This connects up with a whole treasury of images which have
grown out of the mystery of eight and we find these fully developed in Justin as early as the second century:

"The sense of the word of God is this [he says in reference to
the texts just quoted], that at the time of the flood, the mystery
of the salvation of man had already been accomplished. For the
righteous Noah together with the others who survived the flood,
his wife, that is to say, and his three sons together with their wives,
making eight persons in all, became, by reason of this number, a
symbol of the day on which our Christ arose from the dead, for
this was the eighth day which nevertheless by reason of its power
will always be the first. For Christ, the first born of all creation, is
become the beginning of a new race, the race of those who by
virtue of the mystery of the cross are born again of him by water
and faith and the wood."[1]

Baptism is thus a rebirth into eternal life. It is the transition to
the state where there is neither change nor decay and all is at rest,
the state which is symbolically indicated under the figure of the
ogdoad; it is of course the opposite to earthly birth. In the excerpts
from Theodotus compiled by Clement we read: "Whoever is

[1] *Dialogus cum Tryphone*, 138, 1, 2 (Otto, II, p. 486); cf. also *Dial.*, 41, 4 (Otto, II,
pp. 138 f.).

born of an earthly mother is cast forth into death and into the world, but whosoever is born again of Christ, he is transported into life and into the ogdoad. Such men die to the world, but live for God so that death may be made nothing through death, and corruption be made nothing through resurrection."[1] The baptismal fountain is the grave of the life that passes away and the womb of the new life of the heavenly ogdoad—though this has to be understood in a different and higher sense than that in which we speak of Mother Earth being both womb and grave.[2] One of the loveliest of the hymns of praise in honour of this μυστήριον τῆς ὀγδοάδος, or mystery of eight, is to be found in Origen and it glorifies Sunday, the eighth day:

"This is the day which the Lord hath made. What could be like unto it? Upon this day God was reconciled to man. On this day the war with the temporal world was ended and earth made worthy of heaven, for man who was unworthy of the earth was made worthy of heaven when the firstling of our nature was exalted above the heavens and Paradise was opened, when the curse was taken away and sin was redeemed and we regained our ancient home. Though God made all the days, he created this day in a special fashion, for on this day he perfected the greatest of his mysteries."[3]

In Alexandria an understanding for this mystery always remained alive. Cyril was still well acquainted with it. "This eighth day signifies for us the resurrection," he says; "it is the day on which Christ, who suffered death for us, regained life. But we are made like unto him in spirit when in holy baptism we die ourselves, so that we may be made partakers in his resurrection. The time which appears to us best suited for such a solemn

---

[1] *Excerpta ex Theodoto*, 80, 1 (GCS, Clement, III, p. 131, ll. 24ff.).

[2] Clement of Alexandria, *Stromata*, IV, 25, 160 (GCS, II, p. 319, l. 12). On the baptismal font as womb and grave, cf. Cyril of Jerusalem, *Catecheses Mystag.*, 2, 4 (PG, 33, 1080 C), also Dionysius Areopagita, *Eccl. Hier.*, II, 2, 7 (PG, 3, 396 C), und Augustine, *Sermo* 119, 4 (PL, 38, 674 D): *"vulva matris aqua baptismatis"*. Cf. A. Dieterich, *Mutter Erde*, p. 114.

[3] *Selecta in Psalmos* (Lommatzsch, XI, pp. 358f.). Cf. H. Rahner, "Taufe und geistliches Leben bei Origenes" (Baptism and Spiritual Life in Origen), in *Zeitschrift für Aszese und Mystik*, 7 (1932), pp. 205–23.

consummation ($\tau\varepsilon\lambda\varepsilon\acute{\iota}\omega\sigma\iota\varsigma$) is the *mysterium Christi* which is signified to us by the ogdoad."[1]

Latin sacramental mysticism was, however, also acquainted with this symbol: the *sacramentum ogdoadis* as Hilary[2] calls it; and as *sacramentum octavi* it was a favourite subject of Augustine's discourses.[3] The number eight is the symbol for the new birth in baptism and also for that new life which begins in the baptismal water and finds its consummation in final rest, blessedness and the beatific vision. Between baptism and the actual beholding of God, however, there is the spiritual ascent of the Christian gnostic, his gradually increasing deification through the power of baptism; and this deification is itself a mystery of the number eight. Clement of Alexandria has this to say on the matter:

"Whoever, as the apostle writes, has grown into the perfect man, to him applies the saying of David, 'They shall rest upon his holy hill.' Such men will gather together in the heavenly Church on high. There the philosophers of God will assemble, men who have pure hearts and in whom there is no longer any guile. For they have not remained within the number seven which is the number of rest, but having by reason of their good works been made like unto God, they have been exalted to the inheritance of the blessedness pertaining to the number eight, their hearts being set on the pure vision of unending contemplation of which there can be no surfeit."[4]

The influence of this mystical symbolism of the number eight extended even to the shape of the earthly place where this great mystery of baptism was celebrated. The Christians of antiquity nearly always built their baptistries—"those humble places yet full of graces"—in octagonal form. An octagonal balustrade also surrounded the baptismal fonts containing the life-giving water. We also possess the copy of an inscription, long since destroyed,

[1] *Glaphyra in Exodum*, 2 (PG, 69, 441 BC).
[2] *Instructio Psalmorum*, 14 (CSEL, 22, p. 12, l. 24).
[3] *Epistula*, 55, 9, 13, 15 (CSEL, 34, pp. 188, 194f., 201). A quantity of other texts in Dölger, *op. cit.*, pp. 165ff.
[4] *Stromata*, VI, 13, 107f. (GCS, II, pp. 485f.).

which St Ambrose composed for the baptistry of the church of
St Thecla in Milan. The following is a rough metrical translation:

Eight are the temple's walls—O number worthy of holy
  Actions performed at the spot; eight are the walls of the font.
Mystical shape of the house that covers the rites of the water
  —Rites for the saving of man—mystical number of eight,
Rites that derive their pow'r from the light of Christ resurrected
  Christ who set all men free, breaking the shackles of Hell,
Who from the blemish of sin releaseth him that repenteth,
  In the crystalline spring cleansing the bather from guilt.

In the final verse—with which we are already acquainted—
Ambrose uses words which show us all the depth of the mystical
paradox enacted in baptism:

> *nam quid divinius isto*
> *ut puncto exiguo culpa cadat populi?*

(What greater proof can ye ask of the power of God who
Acting at one small point loosens the guilt of the world?)[1]

2

From here we can penetrate a little further into the mystery of
baptism as the Christians of antiquity conceived it. Baptism is only
the "mystery of eternal life", the "*sacramentum octavi*" because the
power of God's death on the cross is effective in it. "What is
water without the Cross of Christ?" Ambrose asks his newly
baptized[2] and answers, "An ordinary element", while Augustine
declares that "the water of the baptismal font is consecrated by the
sign of the cross".[3] A post-Augustinian sermon[4] is even more
specific: "*Per signum crucis in utero sanctae Matris Ecclesiae concepti
estis* – Through the sign of the cross you are conceived in the
womb of your holy Mother, the Church." In other words it is
only by the procreative power of the cross that the Church is
fructified.

[1] Text in Dölger, *op. cit.*, p. 155.   [2] *De Mysteriis*, 4, 20 (PL, 16, 394 C).
[3] *Contra Iulianum*, VI, 19, 62 (PL, 44, 861 A). Cf. also *De Catechizandis Rudibus*, 20 (PL, 40, 325).
[4] Pseudo-Augustinus, *De Symbolo ad Catechumenos* (PL, 40, 659 D).

To put the matter as succinctly as possible, what we are witnessing here is a piece of Pauline theology taking shape as a mystery; it is the theology of the Epistle to the Romans in which baptism and the cross are viewed as a single whole. Baptism is "the mystery of the wood in the water".[1] This is, of course, only one aspect of the whole mystery of Christ, but without some understanding of that aspect neither the Christian mysticism of antiquity nor the liturgy of antiquity nor the great body of Christian art right up to the Middle Ages, can really convey very much to us.

If we are to trace the development of this mystery, we must go back to Jesus' own baptism in the Jordan, an event which from the earliest times Christians regarded as the essential *paradigma* of the mystery of baptism. There is a famous passage in Ignatius of Antioch which says, "Jesus Christ was born and was baptized, so that he might sanctify the water by his passion."[2] God himself took human shape and stood in earthly water and at this moment there took place the theophany of the divine voice testifying to his Sonship. For the Christian of antiquity this event was a manifestation—as it were in a single flash—of the great mystery, the great paradox; it was an anticipation condensed into a single moment, of all the subsequent sequence of suffering on the cross and of that suffering's effects; it was the decision between light and darkness, the transformation of the cosmos, the raising of the earthly to the level of the divine, the breaking in of the next world into the present one.

At a quite early stage this belief began to clothe itself in concrete and visible imagery; we hear of fire bursting forth from Jordan, of the terrified river flooding backwards, of angels that hurry to the spot to give the Son of God the white garment of his divine, essential light. But I cannot here dwell on these embellishments of the story of Christ's baptism, interesting as they may be for the historian of religion.[3] Rather will I concentrate on this one

---

[1] What follows is based on the erudite work of P. Lundberg, *La Typologie baptismale dans l'ancienne Eglise (Acta Seminarii Neotestamentici Upsalensis*, X), Uppsala-Leipzig, 1942, pp. 167ff.: "La Croix dans le fleuve".

[2] *Ad Ephesios*, 18.2 (Funk, I, p. 228, l. 1).

[3] Cf. J. Kosnetter, *Die Taufe Jesu: Exegetische und religionsgeschichtliche Studien* (The Baptism of Jesus: Studied in relation to Exegesis and the History of Religions), Vienna, 1936, pp. 223 ff.

simple fact: that in this baptism of Christ there was symbolically enacted all that became reality upon the cross, all that in the mystery of baptism passes back its effects from that cross to man.

Jesus submerged in Jordan is a symbol of that divine humility which later moved him to allow himself to be submerged in the waters of death—to rise again as the glorified Son of God. Cross and baptism gradually pass into the framework of a single picture. Baptism, the cross and the descent into the darkness of the nether world, together form the mystery of the divine extinction, out of which the new life breaks forth, much as the new day arises from out the setting of the sun. You may perhaps know the wonderful words in which Melito of Sardis compares God's descent into the baptismal water and into the world of the dead with the sinking of the sun into the Western ocean.[1]

A Syrian baptismal liturgy contains the following prayer: "Therefore, O Father, by thy will and that of the Holy Ghost, Jesus inhabited three earthly dwellings, the fleshly womb of his mother, the womb of the baptismal water and the dark sorrowful caverns of the nether world. Make us worthy through these things to be raised up out of the deep abyss into the glorious dwellings of the Holy Trinity."[2] The submerging of God under the water is both the source and the prefiguring image of our own rising up in baptism. Ambrose expresses this with typical Latin pregnancy: "*Unus enim mersit, sed elevavit omnes. Unus descendit ut ascenderemus omnes*–One was immersed and so raised up all; one descended that we might all rise."[3] Jesus' baptism is effective through Jesus' death.

In order to give effect to this mental juxtaposition of cross and baptism in a visual image, it now becomes customary in art to place the cross in the middle of the Jordan and the same notion is also expressed in literary form. One of the ideas at work here is certainly that which we examined earlier—the idea of the tree of life standing by the source of the rivers of Paradise. Primarily,

[1] Cf. *Eranos-Jahrbuch*, 1943, pp. 335ff.; also, here below, p. 115.

[2] James of Sarug's blessing of the baptismal font, published by H. Denzinger, *Ritus Orientalium*, Würzburg, 1863, p. 244.

[3] *Commentary on St Luke*, II, 91 (CSEL, 32, 4, p. 94, ll. 14f.).

however, this cross in the River Jordan is the symbol of the crucified Christ himself who makes the baptismal water fruitful with his blood. From the travel descriptions of the writer known as Antoninus Placentinus we know that a wooden cross had been erected in the Jordan at the spot where, according to tradition, the baptism of Jesus had taken place and where, according to the legend, the river had turned and flowed backwards: "*et in loco ubi redundat aqua in alveum suum, posita est crux lignea intus in aquam ex utraque parte marmoris*–and in the place where the water overflows into its bed is set up a wooden cross in the middle of the water on either side of the marble [socket]".[1] The original wooden cross of the Jordan, to which there are references in the accounts of pilgrims from all over the world, was reproduced in many works of art. We encounter such a representation on the doorway of St Paul's in Rome, in St Mark's in Venice, on an ivory at Salerno, in the Chludof Psalter and even in the picture of Christ's baptism in the *Hortus Deliciarum* of Herrad of Landsberg.[2] This cross symbolizes the fact that the baptismal water has through the death of Christ been made a bestower of life—it is the tree of life. In many Eastern liturgies the baptismal font is actually called Jordan and— as an expression of the same basic idea—a wooden cross is dipped in the water during consecration, an act intended to signify much the same thing as that expressed by the wooden cross of Jordan. A hymn in the Greek liturgy at Epiphany runs as follows:

> Come and see how the shining sun
> Is baptized in the waters of a humble river.
> A mighty cross appeared over the water of baptism.
> The servants of sin descend
> And the children of everlasting life ascend.
> Come ye, therefore, and receive the light.[3]

[1] *Itinerarium*, c. 11 (CSEL, 39, p. 200, ll. 14–16).
[2] Cf. G. de Jerphanion, *La Voix des monuments*, Paris, 1930, pp. 183 ff.; K. Künstle, *Ikonographie der christlichen Kunst* (Iconography of Christian Art), Freiburg, 1928, pp. 377 f.; J. Wilpert, *Die römischen Mosaiken und Malereien* (Roman Mosaics and Paintings), II, Freiburg, 1916, pp. 777–80.
[3] Text in F. C. Conybeare, *Rituale Armenorum*, Oxford, 1905, p. 427, and Lundberg, *op. cit.*, pp. 170 f. In respect of the whole, cf. A. Franz, *Die kirchlichen Benediktionen im Mittelalter* (Ecclesiastical Benedictions in the Middle Ages), I, Freiburg, 1909, pp. 70–5.

The humble river, the mighty cross which produces everlasting light—here you have a mystery which is both Christian and Greek. We must, however, note a new element. The wooden cross, the symbol of Christ crucified in his humility, is a giver of light. The same fire bursts forth from it that was associated with Jesus' baptism in Jordan. The cross is also a bringer of light, and when men seek to express this mystery in explicit liturgical form, they do so by lowering a burning candle into the baptismal font as a sign that, by the power of the cross, the water is a source of the *lux perpetua*, the everlasting life of light. In a word the cross is both the tree of life and the light-bringer and both symbols represent Christ himself who "by his Passion sanctified the water" by giving to it the δόξα, the glory which he had won upon the cross, the power of the Holy Ghost. When therefore even to this day in the Roman liturgy the priest in consecrating the baptismal water breathes upon it in the figure of a Greek Ψ, this has nothing to do with any imperfectly understood Hellenistic sign of life; it is simply—as the most recent scholarship has clearly shown[1]—the sign of the tree of life, in other words, the sign of the cross. And when the priest, before so breathing, dips the candle in the water, uttering, as he does so, the words: "*Descendat in hanc plenitudinem fontis virtus Spiritus Sancti,*" this piece of symbolism—which, by the way, only came into use in the ninth century[2]—is not, as was once supposed, a phallic survival from the cults. Indeed any such interpretation implies a complete failure to understand[3] what the historic process can and cannot do. What we witness here is a symbol of Christ crucified giving to the water the illuminating power of the Spirit and those who insist on seeing a phallic symbol in the candle appear to be completely oblivious of what not only the Roman, but all other liturgies have to declare on this particular point, of what, in point of fact, they declare with considerable emphasis. It is that the baptismal font is *immaculatus uterus* and

[1] R. Bauerreiss, *Arbor Vitae: Der Lebensbaum und seine Verwendung in Liturgie, Kunst und Brauchtum des Abendlandes* (The Tree of Life and its Use in the Liturgy, Art and Custom of the West), Munich, 1928, pp. 48–50.

[2] Cf. A. Franz, *Die kirchlichen Benediktionen*, I, pp. 549–51.

[3] Thus H. Usener, *Archiv für Religionswissenschaft*, 7 (1904), pp. 294ff.; A. Dieterich, *Mutter Erde*, p. 114; C. G. Jung, *Seelenprobleme der Gegenwart* (Modern Man in Search of a Soul), p. 172.

that, like Mary, the Church bears her children solely by the power of the Spirit.[1]

No, the candle used in the baptismal ritual has the same meaning as the dipped cross in the Greek liturgy and we actually have examples of Christian art which show us not a wooden cross, but in its place a great candle standing in the Jordan—as, for instance, in the monastery of the Archangel in Djemil in Cappadocia.[2] The Easter candle is the symbol of the Crucified: that is why five incense grains are placed in it like five wounds. It represents the tree of life which is the cross, and that is why it is decorated with flowers as we can see on the pictures in the South Italian Exsultet scrolls. Both the cross and the tree of life communicate the life of light, and that is why the candle is dipped into the water of the font.

On the magnificent stand for the Easter candle in St Paul's in Rome there is an inscription that reads as follows:

Arbor poma gerit, arbor ego lumina gesto.
Surrexit Christus. Nam talia munera praesto.[3]
(A tree bears fruit. I am a tree but I bear light.
Christ is risen. Such is the gift that I bring.)

I have followed the ramifications of this matter rather more closely than I might have done if the phallic explanation of the Easter candle suggested by Usener and Dieterich did not enjoy so considerable a currency. Also I wished to demonstrate by the light of at least one clear example how the Christian mystery of baptism should be interpreted, and in particular how it should *not* be interpreted. Baptism and the cross must never be separated; whatever mystical and liturgical forms may cover it, it is still the theology of the Epistle to the Romans that is at the bottom of them all.

[1] Cf. the sources quoted in H. Scheidt, *Die Taufwasserweihegebete im Sinne vergleichender Liturgiegeschichte* (Prayers for the Consecration of Baptismal Water in the light of Comparative Liturgical History), Münster, 1935.

[2] Illustration in *Lexikon für Theologie und Kirche*, IX, Freiburg, 1937, plate following col. 1020. Two candlesticks in the Jordan on an ivory carving in the British Museum, see illustration in *Dictionnaire d'archéologie chrétienne*, II, Paris, 1910, p. 363, fig. 1297.

[3] Cf. R. Bauerreiss, *op. cit.*, pp. 50-7: "Symbolik der Osterkerze als Lebensbaum und Kreuzsymbol" (The Symbolism of the Easter Candle as the Tree of Life and Symbol of the Cross).

In a sermon by an anonymous Greek, delivered on the occasion of the Easter baptism we find the unmistakable thinking of St Paul strangely enshrined in the idiom of the Hellenistic mystery cults:

"Thou newly illuminated one [he cries], an earnest of the resurrection has been made thy portion through this mystery-initiation of grace. Thou hast imitated the descent of thy Lord into the grave but thou art risen again from the depths and now thou dost behold the works of the resurrection. May what thou hast seen under the form of a symbol become thine in reality."[1]

3

We have discussed two aspects of the mystery of baptism. We have discussed its purpose and its operative cause. Its purpose is the ogdoad of eternal life, its operative cause the redeeming power of the cross. Before the final end of this mystery is achieved, however, those who partake in it have their earthly lives to live. In those lives the heavenly power released in the initiation of baptism is already operative though it has not yet reached "fulfilment" in its complete and final form, for its ultimate end and purpose is nothing less than the eschatological vision of God in our glorified flesh. Whosoever therefore has received the initiation of baptism already possesses eternal life, he has already entered into the ogdoad though it is still invisible: "It hath not yet appeared what we shall be. We know, that, when he shall appear, we shall be like to him: because we shall see him as he is" (I John 3. 2). Yet what we possess during our life on earth is an imperilled possession, and the mystery of baptism therefore involves a continuous process of decision—and one that lasts throughout our earthly lives—between light and darkness, between Christ and Belial, between life and death.

To put the matter another way and use a metaphor much favoured by antiquity, the man who has partaken of this mystery has already made harbour in the next world and is nevertheless still upon a perilous voyage; he carries upon his soul the seal that gives him a clear passage upon his heavenward journey, yet during that

---

[1] Pseudo-Athanasius, *De Pascha* (PG, 28, 1080f.).

journey his enemies, the evil spirits, still lie in wait for him. It is here that the paradox of the mystery again resides, and at this point we should really spend some time exploring the profound thoughts and wonderful images which this "mystery of the time between" inspired in the Christian of antiquity. Also I should really say something about the mystery of decision (i.e. renunciation and adherence) in the rite of baptism and how the candidate turns from Satan, the "black one", towards Christ, the King of Light, who comes like the sun from the East and imparts to him the illumination (φωτισμός) of baptism.

Such an examination is certainly well worth while, for it is precisely at this point in the fashioning of the words and gestures of the ritual of baptism that the expression of the profoundly Christian decision which that ritual embodies, was assisted by a plenitude of excellent but extraneous things, things that came from that common territory whence many of the symbols and usages of the mystery cults are also derived. It is to that territory that we must assign the image of Satan living in the darkness of the West, the practice of breathing and spitting upon the foul fiend, the choice of milk and honey as the candidate's food, the symbolism of salt. We must, however, content ourselves with this brief mention of the subject, which has been very fully covered by F. J. Dölger in his *Die Sonne der Gerechtigkeit und der Schwarze* (The Sun of Righteousness and the Swart One), which is an historical study of the baptismal vow.[1]

I could say many similar things about the journey to heaven which begins in baptism, but admirable studies[2] already exist on this subject also and I can do no more here than refer you to them. The paradox to which I have been alluding finds expression at an even more profound level in a wealth of ideas concerning the mystical journey to the haven of rest. The Christian's voyage is made

---

[1] Münster, 1918 (*Liturgiegeschichtliche Forschungen*, II).

[2] Cf. W. Bousset, "Die Himmelsreise der Seele" (The Heavenly Journey of the Soul), *Archiv für Religionswissenschaft*, 4 (1901), pp. 136ff., 229ff.; R. Reitzenstein, "Himmelswanderung und Drachenkampf in der alchemistischen und frühchristlichen Literatur" (The Journey to Heaven and the Fight with the Dragon in Alchemistic and Early Christian Literature), *Festschrift für Fr. C. Andreas*, Leipzig, 1916, pp. 33–50; *Vorträge der Bibliothek Warburg* edited by Franz Saxl, 1928–9: *Über die Vorstellungen von der Himmelsreise der Seele* (Conceptions of the Soul's Journey to Heaven), Berlin-Leipzig, 1930.

in the ark—the ship of the time of the world's beginning—which is built of the wood of the cross and it traverses the dark, bitter sea of the world amidst fearful perils. Nevertheless it has already reached harbour, nevertheless it can suffer no shipwreck so long as the mast, which is the cross, remains unharmed. Again we hear an echo of the "mystery of the wood" and of the "mystery of decision": Christ on the cross has already won his final victory, he has passed into his rest, and that is why the Christian who, like Odysseus upon his mythical voyage, suffers himself to be lashed to the mast which is the cross, is sure of return to his home. "In the dark vale of the earth thou voyagest as upon a sea, O thou who art not yet baptized; hasten to make the glorious port of baptism. It leads thee to a safe anchorage, for we have arrived at the glorious resurrection of Christ, our Redeemer." These are the words of an Eastern baptismal liturgy.[1] Lundberg[2] has made a particularly careful examination of the symbolism of this baptismal voyage, and I myself in my essays on the *antenna crucis* have gathered together some of the wonderful treasures of ancient imagery.[3] Here I cannot even make the briefest mention of them. Yet every one of these mystical baptismal symbols is directed towards a specific end which, amid all this colourful variety, is always the same. It always points to the ultimate substance of the Christian mystery of baptism, to the resurrection of God who has been made man and to the consequent deification of man through his partaking in the nature of his glorified Lord. "Such are the mysteries of the Christians," says a Greek Christian. "We celebrate this joyous solemnity because of the resurrection of the dead and because of life everlasting."[4]

The mystery of baptism and the mystery of the cross! If we try,

---

[1] Text in F. C. Conybeare, *Rituale Armenorum*, p. 335.

[2] *La Typologie baptismale*, pp. 73 ff. Cf. also the prayers in C. R. Allbery, *A Manichaean Psalm-Book*, Stuttgart, 1938, pp. 132 and 166; A. Rücker, "Die 'Ankunft im Hafen' des syrisch-jakobitischen Festrituals und verwandte Riten" (The "Arrival in Harbour" in the Syro-Jacobite Festival Ritual and Similar Rites), *Jahrbuch für Liturgiewissenschaft*, 3 (1923), pp. 78–92; T. Arvedson, *Das Mysterium Christi*, Uppsala, 1937, pp. 204 ff.

[3] "Odysseus am Mastbaum" (Odysseus at the Mast), in *Zeitschrift für katholische Theologie*, 65 (1941), pp. 123–52; "Das Meer der Welt" (The Sea of the World), *ibid.*, 66 (1942), pp. 89–118; "Das Schiff aus Holz" (The Ship made of Wood), *ibid.*, 66 (1942), pp. 196–227; 67 (1943), pp. 1–21.

[4] Pseudo-Chrysostomus, *In Triduanam Resurrectionem Domini* (PG, 50, 824).

as I have been endeavouring to do, to enter into the feelings which these aroused in the minds of the Greek and Roman Christians, we shall be able to appreciate to what a degree the very word "mystery" had gained a wholly new and revolutionary significance. When in the *pannychis* of Easter these Christians of Greece and Rome celebrated their mystery, when under the blaze of lights and amid the sheen of white garments they beheld the cross, the tree of life plunged into the life-giving water, then surely the certainty must have forced itself upon their minds that, with the coming of this new mystery, the old mystery cults were finished and done with and had no further part to play. They may have felt as Gregory of Nazianzus felt at the beginning of his brilliant sermon "For the Lights—*Εἰς τὰ Φῶτα*": "Jesus is here again and once again we stand before a mystery, but it is not the mystery of Hellenic [i.e. pagan] intoxication; it is a mystery from above, a divine mystery."[1]

In his poem on the holy night of Easter the poet Drepanius passes once more all the ancient mysteries in review: "See how the people in their bright multitudes hasten to our mysteries to adore the Triune God—not after the manner of Ida's Galli when they imitate Dindyma, not after that of the vigil of Attic Eleusis in honour of the Grecian foster-mothers, nor after that of the nocturnal orgies of Theban Cithaeron. These mysteries are of a different kind. Here there is no thick smoke of incense nor any shedding of blood. Here in pure prayer and simple devotion, and with hands lifted up to heaven, we adore thee and thy Son."

> *Non sicut Idaeis simulatur Dindyma Gallis*
> *Attica nec Grais nuribus vigilatur Eleusis,*
> *Orgia Thebanus vel agit nocturna Cithaeron.*
> *Nil habet insanum strepitu, nil thure vaporum,*
> *Sanguine nil madidum, nil cursibus immoderatum*
> *Nox sacris operanda tuis. Tantum prece pura*
> *Simplicibus votis manibusque ad celsa supinis*
> *Te colimus natumque tuum.*[2]

[1] *Oratio* 39, 1 (PG, 36, 336 A).
[2] *De Cereo Paschali*, Verses 17–26; *Analecta Hymnica*, 50, p. 217, Leipzig, 1907.

As new life is generated from the cross in the water, the gaze of the Christian travels upward from these mysteries to the land of light itself and his joyous cry is: "*Χαῖρε νέον φῶς!* – Hail, thou new light!"[1] In heaven all that was hidden here below under the symbols of baptism and the cross will be made plain, and in the kingdom of the ogdoad, the kingdom of perfection and rest, the full truth will be revealed. Christ has opened that kingdom to us with his cross, he has "crucified death unto life". The baptized Christian will experience in a Christian form that which Plato vaguely guessed when he wrote of that happy realm from which our souls proceed and to which the good return. "There the souls in the midst of their blessed dance could still perceive a shining beauty as they looked upon the wonderful archetypes of truth."[2] Clement of Alexandria had a particular genius for interpreting the Christian mystery by the imagery of Greece, and it is perhaps proper that he should have the last word, as with his spiritual eye he beholds the radiance of this new and heavenly light:

"Let us put off, let us put off our forgetfulness of truth! Let us remove ignorance from our eyes, and the darkness that shuts us in like a thick fog, and fix our gaze upon the living God! Let us call out to him with these words of praise: Hail to thee, O light! To us that lay buried in darkness and were imprisoned by the shadow of death, there appeared a light in heaven, purer than the light of the sun and sweeter than our very life below. This light is called eternal life, and all that partakes of it has life. All has become light that no longer wishes to slumber and our decline has become an ascent. This is the new creation; for the sun of righteousness that hastens across the world has changed our decline into an ascent and has crucified death unto life. It has snatched away man from his ruin and lifted him up into the upper air and made earth into heaven."[3]

"Such are the mysteries of the Christians"—and such the glory they veil.

---

[1] Cf. F. J. Dölger, "Lumen Christi", in *Antike und Christentum*, 5 (1936), pp. 1–43.
[2] *Phaedrus*, 250 B.
[3] *Protrepticus*, XI, 11, 114 (GCS, I, p. 80, ll. 13–29).

IV

THE
CHRISTIAN MYSTERY OF SUN AND MOON

INTRODUCTION

I

As we survey the vast panorama of the ancient cults two very powerful impressions are borne in upon us and they are surely impressions which, as he contrasted the virginal simplicity of his gospel with the bright confusion of Hellenistic piety, the Christian of those days would have shared. The first of these impressions is of the seemingly inexhaustible variety of religious teaching, though it was teaching marked everywhere by a certain unmistakable air of fatigue. At the bottom of it all there is a genuine religious longing; but that longing expresses itself with a sort of drunkard's incoherence in a wild multiplicity of tongues, a multiplicity that still somehow contrives to achieve an effect of monotony.

Now this longing tended vaguely to centre upon the sun as the true embodiment—or at least the supreme symbol—of all that the men of antiquity so hungrily desired, and here again we encounter this character of variety. We have the night-travelling sun-barque of the Egyptians that was bound up with their beliefs concerning the next world; we have the sun-worship of the Roman peasant—essentially a religion of men with their feet upon the ground—; we have the *Helios Pater* of Greek tragedy, the sublime transcendencies of Plotinus' solar mysticism and the brilliance of Roman State religion; we can pass from Plato's myth of the cave down to the debased levels of the magic papyri, and up again to the visionary utterances of Hermetic literature that often truly penetrate to the secret places of the heart; and I want to tell you how Christianity, as it developed within this area of Mediterranean culture, reacted to the solar beliefs of the various peoples among whom it conceived its mission to lie.

Having spoken of the sun I must necessarily also speak of the moon upon whose surface the sun's rays are refracted—a fact whose symbolic significance will soon be made apparent. The quality of moonlight was something to which the ancients were deeply sensitive—as no doubt we are ourselves. "The light of Helios' rays is sharp and clear," sang Empedocles,[1] "but Selene is gentle and mild", and Philo in the spirit of Stoic nature mysticism speaks of Selene's womanlike dew-bringing quality and of her power both to nourish and enchant us: *"Luna debiles namque et magis femineos emittens splendores necnon serenos et rore praeditos optime lactat enutriendo."*[2]

The ancient theologians predicated these qualities of the Church herself, the Church which was, in Origen's words, "in a figurative sense spoken of as the moon – τροπικώτερον λεγομένη Σελήνη"[3]— and this because of the gentle light she shed and the motherly nourishment afforded by her. In the pages that follow I shall endeavour to show how Christianity both rejected and absorbed the light of this solar devotion, how in reflecting it, it changed and transfigured it, and how finally it guided that confused mass of belief, practice and aspiration back to the gentle simplicity of the truth, the truth that had been found at last.

But I spoke of yet a second impression that would surely be left with us and it is one which certainly corresponds to the feeling expressed in Christian theological writing from the second to the fourth century. As we contemplate the strange and devious roads followed by the religions of antiquity the conviction must surely grow in us that all these things are more than what they seem, that they are, in fact, as Eusebius says, a *"praeparatio evangelica"*.[4] With the aid of the material previously dealt with we are in a

---

[1] Diels, *Fragmente der Vorsokratiker* (Fragments of the Pre-Socratics) (4th edition), 21 B 40; preserved in Plutarch, *De Facie quae in Orbe Lunae Apparet* (On the Face on the Surface of the Moon), 2 (Bernadakis, V, p. 403, l. 10).

[2] *De Providentia*, II, 77 (Aucher, p. 96).

[3] *Commentary on St John*, VI, 55 (GCS, IV, p. 164, l. 21).

[4] This is the title of his work on the history of religion published by Migne, PG, 21, col. 22–1408.

position to follow the development of this Greek devotion to the sun; we can observe it rising to great heights of spirituality under the influence of Plotinus and the later Platonists; we can marvel—indeed we shall probably always marvel—at that spirituality which was so symptomatic of the dying soul of antiquity, the spirituality which so admirably prepared the ground for Christianity and which at the same time—like all things which love and are loved in secret—was one of its gravest perils. Nothing is more indicative of that peculiar mood than the cry of the dying emperor Julian, whom Christians call the "Apostate": "Helios, thou hast forsaken me."[1] For Julian's solar mysticism was really little more than Christianity in disguise, and in the comforting hymn to the sun which was sung to the dying man, the hymn that glorified the shining chariot of Helios that would receive his soul, we can surely detect a hidden Christian note:

Helios gives thee release from every pang of the body
Leading thee up to the Father and light eternal of Heaven.[2]

We can never really tell how far this cult of Helios was anything more than a piece of drunken nature mysticism and how far it was a really transcendent vision, embracing all creation, which was, as it were, simply touched off by the symbolism of a physical heavenly body. It certainly could inspire ecstasy. The philosopher Secundus, an expounder of the later Platonism, expressed something essential to its spirit when he cried out: "Helios, eye of the world! Joy of the daytime! Loveliness of heaven! Darling of nature! Jewel of creation."[3] Ambrose, Bishop of Milan, quotes these words on one occasion and in following up his quotation, boldly exploits the feelings they arouse in the sensitive pagan in order to win followers for Christ. "When thou seest the sun," he says, "think of its Lord! When thou marvellest at it, sing praises to its Maker. If the sun shines in so beneficent a fashion, though it is but a part of nature and must share its fate, how lovely must be

---

[1] *Ammianus Marcellinus*, XXV, 3, 6–9. Cf. Joseph Bidez, *Julian der Abtrünnige* (Julian the Apostate), Munich, 1940, p. 347.
[2] Quoted by Bidez, *op. cit.*, p. 348.
[3] *Fragmenta Philosophorum Graecorum* (ed. Mullach, I, p. 518, ll. 25ff.).

Christ, the Sun of Righteousness!"[1] One could trace the development of the same "tutoring for Christ" (Gal. 3. 24) in all the sun-cults of Rome and Italy, ranging from the devotions of the down to earth Latin peasantry to that "transcendent heliolatry" of late Roman times which we can learn about from Macrobius. It may quite possibly have been Macrobius who composed that hymn to the sun which even Christianity could not forget:

> *Sol mundi caelique decus, Sol omnibus idem,*
> *Sol nocti lucique decus, Sol finis et ortus.*[2]

(Glory of earth and sky, the sun is the same for all,
Glory of light and darkness, the sun is beginning and end.)

It was at this time that Ambrose was teaching his Christians the new solar hymn to Christ:

> *verusque Sol illabere*
> *micans nitore perpeti.*[3]

Cumont has shown great insight, in his description of this late pagan devotion to the heavenly bodies, and a real grasp of its emotional quality. It was indeed a devotion with which Christianity had necessarily to concern itself during the first four centuries of its life. Citing a passage from Vettius Valens he writes: "Transported on the wings of his enthusiasm the man of antiquity ascends to the holy choirs of the stars and follows their harmonious movements; he partakes of their immortality and even before death has converse with the gods."[4]

I will try to show how the Church faced the not inconsiderable residual power of this world of the spirit, rejecting this, sublimating and purifying the other, battling and yet beckoning, sure in the knowledge that revealed truth was in her possession and yet receptive to every seed of the Logos that she saw germinating

---

[1] *Exameron*, IV, 1, 2 (CSEL, 32, 1, p. 111, ll. 22–5).

[2] From an anonymous sun-hymn (possibly Macrobius or Dracontius): *Anthologia Latina*, ed. Riese, I, 1 (2nd edition), pp. 300f. In regard to the solar theology of Macrobius, cf. his *Saturnalia*, I, 23 (Eyssenhardt, pp. 127f.).

[3] Second strophe in the hymn "*Splendor paternae gloriae*". The most convenient text in H. Lietzmann, *Lateinische altkirchliche Poesie* (Ancient Latin Ecclesiastical Poetry), Berlin, 1910, 10; or *Analecta Hymnica*, 50, Leipzig, 1907, p. 11.

[4] *Die orientalischen Religionen im römischen Heidentum* (3rd edition), Leipzig, 1931, p. 163.

within the kingdom of the Greek spirit. The nature of her reactions to this world and of her relationships with it is far from being hidden in obscurity, for there is no lack of illustrative material. Indeed the manner in which over the first four centuries the Christian Church dealt with the Greek spirit's final outburst of vigour, the attitude she took towards solar monotheism, towards Neoplatonism's theosophical mysticism of the stars, towards the ideas of Neoplatonism's intellectual predecessors—all this is superbly documented. All the complex phases of this encounter lie plainly before us and can be traced in detail.

One thing stands out from all this beyond any possibility of error or denial. The result of the Church's encounter with the sun-cult of antiquity was nothing less than the dethronement of Helios. There had never been even a suggestion of compromise. From the very beginning the Church had entered the Hellenic world with the clear and certain knowledge—knowledge that rested on biblical revelation—of a God who created the sun and the stars. The implications of that conviction were irresistible and nothing is more palpable—particularly in the apologetic writings of the second century—than the utter rejection of anything like a veneration of the sun. Therefore when I speak of the dethronement of Helios, I mean nothing less than the most brusque and determined correction of all Stoic pantheist, or Platonic mystical, devotion to the sun into transcendent monotheism. Had not the Church with ruthless intellectual clarity insisted on this separation and held herself thus apart, it would never have been possible for her to bring dethroned Helios back to his home.[1]

But before touching on that, I have this further thing to say. The dethroning of Helios involves a definitive and uncompromising sublimation of all things on to the supernatural plane. The Church enters the confusion of pious Hellenistic aspirations with a piece of concrete knowledge. She knows that man is called to a fellowship,

[1] These general ideas are here developed in accordance with the principles of my late teacher, Franz Joseph Dölger, along lines suggested by the two works of Karl Prümm, *Der christliche Glaube und die altheidnische Welt* (The Christian Faith and the World of Ancient Paganism), Leipzig, 1935, 2 vols, and *Das antike Heidentum nach seinen Grundströmungen: ein Handbuch zur biblischen und altchristlichen Umweltkunde* (The Basic Tendencies of Ancient Paganism, a Handbook for the Study of Biblical and Ancient Christian Environment), Munich, 1941.

based on faith and grace, with the God who was made man in Jesus Christ, and the implications of that certitude are as joyous as they are compelling. It was this Christian knowledge of the blessed freedom of the new calling that made Paul utterly repudiate all religious service to the "*stoicheia*", or stars of this world (Gal. 4. 3, 9).

The psychological effects of this change are immediately apparent. The Christian no longer feels that mysteriously oppressive sense of dependence on the everlasting and fatefully determined courses of the stars, a sense which, precisely because of its oppressive character, generates piety of a kind; for, as the apologist Tatian says: "We are exalted above fate, and in place of the planetary daemons, we know but one ruler of the world, and him immovable."[1]

Finally—and here we approach that other matter of the "homecoming"—the dethronement of Helios meant for Christian theology that the mysticism and symbolism which had been developed in Hellenistic devotion, were referred back to the concrete, historical and visible person of the man Jesus Christ. But here too the Church is uncompromising and as she begins to take over images, words and ideas from the devotional life of the sun-worshipping Greeks, she interprets them in a manner that only has relevance to the historically clear-cut figure of her founder, Jesus of Nazareth; it is he who from the very beginnings of Christian theology is "the Sun of Righteousness" (Malachi 4. 2), the "Dayspring from on high" (Luke 1. 78).

On fundamental matters then, on such matters as monotheism, belief in the supernatural and the historic humanity of God in Christ, there was, as I have already said, never any question of compromise. Once we have grasped that, we need have no hesitation in directing our study towards that other phenomenon to which I have alluded and which I have called the "homecoming of Helios".

Yet before we do so, there is admittedly a question to be answered. When, in the manner already briefly indicated, the Church appropriated to her own use the substance of Greek ideas and made

---

[1] *Oratio adversus Graecos*, 9 (Otto, *Corpus Apologetarum*, VI, Jena, 1851, p. 42). Cf. also H. Rahner, "Mysterium Lunae", in *Zeitschrift für katholische Theologie*, 64 (1940), pp. 126 f.

it part of her own thought and part of her own cultic activity, was this mere syncretism? Was it a mere easy-going falling into line? Was it—if I may come to my main point—a "hellenization" of the simple original Christian faith when the Church Fathers raised their voices in praise of Christ the sun and spoke of the Church as the pneumatic Selene? Surely the answer is in the negative. Are we not simply witnessing that unique process in which whatever is endowed with supernatural life must needs absorb all that is truly alive in history or nature and must do so with the sureness and the power that is the unfailing attribute of life and truth? The fact is that primitive Catholic theology did not think it in the least necessary to make a root and branch rejection of everything that pre-Christian genius had discovered or thought to be worthy of honour. For Christianity never looked upon itself simply as a "doctrine", it did not look upon itself as "just another" form of religion; it held itself to be the divine revelation in Christ that had taken living form, and embraced all humanity both in the sense of ethnographical extension and in that of all the variegated potentials of the human soul—and that is precisely the reason why the Church with a gesture of supreme self-assurance could gather home to itself all the truth and all the good things that the spirit of Greece had made its own, and could do so, as though all this had from the beginning secretly already belonged to herself. That is what the apologist Justin is really telling us in the famous sentence which constitutes the dominant theme of his history of the Catholic religion. Christ is the Logos in whom the whole human race has a portion, and all who have lived according to the Logos are Christians, even though, like Socrates and Heraclitus among the Greeks, they are accounted godless.[1]

Newman was one day to voice very similar ideas when he dealt with Milman's *History of Christianity*, a work which like so many others denied the uniqueness of the Christian faith, because of a certain common ground which it shared with other religions.

---

[1] *Apologia*, I, 46 (Otto, *Corpus Apologetarum*, I, Jena, 1876, p. 128), *Apologia*, II, 8 and 13 (*ibid.*, pp. 222; 236f.). In reference to Justin's doctrine of the "seed-like Logos" which was afterwards developed by Clement of Alexandria and Origen, cf. Prümm, *Das antike Heidentum*, pp. 190ff.

"Now, the phenomenon, admitted on all hands, is this," he wrote, "that great portion of what is generally received as Christian truth, is in its rudiments or in its separate parts to be found in heathen philosophies and religions. . . . Mr Milman argues from it,—'These things are in heathenism, therefore they are not Christian': we, on the contrary, prefer to say, 'these things are in Christianity, therefore they are not heathen'. That is, we prefer to say, and we think that Scripture bears us out in saying, that from the beginning the Moral Governor of the world has scattered the seeds of truth far and wide over its extent; that these have variously taken root, and grown up as in the wilderness, wild plants indeed but living. . . ."

The Church claims for her own what the heathen said rightly, "correcting their errors, supplying their defects, completing their beginnings, expanding their surmises, and thus gradually by means of them enlarging the range and refining the sense of her own teaching. So far then from her creed being of doubtful credit because it resembles foreign theologies, we even hold that one special way in which Providence has imparted divine knowledge to us has been by enabling her to draw and collect it together out of the world, and, in this sense, as in others, to 'suck the milk of the Gentiles and to suck the breast of kings.' . . ." Our opponents think, Newman continues, that Christian doctrine consists of "some one tenet or certain principles given out at one time in their fulness, without gradual accretion before Christ's coming or elucidation afterwards. They cast off all that they also find in Pharisee or heathen; we conceive that the Church, like Aaron's rod, devours the serpents of the magicians. They are ever hunting for a fabulous primitive simplicity; we repose in Catholic fulness."[1]

It is in the spirit which these words express that we shall try to follow to its completion the process we have agreed to call "the homecoming of Helios". The world into which the Church entered was the pious world of the Hellenistic star cults; it was natural enough that, equipped as she was with the knowledge—

[1] *Essays Critical and Historical*, 12, "Milman's Christianity", London, 1871, vol. II, pp. 231–4.

resting purely upon divine revelation—of the one God who was the sun and moon's creator, she was able to find in antiquity's deep awe for Helios and Selene something which she could absorb and utilize in her theology and in her cultic activities. Sun and moon are the wonderful creatures of the Unseen. That thought is expressed in the lofty reasoning of the Book of Wisdom, taken up again by Paul in Romans: "If they being delighted . . . with the lights of heaven . . . took them to be gods, let them know how much better the Lord of them is; for the first author of beauty hath created them" (Wisdom 13. 1–3).

Helios and Selene were far from being "contemptible nothings"[1] for the Christian of antiquity, as the Platonist Celsus so scornfully alleged, for, says Origen in his refutation of that same Celsus, when we Christians say of Helios and Selene that they are only creatures, "we do not wish to express contempt for these glorious works of God or to say with Anaxagoras that sun, moon and stars are nothing more than fiery lumps of matter; we speak as we do because we know that the inexpressible majesty and greatness of God and of his only-begotten Son surpasses everything else. But we are sure that Helios and Selene through his only-begotten Son offer their prayers to Almighty God."[2] By the sun and the moon the Christian reads as though by means of "heavenly letters" the text of the beauty of God,[3] and what takes place in the world of the stars is for him an intimation of the mystery, revealed and fulfilled, of the Logos made flesh. It was natural that the Church, possessing, as she did by revelation, a knowledge of man's calling to the supernatural life, should see when she entered the world of nature, so beloved by the Greeks, in the all-illuminating sun, a profound symbol of that supernatural grace "which illuminates all who come into the world". The Logos is like the sun, says Hilary of Poitiers; his rays are ever ready to give light where the windows of the human soul are opened.[4] Moreover the Church, again basing herself on biblical revelation, does not regard this outpouring of grace upon man as the mystical and esoteric inward

---

[1] In Origen, *Contra Celsum*, V, 13 (GCS, II, p. 14).
[2] *Contra Celsum*, V, 11 (GCS, II, p. 12).
[3] Origen, *Commentaria in Genesim* (Migne, PG, 12, 84 B).
[4] *Tractatus in Psalmum* 118, *Lamed*, 5 (CSEL, 22, p. 459, ll. 17–19).

illumination of some soul yearning for the light. She sees the advent of this sunlight, this "true light that enlighteneth every man that cometh into the world" (John 1. 9), fulfilled in the text about the Logos made flesh; so she is ready to compare the concrete historically factual work of the man Christ with the power of the created sun which fills the whole world. "The whole earth is full of the mercy of the Lord," says Ambrose, "and as the sun rises daily for all, so the mystical Sun of Righteousness rises for all: he appeared for all, he suffered for all, he rose again for all."[1]

From what has already been said, it is obvious enough what our guiding principle must be when as historians of religion we seek to determine the nature of the relationship between antiquity and the Church. We have to make a sharp distinction between the actual, unalterable dogmatic beliefs which Christianity, relying on the revelation of Jesus, carried into the Hellenistic world, and the trappings of speech, imagery and symbolism which she appropriated from the overflowing treasury of Greek genius and—as lawful possessor of these *spolia Aegypti*—used for the expression of these truths.

Yet we must not look upon such a wedlock between form and substance as comparable to the relationship between a garment and the human form beneath. We must not imagine that as historians of religion we can step in *post eventum*, so to speak, strip off the wrappings of supposed hellenization and expose the naked body of "pure" Christianity. What we have before us here is a unique phenomenon and one involving a very profound problem of Christian theology; for this is really another instance of the divine becoming human, this is a union between thought and form, between dogma and expression which is like the union of body and soul. Such a union, in which there is nothing in the nature of an actual mingling, is made possible, in the last resort, thanks to the reciprocal attraction existing between nature and grace, two things which our Creator and Redeemer has perfectly attuned to one another. That is why the Catholic Church, without ever losing the essential form that Christ has imparted to her, can absorb into herself every good thing and every fragment of truth

[1] *Expositio Psalmi* 118, Or. 8, 57 (CSEL, 62, p. 186, ll. 14-17).

that she finds scattered about the world into which she has been sent. It is thus that we must visualize her, as, with an unparalleled tact, she pronounces her "Yea" and her "Nay" upon the solar devotions of the Greek world—a world she had entered from the temple at Jerusalem in which all graven images had been abhorred.

2

After this preliminary survey which has confined itself to matters of broad general principle, let us see what kind of a relationship the Church ultimately came to establish between herself and these ancient sun-cults. Once that has been determined, the scope of this book will obviously be more clearly defined. It will immediately be apparent that two distinct aspects of this relationship must be examined. We may call them the theological and the cultic; and the theological aspect can again be subdivided into that concerned with the role of the sun in theological speculation and that concerned with its role in spiritual experience. On these last two subjects I will only touch very briefly.

Under the heading of "the sun in theological speculations" I could describe the various instances in which Christian theologians have from the very beginning used the sun to express the fundamental truths of their revelation. There is a clear line of development, starting with the sentences of St John's Gospel (1. 9; 8. 12) that speak of the light of the world, and then going on through the speculations on the Logos by the theologians of Alexandria, right down to the definitions of the Council of Nicaea, which spoke of the everlasting Word as "*lumen de lumine*" and ultimately to the wonderful thoughts in Augustine's theology of the Trinity.[1] Actually all this theological activity is part of a continuous dialectic with the solar theosophy of Neoplatonism and the solar mysticism of the Manichees.[2] Side by side with it runs the story of Christian

[1] Cf. F. J. Dölger, "Sonne und Sonnenstrahl als Gleichnis in der Logostheologie des christlichen Altertums" (Sun and Sunbeam as Similes in the Logos Theology of Christian Antiquity), in *Antike und Christentum*, I (1929), pp. 271–90; M. Schmaus, *Die psychologische Trinitätslehre des hl. Augustinus* (The Psychological Doctrine of the Trinity in St Augustine), Münster, 1927.

[2] F. J. Dölger, "Konstantin der Grosse und der Manichäismus, Sonne und Christus im Manichäismus" (Constantine the Great and Manichaeism, the Sun and Christ in Manichaeism), in *Antike und Christentum*, 2 (1930), pp. 301–14.

interpretation of the solar piety of the Old Testament which we can see in such passages as Psalm 19(18). 6–7, Psalm 104(103). 19 and Malachi 4. 2 (LXX). Every one of these passages has an incredibly rich history in Christian theology and symbolism. Dölger's *Sol Salutis*[1] has made this plain enough.

The story of the role of "the sun in spiritual experience" would be equally interesting. Max Pulver has told us how things developed in this respect in the Christian East, and it would be tempting to try and do the same for the Christian West. We should have to start out with the echoes of Plotinus in Augustine and with the latter's theory of illumination[2] which really laid the basis for the subsequent development of mysticism. We should then follow these tracks right down to the theosophy of Scotus Eriugena[3] and his influence on Meister Eckhart. We could continue the story much further than that. What Clemens Bäumker has to tell us of the light-mysticism of Witelo, a theologian and naturalist of the thirteenth century,[4] what we can read in the writings of Hildegard of Bingen about her strange solar mysticism[5] —influences that remained a living force right up to the days of Jakob Böhme—, all this would build up into a wonderful account of this inner experience which always seemed to find its most articulate expression in the symbolism of light and the sun; but this is another subject that I must refrain from pursuing.

In considering this question of Christianity and the solar cults, however, I prefer to confine myself to the cultic relationship between the two and the wide variety of the forms it assumed; for

[1] F. J. Dölger, *Sol Salutis: Gebet und Gesang im christlichen Altertum* (Sol Salutis: Prayer and Song in Christian Antiquity) (*Liturgiegeschichtliche Forschungen*, 4–5), Münster, 1925; Dölger, *Die Sonne der Gerechtigkeit und der Schwarze: Eine religionsgeschichtliche Studie zum Taufgelöbnis* (The Sun of Righteousness and the Swart One, an Historical and Religious Study Relating to the Baptismal Vow), Münster, 1918.

[2] R. Jolivet, *Dieu soleil des esprits: la doctrine augustinienne de l'illumination*, Paris, 1934.

[3] H. Dörries, *Zur Geschichte der Mystik: Erigena und der Neuplatonismus* (Study in the History of Mysticism, Erigena and Neoplatonism), Leipzig, 1925.

[4] Cl. Bäumker, "Witelo, ein Philosoph und Naturforscher des XIII. Jahrhunderts" (Witelo: a Philosopher and Natural Historian of the Thirteenth Century), *Beiträge zur Geschichte der Philosophie des Mittelalters*, III, 2, Münster, 1908, pp. 357–467.

[5] Hildegard of Bingen, *Scivias*, I, Third Vision (Migne, PL, 197, 405 f.); *Liber divinorum operum*, I, Second Vision, No. 35 (PL, 197, 781 f.); II, Fifth Vision, No. 37 (PL, 197, 935–7). Cf. H. Leibschütz, *Das allegorische Weltbild der hl. Hildegard von Bingen* (The Allegorical World Picture of St Hildegard of Bingen), Leipzig, 1931, pp. 83 ff.

the sun cult which confronted the Church—and this is especially true of the third and fourth centuries—was a highly developed affair, an institution that had been heavily underpinned by the theosophy of late antiquity. Because of this, the Church's reaction to these forms of devotion had in it a dynamic element that contrasts with its relatively static attitude in the never-ending debate on matters of dogma.

Another point we shall have to consider—and it is surely one of great interest—is that even today in certain cultic usages of the Catholic Church we can trace the after-effects of this dethronement and homebringing of the ancient Helios. Actually it will pay us to press this matter a little further, for it is precisely in the sphere of sacramental words and gestures that we can see with quite especial clarity how close to nature the Catholic Church has from its earliest beginnings remained. When she expresses her transcendental beliefs by enacting and, as it were, "living" them liturgically, she makes use of natural things—water, oil, bread and, by the same token, the sun and the moon.

Once we have grasped the significance of this, we can see how vivid, one might almost say how moving, a demonstration is provided by this particular chapter of man's religious history, of a simple but important truth; for it shows us how deeply the Church is embedded in the general stream of man's cultic development. But we can also see, if we study the matter, how this story of the Church's own cultic growth can only lead to one conclusion—even when treated as a theme for comparative religion—; it can only compel us to recognize that all attempts at comparison must inevitably end by proving Christianity incomparable.

You will now be able to gather what, broadly speaking, I am going to discuss in the succeeding chapters. In her cultic mysteries the Church expresses the fundamental facts that are the basis of her own existence: the mystery of Christ the Redeemer, the mystery of the gathering home of the human race into the Church, the μυστήριον τὸ μέγα of which Paul speaks (Eph. 5. 32) towards which all human history is directed and which is epitomized in the words: "I speak in Christ and in the Church."

The Church seeks to give visual expression to this mystery, and the relation between the sun and the moon afford her a well-nigh perfect way of doing so. Helios is Christ and Selene is the Church. The great men of the ancient Church were always making use of this imagery, and were moved in doing so by a truly Graeco-Roman reverence for the wonders of the starry heavens, a wonder that had received Christian baptism in the certitude that God had only lit these lights in the sky and was only guiding them along the paths of their respective spheres as a sign of what was happening on a higher level of reality between Christ and his Church—and so in that supernatural kingdom which is also a cosmos in itself and which Origen has called "the heaven of our heart".[1]

I am therefore first going to speak of the mystery of the sun, which is Christ. This mystery found its cultic expression in the manner in which the Christian Sunday and the Christian feast of Easter came into being; thereafter when the argument with the cult of *Sol invictus* was finally settled, it took shape as the Christian feast of Christmas. I am therefore choosing "The Easter Sun" and "The Christmas Sun" as the titles of my first two lectures.

After that again, I will endeavour to show you how the mystery of the Church and of her relations with Christ took visual form in the figure of the spiritual Selene—which is the Church. I will try to make you see how, irradiated by the Easter sun, she illuminates, like the full moon, the darkness of this world with her spiritual splendour, being, as she is, the epitome of the whole human race which, receiving, conceiving and giving birth after the fashion of a mother, reflects and pours forth the light of the sun of Christ, that light which first came into being when Christ was born at Christmas.

I will further try to show you how the Christians of antiquity and of the early Middle Ages saw the mystery of the Church's motherhood both signified and perfected in the figure of Mary the virgin mother, from whom proceeded "the Sun of Righteousness even Christ our God".[2] Mary is the true Selene, in whom all the yearning of antiquity after the ideal of motherly womanhood found its fulfilment. Mary is the moon of Christmas.

[1] *Homilia in Genesim*, I, 7 (GCS, VI, p. 8, l. 21).

[2] *Breviarium Romanum*, Antiphon to Magnificat for the feast of the Nativity of Our Lady, September 8.

To conclude the series I will endeavour to show how the mystery of Easter is fulfilled in the resurrection of the body and how the ancient Church saw a symbol of this in the brightness of the moon at Easter. Ambrose had Mary and the Church in mind when he sang in his hymn to the sun and moon: "Truly blessed art thou, Luna, who hast been found worthy of such honour. For Luna hath declared unto us the mystery of Christ."[1]

I THE EASTER SUN

(i) Sunday

Two things belonged to the basic content of the Christian message with which the young Church made its entry from Jerusalem into the Hellenistic world—the belief in the Resurrection[2] and the acceptance of the Eucharist as a feast commemorating to the end of time the death and glorification of the Lord.[3] Now it was an unquestionable fact that the Lord died on what was a day of preparation for the Great Sabbath, that is to say, on a Friday. Moreover, he rose from the dead on what was called in the Jewish enumeration of the days of the week, the $\mu i\alpha \ \tau \tilde{\omega} \nu \ \sigma \alpha \beta \beta \dot{\alpha} \tau \omega \nu$,[4] or first day of the seven. This designation remained in existence for some time among the primitive Christians, as we can tell from Luke and Paul.[5] At a fairly early stage, however, a new name was obviously found for the day, and this change really marks the point at which the young Church severed itself from its native Jewish soil. The day on which Jesus rose begins, as we know from the *Didache*, the Apocalypse and Ignatius of Antioch,[6] to be designated by the adjective $\kappa \nu \rho \iota \alpha \varkappa \dot{\eta}$,[7] which in the Hellenistic usages of the time would have conveyed the meaning "imperial". The day

---

[1] *Exameron*, IV, 8, 32 (CSEL, 32, 1, p. 138, ll. 15–20).

[2] Cf. Acts 2. 31–6; 3. 15; 4. 10; 17. 3; Romans 1. 4; 6. 5–11; I Cor. 15. 12–19. In the history of religion Paul's sermon on the Areopagus concerning Jesus and the resurrection is particularly remarkable. His words caused him to be taken for a "setter forth of new gods" (Acts 17. 18, 31–2).

[3] I Cor. 11. 26.   [4] Matthew 28. 1; Mark 16. 2, 9; Luke 24. 1; John 20. 1, 19.

[5] Acts 20. 7; I Cor. 16. 2.

[6] *Didache*, 14, 1 (F. X. Funk, *Patres Apostolici*, I, Tübingen, 1901, p. 32)); Apoc. 1. 10; *Ad Magnesios*, 9, 1 (Funk, I, p. 236).

[7] On the Hellenistic sense of $\kappa \nu \rho \iota \alpha \varkappa \dot{o} \nu$, cf. A. Deissmann, *Neue Bibelstudien* (New Biblical Studies), Marburg, 1897, pp. 44 ff.; A. Deissmann, *Licht vom Osten* (Light from the East), Tübingen, 1909, pp. 258 f.

following the Sabbath has been turned into the Lord's day and on that day the primitive community celebrates the "Lord's supper", the δεῖπνον κυριακόν,[1] the intention being to give cultic expression to the two beliefs I have just named.

Since the first century before Christ, however, the custom had become universal of naming the days of the week after the seven planets;[2] it was a custom that may have originated in Chaldaean and Egyptian astrology—possibly under the powerful influence of the book of Petosiris. Under the dictates of this custom the first day after the Jewish Sabbath was made into the ἡμέρα τοῦ ῾Ηλίου, the *dies Solis*, or day of the sun, and it may well be here that we should see the first encounter between Christianity and a form of the Hellenistic sun-cult. The members of the early Church must have observed that Christ had risen from the dead on the day sacred to Helios, the second day of the planetary week which began with Saturn. Their great day, therefore, the day on which they solemnized the mysteries of the *anastasis* or resurrection and the *eucharistia*, was not the Sabbath of the Jews nor the day of Saturn which began the pagan week, but the day of Helios. There is a sentence in Ignatius of Antioch's letter to the Magnesians which clearly shows how strong was the impression made on men's minds by the basically coincidental circumstance, how sharply it marked off the Christians as a people with a strong independent identity of their own. Ignatius speaks of the Christians as "those who no longer adhere to the Sabbath but live according to the day of the Lord on which our life ascended". [3]

[1] I Cor. 11. 20.

[2] On the history of the Christian Sunday which is here briefly outlined the following works I have used are recommended: T. Zahn, "Geschichte des Sonntags vornehmlich aus der alten Kirche" (The History of Sunday with particular reference to the Ancient Church), see *Skizzen aus dem Leben der alten Kirche* (Sketches from the Life of the Ancient Church), Erlangen–Leipzig, 1894, pp. 196–240; E. Schürer, "Die siebentägige Woche im Gebrauche der christlichen Kirche der ersten Jahrhunderte" (The Seven-day Week in the Usage of the Christian Church in the First Centuries) in *Zeitschrift für die neutestamentliche Wissenschaft*, 6 (1905), pp. 1 ff.; F. Boll, "Hebdomas", in *Realenzyklopädie der klassischen Altertumswissenschaft Pauly-Wissowa-Kroll*, VII, Stuttgart, 1912, col. 2547–78; F. Boll and A. Bezold, *Sternglaube und Sterndeutung* (Belief in the Stars and Interpretation of the Stars), (3rd edition edited W. Gundel), Leipzig, 1926, pp. 183 ff.; H. Dumaine, "Dimanche", in *Dictionnaire d'archéologie chrétienne et de liturgie*, Cabrol-Leclercq, IV, Paris, 1921, col. 858–994. (N.B.—This has an ample bibliography.)

[3] *Ad Magnesios*, 9, 1 (Funk, I, pp. 236 f.)

Now it is significant and certainly more than coincidence that the word here translated "ascended" (ἀνέτειλεν) is the word which would naturally be used by a Greek to denote the rising of the sun —it is, incidentally, the noun corresponding to this verb that is used in Luke 1. 78, where the evangelist speaks of the "sunrise" or "dayspring from on high – ἀνατολὴ ἐξ ὕψους".[1] In both passages we see a new metaphor gaining currency and one that surely would have come less readily to mind had not circumstances brought it about that the day of the sun should in a special manner be associated with Christ, but those circumstances had obtained and the new imagery had taken hold of the Christian mind. Thus the Christian had begun to think of Christ rising under the figure of the rising sun and of his death under that of a sunset—to be followed of course by the sunrise of his glory. Ignatius applies the same idea to the Christian who dies for Christ: "It is a fair thing to sink like the sun from this world, so that I may have my sunrise with God."[2]

During the next few decades a great deal of thinking was obviously done on the subject of the significance of Sunday, as we can see from Justin's description of the eucharistic celebration: "On the day that is called Sun's day," he writes, "the general gathering takes place, . . . this being the first day, the day on which God created the world by transforming primal matter and the darkness, and also the day on which our redeemer Jesus Christ rose from the dead, for on the day before Saturn's day he was crucified, and the day after Saturn's day, which is the day of Helios, he appeared to his apostles."[3] Here Sunday is at one and the same time regarded from two points of view, that of the first of the six biblical days of creation and that of its Greek significance as the day of Helios, and in both aspects is already perceived something of the character that it was ultimately to possess for the Christian. It is both "Sun" day and creation day because it is the day of Christ's resurrection. The younger Pliny had obviously heard of this Christian

[1] For the interpretation of Luke 1. 78 in Christian sun symbolism cf. F. J. Dölger, *Sol Salutis* (2nd edition), Münster, 1925, pp. 149–56: "Oriens ex alto: Christus im Bild der Morgensonne" (Christ in the Figure of the Rising Sun).

[2] *Ad Romanos*, 2, 2 (Funk, I, p. 254).

[3] *Apologia*, I, 67 (Otto, *Corpus Apologetarum*, I, pp. 18 f.).

celebration which also partook of the character of a religious service; indeed it was an institution which must have attracted notice simply because it was held on a working day, namely on the day following Saturn's day which was a day of rest. He writes of the Christians to the emperor Trajan: "They declared that they were accustomed on a certain day to forgather before daylight and to sing a hymn to Christ as to a God."[1] The "certain day" was the day of Helios and on that day the Christians turned in prayer to the rising sun as a symbol of Christ arising from the dead and ate, as Pliny tells us, "an ordinary and innocent meal". So unusual was the Christian worship on the day of Helios to the pagan way of thinking that they regarded the Christians as a species of sun-worshippers. This is clear from the lively account of Tertullian in which he defends the Church against this accusation—a relatively humane one compared with others that were made. "Others", he says, "hold more humane opinions about us and mistake Sol for the Christian God because they have heard that in praying we turn towards the rising sun and because on the day of Sol we give ourselves over to joy—though this last has nothing to do with any religious honour paid to the sun."[2]

Now, from the very beginning the Church was most certainly opposed to the unreflecting acceptance of the planetary designation of the days of the week, if only because she saw in it an aid to that astrological superstition which she always so passionately resisted. We know that her opposition was vain. Even today the Romance languages preserve their "Chaldaean" nomenclature, the Anglo-Saxons have their "Saturday" and the Germanic races use the names of their own corresponding heathen deities.[3] Even Augustine could already see that the struggle was hopeless.[4] But Sunday had always been a rather special case. Deep down the Christian felt that the coinciding of the day of the resurrection

[1] *Epistolarum*, X, 98 (ed. Merrill, p. 301, ll. 1–13). For the interpretation of the passage from Pliny cf. F. J. Dölger, *Sol Salutis*, pp. 103 ff., on the song to Christ by the Christians of Bithynia and the liturgy before sunrise.

[2] *Ad Nationes*, I, 13 (CSEL, 20, pp. 83 f.); *Apologeticum*, 16, 9–11 (CSEL, 69, pp. 43 f.).

[3] Cf. texts and bibliography in F. Boll, *Realenzyklopädie der klassischen Altertumswissenschaft*, VII, col. 2578; F. Cumont, *Die orientalischen Religionen im römischen Heidentum* (3rd edition), Leipzig-Berlin, 1931, pp. 152 f. and p. 295, n. 25.

[4] *Enarratio in Psalmum* 93, 3 (PL, 37, 1192).

with that of Helios was not a coincidence at all, but that Providence in its profound wisdom had had a hand in this.

It is true that Christians never quite lost the feeling that it would be more truly Christian to speak of "the Lord's day" and actually this feeling ultimately won through so far as the Romance languages were concerned, yet so attached had the faithful grown to the idea of a mysterious secret connexion between the Lord's day and the sun that they were less inclined to depart from what was becoming accepted practice in the case of Sunday than in that of any other day of the week. Further, there is evidence to show that the Romans themselves had begun to count Sunday and not Saturday as the first day of the week,[1] and this seems to have happened, not as the result of Christian influence, but of the growing spread of sun-worship in the late Roman empire. This would seem to explain why Constantine himself when giving orders for the celebration of the Lord's day among the people and in the army, expressly refers to it as "Sunday" in his edicts.[2] Eusebius lays some stress on this: "He instructed his whole army", he writes, "to celebrate with zeal the day of the redeemer which was also named after the light and the sun."[3]

It is clear from all this that the after-effects of certain pagan conceptions had lingered on, conceptions according to which Sunday was regarded as a day of light and good fortune. There was a blessing on "Sunday's child" for heathen and Christian alike, and we have epitaphs even from Christian times which expressly mention that death or birth occurred on the *dies Solis* and which refer to a Christian child born on a Sunday as Ἡλιόπαις or "Sun-child".[4] Yet all this could be interpreted in a purely Christian and even edifying sense, and in the echoes of the Christian preaching of this time which still reach us we continually hear mention of the mystery of the sun's significance for this day, though this is

---

[1] F. Boll, *Realenzyklopädie der klassischen Altertumswissenschaft*, VII, col. 2577, ll. 30–67.

[2] P. Batiffol, *La Paix constantinienne et le catholicisme*, Paris, 1911, Excursus A: "Sol invictus", pp. 69–76. Excellent material also in Dumaine, *Dictionnaire d'archéologie*, IV, col. 874–6.

[3] *Vita Constantini*, IV, 18 (GCS, I, p. 124; PG, 20, 1165).

[4] Roman second-century inscription published in *Dictionnaire d'archéologie chrétienne et de liturgie*, II, Paris, 1910, col. 629. For other inscriptions dating from Christian times and mentioning the day of Helios, cf. *Dictionnaire d'archéologie*, IV, col. 873 f.

always accompanied by the cautionary observation that the name "Sun" day is of pagan origin.

Even so rigidly orthodox a Christian as Jerome says to his monks at Bethlehem: "The Lord created all the days of the week, and the ordinary weekdays could be the days of Jews, of heretics or of the heathen; but the Lord's day, the day of the resurrection, the day of the Christians, is our own. And if the heathen call it the *dies Solis*, we are quite ready to accept this description too, for on this day the light appeared, on this day the Sun of Righteousness shone forth."[1] In the fifth century Bishop Maximus of Turin says much the same thing: "The people of the present world call this day Sunday *quod ortus eam Sol iustitiae illuminat*–because the risen Sun of Righteousness shines upon it."[2]

That competition between the two names continued to be active is evident from Gregory of Tours' history of the Franks. The author rather contemptuously records that this barbarian race would cry out: "*Ecce enim dies solis adest; sic enim barbaries vocitare diem dominicum consueta est*–Lo the day of the sun is here; for thus the Barbarians are wont to name the day of the Lord."[3] Isidore of Seville repeats the standard argument with a slight difference: Sunday derives its name from the fact that "the sun is the chief of all the stars", and it is with the sun of Christ that the week begins.[4]

In most countries Sunday has triumphed over its rival and perhaps Boll is right when he says that the name of Sunday is the most lasting legacy which astrology left us centuries ago and which lives on even after astrology's demise. On the whole it is not such a bad legacy, since for millions of people—though they may be quite unaware of the fact—the day of the Lord is illuminated by a sense of the beneficent physical brightness of the day of the sun.[5]

The author might, however, have added that this is only so, because the early Church gave new content to this day of Helios by filling it with her own mystery of the resurrection. Actually the

[1] *Anecdota Maredsolana*, III, 2 (ed. G. Morin, Maredsous, 1897), p. 418, ll. 7-19.
[2] *Homilia 61* (PL, 57, 371).
[3] *Historia Francorum*, III, 15 (PL, 71, 254).
[4] *Etymologiae*, V, 30 (PL, 82, 216).
[5] F. Boll, *Realenzyklopädie der klassischen Altertumswissenschaft*, VII, col. 2578, ll. 61-7.

Russians speak of Sunday in just this fashion, calling it *voskresenje*[1]
or resurrection day, and in this they follow a very ancient
tradition of whose existence there is evidence both in Greek and
Latin sources.[2]

We have now examined the first manifestation of the process
of interaction between Christianity and the ancient sun-cults. To
form an accurate estimate however of that process's real nature and
development, we must draw a very sharp line of distinction between the fundamental dogmatic content of the Christian faith
and the garment in which it came to be arrayed, a garment which
used, and consecrated by its use, the simple stuff of everyday life.

(ii) Easter Day

From the early history of the liturgical celebration of Sunday as
a commemoration of the death and resurrection of Jesus, it is easy
to gauge the crucial importance attached by Christians to a belief
in this mystery. Yet the death and resurrection of Jesus were not
regarded by the earliest Christians in the light of an enacted myth;
they were not the δρώμενον, the thing "enacted", of some
mystery cult; they were a divinely simple, historical fact: *Sub
Pontio Pilato passus et sepultus est et resurrexit.*

So long as we are quite clear about this, it is not hard to understand why the primitive Church should have been anxious to observe the actual anniversary of the resurrection. In this way it
would do something more significant than give Christian consecration to one day of the pagan planetary week, it would also give
such consecration to the Jewish Pasch into which Jesus had so
firmly built his own redemptive work that the two could no
longer be separated. Thus not only the *dies Solis*, but the cycle of
the solar year should do their service to the true sun, Christ.

Now we know from the data in St John's Gospel[3] and from

[1] My attention was drawn to this point by Dr M. Pulver.

[2] For the Greek tradition, cf. *inter alia*, Eusebius, *Commentaria in Psalmos*, 21, 30 (PG, 23, 213); Basil, *De Spiritu Sancto*, 27, 66 (PG, 32, 192). Other material in H. Dumaine, *Dictionnaire d'archéologie*, IV, 884–6. For the Latin tradition it suffices to name Tertullian, *De Oratione*, 23 (CSEL, 20, p. 196). To this day in the language of the Byzantine liturgy ἀναστάσιμος means "appertaining to Sunday".

[3] John 18. 28; 19. 14.

the ancient tradition of Asia Minor[1] which goes back to John as an eye-witness of the crucifixion and of the events that followed it, that Jesus died on the fourteenth of Nisan. This day fell on this particular occasion, which may have been in the year 30 or 33, upon a Friday, that is to say on the παρασκευή, the day of preparation on which the Jews, in accordance with the law, eat the Easter lamb (Exodus 12. 6, 18).

Nisan for the Jews however is the first month of the year and the commencement of the year is determined by observation of the waxing moon. The first of Nisan fell on the day after the appearance of the new moon following the vernal equinox, so that the fourteenth of Nisan coincided with the spring full moon. From this we see how, in contradistinction to the planetary week and the Julian solar year, the Jewish Pasch with its ever-varying date moved in rhythm with the dance of the heavenly bodies.[2]

Transposed into the Hellenic time-reckoning—and such reckoning was always more than a mere matter of the calendar, it was a kind of time cult, a living with nature—transposed, I say, into this Hellenic reckoning of time, the foregoing amounts to this: Jesus died on the day of Venus, lay in his grave on the day of Saturn and arose from the dead on the day of Helios. Jesus arose on the middle day of the month whose beginning fell in the Roman Martius which, be it noted, was in the Roman empire also the first month of the year. He arose on the day on which, in the waxing light of Helios as he began to move towards his summer zenith, his sister star Selene, irradiated by his light, stood before her brother and bridegroom. Because of this, the coincidence that Christ rose on the day of Helios gains even deeper significance.

How deeply such thoughts engrossed the minds of the first Christians when they received the institution of the Pasch, now filled with a new Christian meaning (cf. I Cor. 5. 6–8), from their brethren that had come out of pious Jewry—all this is made plain by the long argument over the date of Easter that fills the whole

---

[1] According to Irenaeus' account in Eusebius, *Ecclesiastical History*, V, 24 (GCS, II, 1, p. 496).

[2] For the complex problems of Jewish astronomy and the calculation of Easter, and the establishment of the day, month and year of Jesus' death, see a detailed account in U. Holzmeister, *Chronologia Vitae Christi*, Rome, 1933, pp. 156–222.

second century.[1] The Christians of Asia Minor, relying on the tradition received from John, insisted on celebrating Easter on the day which the Jews, on the basis of astronomical observation, reckoned to be the fourteenth of Nisan. But this went counter to the practice that had grown up over almost the whole of the empire. Here, though Easter was similarly celebrated during the days of the vernal full moon, the times were so fixed that the day of the resurrection—the next day but one, that is to say, after that commemorating Christ's death—fell on the day of Helios; in a word, it fell on the day which we still call Sunday and which from the very beginning had been a day of celebration.

This conflict may be regarded as the second phase of the encounter between Christianity and the ancient sun-cults. It ended in the prevailing of the Roman practice, the decisive moment being when Constantine in a rescript[2] after the Council of Nicaea made this practice obligatory over the whole empire. As a result, the Church now indirectly sanctifies, among other things, the cycle of the Julian solar year, and ever since, she has accepted this ordering of things, and the whole world, not excepting that part of it which has ceased to be Christian, celebrates Easter on a Sunday. In doing so it follows and is guided by the rhythmic movement of the heavenly bodies. It is as though Helios and Selene were only created in order—to quote Origen—"to carry out their stately dance for the salvation of the world".[3]

There is an enchanting song that echoes down all the centuries of early Christianity and tells of the sun mystery of Easter day. Before however I deal with it in detail, as I propose to do later, may I quote to you an example of this lyrical early Christian Easter mood? I do so because it will enable you to grasp what the bringing home of Helios to Christ really meant. An anonymous preacher of the fifth century spoke these words to his flock at Easter:

"Now the germinating power of the earth breaks forth. Her face is made lovely by all that stirs upon her and she lets us see her

[1] Cf. H. Leclercq, "Pâques", in *Dictionnaire d'archéologie chrétienne*, XIII, Paris, 1937, col. 1522–31, and ample bibliography, col. 1571–4.

[2] *Vita Constantini*, III, 17–20 (GCS, I, pp. 84–7).

[3] *On Prayer*, 7 (GCS, II, p. 316, ll. 10f.). Cf. H. Rahner, "Mysterium Lunae", in *Zeitschrift für katholische Theologie*, 63 (1939), p. 327.

joy. The whole of nature, which till this moment had had the semblance of death, celebrates the resurrection together with her
Lord. The enchanting loveliness of the trees, as they put forth
their leaves and are set about, as with gems, by their blossoms,
blossoms which together are like a single birth of gladness—Oh,
it is as if all things were hastening to join us in the joy of this feast!
Till today the sky was dark and sad with hurrying clouds; now
it greets the earth with a sweet mild smile. The round earth and
the vaulted sky join in a common song of joy to Christ, God and
man, who brought peace to heaven and earth and made of two
things one. Sol, the focal centre of all the stars, lifts up his face and
lets it shine, and, like a king in his glory, sets on his head the
diadem of the stars, for this is his wedding day and the day of joy
for his heart. Luna when barely born begins to die a little day by
day. Yet today Luna decks herself for Easter with her full garment
of shining light. Thus, my brethren, every creature seems to join
in his holy service of love, and greets with rejoicing this day of
our salvation."[1]

Wholly secure as he was in his conviction that Christ had truly
risen from the dead, the Christian whose mind had been formed
by the genius of antiquity, enjoyed, by reason of that very security, a truly marvellous freedom. He could, with untroubled mind,
draw his risen Lord into the circle of visible and sensible beauty
that had always been his own. Among other things he was free to
let his thought elaborate the hidden significance of the sun in the
mystery of his faith. If Jesus had risen on the day of Helios, if in
every year the day of waxing vernal light, the day when the moon
was irradiated with the new brightness of the vernal sun, signified
the resurrection of Christ, then the whole sequence of the *tri-
duum sacrum*—the Friday when Christ died, the Saturday when
he rested in the grave, the Sunday when he rose from the dead—
might be considered to have a kind of counterpart in the setting
of the sun, in his nocturnal journey and in his rising on the following day.

I have tried to show you how the biblical and historical events

[1] Pseudo-Augustinus, *Sermo* 164, 2 (PL, 39, 2067).

which are the centre of the Christian faith, assumed in the course of time a symbolic dress. I have tried to show you how the Church of antiquity came more and more in its preaching and in its cultic forms to represent the events of Easter as the λεγόμενον and δρώ- μενον, the spoken and the enacted parts, of a mystery that took place on the supernatural plane, and with this we touch the really central point of the encounter between Christianity and the sun-cults.

I have now to say something about another matter, namely the manner in which the death of Jesus and his descent into hell were conceived of under the figure of the setting sun and its journey through Hades. In ancient Greek thought Helios was the epitome and symbol of life. By the same token, the daily setting of this shining star was a symbol of death.[1] Homer already says that the dying man "must leave the light of the sun".[2] In the uttermost West, where Helios sinks into the sea are the "Gates of Hades" through which the sun-god enters to make his way by a hidden road back to the East and rise again with the freshness of youth restored.[3] The West is identified with darkness, death and the demonic powers.

For the men of antiquity, Christian and pagan alike, the noc- turnal road travelled by Helios from West to East was a matter steeped in the deepest mystery. Jerome can still say: "When the sun has dipped his fiery orb in the ocean, he returns by an unknown way to his starting-point and, on completing his nightly course, hastens to come forth once more from his chamber."[4]

Now, whatever conceptions men formed of this road, whether they believed that, having submerged under the ocean, the sun gave light to the dark kingdom of the manes, or whether they imagined that it passed by a hidden path over the North and so back to its rising, all this made little difference to their general ideas in the matter. In either case the darkness that follows the sunset was the symbol of death and the sun's nocturnal journey an image of what befell the soul in the next world. "The sun had sunk into

---

[1] Cf. the article on "Helios", *Realenzyklopädie der klassischen Altertumswissenschaft*, VIII (Stuttgart, 1912), col. 58–93, esp. col. 90–3: Helios as the Nocturnal Sun.

[2] *Iliad*, XVIII, 11.

[3] Texts in F. J. Dölger, *Sol Salutis* (2nd edition), Münster, 1925, pp. 336–64.

[4] *Commentary on Ecclesiastes* (PL, 23, 1067).

the ocean and was illuminating the subterranean regions of the earth," says Lucius the *mystes* in the *Metamorphoses* of Apuleius, and in the course of an initiation into the Isis mysteries it is given him "to see the sun at midnight in its radiant light".[1] For both Egyptian and Greek such ideas as these are of the very stuff of which their religious life was made. Observation of nature, combined with a kind of awe for the myths to which the processes of nature give rise, was a universal ingredient of the religious feelings of antiquity.

Of this universal inheritance the Hellenistic Christians brought along their share and when their minds began to dwell deeply on the redeeming death of Christ and on his resurrection, it was natural enough that they should think of them as the divine fulfilment of those intimations which had been preserved in the myths of their Greek ancestors and that the shape their conception of them assumed should not be unaffected by this. They read in the New Testament account of the death of Jesus that "there was darkness over the earth" (Mat. 27. 45) and that "the sun was darkened" (Luke 23. 45); but to the mind of a Greek reader, steeped as it was in symbolism, this would always be something more than the account of an event in nature; it would be a profound and meaningful symbol. The death of Jesus is the true sunset, for he alone is "the light that lighteth all the world". Indeed as they read their way back into it, the old Church Fathers even carried their sense of symbolism into the Old Testament, and the words about the sunset in Psalms 103. 19 and 67. 5 were held by them to refer to the death of Christ: "the sun knows the time for its setting" meant that the divine wisdom of Jesus knew of his coming death; his "ascent upon the west" was a reference to Christ's glorious resurrection.[2] Athanasius says: "As the sun returns from the West to the East, so the Lord arose out of the depths of Hades to the Heaven of Heavens",[3] and using a thought that had already been uttered by Ambrose,[4] Augustine delivers the pregnant saying: "*Occasus*

[1] *Metamorphoses*, IX, 22 (ed. Helm, I, p. 220, ll. 3 f.); XI, 23 (Helm, p. 285, ll. 14 ff.).

[2] E.g. in Hilary, *Tractatus in Psalmum* 67, 6 (CSEL, 27, p. 280, ll. 7 ff.). Similarly Pseudo-Origen, *Commentary on Job*, 1, 3 (PG, 17, 399 f.). Cf. H. Rahner, "Mysterium Lunae", *loc. cit.*, pp. 433, 440.   [3] *Expositio in Psalmum* 67, 34 (PG, 27, 303 D).

[4] *Exameron*, IV, 2, 7 (CSEL, 32, 1, p. 115, ll. 5–9).

Christi passio Christi – the passion of Christ is the setting of Christ."[1]
Perhaps the most moving application to the Christian mysteries
of the old pagan feeling about the setting of Helios is to be found
in Melito of Sardis a second-century theologian of Asia Minor:

"When drawn by his fiery steeds the sun has completed his
daily course [he writes], then by reason of his whirling passage he
takes on the colour of fire and becomes as a burning torch. When
he has completed half his fiery journey, he appears so near to us
that it is as if he would burn up the earth with his rays. Then,
almost lost from view, he descends into the ocean. Now if we take
a copper ball that is inwardly full of fire and radiates much light
and plunge it into cold water, it hisses mightily but is made bright
by the sheen of it, yet the fire within it is not extinguished but can
blaze forth again and give a great light. So also is the sun; burning
like the lightning, he is not extinguished when plunged into the
cold water but keeps his fire alight without for a moment letting
it die. Bathing himself in the mysterious depths he shouts mightily
for joy, for water is his nourishment. He remains one and the same,
yet he comes forth strengthened out of the depths, a new sun, and
shines his light upon men, having been cleansed in the water. And
now he has made the darkness of night to flee away and brought
us the shining day.

"There follow him in due course the dancing ranks of the stars
and by reason of him the moon puts forth her power. They bathe
in the baptistry of the sun like those who are obedient under
instruction and it is only because moon and stars follow the course
of the sun that they shine with a truly pure light. If then the sun
and the stars and the moon all bathe together in the ocean, why
should not Christ have been baptized in the River Jordan? King
of Heaven, prince of creation, sun of the eastern sky who appeared
both to the dead in Hades and to mortals upon earth, he, the only
true Helios, arose for us out of the highest summits of Heaven."[2]

[1] *Enarratio in Psalmum* 103, *Sermo* 3, 21 (PL, 37, 1374 CD).

[2] Fragment of a lost work *On Baptism*, edited by J. B. Pitra, *Analecta Sacra*, II, Paris,
1884, pp. 3–5. Text also in E. J. Goodspeed, *Die ältesten Apologeten* (The Oldest Apologeten), Göttingen, 1914, pp. 310f. Translation and exhaustive commentary in F. J.
Dölger, *Sol Salutis*, pp. 342–5.

All the mysteries of the Christian faith are to be seen in this marvellous sunscape: the baptism of Jesus and the baptism of the faithful, the latter deriving its power from the sunset which is Christ's death upon the cross and from his glorious rising after his redemptive journey through Hades. Above all there is a reference here to the Church's dogmatic conviction concerning Christ's descent into Hell (I Peter 3. 19; 4. 6—possibly also Apoc. 1. 18—Eph. 4. 9), that redemptive act, faith in which is firmly embedded in the creed, whereby the dead Jesus imparted to the just men of old the saving grace which he had won for them on the cross.[1] The Christian of antiquity who so naturally thought in terms of his solar symbolism was only too ready to enliven this teaching with the imagery of Christ the sun journeying through the nether regions.

In the original version of the so-called *Acts of Pilate* these ideas find expression in something very like the simple idiom of a folktale:

"As, together with all our fathers [the passage runs], we were sitting in the deepest darkness, there was suddenly a golden shining of the sun and a royal, purple-coloured light shone over us, and immediately the father of the human race together with all the patriarchs and prophets sent up a shout of joy, saying, 'This light is none other than the Creator of everlasting light and we have been promised that there shall be sent unto us light that is equally everlasting.' And Isaiah called out, 'This is the light of the Father which is the Son of God, of which I prophesied when I was still alive and walked the earth . . . and now it has come and shines upon us who sit in death.' "[2]

Thus the sun has its part to play in the preaching of that time, and more particularly on the days devoted to the commemoration of Jesus' death and of his descent into Hell, i.e. the Friday and Saturday preceding the actual "Sun" day of Easter. The darkening

[1] The most important works on Christ's descent into Hell: K. Gschwind, *Die Niederfahrt Christi in die Unterwelt*, Münster, 1911; J. Kroll, *Gott und Hölle*, Leipzig, 1932; L. Ganschinietz, "Katabasis", in *Realenzyklopädie der klassischen Altertumswissenschaft*, X (Stuttgart, 1919), col. 2359–449 and above all K. Prümm, *Der christliche Glaube und die altheidnische Welt*, II, pp. 17–51.

[2] *Evangelia Apocrypha* (ed. H. Tischendorf, 2nd edition) Leipzig, 1876, pp. 391 f.

of the sun, for instance, at the time of Jesus' death is regarded by Jerome as a sign of its shame at the setting of the true sun, Christ.[1] This symbolism of the Church Fathers continues right into Carolingian times when in miniatures of the crucifixion the sun is shown growing red with shame and hiding its head.[2] Indeed we find this idea in the Good Friday hymn of Abelard, which tells how while "the true sun" sustains the cross the material sun suffers along with him:

> *Dum crucem sustinens Sol verus patitur*
> *Sol insensibilis illi compatitur.*[3]

By the same token we find in twelfth-century art such words as these inscribed near the figure of Sol which, in faithfulness to the ancient Alexandrine pictures of the heavens, is still placed above the cross in pictures of the crucifixion:

> *Igneus Sol obscuratur in aethere*
> *Quia Sol iustitiae patitur in cruce.*[4]
> (The fiery sun grows dark in the heavens
> because the Sun of Righteousness suffers on the cross.)

The same ideas were made to apply to Holy Saturday. This day is marked by the stillness of rest in the grave, for on this day Christ the sun is on his nocturnal journey through the other world "Christ, sun and God, has descended under the earth" are the words of an anonymous preacher whose homily is sometimes attributed to Epiphanius:

"The darkness of the night spreads over the Jews [the preacher continues] . . . the doors of Hades open. Rejoice, ye that have

---

[1] *Commentary on St Matthew*, IV, 27 (PL, 26, 212 A). Before this Cyril of Jerusalem, *Catecheses*, IV, 10 (PG, 33, 469 A) and XIII, 3 (PG, 33, 813 B).

[2] Cf. L. Hautecour, "Le Soleil et la lune dans les crucifixions", in *Revue archéologique*, 2 (1921), p. 13; J. Reil, *Christus am Kreuz in der Bildkunst der Karolinger* (Christ on the Cross in Carolingian Art), Leipzig, 1930, pp. 98 ff. Cf. also the pictures of Sol in G. Thiele, *Antike Himmelsbilder*, Berlin, 1898. With reference to the representations of Sol in a sun chariot in ancient Christian mosaics, cf. J. Wilpert, *Die römischen Mosaiken und Malereien*, vol. I, Freiburg, 1916, pp. 265 f.

[3] Petri Abaelardi, *Hymnarius Paraclitensis*, Paris, 1891, p. 113. Dölger also quotes this in *Sol Salutis*, p. 353.

[4] Cf. H. Detzel, *Christliche Ikonographie*, I, Freiburg, 1894, p. 418.

departed this life! Ye that sat in darkness and in the shadow of death, receive the great light.... Yes; sing and hearken to a song of joy! Proclaim that the old law has passed away and that now grace is blossoming forth. Tell how the prefigurings of ancient times give place to new things, and how the shadows hurry away. Tell how the sun fills the world. . . . The Jews still stare into the shadows, but the heathen walk towards the sun which is God."[1]

Here, in the appropriation of all the glorious fantasy that surrounded the Greek sun-god, we have something that shows us, even more clearly than the story of the development of the Christian Sunday, the true nature of the interaction between the Church and the ancient sun-cults—something that really shows us how Christianity dethroned Helios and yet at the same time brought him back to his home. There is no hint here that the beliefs of Christianity are in any sense derived from the ancient myths. All that happened was that Christians borrowed symbols and images from the thought and fantasy of that world of antiquity in which they had grown up and made them serve their own precisely defined biblical and traditional faith. If this implied anything, it implied a belief that the things of which the pious pagan had had a vague intimation had in Christ become a higher order of reality; or, to express the matter in the words of my teacher, Dölger: "When the *descensus ad inferos*–the descent into Hell, as an article of primitive Christian faith, began to penetrate the world of Graeco-Roman culture, it encountered the notion of the sun descending into the underworld and, almost involuntarily, this image was used in missionary preaching in order to enliven and embellish the picture (*zur Ausmalung*) of Christ's descent into Hades." Answering objections by the critical school, he adds, "For my part, I am convinced that in saying this, I am doing no more than my duty as a critical historian",[2] and in my own view this is the only possible conclusion to which a conscientious historian of religion can come.

Let us however regard this figure of the sun which is Christ

---

[1] Pseudo-Epiphanius, *Homily on the "Great Sabbath"* (PG, 43, 440 C, 441 B).
[2] *Sol Salutis*, p. 354, n. 4.

under yet another aspect. Helios, travelling at night by a mysterious road passes, as we have seen, from West to East. But Christ, who died and came to life, unites the darkness of the West, the darkness of death and of the diabolical powers, with the East, the region of rising light, the symbol of life, of Paradise—for Paradise stood planted in the East. "*Devicto mortis aculeo aperuisti credentibus regna caelorum* – Thou hast conquered the sting of death and opened the kingdom of heaven to believers."[1] That for the Christians of antiquity was the tremendous content of the Easter vigil, the mightiest of all nocturnal solemnities whose original form we still possess and follow—after seventeen centuries—in the Roman missal. Clement of Alexandria gives us an excellent picture of the main features of this Christian way of thinking about the Easter sun when he writes:

"To us, who were buried in darkness and shut in by the shadows of death, there shone a light from heaven, purer than the sun and sweeter than this earthly life; for the light that shone on us is life eternal and whatsoever has a part in it is alive. But night draws back from this light, it hides itself in fear and makes way for the day of the Lord. All creation has become a light that will never be extinguished and sunset has become the rising of the sun. This is what is meant by 'the new creation'. As the Father makes the sun shine upon all men, and causes the dew-drops of truth to fall upon them all, so the Sun of Righteousness upon his journey passes over all mankind. He indeed it is who has reunited the West with the East and has crucified death unto life."[2]

This Pasch from the death on the cross to the life of the resurrection—in Christian symbolism Pasch always denotes the "passover" from death to life[3]—was fashioned by the ancient Church in the liturgy of the Easter vigil into a marvellous sun mystery. The solemnities of Easter night are, as was truly said by Zeno of Verona, "a sweet vigil through the night that is made bright by

---

[1] From the hymn "*Te Deum*" which must almost certainly be ascribed to Nicetas of Remesiana (end of fourth century). Critical text in A. E. Burn, *Niceta of Remesiana*, Cambridge, 1905, pp. 83–91. [2] *Protrepticus*, XI, 114, 1–4 (GCS, I, p. 80).
[3] Cf. Augustine, *Epistola* 55, 1, 2, 5 (CSEL, 34, pp. 170f.; 174); H. Rahner, "Mysterium Lunae", *loc. cit.*, pp. 435–7.

its own sun—*clarissimae noctis suo sole dulces vigilias*".[1] It is symptomatic of the way—in itself highly significant—in which Constantine, the sometime sun-worshipper, furthered the cause of the
Christian Church, that he laid special stress on the splendour and
brightness of the Easter vigil. Eusebius tells us that "Constantine
turned night into day during these nocturnal solemnities by setting
up enormous pillars of wax which burned all through the night
before Easter. They were like flaming torches which made this
nocturnal vigil brighter than the shining day."[2] Christ then is
the sun shining in the night of this Christian mystery that is
celebrated in the silence of the night.

Firmicus Maternus has a passage in which he compares the mystery of Easter Eve with some pagan nocturnal mystery the identity of which is not exactly known to us and in which the initiates
mourn before a picture of the dead god; after this they greet their
new salvation which is brought in to them under the symbol
of a light while the priest whispers to them the mystic words:

θαρρεῖτε μύσται τοῦ θεοῦ σεσωσμένου
ἔσται γὰρ ὑμῖν ἐκ πόνων σωτηρία.[3]
(Be of good cheer, ye initiates of the saved god,
for ye too shall be saved from your sufferings.)

Herein lies no salvation, Firmicus continues; salvation is only to
be found in the Easter mysteries of Christ, who like a sun gives
light to the nether world and who, radiant as the sun, rose from
the dead on Easter day.

"He broke the everlasting bolts and the gates of brass were
shattered at his command. Lo, the earth trembled, and, shaken to
her foundations, beheld the power of Christ when he appeared.
Before the appointed time, the turning of the world hastens the
end of day, and the sun speeds on his downward course towards
the night before the measure of the daily hours is complete. . . .
But see, after three days there rises a more glorious dawn, the sun
has the beauty of his earlier light restored to him. Christ, the

---

[1] *Tractatus*, II, 38 (PL, 11, 483).
[2] *Vita Constantini*, IV, 22 (GCS, I, p. 125, ll. 26–30).
[3] *De Errore Profanarum Religionum*, 22, 1 (CSEL, 2, p. 112, ll. 3 f.).

almighty God, stands forth illuminated by yet brighter rays. The redeeming Godhead is full of joy and the multitudes of the just and the holy accompany his triumphal chariot."[1]

Here with the boldness of complete self-assurance the risen Christ is depicted entirely after the manner of the conquering Helios, rushing across the heavens in his shining chariot. Similar ideas may well have come to the Christian of this time when during his night-long Easter vigil the *lumen Christi* was carried in, when, before the celebration of the holy Eucharist with which the mystery ended, he heard the clear and joyous voice of the deacon say the words of the Easter Gospel: "ἀνατείλαντος τοῦ ἡλίου–*orto iam sole*–the sun being now risen" (Mark 16. 2). For now the true Helios has risen. Now is fulfilled, but in a much more profound sense, that for which the Greek mysteries had longed; and when a Christian bishop rose to speak and sought to express something of Easter's joy in the sun, it may well be that words came to him very much like those preserved for us in the homilies of Zeno of Verona. In these homilies the Christian mystery is inextricably bound up with the joy of the new Easter sunlight and in them we can still relive the past and feel what it meant truly to consecrate the solar year, to make holy the cycle of Helios. "The driver of the everlasting chariot, yearly completing his prescribed cycle, yet ever turns his steps about his goal, the day of salvation is come upon us. It follows itself and goes ahead of itself, it is old yet ever young, it is the begetter of the year and its offspring . . . God our Lord descended and arose, never to descend again; for this is the day on which the darkness of death was torn asunder."[2] Here is a passage from yet another of his Easter homilies: "Completing its cycle, the blessed day bears down upon us. It drives forward in its unbroken course towards the fulfilment of its task in the world, drawn by the four horses of the seasons and made rich by the changing of twelve moons. It knows no halting for its journey is everlasting life."[3]

Christian poesy also seized on that climactic moment in our

---

[1] *Ibid.*, 24, 2 and 4 (CSEL, 2, pp. 114f.).

[2] Zeno of Verona, *Tractatus*, II, 49 (PL. 11, 504f.).

[3] *Tractatus*, II, 52 (PL, 11, 508).

redemption, that moment so wonderfully dramatized in the Easter liturgy, and visualized it under the image of the sun. I quote Prudentius' wonderful poem on Easter Eve:

Illa nocte sacer qua rediit deus
Stagnis ad superos ex Acheronticis,
Non sicut tenebras de face fulgida
Surgens Oceano lucifer imbuit,
Sed terris Domini de cruce tristibus
Maior Sole novum restituens diem.[1]

(That night when the holy God
Returned to the upper air from the foul swamps of Acheron,
He did not, like the morning star rising from the ocean,
Fill the darkness with his glowing light,
But to earth mourning for the Lord's cross,
As a greater light than Sol, bringing a new day.)

And because according to the Christian conception the resurrection is a victory over death and so over the devil "who has the empire over death" (Heb. 2. 14), the Christian of that day saw in the hero of Easter morning the sunlike Apollo-Helios who had slain the dragon Python. Here, for instance is an Easter hymn attributed by tradition to Paulinus of Nola. It is a composition in which many may feel that the solar allegory has gone rather too far, yet under the cloak of this allegory the lasting substance of Christian dogma is evident enough:

Salve, O Apollo vere, Paean inclyte,
Pulsor draconis inferi!
In triumpho nobilis!
Salve beata saeculi victoria,
Parens beati temporis![2]

(Hail, O true Apollo! Renowned Healer!
Victor over the dragon of hell!
Glorious in thy triumph!
Hail thou happy victory of this age!
Parent of the blessed days to come!)

---

[1] *Cathemerinon*, V, 127-32 (CSEL, 61, p. 30).

[2] Appendix to the poems of Paulinus of Nola, *Carmen*, II, Verses 51 f.; 60–63 (CSEL, 30, p. 349). Cf. on the whole passage Dölger, *Sol Salutis*, pp. 364–79.

Firmicus Maternus tells us that in the ancient mysteries the sunlight was greeted with the cry, "Hail, bridegroom, hail, thou new light!"[1] and we learn from Macrobius[2] who has preserved a Greek sun litany for us, that this litany contained the following prayer: "Helios, ruler of the world, spirit of the world, power of the world, light of the world!" But the Christian knew of another "light of the world" (John 8. 12) and Firmicus has this to say to the pagans: "There is only one light and one bridegroom. It is Christ who has received the grace of these names. If thou desirest that even a gleam of this light illuminate thee, lift up thine eye, leave thy darkness and go to him who has said: 'I am the light of the world'."[3]

The essential thing about the Easter mystery of death and resurrection is that it is something more than an act commemorating the historic redemptive act of Jesus which took place on the fourteenth of Nisan; it involves the actual, supernatural presence; for the new sunlight is imparted in a sacramental initiation, in baptism which takes place on Easter Eve and which from the very earliest beginnings of the Church was called φωτισμός, that is to say, "illumination". In baptism the mystery of Jesus' death, rest in the tomb, and resurrection is prolonged, so that we once again find ourselves in contact with the unalterable content of primitive Christian belief: "Know you not that all we, who are baptized in Christ Jesus, are baptized in his *death*? For we are *buried* together with him by baptism into death: that as Christ is risen from the dead by the glory of the Father, so we also may walk in *newness of life*" (Rom. 6. 3–4). This is where the Christian symbolism of baptism as enlightening by the sun has its origin.

Let me very briefly illustrate my point. For the Christian of antiquity baptism meant, firstly and negatively, the renunciation of Satan.[4] Now it was already an idea familiar to pagan thought that the kingdom of the demons and of death was in the West, the region of the gates of Hades and the sunset. These words of the

---

[1] *De Errore Profanarum Religionum*, 19, 1, (CSEL, 2, p. 104, l. 28).
[2] *Saturnalia*, I, 23, 21 (Eyssenhardt, pp. 127f.).
[3] *De Errore Profanarum Religionum*, 19, 1, 2 (CSEL, 2, p. 105, ll. 2–9).
[4] Cf. H. Rahner, "Pompa diaboli", in *Zeitschrift für katholische Theologie*, 55 (1931), pp. 239–73; F. J. Dölger, *Die Sonne der Gerechtigkeit und der Schwarze*, pp. 1–10.

Christian writer Lactantius, for instance, are typically Graeco-Roman in feeling: "As light belongs to the East, and as light is the cause of life, so darkness belongs to the West and in darkness there is decline and death." He continues with these words that are wholly Christian in sentiment: "The sunset is ascribed to that evil fallen spirit because he shuts out the light, brings in the darkness, leads men to death and causes them to sink down in their sins even as the sun sinks."[1] Since the sin of Adam his whole progeny is, so to speak, on its way towards the West, so that Severianus of Gabala can write: "Adam ran towards the West and sank like the sun into his grave. Christ came and made man who had thus descended rise again . . . in Adam man sank down, in Christ he ascends again."[2]

Now the individual Christian is endowed with this power of rising at his baptism on Easter Eve, and it is in this sense that baptism is a renunciation of the sunset which means of the demoniac powers. Thus we find Cyril of Jerusalem addressing these words to his newly baptized Christians:

"First you went into the antechamber of the baptistry and there facing the sunset, you listened to certain precise instructions. You stretched forth your hand and with this gesture you renounced Satan as though he were actually present. . . . I will tell you why you stand with your faces towards the sunset, and indeed it is most necessary that you should do so, for the sunset is the region of visible darkness while Satan is darkness itself and has the empire over darkness. To express this by means of a symbol you look towards the sunset and in this wise you renounce this dark and sinister ruler."[3]

In much the same spirit Jerome speaks of baptism as of a mystery of light: "In the mysteries we renounce him who is in the West and who together with our sins becomes for us as one dead; then turning towards the East, we enter into a covenant with the Sun of Righteousness and promise that we will serve him."[4]

On the positive side then, baptism means a turning towards the

[1] *Divinarum Institutionum*, II, 9 (CSEL, 19, pp. 142 f.).

[2] *De Mundi Creatione, Oratio* 5, 5 (PG, 56, 477).

[3] *Catecheses Mystagogicae*, 1, 2, 4 (PG, 33, 1068 f.).   [4] *In Amos*, III, 6, 14 (PL, 25, 1068).

East, it means a covenant with Christ the sun and so an illumination by his Easter light. We can see all this clearly enough in
the fragment of a hymn—the oldest we possess—that goes back to
the very earliest days of the Church. Paul has preserved it for us
(Eph. 5. 14) and both Soden and Dibelius have advanced convincing reasons for supposing that it is part of a baptismal hymn:

> ἔγειρε ὁ καθεύδων,
> καὶ ἀνάστα ἐκ τῶν νεκρῶν,
> καὶ ἐπιφαύσει σοι ὁ Χριστός.[1]
> (Rise thou that sleepest,
> And arise from the dead;
> And Christ shall enlighten thee.)

Clement of Alexandria shows us the meaning that the Church
read into these words that echo down to us from remotest times.
He quotes the hymn and then continues thus:

> ὁ τῆς ἀναστάσεως ἥλιος
> ὁ πρὸ ἑωσφόρου γεννώμενος
> ὁ ζωὴν χαρισάμενος ἀκτῖσιν ἰδίαις.[2]
> (The sun of the resurrection
> Begotten before the morning star
> Granting life by the light of his rays!)

Thus Christ, the shedder of light, is "the sun of the resurrection", and so, to be baptized is to partake of the light of this sun.
The conversion of the heathen to the mysteries of Christ is interpreted by Clement as a fulfilment of a very ancient prophecy,
which he believed he had found in some verses of the Sibyl:

> See, he is there to behold, beyond all chances of error
> Come therefore, seek no longer the gloom nor follow
>   the darkness
> Look to the sun and behold his bright delectable smiling.[3]

[1] Cf. Dibelius quoted by Lietzmann, *Handbuch zum Neuen Testament*, III, 2, Tübingen, 1913, p. 118; F. J. Dölger, *Sol Salutis*, pp. 365 f.
[2] *Protrepticus*, IX, 84, 2 (GCS, I, p. 63, ll. 15–20).
[3] *Oracula Sibyllina*, Fragment I, Verses 28–30, in Theophilus of Antioch, *Ad Autolycum*, II, 36 (Otto, *Corpus Apologetarum*, VIII, Jena 1861, p. 168). Quoted in Clement of Alexandria, *Protrepticus*, VIII, 77, 2 (GCS, I, p. 59); critical text in J. Geffcken, *Oracula Sibyllina* (Berlin edition, Leipzig, 1902), p. 229, ll. 29 f.

We possess yet another baptismal hymn that dates back to very early Christian times. It is to be found among the so-called *Odes of Solomon*. In it a Christian who has been deeply moved by the experience of baptism, speaks of his illumination through grace and of the change that has been wrought in him by reason of the mystery:

As the sun is a joy to those who seek the daylight
So is my joy in the Lord, for he is my sun.
His rays have raised me up,
His light has wiped all darkness from my face.
Through him have I received eyes and now I behold the day
I have left the ways of error: to him have I gone.[1]

The *Acts of Thomas* have, as Dölger points out, so strongly developed this thought that they represent Jesus after his baptism, as a youth with a torch—exactly as the sun-god is represented in Graeco-Roman art.[2] I admit that the example I have just cited is mainly representative of a group of men who mixed up paganism and Christianity into a sort of syncretistic Gnosticism. Yet such mongrelization would have been impossible had not Christians already been familiar with the idea of baptism as illumination by Christ, the Easter sun. I could adduce an overwhelming mass of evidence to prove the existence of this baptismal "photism". Baptismal sermons are full of it and the liturgies of every language, Greek, Syriac, Latin and the rest, bear witness to the same thing.

In this connexion I will only make the briefest of references to the Roman Church's liturgy for Easter Eve, which is still in essence, the night for baptism. In that liturgy you will still find such ideas as that of the sunrise and the nocturnal sun very much alive, and no cultic drama has ever expressed the contrast between darkness and light, between night and the sun with such wonderful effectiveness of word and gesture. When at the words: "*Lumen*

---

[1] *The Odes of Solomon*, 15, 1, 2, 6 (German translation from the Syriac in Ungnad-Staerk, *Die Oden Salomos* [H. Lietzmann's Kleine Texte, 64], Bonn, 1910, pp. 16f.; also in H. Gressmann, *Die Oden Salomos* [E. Hennecke, Neutestamentliche Apokryphen], second edition, Tübingen, 1924, pp. 450f.).

[2] *Sol Salutis*, p. 367; "Acta Thomae", 27, in *Acta Apostolorum Apocrypha*, II, 2 (ed. Bonnet, p. 143, ll. 4–10); German translation in Hennecke, *op. cit.*, p. 266.

Christi—Deo gratias",[1] the new light is brought into the darkened church, the *Exsultet* rings out from the hearts of the faithful, it is the great hymn in praise of the Easter candle which is the symbol of Christ, for Christ is the sun of this night, the true *Sol invictus* who ascends as victor out of the depths of the nether world: "*Haec nox est, in qua destructis vinculis mortis Christus ab inferis victor ascendit.*"

The light of this candle is then dipped into water, from which, as the Spanish liturgy expresses it,[2] the "sons of light" are to arise. Through this sunlight of Christ's the baptismal water becomes "fiery water". The same idea is rendered by one of the Syrian liturgies in the words: "The sun inclined its rays downward into this water."[3] From these primal elements which are united on Easter Eve—the sunlight of Christ and the water which is man—there arises the new creature, the Christian; and so the mystery of the Roman Easter Eve ends with the classical prayer:

Deus, qui hanc sacratissimam noctem gloria Dominicae resurrectionis illustras: conserva in nova familiae tuae progenie adoptionis spiritum quem dedisti.

And when the newly baptized Christian stepped forth into the daylight that had been made bright by the Easter sun, he must have become newly alive to what the Church meant by the bringing home of Helios and of *Sol invictus* and by the consecration of the renovating cycle of the sun. For had he not himself taken part in this renewal, had he not himself become a new man in Christ? Had he not become even as one of those happy ones whom long

---

[1] See on this F. J. Dölger, "Lumen Christi: Untersuchungen zum abendlichen Lichtsegen in Antike und Christentum. Der feierliche Lichtruf in der römischen und mozarabischen Liturgie" (Research into the Evening Blessing of the Light in the Ancient World and the Christian Church. The Solemn Acclamation of the Light in the Roman and Mozarabic Liturgies), in *Antike und Christentum*, 5 (1936), pp. 1–43.

[2] *Liber Mozarabicus Sacramentorum* (ed. M. Férotin), Paris, 1912, col. 250, l. 7; cf. H. Rahner, "Die Gottesgeburt: die Lehre der Kirchenväter von der Geburt Christi im Herzen des Gläubigen" (The Divine Birth: Patristic Teaching on the Birth of Christ in the Heart of the Believer), in *Zeitschrift für katholische Theologie*, 59 (1935), p. 396.

[3] Quoted in reference to Justin, *Dialogus cum Tryphone*, 88, in Otto, *Corpus Apologetarum*, II, Jena, 1877, p. 321, note 9. Cf. F. J. Dölger, "Aqua Ignita: Wärmung und Weihe des Taufwassers" (Fiery Water: Heating and Blessing of Baptismal Water) in *Antike und Christentum*, 5 (1936), pp. 175–83; H. Rahner, "Mysterium Lunae", in *Zeitschrift für katholische Theologie*, 64 (1940), p. 73.

ago a bishop had called the children of the new spring? "Ye sprigs of verdant holiness, ye who are my pious seed corn, my new-born swarm of bees, the wreath of blossoms that crowns my honour."[1] Wherever the Christian transfiguration of nature has found lyrical expression, we can safely seek the parentage of such a birth in the sun mystery of the Easter liturgy and the spiritual experience of baptism.

There is a multitude of such choral songs which are both Christian and—in the very best sense of that term—Graeco-Roman in spirit, though here I can only let you hear two of them. One of them is Greek, and dates from the classical period of theology; in the other, which is Latin, we can discern a mingling of the Graeco-Roman way of thinking with a Germanic love of nature. Cyril of Alexandria, bishop of the Church whose task it was to make known in every year the astronomical calculations of the date of Easter, has left us an Easter homily preached in the rippling swift-flowing Greek of his day:

"Spring is the name of the time that is now breaking in on us. Surely a man with a poet's tongue and a lofty spirit cannot but weave a precious garland in honour of it! Gone is the sad spectacle of winter. Helios sparkles as though all the dust had been wiped from his face, and with new lights pours his beauty over hill and dale, over valley and field. All becomes young again and the spring winds itself a garland of young blossoms. . . . And yet I think all this would be but little, were there not another thing that made the spring worthy of praise beyond all other seasons. Together with nature one creature especially celebrates its resurrection; it is a creature that gathers all nature into itself. That creature is man. For spring brings along with it the resurrection of man's redeemer through which we are all changed in newness of life and saved forever from the corruption of death."[2]

[1] Among the pseudo-Augustinian sermons, probably by Caesarius of Arles, *Sermo* 172 (PL, 39, 2075).

[2] *Homilia Paschalis*, 9, 2 (PG, 77, 581). See further texts in H. Rahner, "Osterlyrik der Kirchenväter" (Paschal Lyricism in the Fathers), in *Schweizerische Kirchenzeitung*, 110 (1942), pp. 169–72; T. Michels, "Das Frühlingssymbol in österlicher Liturgie: Rede und Dichtung" (The Spring Symbol in Paschal Liturgy: Preaching and Poetry), in *Jahrbuch für Liturgiewissenschaft*, 6 (1926), pp. 1–15.

The Latin Easter hymn to which I referred is a gift to us from the monk of St Gall, Notker the Stammerer; it is his wonderful Easter sequence to Christ the thunderer, who, as the true sun, completes his thundering Easter journey:

> Therefore now in honour
> Of the resurrected Christ
> All things joyfully,
> Flowers and seeds,
> Burst forth and grow in their colours,
> And flocks of birds
> Sweetly rejoice.
> Brighter now
> Are moon and sun
> Who were so mournful
> At Christ's dying.
> Let stars, earth and sea,
> Shine with brightness,
> May all
> The choir of spirits
> Sing songs of joy in heaven,
> To the thunderer.[1]

2 THE CHRISTMAS SUN

The second illustration from which we can learn what was—and above all what was *not*—the true relationship between the

[1] Easter Sequence, verses 18–22 (*Analecta Hymnica*, 53, Leipzig, 1911, p. 66). As a reflexion of this ancient Christian lyrical joy in the Easter sunlight much value attaches to the pictures on the Exsultet rolls which, in correspondence with the text of the *Exsultet* of the Roman Easter Eve ("*Gaudeat et tellus tantis irradiata fulgoribus: et aeterni Regis splendore illustrata, totius orbis se sentiat amisisse caliginem . . . nox sicut dies illuminabitur*") show how Christ as the sun illuminates the darkness of the earth. Cf. M. Avery, *The Exultet Rolls of South Italy*, Princeton, 1936, vol. II, Plate 100, 4; Plate 131, 3, and Plate 156, 7. In this connexion I should also like to mention the Christian bronze lamp from Selinus, which has been described by Dölger (*Antike und Christentum*, 5 (1936), pp. 33 ff.), and reproduced on Plate 2. This lamp carries the inscription *Deo gratias* and was therefore probably used in the evening benediction of light out of which the liturgy of the bringing of light at Easter was developed: *Lumen Christi, Deo Gratias*. Around the inscription is what Dölger takes to be a circular wreath of flowers. But as H. Leisegang pointed out in the *Eranos-Jahrbuch* for 1939 (p. 154), it seems more likely that this wreath is nothing other than the circle of the sun with rays coming out of it, that is to say a symbol of the *lumen Christi* the "light without evening" for which the Christian offers up his *Deo gratias*.

Christian cult and the solar devotions of antiquity, is to be found in the early history of the two feasts celebrating Christ's birth—Epiphany and Christmas.[1] Since the facts in this case are exceptionally well documented, it is all the easier to get the picture clear.

Before we explore the actual points of cultic contact, however, we shall again have first to outline the basic tenets of Christian dogma around which the cultic garment came gradually to drape its lovely classical folds. Certain words in the Apostles' Creed were from primitive times among the fundamentals of the Christian faith: *conceptus de Spiritu Sancto, natus ex Maria Virgine*, and the accounts in Luke and Matthew which constitute the biblical foundation of this belief are like great blocks of hewn stone. The variegated systems of so-called critical thought which have sought to explain the belief in the Virgin Birth as myths or products of theosophical systems and of the general atmosphere of the surrounding Hellenistic world, have for the most part already proved their own undoing.[2] Their authors have from time to time had really new insights which have proved of genuine value, but because such men were never able to see the picture as a whole, those very insights have merely provided serviceable tools for the demolition of the theories of predecessors—predecessors who had trodden the

[1] The most important works, all of which have been used here, are the following: for antiquity in general, F. Pfister, "Epiphanie", in *Realenzyklopädie der klassischen Altertumswissenschaft*, IV, col. 277–323; W. Schmidt, "Geburtstag im Altertum" (The Birthday in Antiquity), *Religionsgeschichtliche Versuche und Vorarbeiten*, VII, 1, Giessen, 1908. For specifically Christian subjects, H. Usener, *Das Weihnachtsfest* (The Feast of Christmas), (2nd edition), Bonn, 1911; K. Holl, "Der Ursprung des Epiphaniefestes" (The Origin of the Feast of Epiphany), *Gesammelte Aufsätze zur Kirchengeschichte*, vol. II, Tübingen, 1928, pp. 123–54; O. Casel, "Die Epiphanie im Lichte der Religionsgeschichte" (Epiphany in the Light of the History of Religion), in *Benediktinische Monatsschrift*, 4 (1922), pp. 13 ff.; Thibaut, "La Solennité de Noël", in *Echos d'Orient*, 20 (1920), pp. 153 ff.; B. Botte, *Les Origines de la Noël et de l'Epiphanie*, Louvain, 1932 (the principal work on which is based what follows); K. Prümm, "Zur Entstehung der Geburtsfeier des Herrn in Ost und West" (The Origins of the Celebration of the Nativity of Our Lord in East and West), in *Stimmen der Zeit*, 135 (1939), pp. 207–25.

[2] The leading works in chronological order are: H. Gressmann, *Das Weihnachtsevangelium* (The Christmas Gospel), Göttingen, 1914; W. Bousset, *Kyrios Christos*, Göttingen, 1921; H. Leisegang, *Hagion Pneuma*, Leipzig, 1922; E. Norden, *Die Geburt des Kindes* (The Birth of the Child), Leipzig, 1931; M. Dibelius, "Jungfrauensohn und Krippenkind" (Virgin's Son and Manger Child), in *Sitzungsberichte der Heidelberger Akademie der Wissenschaften*, Hist.-Phil. Klasse, 22 (1932).

same thorny path and sought to treat the Virgin Birth as a classifiable phenomenon of comparative religion.[1]

In actual fact the true relation between dogmatic Christian belief and its external cultic garment is in the present instance even easier to grasp than it was in the case of the Easter sun; for it is a well-established fact that the earliest instances of anything in the nature of a cultic enactment of the Christmas mystery do not occur till more than two centuries after the first beginnings of Christianity. The inference seems clear enough. Since the mystery of the human birth of Jesus at first found no expression whatever in any kind of cult or visual imagery—though its dogmatic propagation was, if anything, all the more positive and insistent—, it is obvious that this article of faith cannot possibly have resulted from contact with sun-cults or any other cults. This circumstance however did not prevent it from being the rock from which the Church, wholly sure of her own doctrine and identity, reached out in the third and fourth centuries, appropriated whatever she found serviceable among the thoughts and longings and cultic forms of solar piety, and then used them to express and illustrate a mystery that was uniquely her own.

Before proceeding to a more detailed discussion, may I establish one point of great importance? The belief that our Lord was born true man but born of a virgin is intimately connected with the mystery of the resurrection and here my argument joins on to the conclusions reached earlier in this book. Jesus' resurrection from the dead was for him the beginning of a new and never-ending life: "Death shall no more have dominion over him" (Rom. 6. 9). Christ is truly *Sol invictus*, his sunrise is a new birth.

Now this was a thought that was also familiar to the pagan of antiquity. Helios is born anew every morning—"*aliusque et idem nasceris*", sang Horace in his *Carmen saeculare* to *almus Sol*. Even the theology of the New Testament already sees resurrection and

[1] K. Prümm, *Der christliche Glaube und die altheidnische Welt*, I, p. 279. The whole passage pp. 255–81 contains a thorough critical examination of the rationalist explanation of the doctrine of the Virgin Birth. Cf. also J. Gresham-Machen, *The Virgin Birth of Christ*, New York and London, 1930; F. X. Steinmetzer, "Jungfrauensohn und Krippenkind", in *Theologisch-Praktische Quartalschrift*, 88 (1935), pp. 15–25, 237–53.

birth as two aspects of the same thing: the victor of Easter morning is also "the firstborn from the dead" (Col. 1. 18; Apoc. 1. 5) and Paul quite explicitly connects the resurrection with the words of Psalm 2. 7: "Thou art my son, this day have I begotten thee" (Acts 13. 33).

We find an echo of all this in Clement of Alexandria, as we have already seen. He refers to Christ as "Sun of the Resurrection, begotten before the morning star, giving life with thy rays". The grave is the womb. Both represent night, out of which the sun rises. "At night was Christ born in Bethlehem," says a Greek sermon for Holy Saturday, "at night he is born again in Sion."[1]

This idea of a similarity between resurrection and birth gains support from the Graeco-Roman habit of regarding birthdays as a kind of sunrise. "Sunlight is the symbol of birth," says Plutarch;[2] and the Christian Clement says much the same. "Sunrise", he tells us, "is the symbol of a birthday."[3] Thus the sunrise of his Easter birth is for Jesus but the completion of that mystery of light that was proclaimed on the night when he was born of Mary. He is "the dayspring from on high" (Luke 1. 78), "a light to the revelation of the Gentiles" (Luke 2. 32).

Nay more, when in the mystery of baptism the grace of the risen Christ is imparted to man, then such a man becomes "a new creature" (II Cor. 5. 17); the grace of baptism is a new birth for in a new fashion Christ is born in the heart of the believer.[4] The Easter vigil, filled with the light of Christ, the nocturnal sun, is the night of birth, and the newly baptized are "ἀρτιγέννητα βρέφη – new-born children – *infantes*", as those who ascended out of the womb which is the baptismal pool were called in the ancient Church (I Peter 2. 2).

Thus, even on the purely dogmatic plane there is an intimate connexion between the mysteries of Easter and Christmas. If we regard the matter from the point of view of cultic development, however, we need have no hesitation in saying that the forms

---

[1] Pseudo-Epiphanius, *Homily on the "Great Sabbath"* (PG, 43, 441 D).

[2] *Aetia Romana*, 2 (Bernardakis, II, p. 251).

[3] *Stromata*, VII, 7, 43 (GCS, III, p. 32, l. 33).

[4] See H. Rahner, "Die Gottesgeburt" (The Birth of God), in *Zeitschrift für katholische Theologie*, 59 (1935), pp. 333–418.

taken by the feast of Christmas, the origin of which is comparatively late, are simply modelled on those of the much older feast
of Easter; and the common cultic basis from which this later imitation derived was the world of solar mysticism, for it is this that
provided both these solemn nights with a fitting imagery. It is,
however, very largely an imagery expressly designed to repudiate and contradict the solar cults of later antiquity, but its affinity
to the forms of the latter is too clear to be wholly denied. Prümm
is surely right when he says, "Christmas touches Easter over a
wide front of common ideas, the idea of redemption and that of
the grace of adoption as children of God. This explains why light-
symbolism enters so powerfully into both."[1]

The meaning of Easter is that the life that began at Christmas
is turned into life eternal. In the case of Christ this change is final
and complete; for the baptized Christian it takes place in a sacramental sense: Jesus is for ever now "the brightness of his [the
Father's] glory" (Heb. 1. 3), but even the baptized Christian whom
this brightness of Christ has illuminated is now "a child of light"
(Eph. 5. 8; I Thes. 5. 5), which simply means "a child of the sun".
The baptized Christian is—to use the words of the inscription referred to above—a sun-child, a ʿΗλιόπαις.

Christmas is therefore nothing but an anticipation of Easter, the
beginning of a marvellous springtime, because at Christmas,
though still deeply hidden, the "Sun of Righteousness" arose. An
anonymous Greek has described this springtime mystery of Christmas in truly wonderful fashion in words that take on meaning
only when read in reference to the springtime feast of the Easter
sun:

"When after the cold of winter we see the mild light of spring,
then the earth begins to put forth grass and green things, then by
virtue of the awakening powers within them, the branches of the
trees begin to beautify themselves and the air shines with the brightness of Helios. The choirs of the birds rise up to the sky and brim
over with melody. But lo! for us Christ has appeared like some
heavenly spring, having risen like the sun from the Virgin's
womb. He has put to flight the cold storm-clouds of the devil and

[1] *Zur Enstehung der Geburtsfeier*, p. 222.

has roused to new life the sluggish hearts of them that slept, having with his sunny rays pierced the mists of ignorance. Let us therefore lift up our spirits towards the bright and blessed glory of this heavenly light."[1]

Now a great deal has recently been written on the cultic origins of this essentially Roman and Latin feast at Christmas, but in order to get a clear picture of them I must, for reasons which will soon be apparent, first say something about the feast of Epiphany.

(i) The Feast of Epiphany

The fixing of the date of Easter and the choice of Sunday as a day for special Christian observance had been determined by certain specific passages in the Gospel record, the result being duly dovetailed into the solar year. The Church, however, could find no such calendar guidance when she sought to give cultic expression to the birth of Christ. The day and even the month when that event occurred are matters on which both Scripture and tradition are completely silent. Scholars are not even unanimous as to the year of Jesus' birth and all attempts to calculate it must rely on uncertain inferences from secondary data.

The Church of antiquity was in this respect quite as badly in the dark as we are ourselves. In these circumstances it sought to rely on a process of laboured speculation, in which Scripture and allegory were uneasily mingled—we can see examples of the thing in Clement of Alexandria[2] and Hippolytus[3]—, or alternatively resorted to even bolder expedients; for it fell back on the solar symbolism with which Easter had already made it affectionately familiar, and which, in point of fact, fits in very well with the actual

---

[1] Pseudo-Chrysostom, *Christmas Homily* (PG, 61, 763).

[2] *Stromata*, I, 21, 145, 6 (GCS, II, p. 90). According to the data supplied by him, many, at that time, had fixed on 20 May as the date of Christ's birth. His own calculations lead to 18 November. According to Epiphanius, the *alogoi* believed 21 May to be the Lord's birthday: *Panarion*, 51, 29, 2 (GCS, II, p. 300, l. 9).

[3] According to the critically doubtful text of his *Commentary on Daniel*, IV, 23 (GCS, I, 1, p. 242, ll. 1–3), and the information on the Paschal table on the statue of Hippolytus (text and reproduction in *Dictionnaire d'archéologie*, VI, Paris, 1925, col. 2423 f.) the latter gave 2 April as Christ's birthday, though it is also possible that he accepted 25 December as that date. There is one thing that seems reasonably sure. It is that he (*c.* A.D. 205) believed Christ to have been born on a Wednesday, the day on which out of the six days of creation God created the sun.

dogmatic content of the nativity. Thus equipped, it first concerned itself with the business of date-fixing—later and very gradually, with the liturgical showing forth of the Saviour's birth.

The most engaging example of such attempts to determine the
date of the nativity under guidance from the symbolism of the
sun is a work composed in the year 243 which probably comes
from the pen of an African priest and is entitled *De Pascha Computus*. At the time this work was written, there was still no trace of
any cultic celebration of the nativity and the Church was still very
much concerned with the dating of Easter. Wholly under the influence of that symbolism of the Easter sun which we have already
discussed, this ingenious piece of mathematical allegorizing proceeds from the assumption that the first day of creation coincided
with the vernal equinox on March 25, so that God would have
created the sun and moon on March 28, this being the fourth
day. The author carries his rather wild speculations right through
the Old Testament and finally concludes: "*ad diem nativitatis Christi
perveniemus qui invenitur . . . quinto Kalendas Aprilis, feria quarta*".
Christ was therefore born on March 28, four days after the vernal
equinox, on the day, that is to say, on which God created the sun.

At this point the author, who till now had been satisfied with
arid calculations, breaks out into the joyous cry: "*O quam praeclara
et divina Domini providentia, ut in illo die quo factus est sol, in ipso die
nasceretur Christus, quinto Kalendas Aprilis, feria quarta. Et ideo de
ipso merito ad plebem dicebat Malachias propheta: Orietur vobis sol
iustitiae.*"[1] It is quite obvious that the guiding thought in all this
calculation is the theological conception of Christ as "the Sun of
Righteousness" which by this time had been very fully developed,[2]
and that the entire "computus" of the nativity is based on this.
Thus we already find ourselves in the presence of a Christmas day
—or at any rate of an anniversary of Christ's birth—held to be the
sun's birthday, long before it had been built up cultically at all.
Indeed to this allegorical way of thinking—both profound and
naïve—the whole life of Jesus, right up to his death and resurrection, is one great sun mystery. Christ is symbolized by the sun,

[1] *De Pascha Computus*, 19 (CSEL, 3, p. 266, ll. 9–12).
[2] The early Christian material for this in Dölger, *Die Sonne der Gerechtigkeit und der Schwarze*, pp. 100–10.

which completes its cycle in 365 days and three hours. After four years the three hours add up to twelve, the intercalary day, and this is the symbol of the twelve apostles, from whose accounts in the Bible we can penetrate the solar mystery of Jesus' own life between the time of his birth and Easter. This mystical, allegorical computation is as follows.

The passion and resurrection of Jesus took place in "the sixteenth year of Tiberius"; Jesus was then "thirty-one years old". Now the mystical number that we can read in the first two letters of Jesus' name (ιη) is eighteen. If we add all these figures together, we get the number sixty-five. If we further add to this number the Greek letter tau which is the mystical symbol of the cross and has the numerical significance of three hundred, then the result is the figure of the solar year, namely three hundred and sixty-five. The author concludes this numerical allegory, in which Christian symbolism mingles with a very ancient Pythagorean heritage, with the following words: "*Ecce iterum iam vere credamus quod quinto Kalendas Aprilis secundum carnem natus sit Christus: in quo die probavimus solem factum.*"[1]

We may well feel that this is rather childish and even rather frivolous, but behind it all is the sublime Christian cosmos and its divine sun; and as during the third century the attractions of heliolatry grew—in the theosophy of Neoplatonism, in the cults of Isis and Mithras, which had also now tended to become solar in character—so the Church must have felt an ever more urgent need to give cultic expression to its own supernatural mystery of the sun. Thus in the Greek East the original liturgical celebration of the nativity was, almost as a matter of course, deliberately devised as a rival to the sun-cults.

The proof-text which gives us our first glimpse of the origins of Epiphany as the feast celebrating the nativity of Christ is the much discussed passage in the *Panarion* of Epiphanius of Salamis. This is not only of great historical value, but highly interesting from the point of view of religious psychology. In it the ardent Eastern adversary of heresy denounces the pagan sun mysteries that were celebrated on January 6 as rival institutions to the Christian feast of

[1] *De Pascha Computus*, 19 (CSEL, 3, p. 267, ll. 7–9).

Epiphany. They are only celebrated, he avers, "so that men who have their hearts set upon error, may be prevented from finding the truth".

Historically, of course, what happened was the exact opposite of this. It is reasonably certain, though not absolutely so, that in the third century the Christian feast was introduced in Alexandria and elsewhere in the East as a protest against pagan solar celebrations which took place on January 6. However, let me quote the passage from Epiphanius which is actually introduced into a polemic against the alogists who were attacking the chronology of St John's Gospel.

"The Redeemer", says Epiphanius, "was born in the 42nd year of the Roman emperor Augustus, the year in which, as the Roman records prove, Octavius Augustus was consul with Silanus for the thirteenth time. . . . Christ was born on the eighth day before the Ides of January, thirteen days after the winter solstice from whence onward the light and the days begin to grow longer.

"On this day, i.e. on the eighth day before the Calends of January, the Greeks—I mean, the idolaters—celebrate a feast that the Romans call *Saturnalia*, the Egyptians *Cronia* and the Alexandrines *Cicellia*. The reason is that the eighth day before the Calends of January forms a dividing-line, for on it occurs the solstice; the day begins to lengthen again and the sun shines longer and with increasing strength until the eighth day before the Ides of January, viz., until the day of Christ's nativity, for to each day is added the thirtieth part of an hour.

"A wise man from among the Syrians, Ephraem by name, says in one of his commentaries: 'The appearing of our Lord Jesus Christ, that is, his birth in the flesh and his complete incarnation which we call *Epiphaneia*, occurred on that day which is thirteen days removed from the beginning of the waxing sunlight. That had to happen thus in order that it might be a type for the number resulting when we add to our Lord Jesus Christ his twelve apostles, for it is the fulfilment of the number thirteen, of the thirteen days since the waxing of the sun.'

"However [Epiphanius continues], many things have happened

and are still happening which serve to confirm and prove these things, I mean the birth of Christ; for the charlatans who are the inventors of idolatrous rites celebrate in various places a splendid feast in order to deceive the idolaters who put their trust in them, and they do so on the night before this same day of Epiphany, and through this they are compelled to confess at least a part of the truth, though their only reason for celebrating this feast is that the truth should not be sought by those who set their hopes upon them.

"The principal of these feasts is that which takes place in the so-called Koreion in Alexandria, this Koreion being a mighty temple in the district sacred to Kore. Throughout the whole night the people keep themselves awake here by singing certain hymns and by means of the flute-playing which accompanies the songs they sing to the image of their god. When they have ended these nocturnal celebrations, then at morning cock-crow they descend, carrying torches, into a sort of chapel which is below the ground, and thence they carry up a wooden image of one lying naked upon a bier. This image has upon its forehead a golden cross and two more such seals in the form of crosses one on each hand and two further ones, one on each knee, making five such golden seals in all. Then they carry the wooden image seven times round the innermost confines of the temple to the sound of flutes, tambourines and to the singing of hymns, and when the procession is over, they return the image to the subterranean place from which it was taken. And if anyone asks them what manner of mysteries these might be, they reply, saying: 'Today at this hour Kore, that is the virgin, has given birth to Aion.'

"Such things also occur in Petra which is the chief city of Arabia and is called Edom in Holy Scripture and the image there is similarly honoured. The hymns they sing are in the Arabic tongue and are in praise of a virgin whom they call 'Chaamu' which is the same as Kore or Parthenos, and in praise of her child 'Dusares' which means 'Only son of the ruler of all.' The same thing happens on this same night in Alexandria, in Petra and also in the city of Elusa."[1]

---

[1] *Panarion*, 51, 22, 3–11 (GCS, II, pp. 284–7).

Let us dwell for a few moments on this most illuminating account. Much in it is of course demonstrably erroneous, the wholly arbitrary identification, for instance, which Epiphanius makes of this feast with a quite imaginary Roman *Saturnalia* on December 25. What the writer is really referring to is the feast of *Sol invictus*; indeed the *Saturnalia* were over by December 23. It has been pointed out—and the contention is quite probably sound—that in his eagerness to accentuate the "diabolical aping" by the heathen of the Christian mysteries, he seems to have turned the pagan liturgy unconsciously into something like a copy of the forms of Christian worship at the Epiphany, which at that time was the only commemorative feast of the birth of Christ.[1] For all that, his account is still first-rate source material and it is certainly reliable evidence for the fact that in the Hellenistic East, and with Alexandria evidently taking the lead, a mystery was enacted that concerned the birth of Aion by a virgin and that this mystery took place on the night leading to January 6. It is quite immaterial whether the object of the cult in question was really Dionysus Aion or some other deity. Epiphanius, quoting other ancient writers,[2] tells us elsewhere that the birthday of Dionysus was celebrated on January 5 and 6, though in the present instance it may well have been that of Osiris or Harpocrates-Horus. It matters very little, since the tendency in these late Hellenistic days was for the identities of gods, all of whom were beginning to take on the character of a solar deity, to become completely merged with one another. We know that Aion was at this time beginning to be regarded as identical with Helios and Helios with Dionysus[3]—a circumstance

[1] Already noted by J. Wellhausen, *Skizzen und Vorarbeiten* (Sketches and Preparatory Studies), 1887, p. 46. Cf. K. Prümm, *Der christliche Glaube*, I, p. 271. It seems, moreover, that in his account of the "virgin" mother of the Arabian Dusares, Epiphanius fell victim to a bad linguistic mistake. Cf. C. Clemen, *Der Einfluss der Mysterienreligionen*, p. 63.

[2] *Panarion*, 51, 30 (GCS, II, p. 301); B. Botte, *Les Origines*, pp. 72–4.

[3] For the religious history of Aion, cf. C. Lackeit, *Aion: Zeit und Ewigkeit in Sprache und Religion der Griechen* (Aion: Time and Eternity in the Speech and Religion of the Greeks), I, Königsberg, 1916; L. Troje, 'Die Geburt des Aion" (The Birth of Aion), in *Archiv für Religionswissenschaft*, 22 (1923), pp. 87 ff.; H. Sasse, "Aion", in *Theologisches Wörterbuch zum Neuen Testament*, vol. I, pp. 197–208; O. Weinreich, "Aion in Eleusis", in *Archiv für Religionswissenschaft*, 19 (1916–19), pp. 174 ff.; R. Eisler, "Das Fest des 'Geburtstags der Zeit' in Nordarabien" (The Feast of the "Birthday of Time" in Northern Arabia), in *Archiv für Religionswissenschaft*, 15 (1912), pp. 628 ff.

that gives added meaning to a text of Macrobius which alleges that Dionysus was given a variety of shapes, one being that of a child, another that of an old man, because Dionysus was the symbol of the sun: he then adds: "*Hae autem aetatum diversitates ad solem referuntur, ut parvulus videatur hiemali solstitio, qualem Aegyptii proferunt ex adyto die certa, quod tunc brevissimo die veluti parvulus et infans videatur*–These differences of age relate to the sun. He is made to appear small at the time of the winter solstice, when upon a certain day the Egyptians take him out of the crypt, because on this the shortest day of the year it is as though he were a little child."[1] The words "*proferunt ex adyto*" leave us in little doubt that the reference here is to the same feast, even though Macrobius transfers it to the day of the winter solstice, December 25.

From this we are led a step further by a text which is admittedly late, but is actually the more valuable for that; for it shows how long the feeling lingered on that the birth of Christ was in some way connected with the sun mysteries of the ancient world. Cosmas of Jerusalem (*c.* A.D. 740), in a commentary on the hymns of Gregory of Nazianzus, discusses the latter's poem on Easter in praise of Christ the sun, Φαέθων ὑψίδρομος[2] or High-riding Phaethon, but the significant thing is that just in this context he should refer to a pagan festival which took place on December 25. This is what he says:

"The pagans had of old celebrated this feast each year and named the day on which Christ was born ἀυξίφωτος–increaser of light'. They held an initiation at midnight, descending into a sanctuary, from which they returned crying: 'The virgin has given birth, now the light begins to wax.' Moreover Epiphanius, the great bishop of Cyprus, tells us that this same feast was also celebrated by the Saracens in honour of Aphrodite whom they greatly revered, and whom in their tongue they call *Chamara*."[3]

[1] *Saturnalia*, I, 18 (Eyssenhardt, p. 112). Cf. also H. Leisegang, *Eranos-Jahrbuch*, 1939, pp. 159–65.
[2] *Carmina de Seipso*, I, 38, vv. 15–18 (PG, 37, 1326). Cf. H. Rahner "Mysterium Lunae", *loc. cit.*, p. 340.
[3] *Collectio Historiarum quarum meminit Divus Gregorius in Carminibus suis*, 52 (PG, 38, 464). The above translation is actually from a more reliable text which K. Holl took from a codex in the Bodleian (*op. cit.*, p. 145).

Here too we are obviously concerned with the same feast as before, and one gains the impression that Cosmas is not only relying on what he has read in Epiphanius, but also on other traditions. As to the dates, Norden has shown that the change from January 6 to December 25 can be explained as the result of the reform introduced by the more accurate Julian calendar into the ancient Egyptian calculation which had fixed January 6 as the date of the winter solstice.[1] Yet the significance of the feast, whether we assume it to have been a single or a double one, was obviously that is was "γενέθλιος Ἡλίου", the birthday of the new sunlight.

But what has all this to do with the origins of the Christian feast of Epiphany? The scanty nature of our source material prevents us from giving a clear answer to that question. One thing, however, seems beyond dispute. It is that this feast of Epiphany was from the very beginning primarily a celebration of our Lord's birthday, and it was introduced in order to give cultic expression to what the Church had believed from the beginning, namely, that Jesus Christ had been born of the Virgin Mary and that with his Epiphany, his "appearance" that is to say, upon earth, the true sunlight had begun to shine. There simply is no other explanation of the polemic of Epiphanius, who surely must have known how the feast of Epiphany originated. Even for the man of Greek culture who was not a Christian, the word "Epiphany" meant the birthday of the god.[2] Christ's appearance in the flesh was therefore the highest form of Epiphany that the Christian could conceive (cf. Titus 2. 11; 3. 4; II Tim. 1. 10).[3] In the fourth century when the character of the feast stands quite plainly before us, the birthday of Christ is called ἐπιφάνεια or θεοφάνεια and these terms are interchangeable with γενέθλια which is also used at times in exactly the same sense.

We must therefore assume that at some point of time which we cannot exactly determine, but which I believe was towards the

---

[1] *Die Geburt des Kindes* (The Birth of the Child), p. 388; B. Botte, *op. cit.*, p. 71; Prümm, *Zur Entstehung der Geburtsfeier*, p. 208.

[2] Cf. the material in F. Pfister, *Realenzyklopädie der klassischen Altertumswissenschaft*, supplementary volume, IV, col. 310; W. Schmidt, *Geburtstag im Altertum*, pp. 86f.

[3] On the much higher sense of the idea of Epiphany in the New Testament, see Prümm, *Der christliche Glaube und die altheidnische Welt*, I, pp. 208 ff.

end of the third century, a day was set apart for the solemn commemoration of the birth of Christ and that January 6 was deliberately chosen as the date for this occasion as a gesture of repudiation
against the solar celebrations which took place on this day among
the pagans. We must surely believe that this was done because
Christians had from the earliest times been accustomed to think of
Christ as "the Sun of Righteousness", whose brightness was
glorified on Sunday and at Easter and whose beauty had always
been praised by theologians of the Alexandrian school. In the
Christian feast of the Epiphany men turned to the true sun and by
that act repudiated his rival and it was the birth of the true son
that this feast now recalled to men's minds.

This contention that Epiphany was essentially a birthday feast
is confirmed by a piece of information preserved for us by
Clement of Alexandria, though at first sight it might be held to
prove the opposite. He tells us that in his day some of the disciples of
the Gnostic Basilides celebrated on January 6, the baptism of Jesus
in Jordan.[1] Some people have inferred from this that in the Church
itself Epiphany had originally been a showing forth of the baptism
of Jesus and not of his birth. But it is really quite inconceivable
that the Church should simply have copied a feast from the
Gnostics whom it so heartily detested. Indeed in my submission
such a contention would be the exact opposite of the truth. The
fact is surely that his "baptismal day" was in the Gnostic view the
true birthday of Jesus; for in the Gnostic system the fleshly birth
of Jesus the man is of no account. Significance only attaches to
his spiritual birth in the Jordan when the Pneuma descended upon
him. The conclusion, if any, seems to be that the day was so firmly
associated with the idea of birth, that even the Gnostics accepted
that association, though they interpreted the idea of birth in a way
that the Church could never conceivably accept.

Now there are admittedly versions of Luke 3. 22 in which the
voice of the Father at Jesus' baptism is made to say, "Thou art my
Son; this day have I begotten thee"—the very words which Paul
applies to the "birth" which is the resurrection at Easter. From
the second century onward this reading occurs again and again,

[1] *Stromata*, I, 146, 1, 2 (GCS, II, p. 90).

but the fact remains that early Christian theology never understood the baptism of Jesus in the Jordan to be a birth in the Gnostic sense; it always saw in this event an epiphany, a divine manifestation of Jesus as the only-begotten Son of God.[1]

When, therefore, we investigate the origins of the feast of January 6 and seek to discover the Church's intentions in instituting it, we must always regard a double protest as being implicit in it: first there was the protest, already noted, against the mysteries of the pagan sun-cults, but there was also the protest against the Gnostics who denied the divinity of Jesus at the time of his birth.

The feast of January 6 thus celebrated the human birth of him who had risen as a new sun upon the world—as indeed can be seen from the very nature of the feast in the fourth century, especially in those places to which the Roman Christmas feast of December 25 had not yet penetrated and which had not yet come under the influence of that institution. Everywhere the Epiphany is still the feast of the nativity, the feast of the rising sun; it is also admittedly the feast commemorating the baptism in Jordan, where the divine nature of Mary's child was proclaimed and, indeed, after the Roman Christmas of December 25 had won the day and secured universal acceptance, it was the latter element that became the dominant feature of the solemnities of January 6, but even if that is so, even if baptism of the faithful took place on this day, the inner meaning of these things was exactly what I have described: baptism is birth, and in the baptism of the faithful Jesus is born anew.

But, as we have seen, birth is sunrise and illumination, and the two ideas are continually in association. For instance, at a time when he had not yet introduced the other feast of the nativity, Chrysostom calls the Epiphany ἡμέρα γενέθλιος,[2] or "the birthday", while an anonymous writer—according to Holl[3] a priest of Jerusalem—in an Epiphany sermon to the newly baptized speaks of Christ's birth as the rising of the Sun of Righteousness and refers to the holy night of the nativity as "a bringer of more light than any 'Sun' day".[4] Even when the Roman feast of

[1] Source material discussed in detail by H. Rahner, "Die Gottesgeburt", *loc. cit.*, pp. 362 f.
[2] *De Sancta Pentecoste*, I (PG, 50, 454).   [3] *Op. cit.*, p. 126; B. Botte, *op. cit.*, p. 14.
[4] *Sermo de Cognitione Dei* (PG, 64, 43–6).

Christmas began to get established, outside Italy, the original asso-
ciations of Epiphany remained and stamped upon it the character
which for so long it continued to bear. Gregory of Nazianzus who
had already glorified the other Christmas feast in one of his sermons, can still exalt January 6 as "the day of holy lights", and can
especially associate that day with "the mystery of the light" which
is Christ and contrast that mystery with all the pagan mysteries
such as those of Dionysus and Mithras and those of Eleusis. The
newly baptized are for him men who have been "touched by a
ray of the sunshine of the one true God",[1] and on the following
day he delivers that famous address in which his joy over the sun
mystery of Epiphany reaches its climax in the quotation of those
words of Plato's which he loved so dearly: "In the realm of spirits
God is as the sun in the realm of sense",[2] words that he had already
quoted in that hymn to the sun which is his second theological
oration.[3]

One must have a feeling for all these things, if one is to understand the spirit that gave the birthday feast of Epiphany its ultimate form—it is the same spirit as that which originally created
it. We see this most clearly in the writings of the Syrian Ephraem
who knew nothing of the feast of December 25 and whose
Epiphany hymns are full of this Christian delight in the sun. We
have already come across a quotation by Epiphanius from one of
Ephraem's works which has since been lost and the note that is
there sounded echoes on in his hymns. I can only touch on this
matter briefly, yet it is clear that for Ephraem Epiphany is the
Lord's birthday because this is the day of the sunlight's triumphant
new beginning, and Ephraem treats it as such, though he knows
that the winter solstice is on December 25 and not on January 6.
From this we see quite clearly that the origins of Epiphany should
really be ascribed to the zeal of the Alexandrian group which instituted a Christian solar mystery on this day in opposition to the
feast of Aion which was customarily celebrated on it, and they
did this though fully aware that the day was strictly speaking not

---

[1] *Oratio 39: in Sancta Lumina* (PG, 36, 336–60).

[2] *Oratio 40, 5: in Sanctum Baptisma* (PG, 36, 364 B). The passage from Plato which
Gregory has changed somewhat, is to be found in the *Politics*, VI, 19, 508 C.

[3] *Oratio Theologica*, II, 29, 30 (PG, 36, 68 f.).

the "right" one at all. The manner in which this latter difficulty was resolved has already been indicated and is apparent in the following lines:

> The sun conquers and the steps by which it approaches
> the zenith
> Show forth a mystery.
> Lo, it is twelve days since he began to mount upward
> And today is the thirteenth day.
> It is the perfect symbol of the Son and his twelve apostles.
> The darkness of winter is conquered,
> To show that Satan is conquered.
> The sun conquers, so that all may know
> That the only-begotten Son of God triumphs over all.[1]

That the sun which is Christ went forth from the Virgin's womb on the fourth day of creation, the day on which the sun was created, is also a subject of one of Ephraem's hymns, and this hymn too is composed for January 6:

"The fourth day alone praises, before all other things, the birth of him who on that fourth day created the two lights of heaven which were worshipped by the foolish and caused them to be without sight or light. The Lord of the heavenly lights descended and like a sun shone forth from the womb of his mother. His rays open the eyes of the blind and his brightness illuminates those who wander in error."[2]

When one reflects on the fact that it was precisely in Syria, in Ephraem's own Baalbek-Heliopolis, in Emesa and in Palmyra, that the ancient sun-cults survived right into the days of Constantine, one realizes how important a part was played by the liturgy of Epiphany in the final issue of the conflict between Christianity with this form of superstition.

(ii) The Feast of Christmas

We have seen that the feast of Epiphany came into being as an

---

[1] "Hymn to the Epiphany" I, Strophe 11, 12 (ed. Th. J. Lamy *Ephraem Syri Hymni et Sermones* I, Malines, 1882, p. 10).

[2] "Hymn on the Birth of Christ in the Flesh", 6 (Lamy, II, p. 498). Cf. also Hymn 2 (Lamy, II, p. 448).

institution specifically designed to counter and weaken the Eastern form of sun-worship and its mystery rituals. In Rome, however, during the course of the third century sun-worship, favoured and protected as it was by the rulers of the empire, had achieved a position of great power and splendour, and had indeed virtually become the official religion of the State. But the concluding chapter in this story of Christianity's ultimate settlement with paganism, the chapter that is laid in Rome, follows much the same pattern as that which we have already studied. The Church opposes, the Church dethrones, the Church consecrates and in the end the Church brings home. The result of all this is the establishment and liturgical development of the feast of Christmas on December 25, the feast, whose magic even to this day enthralls the hearts of Christian and non-Christian alike.

During the lull between the persecutions of Decius and Diocletian the Church must surely have regarded the rise of the imperial sun-cult as an ever-increasing menace. To catch something of the spiritual atmosphere of that time, we should have to imagine ourselves in that vast temple of Sol on the Campus Agrippae, the temple built by the Emperor Aurelian after his victory over Palmyra, with its solemn *collegium* of the *Pontifices Solis*. We should have to witness the brilliance of the new feast of *Natalis Invicti* that was to be celebrated from now on, on each December 25,[1] the day of the winter solstice. Certain fragments of Cornelius Labeo which have been preserved for us by Macrobius,[2] are very much worth reading in this general connexion, and it is particularly worth noting that this writer identifies Helios-Sol with the Jewish Yao and with Dionysus. Even if we disregard the triumphant rise of Mithras-worship, at least in the Roman army, this shows us how great was the danger that confronted the Church, from this kind of solar syncretism.

Something like a symbol of the time, and of the conditions

---

[1] F. Cumont, "Le Natalis Invicti", in *Académie des Inscriptions et Belles-Lettres, Comptes rendus*, Brussels, 1911, pp. 292–8; Cumont, "La célébration du Natalis Invicti en Orient", in *Revue d'histoire des religions*, 82 (1919), pp. 85 ff.; J. Noiville, "Les origines du Natalis Invicti", in *Revue des Études anciennes*, 38 (1936), pp. 145 ff.

[2] Cf. R. Ganschinietz, "Jao", in *Realenzyklopädie der klassischen Altertumswissenschaft*, IX, col. 708, ll. 1–33. On Cornelius Labeo, see *ibid.*, IV, col. 1351.

prevailing in it, is preserved for us in the so-called chronographer's record for the year 354. It contains a notice, a double one, relating to the same day, December 25, and reads:

VIII Kalendas Ianuarias Natalis Invicti.[1]
VIII Kalendas Ianuarias natus Christus in Bethlehem Iudeae.[2]

This chronographer's notice proves that by the year 354 a regular liturgical feast of the birthday of our Lord was being celebrated in Rome on December 25. Indeed from other statements of the same chronographer it can be shown that this was already the case in 336, while the fact that the African Donatists celebrated this feast makes it reasonably certain that before the time of the persecution of Diocletian it had already been brought over from Rome.[3] It would seem then that this feast was first instituted at some time towards the close of the third century, at the very time, that is, when the feast of Epiphany originated in the East, and both feasts came into being as the result of the liturgical and apologetic needs of that long period of tranquillity that preceded the final persecution; both are the Church's answer to that spiritual hunger that lies at the bottom of the sun-cults.

This attempt at dating may seem a little bold. Yet one thing emerges quite plainly from all the relevant fourth-century texts: it is that the nativity feast of December 25 was always regarded as a Christian solar feast and that men saw in it the Church's answer to the sun-cults of the fading Graeco-Roman world. A highly interesting Latin treatise which is assigned by Dom Wilmart,[4] its discoverer, to the end of the third century but which in my opinion probably comes from the early part of the fourth, deals with the question of the winter solstice and its relation to the nativity of Christ. In reference to December 25 we find the author saying this:

"Sed et Invicti Natalem appellant. Quis utique tam invictus nisi Dominus noster qui mortem subactam devicit? Vel quod dicant Solis esse

[1] *Corpus Inscriptionum Latinarum*, I, 1, Berlin, 1893, p. 256.
[2] T. Mommsen, *Chronica Minora* (*Monum. Germaniae Hist., Auct. Ant.*, IX, p. 71).
[3] Cf. G. Brunner, *Jahrbuch für Liturgiewissenschaft*, 13 (1935), pp. 178–81; K. Prümm, *Zur Entstehung*, p. 215.
[4] A. Wilmart, "La collection des 38 homélies latines de St Jean Chrysostome", in *Journal of Theological Studies*, 19 (1918), pp. 305–27.

Natalem: ipse est Sol iustitiae, de quo Malachias Propheta dixit: orietur vobis timentibus nomen ipsius Sol iustitiae et sanitas in pennis eius."[1]

(But they also call [this day] the birthday of the unconquered sun. Yet who is as unconquered as our Lord who threw down death and conquered him? They may call this day the birthday of Sol, but he alone is the Sun of Righteousness of whom the Prophet Malachi said: There shall arise to you who fear his name the Sun of Righteousness and there shall be healing under his wings.)

Here we can detect that same cry of victory which Ephraem uttered in distant Syria when he sang of the feast of Epiphany: the sun has conquered. This Christian cry of joy will never again be silenced. Let us call back to life some of the voices of the great chorus that uttered it; we can still hear its echoes in the classical phrases of Rome when the Catholic liturgy celebrates its nocturnal mystery at Christmas.

The inner meaning and purpose of the Roman feast of Christmas find particularly explicit expression in those places where during the course of the fourth century this new liturgical creation had already begun to penetrate in its triumphant advance through the Church; this is particularly true of the Greek East where it was gradually displacing the strongly rooted feast of the Epiphany. We are plunged into the midst of this particular debate by a sermon delivered by Jerome to his monks in Bethlehem. Jerome had brought from Rome the new custom of celebrating the birth of Christ on December 25 whereas in the East the practice of celebrating this on January 6 was still universally observed. Jerome reproves the presumption of the Christians who had for generations inhabited Jerusalem and Bethlehem—and does so with a certain mocking humour—because these insisted that their dating of this feast followed a genuine local tradition that had real historical value. Then he points out that even nature with her solstice supports the Roman practice and says:

"Even creation justifies our preaching and the cosmos testifies to the truth of our words. Up till this day the days have continued

---

[1] Critical text of the dissertation "De solstitiis et aequinoctiis" in B. Botte, *op. cit.*, pp. 93–105. Passage quoted is on p. 105, ll. 434–9.

to wane, but from this day onward the darkness grows less. The light grows, the nights diminish. The day grows greater, and error grows less; up rises truth. For today there is born unto us the Sun of Righteousness."[1]

When Jerome speaks, as he does here, of the darkness of error receding, he is thinking of the pagan cult whose sun mysteries were still very much alive; Emperor Julian's attempt to make Helios once more into the *Dominus Imperii* had shown that plainly enough, and in Jerome's day the sanctuary of Adonis on the Janiculum in Rome could still be visited by devotees seeking solace in that solar pantheism which by now had absorbed the figures of the Syrian gods.[2] It is therefore not difficult to guess the nature of Jerome's thoughts when he celebrated the nocturnal solemnities commemorating the birth of Christ in the cave at Bethlehem, for that same cave had since Hadrian's day been a sanctuary of Adonis.[3] He writes of this in one of his letters: "Bethlehem, which is now ours and the most venerable place in the whole world, was once overshadowed by the grove of Tamuz, that is to say, of Adonis, and in the cave where once Christ whimpered as a little child, there sounded lamentations for the beloved of Venus."[4] Truly the Christians must have felt that their nocturnal sun-feast of December 25 was a victory over all the pagan mysteries. You will recall that Gregory of Nazianzus spoke in this sense on the day of Epiphany and you can hear the same note in the words which Firmicus Maternus puts into the mouth of the sun—another proof by the way, of the manner in which all mysteries at this time got drawn into the orbit of heliolatry:

"If the sun [he says] were to call the whole human race together and address it, he might well shatter you with his words. He would surely say, 'Who has driven you to this infamous deed,

[1] "Homily on the Birth of the Lord": G. Morin, "Hieronymi Presbyteri Tractatus sive Homiliae" (*Anecdota Maredsolana*, III, 2), Maredsous, 1897, p. 397, ll. 9–13.

[2] On these late solar forms of the Syrian cult, cf. F. Cumont, *Die orientalischen Religionen im römischen Heidentum*, pp. 122 f.; on the cave of Adonis on the Janiculum, cf. Prümm, *Das antike Heidentum*, p. 267.

[3] This according to Paulinus of Nola, *Epistola*, 31, 3 (CSEL, 29, p. 270, ll. 1–4).

[4] *Epistola*, 58, 3 (CSEL, 54, p. 532).

150   *Greek Myths and Christian Mystery*

O ye sons of men that perish, in that in your impious passion and unheeding madness you let me die and be born. . . ? Bewail Dionysus, bewail Proserpina, bewail Adonis, bewail Osiris, but do not offer this insult to my own dignity. At the beginning of days I was created by God and that is sufficient for me.'"[1]

Christmas served both to combat and consecrate the old Graeco-Roman feeling for the sun, and it continued to do so even when the ancient mystery cults were already dead; for to the soul of the people December 25 meant something more than the fact that it happened of old to have been designated as the day of *Sol novus* or *Natalis*. What lived on was the feeling of religious awe with which such men followed the happenings in the starry heavens and the paths of the sun. The Church sanctified this feeling through the mystery of Christmas. "Born of his Father," says Augustine in a Christmas sermon,[2] "Christ created all the days. Being born of his mother he consecrated this one"—and by consecrating it drew towards himself and gave form and direction to the vague and inchoate feeling of awe with which that day was already associated.

The story telling how Christian truth filled up the measure of this ancient reverence for the new-born sun is easy to follow. Let me deal first with the Greek East where the Roman feast was accepted towards the end of the fourth century. Gregory of Nazianzus personally introduced it in Constantinople and proudly referred to himself as the ἔξαρχος, or chorus leader, of the new mystery.[3] Superb indeed is that first Christmas sermon of his, so full of the characteristic rhythms of Gregory's Greek: "Once again the dark shadows of winter draw away, once again the light rises towards the zenith."[4] Chrysostom, who first celebrates the feast in Antioch, calls it the μητρόπολις, the source of light and starting-point for all the coming feasts,[5] while in Alexandria, where once were celebrated the mysteries of the new-born Aion, the feast of Christmas is introduced after the Council of Ephesus

[1] *De Errore Profanarum Religionum*, 8 (CSEL, 2, pp. 89f.).
[2] *Sermo* 194: *in Natali Domini*, 11, 1 (PL, 38, 1015 C).
[3] *Oratio* 39, 14 (PG, 36, 349 B).   [4] *Oratio* 38, 2 (PG, 36, 313 A).
[5] *Homilia in S. Philogonium* (PG, 48, 752 D).

in 431. No longer now does the cry: "The virgin has given birth, now the light begins to wax", go up in the Koreion, instead it is in the basilica, now radiant with light, that, speaking of a very different virgin, Paul of Emesa, the age-old city of the sun, breaks out into the cry, as he preaches his first Christmas sermon, "Oh the wonder of it! The Virgin has given birth—and remains a virgin!"[1]

Turn now to the Roman West where the feast of *Natalis Invicti* was a more homely and popular affair than the corresponding feast of the Greeks. While in Rome the competitors in the thirty races of the *Agon Solis* were tearing round the arena, while bonfires were being lit in honour of the sun's birthday by men who had reverently bowed their heads towards the sunrise, the Church was celebrating a true solar feast. While the pagans were giving noisy expression to this festive spirit before the church, Augustine was telling his flock of the mystery of the new-born sun which is Christ. "*Natalis dies quo natus est dies* – Christ is the true day of the sun."[2] "Let us rejoice, my brethren," he says, "however much the pagans may shout, for it is not the visible sun that makes this day holy, but its invisible maker."[3] "Yes, my brethren," he says on the Christmas following, "we will keep this day holy, but not like the unbelievers because of this sun, but because of him who is the sun's Creator."[4]

The extent to which this day of *Natalis* provided an opportunity for settling matters with the residual vestiges of the ancient sun-cults, which were apparent even among Christians, is evident from the words addressed at Christmas by Pope Leo to the faithful in the middle of the fifth century. There are those, he says, "who think that these solemnities of ours should be held in honour not so much because of the birth of Christ as because of the rising of the new sun".[5] Indeed he finds that he must reprove his Christians for bowing their heads towards the rising sun from the very

---

[1] *Christmas Homily*, 1 (PG, 77, 1436 A). Critical text in E. Schwartz, *Acta Conciliorum Oecumenicorum*, I, 1, 4, Berlin-Leipzig, 1928, p. 10, l. 4.

[2] *Sermo* 196, 1 (PL, 38, 1019 A). Cf. W. Roetzer, *Des hl. Augustinus Schriften als liturgiegeschichtliche Quelle* (The Writings of St Augustine as a Source for the History of the Liturgy), Munich, 1930, pp. 38–43.

[3] *Sermo* 186, 1 (PL, 38, 999 A).   [4] *Sermo* 190, 1 (PL, 38, 1007 C).

[5] *Sermo* 22: *in Nativitate Domini*, 2, 6 (PL, 54, 198).

steps of St Peter's Basilica. "For before they enter the basilica of the holy apostle Peter, they mount the steps, turn round, and with their heads bent down they bow in honour of the shining disc."[1] And he closes his Christmas homily with a hymn to the beauty of the heavenly bodies, pointing out that these are only a pale reflexion of the light of Christ: "Let the light of the heavenly bodies work upon thy fleshly sense, but embrace with all the glow of love which thy soul can bring forth the light that lighteth every man that cometh into the world."[2]

We have yet another and somewhat later witness, who, despite a rather naïve over-simplification of the issue, has grasped and preserved for us the real inwardness of the relationship between the sun-cult and the Church. A Syrian writer of glosses on Dionysius, Bar Salibi, tells us of the reason why the date of the Lord's birthday was set back to December 25 from January 6 and explains it thus:

"The reason why the Fathers changed this feast from January 6 to December 25 was, it is said, as follows: The heathen were accustomed on December 25 to celebrate the feast of the birthday of the sun and to light fires in honour of the day, and even Christians were invited to take part in these festivities. When the doctors of the Church observed that Christians were being induced to participate in these practices, they decided to celebrate this day as the true anniversary of Christ's birth and to keep January 6 for the celebration of the feast of Epiphany, and this custom they have continued to observe to the present day together with the practice of lighting fires."[3]

I should like to present to you one more piece of evidence. It provides us with yet another illustration of how in the West Christianity and Graeco-Roman ideas interacted with one another in regard to the institution of Christmas. It also shows us how from a certain point of time Christian thought and teaching got the upper hand, so that what had been happening before in

---

[1] Sermo 27: *in Nativitate Domini*, 7, 4 (PL, 54, 218 f.).
[2] Ibid., 7, 6 (PL, 54, 221 A).
[3] Text in J. S. Assemani, *Bibliotheca Orientalis*, II, Rome, 1721, p. 164.

the domain of the spirit began, so to speak, to happen in reverse. The "masses" are now Christian, and the few pagans that still live among them seem actually to be getting their ideas about the sun from Christianity. In the middle of the fifth century Bishop Maximus of Turin delivered a Christmas homily which opened with the following words:

"It is good that the people should call this birthday of our Lord the day of *Sol novus*, for they certainly do so and are so determined in the practice that even Jews and pagans use the same term. Let us by no means seek to change this, for with the resurrection of our Saviour there is a renewal not only of salvation for the whole human race, but of the brightness of the sun. If the sun grew dark at the passion of Christ, it must of necessity shine more brightly at his birth."[1]

This brings us to the threshold of the Middle Ages. And now the Church, having consecrated antiquity's love of the sun, passes it on in her Christmas liturgy to the peoples of the North. The *Missale Gothicum* from which in the seventh century the Franks learnt how to pray begins the Christmas midnight mass with these words: "Thou hast risen for us, O Jesus Christ, as the true Sun of Righteousness, thou hast descended from heaven as Saviour of the human race."[2] And even to this day the classic cadences of the Roman liturgy tell of this same mystery of the new sunlight that arose in Christ. It is the great gift from the treasury of antiquity, transfigured by the Christian faith. I will not impair by translation the loveliness of this Latin prayer, the prayer that goes up at midnight on Christmas:

Deus, qui hanc sacratissimam noctem veri luminis fecisti illustratione clarescere: da quaesumus; ut, cuius lucis mysteria in terra cognovimus, eius quoque gaudiis in caelo perfruamur.

Whenever we open the liturgical text for Christmas, we encounter the sparkle of this Christian mystery of the sun. "The

---

[1] *Christmas Homily*, 2 (PL, 57, 537). This contains at the end a hymn-like song of praise to Christ as *Sol novus* (539, BC).

[2] *Missale Gothicum*, "In Nativitate Domini" (PL, 72, 227 A).

Saviour of the world shall arise like the sun and descend into the Virgin's womb", says an antiphon of the vigil, while at vespers of the eve of this new "Sun" day there is sung, "When heaven's sun has arisen, ye shall see the King of Kings coming forth from his Father, as a bridegroom comes forth from his chamber."

What is here said concerning the mystery of the true sun, what is here cast in the noble speech of Rome for all the peoples of the future to read, was proclaimed in Greek by Chrysostom during his Christmas sermon at Antioch—with a vividness that is peculiarly his own. Let me close this section with these words of the Golden Mouth:

"Consider what it would mean to see the sun descend from the heavens and walk about the earth. If this could not happen, in the case of the shining body that we can see, without causing all who saw it to be amazed, then think what it means that the Sun of Righteousness should send forth its rays in our flesh and should shine into our souls."[1]

3 THE MYSTERY OF THE MOON

From the point of view of Christian dogma the content of the two ancient Christian feasts of Christmas and Easter can best be expressed in terms of those twin concepts so dear to ancient theology: *natus* and *renatus*, γέννησις and ἀναγέννησις. Christ was born as a man from the Virgin Mary for the unfolding of his life up to the point of his death, and Christ was reborn in the resurrection unto the everlasting transfiguration of his flesh. These two facts are the foundations which support the two pillars of the Christian life—two pillars, each of which corresponds exactly with the foundation on which it rests; for, to the birth of Jesus corresponds exactly the Christian's birth of the virgin mother which is the Church, the birth that takes place in the sacrament of baptism, while to the resurrection of our Lord corresponds the rebirth of all flesh at the end of days.

Born in baptism, reborn to life eternal—such is the Christian;

---

[1] *Christmas Homily* (PG, 49, 351 A). Cf. H. Usener, *Das Weihnachtsfest* (The Feast of Christmas), (2nd edition) Bonn, 1911, pp. 379–84.

or, to use the words of the lofty dialogue that is the beginning of the baptismal liturgy, *fides* and *vita aeterna*—eternal life, veiled in faith and revealed in eternity—such is the gift of Christ, born and reborn. Yet just as Christ's birth and the ultimate transfiguration of his human flesh could only become possible through the instrumentality of a mother whose task it was to bear him, so the granting of birth in baptism and ultimately of life eternal to the Christian is only possible through the womb of a mother, that mother being the Church. If, therefore, we are to try and see the Christian mystery as a whole, we must think of it as taking place at two levels. From above descends the gift "from the Father of lights" (James 1. 17) through Christ our Lord; below Mary and the Church await it in motherly readiness.

This piece of Christian teaching can be clothed in a wonderful symbolic dress. To the ancient theologians it was known as the *mysterium Lunae*,[1] and its symbolism is really complementary to that of the Christian mystery of the sun. The Christian of those days was still moved by the typically Hellenistic awe for the mystery and hidden meanings of the starry heavens. Not only did he see in Helios the shining image of the Sun of Righteousness, Selene too was a symbol, a symbol of that being which humbly receives and absorbs the light, the being that came alive in the person of Mary and the Church. The way in which inexorable cosmic forces acted on Luna and shaped her nocturnal appearances, the phases of her ever-repeated waxing and waning which ended in the darkness that preceded the coming of the new moon, the brightness of the night when the moon was full, the terrestrial germination and fertility which were governed by the rhythms of the mother-like Selene—this was for the Christian of that day, in Ambrose's words, a *"grande mysterium"*.[2] It is this same Bishop Ambrose who enjoins his flock to watch this star of the night, "not only with the fleshly eye, but with the living and penetrating power of the spirit—*noli ergo Lunam oculo tui corporis aestimare*

---

[1] This subject is treated in detail in my series of essays bearing the title "Mysterium Lunae", in *Zeitschrift für katholische Theologie*, 63 (1939), pp. 311–49, 428–42; 64 (1940), pp. 61–80, 121–31. All the source material both pagan and Christian is contained therein that applies to what is written here.

[2] *Exameron*, IV, 7, 29 (CSEL, 32, 1, p. 134, l. 26).

sed mentis vivacitate";[1] for the Creator has granted this bridal sister-star of Sol the power of showing forth the mystery of Christ.[2]

I want to speak of these things in more detail, for it is only after we have understood how the light of the sun Christ is passed on to the dark earth through the motherly mediation of Mary and the Church that we can truly grasp the Christian mystery.

In this matter of moon symbolism I have selected two very distinctive ideas from out the abounding wealth of ancient theological thought on the subject—ideas which grow out of, and complete, what I have tried to tell you about the Christmas and the Easter sun. The basic dogmatic conception from which both these systems of symbolism derive their form is as follows.

The redemption of man in Christ is something other than a creative fiat coming from above, and in this respect it differs from the act of creation itself. It is an act of God that includes within itself the co-operation of man, though that co-operation is itself a matter of grace and does not imply any impairment of God's sovereign power. Man was not to be merely the object of redemption but a partner therein. The descent of God was to be met by a receptive and answering "Thou", the unconstrained "Yea" of the creature: in a word, by love.

This divine activity takes place above all in the Incarnation, which is not some radiant epiphany in which a man appears in the full power of his manhood; it is a birth from the womb of a virgin, who, as the epitome and representative of an earth that was ready for redemption, receives into herself the coming of God: the sun of Christmas forms a union—for so I may now express the matter —with the Christmas moon and from this conjunction, both bridal and motherly, from this supernatural *synodos*, comes the procreation of all divine life for all the days to come; that union continues its effectiveness in the baptismal birth of those who in the Church form the mystical body of Christ on earth. Further, after Christ had completed the redemption of mankind through the sunset of the cross and the sunrise on Easter morning, he was free there and then to possess for himself the sunlight of his flesh

---

[1] *Exameron*, IV, 8, 32 (CSEL, 32, 1, p. 137, ll. 18 f.).
[2] *Ibid.*, IV, 8, 32 (CSEL, 32, 1, p. 137, ll. 27 f.).

glorified unto all eternity. The redemption of the human race, however, is a process that develops organically, a process in which the Church to the end of time must ever anew be giving birth and must ever be dying, for it will only be at the end of days that the whole Church will be truly flooded with the light of the Easter sun. Then the Easter sun will be united with the Easter moon in a perpetual spring. Meanwhile, with her eyes set upon the coming transfiguration of all things, the Church endures the changing phases of her fortune in the night of her earthly days, sends forth to all men the reflexion of the sunlight of Christ, and is the motherly queen of all that are born.

(i) The Christmas Moon

Let me deal first with the mystery of the Christmas moon. The world of moon symbolism, which was the world of the Christian of Graeco-Roman culture, was indeed a strange one. The Middle Ages could still understand it, but to make it come alive to people of our own time is difficult indeed. For are we not all of us nowadays to be numbered among those who, in Origen's words, see nothing in the stars above us but so many "fiery lumps"? At best they are for us merely the subject-matter of astronomical calculation. Heathen and Christian alike, the man of antiquity felt differently.

We encounter the basic pattern of this symbolism to which I refer in the apologist Theophilus of Antioch. "These lights," he says, "the sun and the moon, enact and show forth a great mystery. The sun is as an image of God, the moon of man."[1] At the time these words were written—and they were written by a Christian in the very earliest days of the Church—lunar symbolism among the Greeks had already undergone a long and abundant development and its last word was spoken by Plotinus not long after Theophilus had set those words down. In his theosophic system the unnameable God is pure original light which, indivisible and invisible, rests over all. By this original light the logos is illuminated and the logos is the sun. And again by this sun there is illuminated the innermost part of man's soul and this

---

[1] *Ad Autolycum*, II, 15 (*Corpus Apologetarum*, VIII, p. 100, ll. 14f.).

innermost "spirit" of man, by means of which he partakes of the divine, is therefore comparable to the moon.

In the fifth Ennead we find the matter put thus: "We see therefore that the One is comparable to the light, the second to the sun, and the third to the moon which receives its light from the sun; for the spirit is something superadded to the soul, and casts a glow over it if the soul itself be spiritual."[1] Thus when the Christian of that day sought to give expression to the kind of relationship which, his faith declared, subsisted between God and man, he was bold enough and free enough to avail himself of this Hellenistic astronomical symbolism and take from it whatever helped him—by way of image or comparison—to visualize the supernatural in some kind of symbolic form.

Here the ideas developed by Greek genius, in its penetrating nature mysticism, on the relation between Helios and Selene, were, he found, particularly suited to his purpose. This Greek genius and its heir, the astronomical mysticism of the Latins, conceived of Helios and Selene as bridal brother and sister carrying out an everlasting dance in the heavens. Selene is illuminated by the mighty masculine light of Helios and she it is who receives this light and passes it on to the other stars. Boethius in his *Consolations of Philosophy* can still sing:

> *Ut nunc pleno lucida cornu*
> *Totis Fratris obvia flammis*
> *Condat stellas Luna minores,*
> *Nunc obscuro pallida cornu*
> *Phoebo propior lumina perdat . . .*[2]

(That now, when she is full
    and encounters all her brother's rays
The moon may cause
    all lesser stars to disappear,
Then, when she is near to him
    and her face is dark, may lose her light . . .)

In these words Boethius gives expression to the dramatic element in this bridal relationship between Luna and Phoebus; that

---

[1] *Enneads*, V, 6, 4.
[2] *Philosophiae Consolatio*, I, Metrum 5, verses 5–9 (CSEL, 67, pp. 13 f.).

element consists in the recurrent changes of light and in a certain contradiction arising from the curious fact that Luna loses her light in just that moment when she is nearest the sun; her path around the sun really does resemble a kind of lovers' dance, as she withdraws from the light and then hurries back towards it. Parmenides had already expressed this in the happy phrase, "Ever looking out shyly toward the rays of Helios is Selene."[1] All antiquity, from Plutarch to Macrobius has something to tell about this lovers' play of the stars.

Nay more, in the loving union of the *synodos*, in the mysterious darkness that precedes the new moon, it is as though Selene became pregnant with the light of Helios, and having thus been made fruitful by the sun, she becomes the birth-giving mother of all living things. In the darkness before the new moon she holds discourse with her bridegroom, her mystical speech being that harmony of the spheres of which Pythagoras tells.[2] Selene becomes τοῦ βίου κυριωτάτη,[3] the mistress of all earthly life. "For Selene, in her love for him, circles continually around Helios," says Plutarch "and it is by the union with him that she receives the power to give birth."[4] And Firmicus Maternus, while still a heathen, prays thus to the nocturnal Luna:

"*Radios luminis sui quasi Solem venerata submittit, ut fraternis ignibus rursus ornata, . . . renata fulgidi splendoris ac renovata luminis ornamenta circumferat. . . . Tuque Luna, quae in postremis caeli regionibus collocata ad genitalium seminum perennitatem menstruis semper aucta luminibus Solis augusta radiatione fulgescis . . .*"[5]

(She dims the rays of her light as it were out of respect for Sol, in the hope that once again graced with her brother's fires, . . . reborn and renewed, she may go her way clad in radiant splendour and light. . . . O Luna, thou art set in the remotest region of heaven and art ever remade with thy monthly-waxing light to ensure the permanence of the seeds of life. Do thou then shine with the royal rays of Sol . . .)

[1] H. Diels, *Fragmente der Vorsokratiker* (4th edition, Berlin, 1922), 18 B, 15.
[2] Cicero, *De Natura Deorum*, III, 11, 27.
[3] Plutarch, *De Facie in Orbe Lunae*, 26 (Bernardakis, V, p. 463, ll. 13 f.).
[4] *Ibid.*, 30 (Bernardakis, V, p. 472, ll. 8 f.).
[5] *Mathesis*, I, 4, 9 (Kroll-Skutsch, I, p. 13, ll. 10ff.); I, 10, 4 (P. 38, ll. 10-13).

And so Selene becomes that heavenly star which hangs as an intermediary between the sublime light of Helios and the dark earth, the great mediator between the world of pure spirit of the fixed stars and the dark sensuality of the earthly elements, the μέσον of Pythagorean teaching. Her task is to mediate, to "harmonize",[1] to pass on the light she receives, but it is now a milder light, "ἱλάειρα – gentle and mild", Empedocles called it in the verse already quoted.[2]

What causes the sun's light to grow more mild is that Selene mingles the fire of Helios with the water of her own being, and I might well at this stage tell you more about the rioting fancies of Greek thought on the subject of "heavenly moonwater".[3] Poets and nature mystics produced an abundance of ideas about it, ideas which lingered on for a thousand years. In the *synodos* of the new moon Selene becomes a giver of water, dew is created which she causes to drip down; because of the mixture of the elements it is "warm and wet" and a begetter of life upon the earth; it brings about the growth of the grass and the growth of beasts and makes it possible for human mothers to bear their children. That is why her light is soft and, as it were, female. She is mistress over all the waters and the vital principle of all birth. John Lydos says the last word on this Greek symbolism that surrounds Selene when he declares: "Selene is the primal cause of all birth."[4]

In view of what has been said, it is not surprising that in seeking to give expression to his own beliefs the Christian should have made use of this lunar imagery with which the whole Hellenistic world was familiar. The relationship between God and man, which Theophilus had professed to see prefigured in the sun and moon, is now translated into Christian terms and serves to describe the relation between Christ and his Church, and the "great mystery" of Ephesians finds symbolic expression in the idea of a supernatural cosmos in which Christ is the sun and the Church is the moon.

And when at Christmas, Christ is born as the true *Sol novus*,

---

[1] Plutarch, *De Iside et Osiride*, 54 (Bernardakis, II, p. 528, ll. 8 f.).
[2] Cf. p. 90.
[3] In addition to the material in "Mysterium Lunae", see also H. Usener, *Kleine Schriften*, II, Leipzig, 1913, p. 252.   [4] *De Mensibus*, IV, 80 (Wünsch, p. 133, l. 8).

when in the dark of Easter Eve he arises as the true *Sol invictus*, there now stands beside him that exalted woman of whom it is written in the Apocalypse that she is clothed with the sun and has the moon at her feet. Mary has given birth to the sun and the Church shines with the light of Easter. It is then that the newly baptized step forth from the baptismal pool, the pool filled with fiery water, to await the *plenilunium* of the coming resurrection. Thus Mary is the spiritual Luna of this Christmas union between God and humanity and the Church is the true full moon of Easter, and in the Christian sense the "primal cause of all birth".

From this wonderful world of Christian symbolism let me first choose this idea of Mary as the Christmas moon, for the dogmatic content of the story of Christ's birth, the story that tells us how he was born of Mary in the night, is the ultimate origin of the rite of baptism in which the Christian is born.

In the *Symposium of the Ten Virgins* which was written by Methodius of Philippi at the end of the third century, we can find the first instance of an interpretation in terms of lunar symbolism, of the twelfth chapter of the Apocalypse, which speaks of the woman clothed with the sun. The tradition by which this passage was interpreted as referring to the Church's giving birth to the mystical Christ is of course much older than this. Already at the beginning of the third century the Roman Hippolytus was having this to say in reference to the aforesaid figure: "Never does the Church cease to give birth to the Logos from her heart . . . the male and perfect Christ, the child of God, God and man."[1]

Methodius, however, takes the matter further. The Church, like a true mother, receiving into herself the rays of the Christmas sun, and being in this respect an imitator of the Blessed Virgin, gives birth to Christ, for in baptism she gives life to the faithful. In doing so she transforms mere earthly "psychics" into the race of "pneumatics", into a people filled with the spirit. By this action the Church becomes comparable to Selene who receives the light of the sun, transforms it after the manner of a mother and so, as mistress of all waters upon the earth, brings new life into the world.

[1] *De Antichristo*, 61 (GCS, I, 2, p. 41). Described in detail in H. Rahner, "Die Gottesgeburt", in *Zeitschrift für katholische Theologie*, 59 (1935), pp. 349 ff.

It should now be possible to understand a passage in Methodius, which is certainly obscure:

"The Church stands upon the moon. By Selene, in my view, the Scripture seeks to indicate, by means of an image, the faith of those who have been cleansed by the power of baptism. For the light of Selene has a kind of relationship to luke-warm water, and all things that are of moist substance are dependent on Selene. Thus the Church—of which Selene is the symbol and prefiguration—stands upon our faith and our [divine] childhood, and until such time as all the nations have returned to their home, she suffers the pangs of child-birth, and, like a mother bearing her child, turns psychics into pneumatics. This makes of her a true mother."[1]

The woman on the moon is Mother Church. Methodius was, however, also acquainted with an interpretation, which was already current in his day, according to which the apocalyptic vision referred to the Virgin Mary, though he himself rejected this view.[2] Actually these two forms of interpretation are closely connected with one another. The reason why the Church can claim to be the virgin mother of the mystical Christ is that once on the night of Christmas a virgin mother gave birth to the Lord. Baptism and the birth of Christ are in the last resort a single mystery. The sun Christ descended into the night of his mother's womb so that Christians might be born from the womb of the baptismal water which had been made fruitful by him who became the Easter sun. That is the sense of the exegesis of Anastasius Sinaita who wrote in the seventh century and in whose writings all the beauty of the Graeco-Christian mind seems suddenly to come alive again. Christ the sun descended into the night of life on earth so that he might give his light to the moon which is the mistress of all birth:

"In the heavens Helios has the first place and leads the dance. Similarly Christ, who is the spiritual sun, is in heaven placed

---

[1] *Symposium*, VIII, 6 (GCS, p. 88, ll. 5-11).
[2] *Ibid.*, VIII, 7 (GCS, pp. 89f.).

over all dominions and powers, for he is the door and the chorus-leader to the Father. On earth, however, whither he descended in humility, taking upon himself the form of a servant, he freely handed over his primacy of place to his body, which is the Church, and he did this in the mystery of baptism. Now, Selene gives men light upon earth, by which I mean the Church, for Selene has power over all water, and the Church has power over the Holy Ghost whom Christ entrusted and gave to the Church, so that she might bear us in our rebirth."[1]

Here the relationship between Mary and the Church is even clearer, and from now on it becomes increasingly the practice to interpret the apocalyptic vision as a reference to Mary, though the conception of a child-bearing Church is never lost from view and the two things really form parts of a single whole. Augustine's theology is particularly important in this connexion. Mary the virgin mother is for him always the prefigurement of the child-bearing Church. Both are "the woman that is clothed with the sun, with Christ, the Sun of Righteousness".[2] The degree to which, in the mystery of the sunlight that was born of the virgin, Mary and the Church—and by the same token Christmas and the night of baptism—were treated as equivalents, as being fundamentally the same, is shown in a Christmas sermon that has been left us by an anonymous pupil of Augustine:

"Let us therefore rejoice, dear brethren. From today the light of the sun begins to wax. Believe on Christ and then the light of day will also wax within thyself. Doest thou believe? See, the day hath begun! Art thou baptized? Lo, Christ hath been born in thy heart! God's word hath been made flesh and dwelleth within us. For our sakes was he born, but we must be born again in him."[3]

Caesarius of Arles puts all this very clearly. "Let the Church of Christ rejoice," he says, "for, imitating blessed Mary, she has

---

[1] *Hexaemeron*, 5 (PG, 89, 913 CD).
[2] *Enarrationes in Psalmos*, 142, 3 (PL, 37, 1846).
[3] Pseudo-Augustinus, *Sermo* 370, 4 (PL, 39, 1659). On Augustine's doctrine cf. H. Rahner, "Die Gottesgeburt", *loc. cit.*, pp. 387-91.

become the mother of a divine child."[1] In Carolingian theology the idea lives on. In the words of Berengaud of Trier, "The Church gives birth daily to the limbs of that body which was once born of the Virgin Mary; for is not Christ ever one and the same?"[2] Here we are still in the midst of that world of symbols by drawing on which Carolingian art and the art of the early Middle Ages, still enlivened as they were by the spirit of antiquity, created those pictures of the virgin standing upon the moon—ever the Virgin Mary and the Virgin Church clothed in Christ's sunlight and giving birth through his power. Typical examples are the miniatures of the Beatus Apocalypses[3] and the exquisite Herrad of Landsberg paintings.[4]

This stream of ideas is joined by another, deriving directly from the mystery of the Christmas sun. If the nocturnal birth of Jesus on the darkest day of the solar year is a symbol of his infinite humiliation, as Augustine maintains in one of his Christmas sermons,[5] then his departure from the heights of his Father, his stepping forth out of the simple primal light of his divine existence, constitutes the true *Sol novus*. His birth from the womb of the Virgin is therefore a coming forth of the sun out of Mary. When the Christian of antiquity read Psalm 19 (18). 6 and saw the words: "He hath set his tabernacle in the sun: and he as a bridegroom coming out of his bridechamber, hath rejoiced as a giant to run the way", then since the very beginnings[6] of Christianity he had thought of the carnal birth of our Lord. Indeed once the Christian feast of *Natalis Invicti* had been established this passage became the key text for Jesus' birth from Mary. Indeed Ambrose incorporates it almost verbatim in his Christmas hymn in which he

---

[1] *Easter Homily*, 3 (PL, 67, 1048).

[2] Berengaud of Trier, *Commentary on the Apocalypse*, Visio 4, 6 (PL, 17, 877 A). For other sources see Rahner, "Die Gottesgeburt", pp. 398 f.

[3] Thus for instance in a representation of the woman of the Apocalypse in a Beatus MS. in the Bibliothèque Nationale (Eranos Archives); cf. W. Neuss, *Die Apokalypse in der altspanischen und altchristlichen Bibelillustration* (The Apocalypse in Ancient Spanish and Ancient Christian Bible Illustration), 2 vols., Münster, 1931; H. Wölfflin, *Die Bamberger Apokalypse*, Munich, 1918, plate 29.

[4] *Hortus Deliciarum*, edited by A. Straub and G. Keller, Strasbourg, 1879–99, plate LXXVI.   [5] *Sermo* 192, 3 (PL, 38, 1013 C).

[6] Sources in F. J. Dölger, *Die Sonne der Gerechtigkeit*, pp. 102–4; others in B. Botte, *op. cit.*, p. 37.

speaks of the "giant" as being "of two substances"—human and divine:

> Procedat e thalamo suo
> Pudoris aula regia,
> Geminae gigas substantiae
> Alacris ut currat viam.[1]

Mary then is bride and mother, and as the words, "*Pudoris aula regia*" show, her womb is "the royal court of modesty", her giving birth being the sunrise of Christmas. There is an echo too of the old classical way of speaking about flaming Sol when a man like Peter Chrysologus, writing in the fifth century, describes the birth of the sun in such fashion as this:

"*Transcursis anni metis dies dominicae nativitatis adventat et virginei partus fulgor toto orbe diffunditur flammeo corusco* – Having passed through its appointed annual course the day of the Lord's nativity arrives and the splendour of the virgin birth is spread in fiery brilliance over the whole earth."[2]

That Jesus at his birth did no injury to the virginal portals of his mother's womb was symbolized in the flooding sunlight, pure in itself and cleansing all it touched. Chrysostom too, in the Christmas homily to which I have already referred,[3] introduces this same metaphor of the sunlight streaming forth in reference to the virgin birth and the sun. Yet perhaps the loveliest expression of reverence for the sunlight that arises from out of Mary, comes from Prudentius. Surely it is one of the most charming conceits of Latin lyric poetry when he bids the "sweet infant boy" to awake, for this being the winter solstice, the sun now leaves his narrow circle. Surely it is Christ himself who lengthens his path in the sky:

---

[1] Christmas hymn, "Intende qui regis Israel", Strophe 5. Text in *Analecta Hymnica*, 50 (Leipzig, 1907), p. 14. Also in H. Lietzmann, *Lateinische altkirchliche Poesie* (Kleine Texte, 47–9), p. 10.

[2] *Sermo* 146 (PL, 52, 591 C).

[3] *Christmas Homily* (PG, 49, 359 BC). Augustine speaks in a similar vein, *Sermo* 186, 1: *in Nativitate Domini*, 3 (PL, 38, 999 A): "*Istum diem nobis non Sol iste visibilis, sed . . . visceribus fecundis Virgo Mater nobis effudit.*" This idiom of the "flowing light" is still used by the Roman liturgy today in the Preface of the Blessed Virgin: "*lumen aeternum mundo effudit Iesum Christum Dominum nostrum*".

Quid est quod artum circulum
Sol iam recurrens deserit?
Christusne terris nascitur
Qui lucis auget tramitem?
Scandit gradatim denuo
Iubar priores lineas.
Emerge, dulcis pusio,
Quem mater edit castitas,
Parens et expers coniugis
Mediator et duplex genus.[1]

The existence of this complex of ideas, which visualizes the sun-light streaming forth from the womb of Mary, is attested by a mass of evidence coming both from antiquity and the Middle Ages, and it connects with something else. It connects with what is in effect the last part of the mystery of the Christmas moon, and here we can see how the image of the Virgin on the moon has influenced and developed in people's minds.

In giving birth to our Lord, Mary gave birth to the Sun of Righteousness. In a certain sense this makes her something like the nocturnal chorus-leader of the morning sun. She becomes Luna who has been united to the sun, a union as the result of which the sun undergoes the nocturnal annihilation of becoming man. She thus becomes the mother of all living things. If Luna is called *humorum mater*—the mother of humidity—which means that she is the maternal principle of all life that comes from water, then, according to the *Clavis Melitonis*, a very important work for symbolical theology, this is a reference to Mary, for Mary is *Mater gratiarum*;[2] and in the earlier miniatures we can see written over the picture of the Virgin Mother words which only become intelligible in the context I have just indicated:

---

[1] *Cathemerinon*, XI, verses 1-4, 11-16 (CSEL, 61, pp. 63 f.).

[2] *Clavis Melitonis*, III, 6 (edited by J. B. Pitra, *Spicilegium Solesmense*, II, p. 65). For other sources for Mary as the moon, see F. X. Kraus, *Realenzyklopädie der christlichen Altertümer*, II, Freiburg, 1886, p. 766, where there is particular mention of Conrad von Megenberg's *Buch der Natur* which is so important for medieval symbolism. Certain material not mentioned by Kraus is to be found in H. Rahner's "Mysterium Lunae", in *Zeitschrift für katholische Theologie*, 64 (1940), p. 80. See also J. Kreuser, *Christliche Symbolik*, Brixen, 1868, pp. 186 and 207 f. This work has been long forgotten, though there is much novel material in it. (The author draws attention to two Gothic "Moon-Mary's" in Ulm and Straubing.)

In gremio Matris residet Sapientia Patris
Luna fovet Solem cui Sol dedit ipse nitorem.[1]
(In the lap of the Mother dwells the Wisdom
   of the Father.
The moon fosters the Sun, from whom she
   herself derived her light.)

As late as the fourteenth century a hymn to Mary sung by the
French flagellants speaks of the supernatural conjunction of Christ
the sun and Mary the moon:

> *Ave Regina pure et gente*
> *Très haulte, Ave maris stella,*
> *Ave, précieuse Jovante,*
> *Lune, ou Dieu s'esconsa.*
> *Se ne fust la Vierge Marie*
> *Le siècle fust pieça perdu.*[2]
> (*Ave Regina*, pure and loving
> Most noble; *Ave maris stella*,
> *Ave*, dear Maid,
> Moon where God took hiding.
> But for the Virgin Mary
> The world had been lost.)

And so to end this section I go to the thirteenth century and
take a poem from a forgotten Latin manuscript. I quote one verse
of which the following is a rough translation:

> From Luna shines the glow
>   Of the sun God's ray
> Her steadfast motions show
>   To men his way.
>   When sun and moon unite
> Darkness doth fly away
> And all things grow more bright.[3]

---

[1] Cf. H. Schwarzenski, *Vorgotische Miniaturen der ersten Jahrhunderte deutscher Malerei*
(Pre-Gothic Miniatures of the First Centuries of German Painting), Leipzig, 1927, p. 43.
[2] M. Vloberg, *La Vierge et l'enfant dans l'art français*, II, Grenoble, 1934, pp. 110f.
[3] Hymn "In rosa vernat lilium", Strophe 2. Text in *Analecta Hymnica*, 20, p. 69.

(ii) The Easter Moon

The last words of the Christian Creed are *et vitam aeternam*. At Christmas Christ was born and the flesh which he had put on was glorified at Easter. Similarly the purpose of the Christian's birth in baptism is the glorification of his flesh in the sunrise of eternity: *lux perpetua luceat eis*. That is why in prayer the ancient Church turned towards the East, for it was from the East that she was expecting the dawning of the φῶς ἀνέσπερον – the light without evening.[1] While, however, we are still on our earthly pilgrimage, it is night and we only see the sunlight of our distant Lord in so far as it is reflected by Selene who has been set up over the darkness, Selene being, of course, the Church.

The Church's fortunes in actual history are, as I have pointed out, comparable to the moon's varying phases. The moon wanes, it disappears, it grows red, as with the bloodshed of persecution. Yet, like the moon, the Church ever renews herself as she circles around the sun which is Christ, and when at every Easter she sees the brightness of the moon when it is full, she knows that she too moves towards a brightness of which there will be no end.

Such is the dogmatic foundation on which is built up the remaining imagery of the Christian moon mystery. The passing away of the light which took place when Christ suffered upon the cross repeats itself in the fate of the Church, and the renewal of the light in the full moon at Easter shows forth the light that, in the end, will be shed most gloriously upon herself. There thus once more passes before our eyes the divine drama of the dying and rising Christ, but now we see it in the mirror of Selene, the Church. Luna suffering and Luna radiant—that was how the Christians of that day loved to picture their virgin Church. That was the majestic figure that could satisfy their longing for immortality in so different a fashion from that of the lunar mother-goddesses, though the cult of the latter had spread over the whole late Graeco-Roman world and was moving enough on the purely human plane.

[1] Cf. F. J. Dölger, *Sol Salutis* (2nd edition), pp. 220–42. The description of Christ as "Sunlight without evening" comes from the hymn at the end of the *Symposium* of Methodius of Philippi (GCS, p. 133, l. 5). Cf. also F. J. Dölger, "Lumen Christi", in *Antike und Christentum*, 5 (1936), pp. 10f.

There is a letter of Ambrose's—written for the benefit of those who still clung to a dying paganism—which seeks to expose the true nature of these motherly goddesses, Cybele, Venus and the Heavenly One of Carthage. In that same letter he also speaks of the Church. The cults of the divinities to whom I have just referred were all very much concerned with devotion to the moon, a devotion which was a clear corollary to the then fashionable transcendent heliotary, and Ambrose takes this occasion to exalt the Church as the true Luna:

"When Luna, in whom, relying on words of the Prophets, we see the image of the Church—when this same Luna is reborn to run her monthly course, she is at first hidden by dark shadows. Slowly, however, her horns are filled with light, and then when she stands opposite Sol, she shines again with the brightness of his beams."[1]

Before all else, therefore, the Church on earth is *Luna patiens*. For the people of antiquity, Christian and pagan alike, it was a hallowed thing to suffer in sympathy with this star of the night. The waning of the moon, or its darkening in an eclipse, made them sad, and in all this there was for the Christian a profound symbolism. When Luna is hidden by darkness, he feels she is "as a sorrowing widow". When periodically she wanes she "lies in pangs because of the change".

Ambrose turns these feelings to good account. "It is for thee", he says, "that Luna suffers, and she waits with ever-growing longing for thy redemption, so as to be free at last from the enslavement that weighs down all creation."[2] Behind these words, of course, lies a deeper meaning. The moon has become the image of the suffering Church which must go down into the dark together with the sun of Christ. It is one of the oldest features of

[1] *Epistola* 18, 24 (PL, 16, 979 B). This letter contains, 18, 30 (980 B) the well-known passage in which Ambrose includes "the Mithra" of the Persians among the lunar mother-goddesses. As Dölger has pointed out, Ambrose probably had Herodotus in front of him, for the latter says (I, 132) that the Persians reverence "Mitra as Aphrodite"; cf. the article "Die Himmelskönigin von Karthago" (The Heavenly Queen of Carthage), in *Antike und Christentum*, 1 (1929), pp. 93 f.

[2] *Exameron*, IV, 8, 31 (CSEL, 32, 1, p. 137, ll. 7-14).

Christian exegesis that mention is made in comments on the crucifixion not only of the darkened sun referred to in Luke 23. 45 but also of the moon sorrowfully hiding its face,[1] an inference made from Isaiah 24. 23, the words, "And the moon shall be confounded and the sun ashamed", being taken as a prophecy relating to Christ's death; and surely the words put into the mouth of Mary by Andrew of Crete in the Greek liturgy for Good Friday might well be the lament of Luna obscured by the dark: "Alas, my child, thou unsetting brightness! Make thy light shine on all, thou sun of glory!"[2] Even in the early Middle Ages the miniatures of the crucifixion preserve this echo of antiquity in the lamenting moon, for the moon appears above the cross "like a sorrowing virgin, veiling the shining horns of her light"[3] and that is why this scene so often bears the superscription—as on the ivory cover of a Munich manuscript:

> *Eclipsim patitur Luna*
> *quia de morte Christi dolet Ecclesia.*[4]

(The moon suffers eclipse
Because the Church mourns for the death of Christ.)

We can, however, find even deeper things in this mystery of sorrowing Luna. Once Origen had formulated the theological concept of the Church which here on earth is continually dying, and had used in this connexion the image of the Church's disappearing in the dark before the new moon, this meaningful metaphor was never wholly lost to Christian memory. The Church's earthly journey is as "the new moon that everlastingly returns". "We call Selene new when she is quite close to the sun, and is so closely united to him that it is as though she disappeared in his brightness. But the Sun of Righteousness is Christ, and when the true Selene, which is the Church, is so intimately united with him that she can say, 'I live, now not I; but Christ liveth in me', then it is

---

[1] This idea is found in so early a writer as Alexander of Alexandria who was certainly drawing on Melito of Sardis, so that mention of the moon sorrowing at the cross goes back as far as the second century: *De Anima et Corpore* (PG, 18, 600 C).

[2] PG, 97, 1409 A.

[3] Gislebert of Westminster, *Disputatio Iudaei cum Christiano* (PL, 159, 1034 B).

[4] H. Detzel, *Christliche Ikonographie*, I, Freiburg, 1894, p. 418.

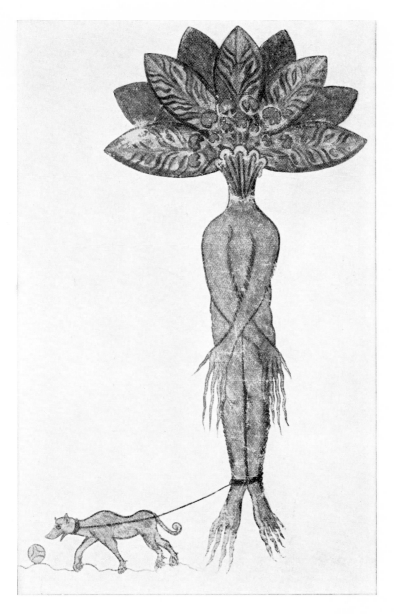

5. Mandrake Root with Dog
From the *Herbal* of pseudo-Apuleius (printed in *Corpus Medicorum Latinorum*,
IV, Leipzig-Berlin, 1927, ed. E. Howald and H. Sigerist, p. 223)

6. Mandrake Root with Dog and Root-gatherer

From a fifteenth-century Italian *Herbal* (pen-and-ink sketch in a private collection, reproduced in *Philobiblion, Zeitschrift für Bücherliebhaber,* 5, 1932, p. 149)

her new moon."[1] Now, this is only so when she is united with him upon the cross and loses her light there, in the setting sun; yet it is only through such a union as this that she becomes fruitful and can bring forth new life.

Methodius of Philippi carries Origen's thought a stage further. In the ecstasy of the anguish of union with the Crucified, Selene becomes the mother of the living who are born in the sacrament of baptism. "The Church lets her spiritual moonlight shine upon the baptized when she recalls his sufferings anew as the season thereof returns, and will continue to do so up to that great day when the sun will rise in his glory and there will be perfect light."[2]

The Church's mystery of the moon thus consists of a lofty dialectic, in that in dying she becomes capable of giving birth. Ambrose has expressed this in classical measures:

> *Minuitur Luna ut elementa repleat,*
> *Hoc est ergo grande mysterium.*
> *Donavit hoc ei qui omnibus donavit gratiam.*
> *Exinanivit eam ut repleat,*
> *Qui etiam se exinanivit ut omnia repleat.*
> *Ergo annuntiavit Luna mysterium Christi.*[3]

(The moon is diminished so that she may replenish
  the elements
This is a great mystery.
He who gave grace to all gave this to her.
He emptied her that he might fill her
Who emptied himself that he might fill all things.
Thus Luna has shown forth the mystery of Christ.)

It is Augustine who finally perfects these thoughts. The Church is the true Luna since she takes part in the sunset of the Crucified and vanishes into it. She is dark with the sinfulness of her members, and blood-red with her martyrs' afflictions.[4] All this, however, is of little account—so runs his threnody to the dying moon —for Luna moves in never-ending circles towards the Easter full

---

[1] *Homily on Numbers*, 23, 5 (GCS, VII, pp. 217f.).
[2] *Symposium*, VIII, 6 (GCS, p. 88).
[3] *Exameron*, IV, 8, 32 (CSEL, 32, 1, p. 137, ll. 19–27).
[4] *Enarrationes in Psalmos*, 10, 4 (PL, 36, 133).

moon of the resurrection. "We know that the Church is growing, however much she may age through the mortality of this life, for, despite it, she still draws nearer the sun."[1]

All dying with the crucified sun—to use another bold expression of Augustine's[2]—is for the Church only a growing towards the resurrection. Therefore Luna is at all times, and even now, secretly *Luna splendens*. In the cosmic fortunes of the visible Selene Christians see, as though in a picture placed before them by God, what their faith may hope for from the Church—resurrection to life eternal.

Antiquity had already had an intimation of these things, and the longings that it experienced lived on in the heart of the Christian, but they lived on transfigured by the firm faith in the promises of Scripture. Above the moon, which hangs as a mediatory being between sublunar darkness and the blessed changeless light of the ether, there is—so many pagans believed—the region of the spirits to which the human soul longs to return. Below the region of Selene all is dark, corruptible and subject to the blind fate of the stars, nor does the providence of the gods reach down into this demonic realm of night. Beyond the moon, however, all is light and freedom: there, says Macrobius, *"omnia sacra, incorrupta, divina sunt*—all things are sacred, incorruptible and divine".[3] But if any man's soul on its journey heavenward towards the divine light reaches the country of Selene, that man is saved, for he there puts off whatever still hampers him in his ascent. And the mystery cults promised their initiates that even here and now they could enjoy this heavenly freedom from the compulsion of the stars and that even here and now they could receive the light from the distant heights of Helios.

The Church consecrated these longings and transformed them. In the mystery of baptism mortal men are born anew and immediately the coming resurrection begins to be effective in them; for the Christian is born out of the "fiery water"[4] which has been

---

[1] *Enarrationes in Psalmos*, 103, Sermo 3, 19 (PL, 37, 1373).

[2] *Sermo* 136 (PL, 38, 753).

[3] *In Somnium Scipionis*, I, 21, 33 (Eyssenhardt, p. 566, ll. 15–21).

[4] This is what Firmicus Maternus calls baptismal water: *De Errore Profanarum Religionum* 2 (CSEL, 2, p. 77, l. 13).

made fruitful by Sol and bestowed by Selene, the Church. This close association of Selene with the new birth in baptism led Anastasius of Sinai to give a Christian twist to an old play on words by Plato which derived "Selene" from σέλας νηπίων, i.e. the light of infants, for all who come out of the baptismal pool are as infants coming from their mother's womb. Indeed the thought of Selene never ceased to be linked with this giving of spiritual birth. It was because Selene was always giving birth to children that her face everlastingly retained the brightness of youth.[1]

In this sense then the Christian too has entered the realm of Selene. In baptism he has already been raised from the dead and become a man freed from all corruption and from the dark compulsions that prevail in the regions that are below the moon, and all through the Christian literature of antiquity one can hear the echoes of the cry of joy: "No longer are we children under compulsion from the stars",[2] or, "Now there are no more horoscopes and there is no longer such a thing as fate."[3] Of course men's minds could not wholly cease at short notice from working in the old ways, and on one occasion Bishop Zeno had to make allowances for certain newly baptized Christians who rather childishly asked him under what horoscope their recent new birth out of Mother Church had taken place. He replied: "I will fall in with your wishes and answer you as I would answer children; I will explain to you the mysteries of this holy horoscope."[4] He then launched out into an edifying exposition in which the signs of the zodiac were reinterpreted in a Christian sense.

Christ the sun thus sheds the simple primal light of his Father upon the Church which is his moon, and the Church in her turn sheds it upon her new-born babes, so that they may be "as lights in the world";[5] but here below that light is not visible, for despite the new birth in baptism, all things in this life are still shrouded by the night of this world. Yet the Christian knows by faith that the resurrection of his body is as certain as that of Christ, his Lord,

---

[1] *Hexaemeron*, 4 (PG, 89, 900 BC).

[2] Justin, *Apologia*, I, 61 (*Corpus Apologetarum*, I, p. 166).

[3] Methodius, *Symposium*, VIII, 15, 16 (GCS, p. 103, ll. 11 f. and in a number of other places in this context).

[4] *Tractatus*, II, 43, 1 (PL, 11, 494 A).   [5] Phil. 2. 15.

which has already taken place. Because he has this faith, he sees his resurrection prefigured in the phases of the moon, and this again is a thought that is part of the substance of the very earliest Christian theology. "Selene", it was said, "is the surety of our resurrection."[1]

There is a treatise on the resurrection by Zeno of Verona in which we can discern all the charm of antiquity's love for Sol and Luna. In it Zeno adduces once more the age-old argument from Luna's ever repeated rebirth in the nocturnal sky:

"Even Luna [he says] shows in herself all the characteristics of humanity. She first appears as a scarcely visible crescent. It is as if she were a child of tender years, just come from the cradle. Then she grows slowly into a girl and then into a damsel, and as she follows her wide course and fulfils her task in the world, so she grows daily older. When she is fully grown and the golden fire of the flaming, light-giving charioteer has caused the small circle of her silver disc to become fully rounded—her own travail having been not less than that of her brother—then she inclines slowly toward old age, until, having been wholly consumed by death, she starts her life afresh. And so, as the fiery seed of her life breaks again and again into flame, she unites the end of that life with the beginning."[2]

So will it be at the end of days, when all will be a beginning and all will be as the full moon of Easter. "And Luna, the Church," says Anastasius, "which once, as teacher, and proclaimer of the truth, cast her nocturnal beam upon the earth—Luna will never again grow old".[3] The day will come when Christ, the eternal sun, and the eternal moon, which is the Church, will give light to the innumerable host of the stars. This is the day longed for by the Christian as he still wanders in the dark, and lovely indeed are the words of Anastasius in which he gives expression to this pagan longing, this longing that has been transfigured by the Church:

[1] Severianus of Gabala, *De Mundi Creatione Oratio* 3, 5 (PG, 56, 453 C).
[2] *Tractatus*, I, 16, 8 (PL, 11, 380f.).
[3] *Hexaemeron*, 4 (PG, 89, 911 D).

Oh, never again vanish into the darkness of the renewing
   moon,
Ever-shining Selene.
Lighten our way through the divinely hidden meaning
Of the Scriptures.
Oh, cease not,
Thou consort and fellow-traveller of Christ the Sun
Who, as thy bridegroom, clothes thee with light,
Oh, cease not
To send forth thy rays which from him have taken
   their brightness,
So that out of himself but through thee
He may give light to the stars
And set them on fire,
Through thee for thyself.[1]

Here is the Christian sanctification of that love for the world of
heavenly bodies which is so typically Greek, and here in that sanctification is the very essence of the Church's mystery of the sun
and moon. With this the drama of redemption returns to its point
of origin—to the everlasting Father, to the source of that primal
light which through Christ the sun shone upon his moon the
Church and through that moon upon the human stars. The author
of the *Divina Commedia* tells us in his *Paradiso* how his gaze
travelled upward to the immortal sun Christ who gives light to
all spiritual stars, even as, in our earthly night, Luna brings brightness to the countless army of stars perceived by the eye:

> *Quale nei plenilunii sereni,*
> *Trivia ride tra le ninfe eterne,*
> *Che dipingono il ciel per tutti i seni,*
> *Vid'io sovra migliaia di lucerne,*
> *Un Sol che tutte quante l'accendea,*
> *Come fa il nostro le viste superne.*[2]

[1] In the hymn of praise to the Church at the end of the work on the *Hexaemeron* in
which Anastasius applies to the Church the *Ave Maria*, the visions of the Protoevangelium
and of the woman clothed with the sun in the Apocalypse (PG, 89, 1076 CD).
[2] *Paradiso*, XXIII, 25-30.

(As, in the still light of the full moon,
Trivia [=Diana=the moon] smiles amid
    the eternal nymphs,
Who paint the heaven in all its parts,
I saw, [bright] above myriads of lamps,
A Sun that enkindled them all
As ours does the upper air.)

In the foregoing pages I think I have shown once again how ancient Christian worship, secure in the knowledge it derived from divine revelation and apostolic tradition, made use of whatever served its purpose in pagan thought, how it did so quite boldly and with a truly Greek largeness of mind, and how it thus fashioned a garment for the mysteries of Christ. Such was the attitude of the great Origen, and it is with a quotation from Origen that I should like to close these lectures:

"For my part, I am firmly assured that God guards, as in a treasury, things far more glorious than any yet seen by sun, moon or angels, and that he will bring these things to light when all creation has been freed from bondage to the enemy, and brought into the liberty of the brightness of the children of God."[1]

[1] *Exhortatio Martyrii*, 13 (GCS, I, pp. 13 f.).

Part Two

THE HEALING OF THE SOUL

V

MOLY AND MANDRAGORA IN PAGAN
AND CHRISTIAN SYMBOLISM

INTRODUCTION

THE Greek frequenter of the mystery cults was driven by a longing to rise from out of the darkness into the light. The Christian found this longing assuaged in "the brightness of the children of God". But this ascent is a weary one, for in it we are transformed. In the course of it there takes place a purifying process which I will deal with under the name, "The healing of the soul", and the symbols which cryptically designate this process are the "soul-healing" flowers moly and mandragora. Antiquity lisped of these flowers in its myths and the Christian saw in them an intimation of Christian truth. For in the contrast between the blackness of the root of these plants and the brightness of their blossoms, the ancients saw a symbol of the spiritual division in man—and it is a division that must needs be healed.

Man is the strangest of all the products of earth, for a great part of his being roots in chthonic darkness and it is only by means of the powers of this black root, as they pass through him, that he can spread before heaven the white flower that is the light of his conscious mind. For this reason there are rhizotomists, root-gatherers or herbalists of the spiritual life who show us how to change ourselves from a black root into a white blossom, but who warn us that even in the flower which Helios has kissed awake that primal power still has dominion, which, in accordance with the mysterious law of the spirit, has ascended out of the root. Man is two things at once: he is both root and flower. He stands ever-lastingly between Uranos and Gaia, between Helios and Chthon, between Hermes and Circe. He is something of everything. That which is of the light in him is never without the sap that comes out of the dark. Yet to man alone is it given to make bright the darkness of his earthly roots with the light that is gathered from the sun. Man is born to be the rhizotomist of the soul, a potential illuminate for whom the true light is always waiting. He must forever be tearing his own roots out of the dark and lifting them up to the light, for only thus do the roots become capable of making him whole.

I shall speak first of the herb which the gods called moly. Hermes himself gave this to Odysseus to protect him from all the deceits of Circe. "Black are its roots and milk-white its flower", and because of this, it has become a symbol of certain deep problems concerned with the spiritual healing of man.

After that I shall speak of the famous magic herb of antiquity mandragora. Mandragora's root is also black, and the men of antiquity called it "man-like", because its curious shape seems to be a clumsy imitation of a human body, but this body is without a head, lacks its flower, and it is this feature which gave rise to the symbolism, now long forgotten, of Christian spiritual pathology, whose final solution for all the problems of the human soul was that, though it might root in the dark earth, the headless mandragora of humanity must be completed and perfected in Christ who is the head of all.

It is a vanished and well-nigh occult world of spiritual symbolism that we enter. Only that small handful of men who today still —or perhaps I had better say "who today once more"—can find their way about in the enchanted territory of the alchemist and its spiritual substrata will, like loving botanists, recognize old acquaintances in the names moly and mandragora. Goethe might well have taken pleasure in this little nosegay that I am putting together here, after long nights of root hunting, but for modern man nature has lost her magic; he has no reverence for the *potentes herbae* to which the ancients prayed, and because this is so, he no longer knows anything of that spiritual symbolism, which could see in nature a "showing forth" of the things that happen in the human soul.

The Fathers of the Church still thought in terms of this unity of body and soul, and when they spoke of roots and flowers, could imply things to which our ears are no longer attuned. "*In occulto est radix*", says Augustine: "*fructus videri possunt, radix videri non potest*–the root is hidden in the ground; its fruits are visible; the root itself is invisible".[1] For Augustine there is something mysterious, one might almost say occult, in the very word "root". It is the most telling symbol which nature in her silent, unchanging majesty provides of what takes place within the soul. Indeed certain words of Gregory the Great seem to formulate a principle which sounds like the very thing towards which depth psychology is feeling its way: "*Quid enim radicum nomine nisi latentes cogitationes accipimus, quae in occulto prodeunt, sed in ostensione operum per apertum surgunt?*–What could we better understand under the name 'root' than those secret thoughts which rise up from the hidden part of us but only show themselves openly in our actions?"[2]

Let me therefore say something of these roots and of the soul-healing flowers that spring from them. We should set out upon this nocturnal expedition of spiritual root-digging with a distinct feeling that we are on the track of very ancient truths, and since only the reverent can make new discoveries, it would be well to start our search with a prayer with which the old root-gatherers were wont to start their work:

"*Nunc vos potentes omnes herbas deprecor, exoro vos maiestatemque vestram, quas parens tellus generavit et cunctis gentibus dono dedit medicinam sanitatis*–Now I call upon you, ye mighty herbs, and I send forth my supplication to your majesty, for your parent the earth hath begotten you and given you to all peoples as a physic of healing."[3]

I MOLY, THE SOUL-HEALING HERB OF HERMES

There is a poem in the *Anthologia Palatina* which uses the imagery of Homer's story of Circe and Odysseus, to describe the

---

[1] *Enarratio in Psalmos*, 51, 12 (PL, 36, 607 C).

[2] *Moralia in Iob*, VIII, 48, 81 (PL, 75, 851 A). Cf. also, *ibid.*, XII, 47, 52 (PL, 75, 1012 A).

[3] R. Heim, "Incantamenta magica Graeca Latina" (*Jahrbücher für klassische Philologie*, Supplementary volume, 19, Leipzig, 1892), No. 129, pp. 505f.; *Poetae Lat. Minores*, I, 140f.; T. Hopfner, *Griechisch-ägyptischer Offenbarungszauber* (Graeco-Egyptian Revelation Magic), I, Leipzig, 1921, pp. 122f.

fundamental spiritual problem of man, for man is eternally placed
between two kingdoms, that of heaven and that of earth. The poet
utters this cry:

Ἔρρε μοι, ὦ Κίρκης δνοφερὸν σπέος· αἰδέομαι γὰρ
οὐράνιος γεγαὼς βαλάνους ἅτε θηρίον ἔσθειν.
ἀλλὰ λαβεῖν θεόθεν ψυχοσσόον εὔχομαι ἄνθος
μῶλυ, κακῶν δοξῶν ἀλκτήριον . . . .[1]

(Depart from me, thou murky cave of Circe, for I am
ashamed,
Belonging as I do to heaven, to eat acorns like a beast.
Rather do I pray to receive from God the soul-healing
flower
Moly, the good physic against evil thoughts.)

Here Odysseus, the supposed utterer of the prayer, is man the
everlasting, placed half-way between the clear heavenly light of
Hermes and the dark and seductive charms of chthonic Circe. He
stands between heaven and the cave. Salvation comes to him from
that "soul-healing flower" which he receives from the hand of the
messenger of the gods and which is in itself a clearly perceptible
symbol of what is here enacted in the realm of the soul. Moly's
root is black its blossom white. By its power man sets himself
free from the powers of darkness among which he has buried his
roots. This he can do because he is a being begotten of heaven
whose flower, whose spiritual self, that is, can open itself upwards,
milk-white and pure. Nevertheless—and this is the real point in
the symbolism of the myth—this is only possible because his help
comes θεόθεν, from God, and because he has encountered the
transforming power of Hermes.

This will suffice to give you the necessary feeling for the pagan
and Christian symbolism of this little herb called moly. Let me
now go into the matter in greater detail.

When the ancients reflected on such an allegory as this, they

---

[1] *Anthologia Palatina*, XV, 12 (presumably, though not certainly, by Emperor Leo the
Wise, 886–912. Cf. what is undoubtedly a genuine poem of his, namely that against the
Muses which also begins with the words ἔρρε μοι, in P. Matranga, *Anecdota Graeca*, II,
Rome, 1850, p. 559).

always called to mind the events of the myth as Homer's immortal verse has described them:

> Thus spake Hermeias and gave me the herb of my healing
> Which he tore from the ground, and showed me its nature;
>   the root was
> Black, and the flow'r milk-white, and the high gods moly
>   have named it.
> Hard, forsooth, is its digging to mortal men, but the gods can
> Do all things.[1]

I am only concerned here with the symbolism of moly and its development. I have no desire to enter the domain of the naturalist or to embark on a learned disquisition therein. There has already been more than enough of that. Whatever may be the degree of factual accuracy achieved in the botanical description and classification of this little Homeric herb which has been so ruthlessly pulled about by commentators, all I am concerned with here is the search for this little article of pharmacology in the broad gardens of spiritual medicine, pagan and Christian. I am afraid, however, that we shall have, before we can proceed further, to submit to a certain amount of botanizing by both ancient and modern experts in the subject. After that I shall try and explain what the Stoics and the Neoplatonists had to say, in their allegorizing of Homer, about the spiritual symbolism of the Hermetic herb. That will bring me to the influence of such ideas in Christian

---

[1] *Odyssey*, X, 302-6. Certain pictorial representations of the moly myth dating back to antiquity are extant. The first is a gem which shows Odysseus holding up in his left hand the herb which he has just received from Hermes. Reproduced in F. Inghirami, *Galleria Omerica*, Fiesole, 1831-6, vol. II, Plate 49. The second is on the Tabula Rondanini, a bas-relief that has now disappeared but which had a close artistic relationship with the Tabula Iliaca in the Capitol Museum in Roma. Both these reliefs were obviously meant to serve an educational purpose and represent various scenes from Homer's tales. In the present instance the subject is the story of Odysseus and Circe and there is an explanatory inscription reading "From the tale told to Alcinous in the tenth book". Between the figures of Odysseus and Hermes there are written the words "*Tὸ Μῶλυ*", while under the figures of Odysseus' companions there is written "The companions who have been turned into beasts". The best reproduction and description are in the work of A. Barthélemy in *Mémoires de l'Academie des Inscriptions et Belles-Lettres*, XXVIII (Paris, 1761), Plate II, between pp. 578 and 579; also in O. Jahn, *Griechische Bildchroniken*, Bonn, 1873, Plate IV, and in A. Baumeister, *Denkmäler des klassischen Altertums*, Munich-Leipzig, 1887, II, p. 783, ill. 839.

times and on men who possessed a Christian conception of the nature of the soul, and I shall pursue this theme right up to the days of humanism with its deep love of the ancient wisdom of Homer.

I

The mighty herb with the black root and the white flower has never wholly ceased from ancient times to the present day to cast its spell on the botanist. With a zeal that is sometimes slightly ridiculous, learned men, summoning to the task all the forces of their professional erudition, have striven to determine moly's exact botanical identity. A small library of books, both old and new, has come into being,[1] but there is little left in these dry herbaria of the colour and fragrance of this "soul-healing plant". To have real knowledge of these we must in one way or another have, somewhere within us, something of Homer himself—"the sovereign poet", as Dante called him.[2] For all that, we have something to learn from the highly knowledgeable specialists concerned about these dried-up children of our Mother Earth, for even here our studies will teach us something of the way in which this symbolism has developed and of the strange way its story hangs together.

Even the ancient botanists never arrived at any very clear conclusions when they attempted to identify the Homeric herb as a plant that could actually be found somewhere in Greece. The unknown author of the ninth book of Theophrastus' *Botany* was a rhizotomist who was particularly concerned with popular herbal

---

[1] Among older writings I have consulted G. W. Wedel, *Propempticon inaugurale de Moly Homeri in specie*, Jena, 1713; D. W. Triller, *Moly Homericum detectum cum reliquis ad fabulam Circaeam pertinentibus*, Leipzig, 1716; J. H. Dierbach, *Flora Mythologica, oder Pflanzenkunde in bezug auf Mythologie und Symbolik der Griechen und Römer*, Frankfurt, 1833, pp. 192f.; C. Senoner, "Über Homers Moly", in *Österreichische Blätter für Literatur und Kunst*, 5 (1848), pp. 37ff. Among more recent studies are J. Murr, *Die Pflanzenwelt in der griechischen Mythologie* (The Plant World in Greek Mythology), Innsbruck, 1890, pp. 208ff.; F. Schmiedeberg, *Über die Pharmaka in der Ilias und Odyssee* (The Drugs in the Odyssey and the Iliad), Strasbourg, 1918, pp. 22ff.; T. Hopfner, *Griechisch-ägyptischer Offenbarungszauber*, I, pp. 115, 126, 137, 192; E. Buchholz, "Die drei Naturreiche nach Homer" (The Three Kingdoms of Nature according to Homer), *Homerische Realien*, I, 2, Leipzig, 1873, pp. 216ff.; A. Abt, *Die Apologie des Apuleius von Madaura und die antike Zauberei* (The Apologia of Apuleius of Madaura and Ancient Magic), Giessen, 1908, p. 103.

[2] *Inferno*, IV, 88.

remedies, and it is he who makes the first attempt of which there is any record to determine moly's botanical identity.[1] It is he who furnished the grounds for an opinion which was passed on and continued to be held throughout the whole life of antiquity. According to this writer, moly was a plant that had a perfectly real existence among the flora of Greece and was chiefly to be found on Mount Cyllene and near Pheneus—in the classical territory of the Hermes cult. Small wonder then that it is just this root that is given to Odysseus by Cyllene's god. It is thus easy to understand what makes Ovid write:

> Pacifer huic dederat florem Cyllenius album,
> Moly vocant superi, nigra radice tenetur.

(The peace god of Cyllene had given him a white flower. Moly the gods name it, and black is the root that holds it.)[2]

As he attempts more exact description, our Pseudo-Theophrastus shows obvious signs of uncertainty: "It is said that this moly is very like that mentioned by Homer." Its onion-like root and its leaves suggest, he thinks, a resemblance to the *Scilla maritima* or sea-onion. It is obvious that the author is doing no more than repeat typical plant folk-lore, but it is precisely this that makes him of interest to us. Actually, all forms of leek and onion which today we classify under the name *Allium*, were, by the ordinary Greek, supposed to be charged with magic and to possess medicinal properties, and this applied particularly to *Scilla maritima* with which moly is here compared.[3]

Clement of Alexandria tells us that the Greeks had a strange feeling of awe for the sea-onion and has preserved for us some verses of the comic dramatist Diphilus which relate how the seer Melampos cured Proetus' daughters by means of this plant, when Dionysus had made them mad.[4] It is clear that the identification of moly as a member of the *Allium* family by the scientific botanists

---

[1] Pseudo-Theophrastus, *Hist. Plant.*, IX, 15, 7 (Wimmer, I, p. 251).

[2] *Metamorphoses*, XIV, 291 f. According to Gregory of Nazianzus the word moly was for the Greeks a name invented by the gods. Cf. *Oratio contra Iulianum*, I, 105 (PG, 35, 641 B).

[3] On the chthonic character of the leek and the onion, see T. Hopfner, *Offenbarungszauber*, I, pp. 136 f. [4] *Stromata*, VII, 4, 26 (GCS, III, p. 19).

does not go to the heart of the matter. The real point is that moly was held to possess magical properties.

Pliny, drawing on Pseudo-Theophrastus, wrote a few words on moly which were still remembered in Christian times, "*Clarissima herbarum est Homero teste, quam a dis putat vocari moly, et inventionem eius Mercurio adsignat contraque summa veneficia demonstrationem. Nasci eam hodie circa Pheneum et in Cyllene Arcadiae tradunt specie illa homerica, radice rotunda nigraque, magnitudine cepae*—Moly is the most famous of all plants according to the testimony of Homer, who believed that the gods themselves gave it its name and that Mercury discovered it and showed it to be an antidote against all poisons. Men say that even today moly grows in the neighbourhood of Pheneus and on Cyllene in Arcadia in the form described by Homer, namely with a round black root of the size of an onion."[1] In what are really already Christian times the writer usually known as Pseudo-Apuleius Platonicus describes the Homeric plant in exactly the same words as Pliny and even makes a drawing of it which the tradition of the codices has preserved in a long succession of volumes.[2] Dioscurides,[3] and after him Galen,[4] describe moly as an onion-like plant that serves numerous medicinal purposes, but they are so vague that what they tell us cannot form the basis for a genuine botanical identification. Linné has picked out two kinds of leeks, calling one *Allium moly* and the other *Allium magicum*, while modern botanists incline towards some plant of this family as the Homeric moly, and show a preference for victor's garlic (*Allium victorialis*) which was also credited with magical properties.[5]

There is yet another school of thought, however, which points to a quite different class of magic herbs and is based on yet another statement of Dioscurides.[6] "Moly is also the name", he says,

---

[1] Pliny, *Nat. Hist.*, XXV, 26 (Mayhoff, IV, pp. 124 f.).

[2] Pseudo-Apuleius Platonicus, *Herbarius*, 48 (*Corpus Medicorum Latinorum*, IV, Leipzig-Berlin, 1927, p. 98).

[3] *De Materia Medica*, III, 47 (Wellmann, II, p. 60, ll. 11 ff.).

[4] XII, pp. 80, 82, 101 (Kühn).

[5] Thus recently Murr, *op. cit.*; Buchholz, *op. cit.*; F. Marzell, "Die Zauberpflanze Moly" (The Magic Plant Moly), in *Der Naturforscher*, 2 (1926), pp. 523 ff.

[6] *De Materia Medica*, III, 46 (Wellmann, II, p. 59, l. 14). Similarly Galen, XII, 940; XIII, 211 E; 257; 605 A. Cf. E. H. F. Meyer, *Geschichte der Botanik* (History of Botany), II, Königsberg, 1855, pp. 192 f.

"given in Cappadocia and Asiatic Galatia to the plant called πήγα-
νον ἄγριον which seems to be identical with what the Germans call
Bergraute or mountain rue. Others call it harmala, the Syrians
besasa, the Cappadocians moly." As Paul de Lagarde has pointed
out, Dioscurides' statement in this matter is quite credible, since
he himself comes from Anazarbus in Cilicia.[1] Moly is thus clearly
a Cappadocian word. Nay, more, the plant which bears this name,
which we know as mountain rue, is for the Persian Saka who lived
in Cappadocia a substitute for their native hôm and we shall later
hear Plutarch discoursing of magical things in this connexion and
calling the plant moly.

In the Syrian tongue, as we have seen, moly is called besasa, and
this leads us still deeper into the history of this ancient plant moly.
The Aramaic term for mountain rue is bešaš and in the Syriac
version of Galen, who has copied his wisdom from Dioscurides,
moly is called bašašo.[2] Galen states that mountain rue has a black
root and a white flower, and thus corresponds to the herb
mentioned by Homer. So it is that rue, famed already for its
magic powers, enters human tradition under the name of moly,
and all the properties ascribed to rue are now assumed to be
possessed by the flower of Hermes.

In a passage interpolated into Pseudo-Apuleius from Dioscurides
we are told: "*Apud Cappadocas appellata est moly, a quibusdam
armala, a Syris besasa*–It is called moly among the Cappadocians,
others call it armala and the Syrians besasa."[3] And even in the sixth
century A.D. we are told by the so-called Dioscurides Langobardus:
"*Alterum genus rutae nascitur in Macedonia et in Galatia Asiae, quam
cives moly appellant. Frutex est ex una radice multas radices habens . . .
florem album habens*–Another kind of rue grows in Macedonia
and in Asiatic Galatia which the inhabitants call moly. It is a shrub

---

[1] "Die persischen Glossen der Alten" (The Persian Glosses of the Ancients), *Gesammelte
Abhandlungen*, Leipzig, 1866, pp. 172–5.

[2] A. Merx, "Proben der syrischen Übersetzung von Galenus' Schrift über die einfachen
Heilmittel" (Tests of the Syriac Translation of Galen's Work on Simple Medicaments), in
Zeitschrift der Deutschen Morgenländischen Gesellschaft, 39 (1885), p. 282; in the Greek
Ducange βήρασσα is equated with μῶλυ. Cf. other references in E. A. Sophokles,
Greek Lexicon of the Roman and Byzantine Periods, Cambridge, 1914, where see under
"βήσασα" and "ἄρμαλα".

[3] *Herbarius*, 90 (*Corp. Med. Lat.*, IV, p. 163, ll. 46f.).

putting forth many roots from its single one . . . and bearing a white flower."[1]

It is very tempting to try and connect the herb moly-besasa with what Hopfner has discovered of the relation between besasa and the popular Egyptian deity Bes.[2] The extent of our knowledge might quite possibly thus be increased and there can be no doubt that this pseudo-botany is rarely far from ordinary herb magic. At this stage we can merely draw attention to the fact that Alexander of Tralles[3] confirms that moly and mountain rue are identical, and most certainly rue with all the demon-repelling powers that have been attributed to it from Pliny[4] till the late Middle Ages belongs in the same magic circle which includes moly; and we find that the Christian credited this plant with powers of driving away the devil in much the same way as moly rendered Circe's poisons innocuous. In a medieval benediction of rue we have these words: "*Benedico te, creatura rutae, ut sis exterminatio diaboli et omnium contubernalium eius*–I bless thee, O offspring of the rue, that thou mayest be the means of exterminating the devil and all his companions."[5] Even in the *Historia Plantarum* of Conrad Gessner of Zürich we get an echo of Dioscurides: "*Vocant etiamnum sylvestrem rutam, quod in Cappadocia et Galatia Asiae finitima moly dicitur*–They still call wild rue the plant which in Cappadocia and Galatia, a part of Asia, is called moly."[6] The importance of the part played by besasa, mountain rue and moly in the literature of alchemy can best be judged by those who have made a pathway for themselves in Circe's luxuriant herb garden. Everywhere there is a riot of moly.

And this brings us to the third kind of attempted identification, of which both ancient and modern times provide examples. In many ways it is the most engaging of the three, for it declines to

[1] III, fol. 84 d (ed. H. Stadler, *Romanische Forschungen*, 10, 1898, p. 399, ll. 9 ff.).

[2] *Offenbarungszauber*, I, p. 127 and II, pp. 62 and 93.

[3] *Therapeutica*, II (Puschmann, I, pp. 133–5). Cf. also E. H. F. Meyer, *Geschichte der Botanik*, II, pp. 379 ff.

[4] *Nat. Hist.*, XX, 131–43.

[5] Cf. the texts in A. Franz, *Die kirchlichen Benediktionen im Mittelalter*, I, p. 417 ff., where there are also other references to the medieval magic of rue. For the devil-resisting powers of the rue see the verses in the *Hortulus* of Walafrid Strabo (PL, 114, 1122 f.) and Hrabanus Maurus, *De Universo*, XIX, 9 (PL, 111, 532).

[6] Conrad Gessner, *Historia Plantarum et Vires*, Basle, 1541, fol. 134 b.

classify this plant with any group of the rue or leek family or with any other family, and declares that the name moly and all that goes with it belong entirely to the realm of myth and that the name itself simply indicates a magic plant with curative and prophylactic powers. Moly is a fairy plant, it is the φάρμακον ἐσθλόν,¹ the puissant physic pure and simple. This is plain from the popular etymology given in the *Scholia Graeca* on Homer: "Moly is a species (εἶδος) of plant, and its name is derived from μωλύειν, from its power as an antidote to poison."² According to Suidas, moly is simply an antidote to drugs,³ while Pliny sees in it the essence of all prophylactics and counter-magic: "*Contra haec omnia et magicasque artes erit primum illud Homericum moly.*"⁴

It is precisely for this reason that, in the course of time, all kinds of quite specific plants were light-heartedly added to the list of those identifiable with moly. Pliny himself, for instance, when speaking of the herb helicacabon which is more potent than opium, and a powerful intoxicant, identifies it with moly: "*Ab aliis morion, ab aliis moly appellatur.*"⁵ Even the Christmas rose (black hellebore), of which both pagan and Christian writers tell us such marvellous and terrifying things, was, on occasion, designated as moly.⁶ We should, I think, do well to accept the statement of Berendes when he says: "My own view is that moly does not refer to anything concrete at all, to any particular plant, that is; the name is one in general use among poets to denote an

¹ *Odyssey*, X, 292. For the semantics of φάρμακον see the important discussion in A. Abt, *Die Apologie des Apuleius von Madaura und die antike Zauberei*, Giessen, 1908, pp. 112–15.
² *Scholia Graeca in Homeri Odysseam* (ed. Dindorf, II, Oxford, 1855, p. 467).
³ *Suidae Lexicon* (ed. Adler, *Lexicogr. Graeci*, III), see μῶλυ. It is, however, to be noted that Suidas also admits the meaning of wild rue. The so-called *Anonymus de Herbis*, a Greek poem of uncertain date about herbs, treats moly (in c. 13) as an antidote with a wide range of application (ed. Fabricius, *Bibl. Graec.*, II, 630 ff.; also Lehrs, *Poetae Bucolici et Didactici*, Didot, II, pp. 173 ff.). Cf. E. H. F. Meyer, *Geschichte der Botanik*, II, pp. 336–40.
⁴ *Nat. Hist.*, XXV, 127.
⁵ *Ibid.*, XXI, 180.
⁶ Thus Triller, *loc. cit.*; Schmiedeberg, *loc. cit.* Cf. also Pliny, XXV, 150 where the Christmas rose is treated as being of equal effectiveness with the mandrake. Similar views in Apuleius, *De Magia*, 32 (Helm, pp. 22 f.). On the Christmas rose in the magic papyri see A. Abt, *loc. cit.*, p. 134. The use of hellebore as a drug is also known to Christian writers, especially against "*insania*". Cf. Irenaeus, *Adv. Haer.* II, 30, 1 (Harvey, I, p. 362); Tertullian, *De Spectaculis*, 27 (CSEL, 20, p. 26, ll. 19 f.); Sulpicius Severus, *Vita Martini*, 6, 5 (CSEL, I, p. 117, l. 2).

antidote. It is derived from μωλύειν which means to cause to weaken or subside."[1]

We can conclude from this that from the very beginning Homer's moly was a thing surrounded by mystery and that it is not the botanists but the mythologists who are really in a position to tell us the truth about it. Unfortunately, it is precisely what the mythologists have to tell us that has tended to be neglected, and even the most recent and learned discussions of the matter are content to relegate the question of this mythical symbolism to a couple of lines.[2] In particular the story of the Christian symbolism connected with the "soul-healing flower" has received deplorably little attention and it is this that I shall make the starting-point of my enquiry.

2

In order better to understand moly's psychic mythology, it will first be necessary to say a few words—and to support them with appropriate evidence—about the spiritual situation in which Odysseus finds himself after receiving the moly. He stands between Hermes and Circe. Both the bright messenger of the gods and the dark mistress of the cave are seeking to win him. These two figures represent the same ideas as the white flower of moly and its black root.

It would be presumption to attempt to say more about Hermes —or to say it better—than has already been done by Karl Kerényi both in his *Eranos* lectures and in his book on *Hermes the Guide of Souls.*[3] I should nevertheless like to accentuate certain lines in his picture. Hermes is and remains the *agilis Cyllenius*, as Ovid once calls him, the bright, the elegant, the light-footed god of Cyllene, the place where moly grows.[4] For the Greeks he is the λόγιος, the personification of all that is bright and clear in thought, he is, one

---

[1] J. Berendes, *Die Pharmazie bei den alten Kulturvölkern* (Pharmacy among the Ancient Civilized Peoples), I, Halle, 1891, p. 131.

[2] See article "Moly" in Pauly-Wissowa, *Realenzyklopädie*, XVI (1933), col. 33, ll. 47–65 (Steiner).

[3] K. Kerényi, *Hermes der Seelenführer* (Hermes the Guide of Souls), Zürich, Rhein-Verlag, 1944.

[4] *Metamorphoses*, II, 720; II, 818, *"velox Cyllenius"*; Virgil, *Aeneid*, IV, 258, *"Cyllenia proles"*. On Mount Cyllene as a cultic centre for Hermes, see W. H. Roscher, *Mythologisches Lexikon*, I (1886–90), col. 2342f.

might say, the logos in its articulate utterances.[1] Hermes is the possessor of knowledge and so the mediator of all hidden wisdom. He is by no means only a heavenly being, he is also of the earth, and for that very reason, since he knows them, able to combat the chthonic powers. Whoever has obtained from him the magic formula is armed against all the powers of darkness. That is why in the Paris magic papyrus Hermes is "the leader of all the magi— πάντων μάγων ἀρχηγέτης".[2]

We know from Apuleius' book on magic that the magicians used to call upon him as the communicator of the sacred spells: "*Solebat advocari ad magorum ceremonias Mercurius carminum vector.*"[3] Mercury whispers the healing formulae to men, and an old altar inscription among the Carolingian foundations of the cathedral at Aix honours him as *Mercurius Susurrio*, Mercury of the happy inspiration.[4]

In this form he lives on even in the mind of Christians, and up to the time of Isidore[5] and Hrabanus Maurus[6] he continues to be the discoverer of magical practices, the soul-guide possessed of all the magic of Thessaly who with his wand can lead human spirits to darkness or to light. It is in this form that Prudentius sings of him:

> *Nec non Thessalicae doctissimus ille magiae*
> *Traditur exstinctas sumptae moderamine virgae*
> *In lucem revocasse animas . . .*
> *Ast alias damnasse neci penitusque latenti*
> *Immersisse chao. Facit hoc ad utrumque peritus.*

(Most learned is he in the magic of Thessaly
And it is said that by the power of the staff in his hand
He calls departed souls up to the light . . .
But others again he condemns to death and plunges
Straight into the hidden chaos below. Of these things
    he can do either.)[7]

---

[1] Roscher, *loc. cit.*, I, 236. On Hermes as logos, cf. *Realenzyklopädie*, XIII (1926), col. 1061 f. (H. Leisegang); E. Orth, *Logios*, Leipzig, 1926, pp. 77 ff. (This deals with Hermes Logios.)

[2] *Pap. Paris.*, 2289 f. Cf. T. Hopfner, *Offenbarungszauber*, II, p. 2; Martianus Capella, *De Nuptiis Mercurii*, I, 36 (Kopp, p. 79).

[3] *De Magia*, 31 (Helm, p. 37, l. 19). On Hermes as a chthonic deity, see A. Abt, *Apologie des Apuleius*, pp. 229 f., pp. 117 f.

[4] *Corpus Inscr. Latin.*, XIII, 12005. Cf. on this *Realenzyklopädie*, XV (1931), col. 996.

[5] *Etymol.*, VIII, 9, 8 (PL, 82, 311 B).   [6] *De Magicis Artibus* (PL, 110, 1097-9).

[7] *Contra Symmachum*, I, verses 89–94 (CSEL, 61, p. 222).

I know of no more apt designation of the character of Hermes-Mercury than this *"ad utrumque peritus"* of Prudentius. Hermes is the magical victor over the powers of darkness because he "knows" everything and therefore "can do" everything; this is an excellent example of the way in which the world of antiquity thought of magic; indeed it is of the very essence of their conception of the thing.[1] Whosoever has been instructed by bright Hermes can resist all the seductions of the dark powers, for he has become one possessed of knowledge.

In the Homeric myth Hermes' foil is Circe, the witch of the dark, seductive cave on the island of Aeaea. She too is a mongrel creature, being the daughter of Helios and the ocean nymph Perse, but the motherly inheritance is the stronger and she is essentially a child of Oceanus, of the deep waters far removed from God that are the very embodiment of chthonic darkness.[2] That is why, like Hecate, she becomes a lunar being, the great nocturnal sorceress. "Circe of the many drugs" Theocritus calls her in his exquisite idyll.[3] She is a close relative of Medea, another initiate in the knowledge of herbs; all poisons of the world grow in her garden and men who are made captive by her seductions turn into wolves and swine.

Circe's figure, like that of Hermes, remains alive for a long time in the Christian mind. To Arnobius[4] she is *"versipellis Circe"*, the "skin-changing", crafty seducer who can assume any part at will. To Augustine[5] she is *"maga famosissima"*, while for Isidore[6] she is *"maga et venefica et sacerdos daemonorum* – sorceress and poisoner and priestess to the demons".

Odysseus then stands midway between these two mythical powers and it is Hermes' moly that saved him. Let me now try to unfold the history of the interpretation of this spiritual drama. In Xenophon's *Memorabilia*[7] Socrates jokingly treats the story

---

[1] Cf. T. Hopfner, *Offenbarungszauber*, II, pp. 1–19.

[2] W. H. Roscher, *Mythol. Lexikon*, II, col. 1193–1214; W. H. Roscher, *Selene und Verwandtes* (Selene and Related Matters), Leipzig, 1890, p. 144; T. Hopfner, *Offenbarungszauber*, I, pp. 115 f.; H. Rahner, "Das Meer der Welt" (The Sea of the World), in *Zeitschrift für katholische Theologie*, 66 (1942), pp. 89 ff.

[3] II, 15.   [4] *Adversus Nationes*, IV, 14 (CSEL, 4, p. 152, l. 3).

[5] *Civitas Dei*, XVIII, 17 (CSEL, 40, 2, pp. 288 f.).

[6] *Etymol.*, XVIII, 28, 2 (PL, 82, 654 B).   [7] *Memorabilia*, I, 3, 7 (Mücke, p. 74).

of Circe and Odysseus as a warning against the dangers of gluttony and claims that thanks to the cautionary advice, ὑποθημοσύνη, of Hermes, Odysseus was preserved from the fate of being turned into a swine. Though this would be no more than a happy simile—it certainly does not amount to an allegory— it shows how ready were the Greeks to find moral applications for scenes from Homer. This practice may often have prevailed in post-Socratic ethics, but we cannot really speak of genuine Homeric allegory till we get to the moral philosophy of the Stoics.[1] At that point great importance begins to be attached to finding hidden moral lessons in the myths of the ancient poet, which Plato so heartily despised. Now, the very essence of Stoic wisdom was the βίος λογικός, life in accordance with the logos, which means the growing awareness in our inner world of the law that is effective throughout the whole universe. The greatest weight was however placed on the control, by means of knowledge, of the πάθη, the dark and purely earthly passions.

Now, the first instance of the Homeric moly mythology's being interpreted in this Stoic sense is to be found in Cleanthes, the pupil of Zeno and the teacher of Chrysippus, and it is obvious that we are here concerned with a genuine piece of old Stoic teaching. We owe the preservation of Cleanthes' words to the sophist Apollonius. "Cleanthes the philosopher", he says, "said that moly was an allegorical representation of the logos, by whose power the lower instincts and passions are made weaker – μωλύονται."[2] Observe here how the popular etymology of μῶλυ and μωλύειν is introduced into the realm of philosophy. The moly of Hermes has become nothing other than the Stoic logos, the law of life for the "rational" man.

From this point onwards the moly allegory adapts itself to all the changes which Hermes turned philosopher—himself a being of infinite variety—proceeds to undergo. In Athenaeus we still

---

[1] Cf. F. Wehrli, *Zur Geschichte der allegorischen Deutung Homers im Altertum* (The History of the Allegorical Interpretation of Homer in Antiquity), Basle, 1928, pp. 52–64; S. Weinstock, "Die platonische Homerkritik und ihre Nachwirkung" (Plato's Criticism of Homer and its After-Effects), in *Philologus*, 82 (1926), pp. 121 ff.

[2] Cleanthes, *Fragment* 526 (Arnim, *Stoicorum Veterum Fragmenta*, I, 118); Apollonius, *Lex. Homeric.* (Bekker, p. 114). On the logos doctrine of Cleanthes, cf. *Realenzyklopädie*, XI (1921), col. 566.

encounter the typical Stoic article. The companions of Odysseus are said to be turned into beasts because they followed their lusts, the Ithacan, however, is saved because he follows the logos of Hermes, for through this logos—which is what moly represents —he becomes "passionless" (ἀπαθής).[1]

The author of the *Scholia Graeca* on Homer must have been drawing on some such source as this when he wrote, "Because Odysseus was a 'wise man' he received the moly, which means the full logos, by whose help he was made safe against every passion."[2] Perhaps, however, the Stoic ideal of the man informed by knowledge striving for virtue is best exemplified in the *Homeric Problems* of Heraclitus, an allegorizing writer of the Augustan period. The essence of the virtues of Odysseus, we are here told, is his φρόνησις, his insight into things, an insight that is illuminated by reason. This, however, only comes to him through Hermes, who is actually called ἔμφρων λόγος, the wise or prudent logos.

Closely following the Homeric text, Heraclitus now develops the allegory of moly. "*Phronesis*", he writes—insight illuminated by reason, that is—"is most appropriately represented by moly. This is a gift which can only be given to human beings, and to very few human beings at that. The most essential thing about moly is that its root is black and its flower milk-white. Now the first steps towards insight, which is a kind of simultaneous comprehension of all that is good, are rough, unpleasant and difficult, but when a man has bravely and patiently surmounted the trials of these beginnings, then, as he progresses, the flower opens to him, as in a gentle light."[3]

Heraclitus' other work, *De Incredibilibus*, shows us in what the opposite of *phronesis* consists—and we have here another typical piece of Stoicism. Circe is the great *hetaira* who turns men's heads,

---

[1] *Deipnosophistae*, I, 10 E (Kaibel, I, p. 23, ll. 14–16). Similar expressions in Pseudo-Plutarch, *De Vita Homeri*, 126 (Bernardakis, VII, p. 400, ll. 11–14): "The prudent man [Odysseus] was not subject to such transformation, for he had received from Hermes, that is to say from the logos, the freedom from his passions—τὸ ἀπαθές."

[2] *Scholia Graeca* (Dindorf, II, p. 467, ll. 19f.). Thus also in Hesychius, *Lexicon*, under μῶλυ (Schmidt, II, p. 135), "Moly represents the logos through which all things are brought to full completion—μωλύνεται."

[3] *Problemata Homerica*, 73 (Editio Bonnensis, Leipzig, 1910, p. 97, ll. 6–13).

but of this temptation also wise Odysseus shows himself the master.[1] The dark urges of sex which the author here has in mind are also alluded to in this connexion in a poem of Palladas, which is preserved in the *Anthologia Palatina*:

> Prudent was Odysseus and fled from the lusts of immature youth.
> But it was not Hermes who gave him the magic-repelling drug
> Rather was it that reason which is an attribute of man.[2]

Here we have reached the ultimate limits of that Stoic allegorizing which finally dispelled all belief in the gods. Hermes has become nothing more than the symbol of human reason and his moly is nothing more than man's self-redemption.

Yet as a result of the transformation of philosophic and religious thought by the Platonic revival, things began towards the end of antiquity to take a very different course. Hermes ceased to be a shadowy abstraction, a mere vague personification of simple human reason. He became a god again—the representative of that heavenly power to which man, seeing himself placed in the centre of the battle between the demonic and the divine, looked longingly for redemption and for grace.

This transition from Stoic enlightenment to that longing for redemption which was the mark of the later Platonism—you can see it in the Neopythagoreans and in the Neoplatonists who begin to be active about this time—this transition, I say, was surely one of the most important events in the spiritual history of man, and the transformation of the figure of Hermes is both a measure and a symptom of the change.

Meanwhile the development of the symbolism connected with this little herb moly becomes a kind of abstract of this whole spiritual upheaval, and particularly so in regard to what may be called its psycho-therapeutic implications. Now the divine is once more recognized, now men once more become alive to the fact that a healing of the soul, a transition from the chthonic root to the

---

[1] c. 16 (*Mythographi Graeci*, ed. Westermann, p. 216, ll. 7–12).
[2] *Anthologia Palatina*, X, 50.

heavenly flower, can only be effected through a power that comes from above.

Actually there is already in Plato—but faint and delicate as the recordings of a seismograph—an indication of the upheaval to come. There is a tendency to personify the world-logos—one can see it in the *Phaedrus*—and Plato seems to look upon Hermes and the logos as being one and the same.[1] The thinkers who, after the emptying of all religion by the Stoics, return to him, do so with that mixture of maturity and weariness that comes from a bitter spiritual experience, but they see in Hermes the embodiment of all that is the object of their religious longings: the power that changes us into creatures of the light must come from above, the god himself must tell us through his emissary how we can extricate ourselves from the cave of Circe. Now men's hearts can find release in such words as those of the fifth Orphic hymn to Hermes, "O thou messenger of God, O thou prophet of the logos for mortal men!"[2] The divine knowledge that frees us from ourselves, the knowledge that comes ἄνωθεν and θεόθεν, from above and from God, is the λόγος προφορικός, the word made audible, and Hermes is that very thing.[3]

It was precisely when this sublime level had been attained in the spiritual development of the Greeks and in Greek thought that the earliest Christian theology was able to lay hold of it and to show how its aspirations might be satisfied. There is surely some significance in the fact that the Greeks and other inhabitants of Lystra should have mistaken Paul for Hermes and cried their joy to heaven in the Lycaonian tongue because they believed they were seeing gods in human form. Paul, as the ἡγούμενος τοῦ λόγου, literally "the leader in speaking", was for that very reason identified with Hermes.[4]

This identification by the Greeks of Hermes with the logos leads Justin to a daring feat of apologetics in which he actually sets the Hermes-Logos and the Christian Jesus-Logos more or less side by side. "In this we are at one with you," he writes, "in that

---

[1] *Phaedrus*, 264 C; *Cratylus*, 407 E.

[2] *Hymni Orphici*, 28, 1, 4 (ed. W. Quandt, Berlin, 1941, p. 23).

[3] Cf. R. Heintze, *Xenokrates*, Leipzig, 1892, pp. 143 ff.; *Realenzyklopädie*, XIII (1926), col. 1057 f. (H. Leisegang).   [4] Acts 14. 12.

we both regard the Logos, whom you call Hermes, as the messenger of God."[1] Hippolytus is another who bears witness to this identity between Hermes and the Logos[2] and a passage in the Pseudo-Clementine *Recognitiones* states that *"Mercurius Verbum esse traditur*–It is said that Mercury is the Word."[3] In this connexion we should also read what Augustine reproduces from Varro in the *Civitas Dei*.[4] One might really say that at the beginning of the Christian era Hermes had just received a new lease of life—and with the change in Hermes' character there also came a change in the significance of his soul-healing flower. Homer and Plato were to be reconciled at last.

One of the writers in whose work we become aware of the strange religious sensitivity of those days is Maximus of Tyre.[5] In his twenty-ninth discourse he says: "God has embedded in human nature something like a living spark of fire, namely his longing and hopeful expectation of the good. Yet the ways toward the finding of this good he has kept profoundly secret."[6] And at this point he remembers Homer's line: "The root was black, and the flow'r milk-white."

Let us, however, note that at this point we are really witnessing a revival of Plato, of Plato who can never die, and of his longing, that transcends all the things of sense, for the ἀγαθόν, the good *per se*. Man can only become a being of goodness and light if he blows into flame the heaven-sprung spark within him which is the memory of the divine goodness that he must imitate. It was the tremendous world-changing discovery of Platonic idealism that man can only escape from the spiritual darkness of his earthly nature if he receives the fire and the power from the divine; for he himself is derived from divinity, even though he has fallen headlong into weakness and the dark. In Maximus we can really already detect the lofty tones of Plotinus and we can find similar

---

[1] *Apologia*, I, 22 (Otto, I, p. 70, ll. 1 f.).

[2] *Elenchos*, IV, 48, 2 (GCS, III, p. 70, ll. 16 f.).

[3] *Recognitiones*, X, 41 (PG, 1, 1441 B).

[4] VII, 14 (CSEL, 40, 1, pp. 321 f.).

[5] On his religious significance, cf. K. Prümm, *Das antike Heidentum*, pp. 94 f., 177; J. Lebreton, *Histoire du dogme de la Trinité*, II, Paris, 1928, pp. 68–80; T. Hopfner, *Offenbarungszauber*, I, p. 9.

[6] *Oratio* XXIX, 6 (Holbein, p. 346, ll. 15–23).

utterances in Augustine though these are of course wholly filled
with a Christian spirit. Man's everlasting situation then is that in
the midst of black chaos he bears within himself the spark of the
Logos and is homesick for the source of this light. It is this that
forms the theme of the wonderful hymn of Synesius, Platonist
and Christian:

> I am filled with the seed
> Of thy noble spirit,
> A glowing spark
> That is embedded
> Deep in matter;
> For thou hast set
> The soul in the world,
> And hast, O my ruler,
> Through this soul,
> Set my spirit in my body.
> Kindle therefore, O my Lord,
> Lights that will lead me on high,
> Let the brightness shine forth
> And blaze as a fire.
> Magnify the tiny spark
> Within the crown
> Of my head.[1]

Yet this upward striving is a battle. Our dark root is sunk in
matter and it is not easy to loosen it from thence, and in Homer's
line: "Hard is its digging to mortal men", Maximus sees an
intimation of this struggle. He adds: "I look at this moly and
understand its deep secret, for I know full well how hard it is to
find the way to the good."

This leads us straight to the kind of symbolic interpretation
given to moly by the Neoplatonists. According to these, moly
stood for the παιδεία, the spiritual education of man that would
enable him to raise the power of the light within him and so dispel
the darkness of his earthly and sensual being. Hermes, the guide of

---

[1] Synesius, *Hymnus*, III, ll. 558–67 and 592–8 (PG, 66, 1601 f.).

souls points the way and grants the strength, for Hermes is the logos. He leads towards the light or plunges us into the darkness, he is *ad utrumque peritus.*

In the *Alexandra* of Lycophron—a distant Alexandrine prelude with, as yet, no trace of Platonism—it is stated that moly is a protection against the malignant powers of evil.[1] The fact is that, in sharp contrast with the enlightened scepticism of the Stoics, those men of antiquity who were truly struggling towards the heights had preserved a kind of instinct for the presence of demonic powers and malignant magic and felt the need to safeguard themselves against these things by heavenly aid.

The idea that it is heaven that thus combats the infernal comes out even in the fables of Hyginus who makes Circe aware of the fact that a supernatural power is acting when Mercury gives Odysseus the remedial herb: "*Tunc Circe intellexit non sine divina voluntate deorum id esse factum.*"[2] The mockers might smile or drag down the Homeric myth into the shallow mud of their obscene verses—one such case is to be found in the *Priapea*[3]—but for the pious a deep human secret lay concealed beneath the poet's fancy. Moly, the gift of Hermes is, as Philostratus once says, the symbol of "fellowship with the logos and of spiritual striving".[4] Moly is a specific against spiritual darkness and against the demons who are the enemies of God.

At this point we could very usefully turn our attention to Plutarch, for he has described this late Platonic theology better

---

[1] *Alexandra*, 678 f. (Kinkel, p. 29). Cf. G. H. Hermann, *Opuscula*, V, Leipzig, 1834, pp. 242 f.; *Realenzyklopädie*, XIII, col. 2340, ll. 32–40.

[2] *Fabulae*, 125, 8 (Rose, p. 90).

[3] *Priapea*, 68, 21 f. (Baehrens, *Poetae Latini Minores*, I, pp. 81 f.):

> Hic legitur radix, de qua flos aureus exit
> quam cum moly vocant, mentula moly fuit.

It is worth noting here that the poet calls the "white" flower of moly "*flos aureus*" or "golden flower". This recalls a remark of Pliny's (*Hist. Nat.*, XXV, 26), that Greek flower-painters painted the flower of moly yellow (*luteum*). Obviously white and gold are interchangeable, both being the symbol of "light". How far all this is connected with the "gold-flower" of the alchemists under which head the chrysanthemum and moly are to be reckoned, I am unable to say; cf. C. G. Jung, *Psychology and Alchemy*, English edition, London, 1953, p. 75, note 30. Presumably the "*flos citrinus*" of the plant "*lunatica*" or "*berissa*" also belongs to this category; this last will be discussed later in connexion with the mandrake.

[4] *Heroicus*, 665 (Kayser, p. 134).

than any other writer and shown how the Greeks who professed
it saw man as one standing between God and the demons. It is
Plutarch who has given us one of the most informative accounts
of the symbolism of moly.

In his book on Isis and Osiris Plutarch discusses the problem of
the dualistic opposition with which man is faced in the sublunar
world, the opposition between good and evil, between darkness
and light. He shows us what the Pythagoreans thought about the
matter, he tells what Plato had to say concerning it and how the
Egyptian myths of bright Osiris gave expression to it. Man is
possessed of an immense longing to ascend into the blessed domain
of Osiris:

"To the souls of men here below, enclosed as they are in a body
and subject to its passions, it is impossible to attain to God's
fellowship; only with the aid of philosophy can they dimly and
as in a dream conceive of him. As soon however as, having freed
themselves from their bonds, they have been transported to that
invisible and imperishable sanctuary, this God is their Lord and
king and they cleave to him and look upon his beauty with
unassuageable desire, a beauty no man can express."[1]

The personification of those dark powers which hinder man's
ascent to this place is Typhon-Seth to whom all harmful herbs
and beasts are subject. The mediator of man's ascent on the other
hand is Horus, the child of Osiris, who is really the Hermes of
Egypt, and on the feast of Hermes, the nineteenth of Thoth,
people eat honey and say, "Sweet is the truth."[2]

Now Plutarch, as becomes a unifying and generalizing expounder of religious psychology, finds a myth of wholly similar
structure among the Persians: Ahura Mazda is the light, Ahriman
the darkness, while Mithras "stands in between the two and is
therefore called the mediator by the Persians".[3] To protect themselves against the powers of darkness, so Plutarch tells us, the
Persians offer a sacrifice to Ahriman. The text, as given by most
editors, reads as follows in translation:

[1] *De Iside et Osiride*, 78 (382 F; 383 A).
[2] *Ibid.*, 68 (378 B).
[3] *Ibid.*, 46 (369 E).

"The Persians, calling on Hades and the dark, pound a certain herb in a mortar; the herb is called omomi. They mix it with the blood of a slaughtered wolf and the mixture is then thrown away in a place upon which the sun does not shine."[1]

This practice, Plutarch expressly tells us, had been taught the Persians by the mediator Mithras.

Now what is this strange herb omomi? In my opinion Paul de Lagarde was here once again on the right track.[2] He has shown that the quite nonsensical word omomi, for the existence of which there is no other evidence at all, is merely a copyist's faulty transcription of moly. Indeed Bernardakis in his edition of Plutarch actually inserts the word moly here, though whether he does this simply relying on Lagarde's conjecture or because he has found other evidence in some manuscript, I do not know,[3] and we must leave it at that.

Actually Plutarch may here be factually quite accurate. Let us cast our minds back for a moment to the Cappadocian tradition which we find in Dioscurides, according to which moly, mountain rue, harmala and the Syrian besasa were all one and the same thing. If this is correct, then moly, even if it originally lacked a botanical identity, must be held in the course of time to have acquired one. Bearing this in mind let us note another interesting fact. In Cappadocia there was a Persian colony in which the religious practices of the old Persian homeland lived on. Plutarch had heard of it, "and so," says Lagarde, "he must have got his information from a writer who knew of the Persian cult in Cappadocia. No doubt the region had before this known Iranian religious ceremonies, but these did not become a matter of special note to the Greeks until the Saka settled there in approximately 130 B.C. and revitalized these institutions."

So then, although there can be no question of connecting etymologically the form *omomi* with the Persian *hôm*, there is, nevertheless, an objective identity between them. What Plutarch,

[1] *Ibid.*, 46 (369 E).
[2] "Die persischen Glossen der Alten" (*Gesammelte Abhandlungen*, Leipzig, 1866, pp. 172 ff.).
[3] Bernardakis, II, Leipzig, 1889, p. 519, l. 21.

in his account, calls moly, is none other than the Persian herb hôm. "Now, Arabian botanists describe a species of harmal—which, as we have seen, is moly—in exactly the same way as the Persians describe hôm: as a shrub with leaves that resemble those of the willow and flowers like jasmine blossoms . . . we see what an excellent substitute moly was for those who no longer had any hôm."[1]

It is, however, reasonable to suppose that Plutarch was led to write as he did not by reason of similarities in actual botanical character but rather because of the way in which the pious Persian regarded the plant in question. Hopfner shows that hôm for the Persian was a "symbol of heavenly nourishment. According to the *Avesta* the plant wards off death, is a protection against evil spirits and ensures the hope of heaven."[2] That Plutarch should have been so ready to identify moly with hôm, using this link as a means of integrating the Persian theological system into his own, shows how great was the significance attached by the later Neoplatonists to Homer's story of the moly of Hermes. Like the Persian hôm, the soul-healing flower of the Cyllenian mediator makes certain the ascent into the divine kingdom of light, and victory over all the powers of darkness. By offering up its black root it is made possible to ban the demon. Man becomes as the blossom of Osiris and mounts into the heavenly light; "for", says Plutarch, "Ahura Mazda is purest light".

The subsequent elaboration of the symbolism of moly is the work of the Neoplatonists in their most fully developed phase. The rare and heavenly gift of moly, says Themistius in one of his speeches,[3] is the heavenly *paideia* by which man, while yet here below, prepares himself for the final ascent into the light. Moly is self-control, circumspection in conduct and that ascetical form of life that has a bitter, black root but a flower that is white and sweet.

The anonymous writer who has left us an allegorical account of the wanderings of Odysseus—those lofty prefigurations of every phase of spiritual ascent—interprets the myth as follows: "Odys-

[1] Lagarde, *op. cit.*, p. 174.   [2] *Offenbarungszauber*, I, p. 127.
[3] *Oratio* XXVII (Petavius, p. 340, A/D). Cf. also *Oratio* XXVI (p. 330 B).

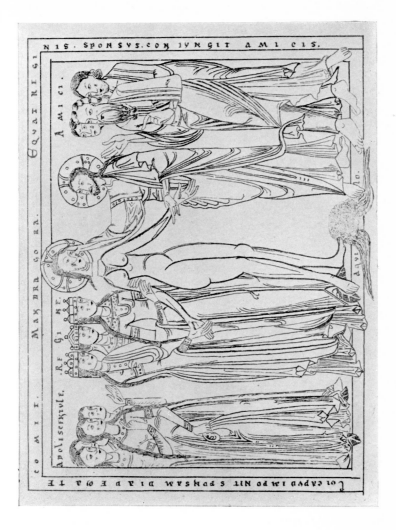

7. The Coronation of Queen Mandragora

From a twelfth-century Miniature, Munich MS Clm 5118 (Honorius' *Commentary on the Song of Songs*)

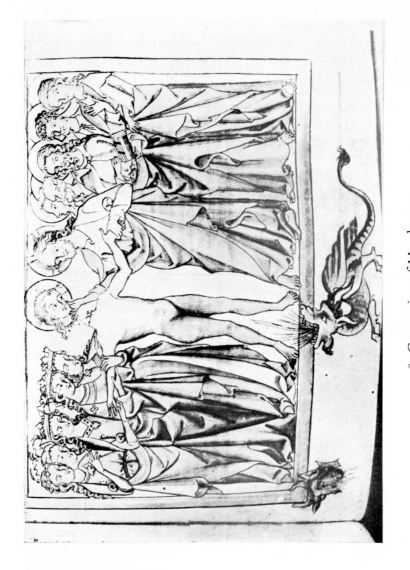

8. Coronation of Mandragora

Miniature of 1301 from St Florian, Codex XI, 80 (Goldschmidt Collection, Basle, Kunstmuseum)

seus, we think, represents the sovereign spirit of our soul, τὸν ἡγεμόνα νοῦν τῆς ψυχῆς, the island of Aeaea the mournful land of earthly wickedness that brings so many tears, Circe the sorceress of ever-changing form is the image of evil, logos-deprived lust. But he who has received the holy physic battles bravely against Circe and is at length changed for the better and raised to the heights of virtue."[1]

And now, at the very end of the process, so to speak, there comes yet a further development in the interpretation of the Homeric myth, and one which makes the symbolism of this soul-healing plant more vivid and impressive. We can see this in the statement of Ptolemaeus Hephaestion: "As to the plant moly that is mentioned by Homer, it is said that its root is made to grow by the blood of the giant who was killed on Circe's island, but it also has a white flower because he who was the helper of Circe and the killer of the giant was none other than Helios himself. This was a difficult and wearying (μῶλος) battle, however, and it is from this that the plant derives its name."[2]

There seems to be some uncertainty about the origin of this myth of the giant-killing,[3] but it was a favourite of the later phases of antiquity because it so admirably symbolized the dual spiritual nature of man, and Photius was still to copy the story from Ptolemaeus.[4] With this we come to the end of our account of the manner in which the symbolic interpretation of the moly story developed under the Greeks, and we will let Eustathius, that great collector of Homeric allegories, have the last word in this matter:

"Here is the essence of the allegory. By Hermes Homer most tellingly indicates the logos and by moly he indicates *paideia*, our spiritual education that is to say; for this can only be developed with great travail, ἐκ μώλου, and by means of suffering and misfortune. The root of moly is black because the beginnings of *paideia* are always dark as shadows and extraordinarily ill-formed.

[1] *Epitomos Diegesis*, 5 (*Mythographi Graeci*, ed. A. Westermann, p. 335, ll. 16-35).

[2] *Mythographi Graeci*, p. 190, ll. 17-22.

[3] It has even been suggested that there was a fraudulent invention by Ptolemaeus Chennus; see W. H. Roscher, *Mythol. Lexikon*, III (1902-9), col. 2506.

[4] *Bibliotheca*, 190 (PG, 103, 620 C).

Therefore our spiritual development is as the carrying of a heavy load and in no wise sweet. Yet moly has a flower and it is white as milk, for the end that *paideia* aims at and seeks to achieve, lies before us in gleaming brightness and all is sweet and satisfying. Hermes it is who gives us this moly, and this is nothing less than those logos-inspired directives which do not by any means lie ready for the human understanding to grasp. For moly comes from God and is a gracious gift."[1]

Then Eustathius—incidentally giving Themistius as his authority—speaks of the ascetic features of this spiritual process of healing. It is difficult, he says, to draw this root out of the ground, especially if you are trying to free it down to the uttermost tip of every fibre, "for the delicate ends of any *paideia*—and any virtue—are difficult to discover". Moreover, this is a mortally dangerous venture, and to confirm that statement the writer follows a train of thought of which we can find traces in the *Scholia Graeca*[2] and of which I shall have a great deal more to say when I come to deal with mandragora. It is reported, he says, that digging for the moly root can bring death to the rhizotomist who sets heedlessly about his task—a highly perceptive description of the rhizotomist of the soul whose attempts at healing can bring death as well as life: he too is *ad utrumque peritus*.

Finally Eustathius develops the story of the battle with the giant in much greater detail than Ptolemaeus. Picolous the giant, he relates, had become inflamed with love for Circe and had sought to steal her from her island, but Father Helios came to his daughter's aid and killed him. "And out of the blood of the giant that ran into the earth grew moly, which acquired its name from the 'labour' of battle, but its white flower that gleams like milk comes from shining Helios who was the victor. The black root grew from the black blood of the giant. Another explanation is that Circe paled with terror."

We now gain a deeper understanding of the meaning of Emperor Leo the Wise's poem that I quoted at the beginning of

---

[1] *In Odysseam*, 1658 (ed. Leipzig, 1825, p. 381, ll. 9–16).

[2] *Scholia Graeca in Odysseam* (Dindorf, II, p. 467, ll. 17 f.): φασὶν θάνατον ἐπιφέρειν τῷ ἀνασπῶντι. For this reason Eustathius compares moly with the equally dangerous mandrake (p. 381, ll. 29–31).

this forgotten chapter of Greek spiritual history because I thought it would set you in the mood for what was to come. The eternal Odysseus stands between bright Helios and the dark cave. Deep within him rages the battle between the black blood of the giant and the shining part of him that belongs to the sun. He himself is the moly with the black root and the white flower, but he can only be healed, saved and lifted up into the light when both strength and caution have been successfully used to loosen the luxuriant root and free it from Mother Earth. Hermes alone can teach this divine art, "for moly comes from God and is a gracious gift".

3

Let us now try to put the necessary Christian brush-strokes upon this spiritual canvas of Odysseus and the Hermetic herb. It should by now be clear to what a considerable degree in thought and prayer this late Hellenic culture, regarding man as one placed midway between God and daemon and as one who, under the guidance of the logos, was homeward bound towards the light, constituted a most effective *paideia* towards Christ. Justin, the apologist, who held that all who truly lived according to the Logos were Christians in secret,[1] did not hesitate to use the figure of Hermes-Logos to help the Greeks towards a better understanding of what he had to tell concerning the Mediator that was made man. If that is so, then we too, who stand in the light of certain knowledge concerning the new and different thing brought us by Christian revelation, may surely use this same Greek freedom in enquiring into the Christian transformation of the Homeric myth. The fruits of this enquiry will perhaps be less abundant than those we shall gather later when we deal with the plant mandragora, but a few contributions will nevertheless be offered to the as yet unwritten history of ancient Christian psychotherapy.

For the Christian too, in an infinitely more precise sense, stands between God and daemon, between heaven and hell. His bodily nature embedded in the earthly, he stands within the power of the Prince of this world and must ever, by exhausting ascetic practice, be freeing himself from the powers of darkness;

[1] *Apologia*, I, 46 (Otto, I, p. 128).

only thus may he lift himself towards the light. He is on the supernatural plane a rhizotomist of the root of his own soul. Yet he has as his guide the Logos that was made man, and in the latter's person and gospel he possesses the "physic of everlasting life".

At the end of his *Stromata*[1] Clement of Alexandria describes this Christian situation, and it is here that the Homeric myth comes once more into his mind, a mind that had been so palpably moulded by the culture of Greece; but this time the meaning of the myth is new. Clement is concerned to explain the ideal of the true Catholic gnosis and to substitute it for the false Gnosis which, basing itself on an interpretation of the Gospel which was little more than self-glorification, taught that man by his own power could force his way into the realm of heavenly light. The Christian is a wayfarer towards his eternal rest; he has left behind him "the life that is turned towards the things of sense"; but the ascent towards that rest is "weary and strait". There, then, stands man with his κρίσις his power of spiritual choice. He stands, as Clement says, between Logos and lust. In some cases he follows the Logos, who seeks to "grasp" him and lead him on. In others he surrenders to his passions.

In all this, of course, we touch upon a truth dimly intimated to Plato. It is that man never was and never will be a simple, homogeneous entity, fashioned by nature into a completed thing of beauty, though this was what the smooth, plausible and supposedly self-evident doctrine of the Stoa declared—and Stoics of all ages have held the same opinion. Man will always be a divided creature, wooed at one and the same time by beasts and angels, a compound of giant's blood and of the light of Helios. He is, in Clement's Christian idiom, either a man of God or a beast of the demon. In this consists his "crisis", and his spiritual health can only be ensured if he becomes a decided ἐραστὴς τῆς ἀληθείας, a man in love with the truth that comes from above. But for this he also needs help from above, help that takes the form both of knowledge and power, and the result of this spiritual guidance which God vouchsafes is, in Clement's striking phrase, a ψυχικὴ

---

[1] *Stromata*, VII, 16, 93–5 (GCS, III, pp. 66–8).

εὐτονία, a spiritual eutony,[1] a vigorous harmony of the soul, the flexible and yet hard and nervous strength that is the mark of a thing truly alive.

The essential thing in this Christian-gnostic psychotherapy is the realization that knowledge and power cannot attain such a eutony from out of man himself; such eutony can only come from above. Man's soul can only be healed within him through obedience to a higher power. In the Christian fulfilment this means obedience to the audible message of God brought by the Mediator, and which, in the Gospels, of which the visible Church is the guardian and expounder, is placed before the "crisis" of man.

Here then we have the Christian transformation of the myth of Hermes and Odysseus and it seizes upon the truth which is fundamental to all true therapy of souls, that man, if he is to be made whole and become a creature of the light, must be guided by the overwhelming truth that comes from above—by the Logos himself. Clement utters what is really the last word on this subject when he says, "It is inevitable that those who attempt the heaviest tasks fall into the greatest errors, unless they receive the rule of truth from the Truth itself – τὸν κανόνα τῆς ἀληθείας παρ᾽ αὐτῆς λαβόντες τῆς ἀληθείας."

"From the Truth itself!" Here we have that essentially Christian meeting between homeward-faring man and the mediating Logos. Odysseus meets his Hermes, and the soul-saving physic which ensures that man shall not be turned into a beast is "the Truth itself". And now Clement once again harks back to the ancient myth:

"If a man were to be turned into a beast, like those who were bewitched by the poisons of Circe, he would be suffering much the same fate as those who give a kick to the tradition of the Church and light-heartedly caper away to the edifices of private opinion; for such men destroy their chances of being men of God and of remaining true to the Lord. Nevertheless he who turns his back upon such aberration, heeds the Scriptures, and turns his life once more towards the truth, such a one, from being a mere man,

[1] *Ibid.*, 94–5 (p. 67, l. 3): δεῖ τῷ τῆς ἀληθείας ἐραστῇ ψυχικῆς εὐτονίας.

is transformed, as it were, into a God. For ours is the source of all knowledge, namely the Lord himself who through the prophets, through his own joyful gospel and through the blessed apostles has spoken to us in numerous and manifold ways. From the first beginnings until the end he is the leader of gnosis."[1]

We need no elaborate apparatus of interpretation to understand the above text which is profound theologically and yet indicates with a certain Hellenic elegance the evangelical truth hidden in the Homeric myth. It is no more than an indication, of course. Like fleeting sketches, like pictures glimpsed in passing on a Greek vase, Hermes, Odysseus and the bewitched companions of Odysseus are seen for a moment and are gone; the saving role of moly is not as much as mentioned, but then everybody would know about that. It is only in what I might term the companion picture in which he speaks directly of Christianity that we can discern his unspoken thoughts. Christ is the true, the only Hermes, ὁ ἡγούμενος τῆς γνώσεως the leader who is filled with and rules over and dispenses knowledge. His soul-saving gift is the moly of the Gospel. And the effect of this physic is to achieve the mystical *teleiosis* in which man becomes a partaker in the divine nature, and is at length wholly saved from his threatened fate of being turned into a beast. Never again in Christian symbolism was such honour to be accorded to the immortal flower moly as was given it by Clement when he compared it to the glad tidings of the Gospel.

If Clement sees fit in his battle with the Gnostics to demonstrate the true nature of Catholic gnosis by means of imagery taken from the Homeric myth, it is because he has a definite apologetic object in view, for everybody knew that the Gnostic teachers outside the fold were very fond of delving into that source. An excellent example of this is the Gnostic system that in the second and third centuries proudly named itself after that Simon Magus of whom we are told a little in the Acts of the Apostles. It is true that scholars now tell us that this late Simonian Gnosis had very little to do with this venerable father of all heretics, though a small

---

[1] *Stromata*, VII, 16, 95, 1-3 (GCS, III, p. 67, ll. 10-19).

number of scattered fragments may conjecturally be attributed to his pen.[1] The finished system itself, however, is well worth our attention, and Hippolytus has preserved great excerpts from its declarations of belief.[2] Allegories from Homer played an important part in the Pseudo-Simonian theosophy and its devotees attached great importance to a peaceful reconciliation between the Bible and the *Odyssey.*

I can only deal briefly with this matter,[3] but the main part in this system was played by Trojan Helen who was regarded as an embodiment of the aeon Epinoia. The latter in due course became the companion of Simon and was drawn upward out of the sensual in which she was sunk. Finally she was actually changed into Selene, the "All-mother and Wisdom".[4] Even the wooden horse acquires, thanks to the Simonites, a mystical significance, and Hippolytus gets quite angry when he talks about the matter: "With such silly little conceits", he says, "Simon has not only malignantly distorted the words of Moses but also those of the poets. He weaves allegories around the wooden horse and spins yarns about Helen with the torch and about a great many other things, all of which are supposed to refer to himself and his Epinoia."[5]

In this Simonian medley of Homer and Moses, in which we must by no means underrate the genuine appeal exercised by the hope of redemption which it promised, we once again encounter our little herb moly. The anonymous Gnostic who is the author of the movement's most important document—written probably in the second century—gives therein a somewhat startling interpretation of the books of Moses. There is apparently a secret meaning in Genesis which is really an allegory of the manner in which man

[1] Cf. L. Cerfaux, "La Gnose simonienne: nos sources principales", in *Recherches de science religieuse*, 16 (1926), pp. 16 ff. See also *Realenzyklopädie*, III A, 1 (1927), col. 180 ff. (H. Lietzmann).

[2] *Elenchus*, VI, 9–18 (GCS, III, pp. 136–45).

[3] See Irenaeus, *Adv. Haer.*, I, 23, 2–4 (Harvey, I, pp. 191–5); Philastrius, *Haer.*, 29 (CSEL, 38, pp. 14f.); Pseudo-Clement, *Homilia*, II, 25 (PG, 2, 93 AB), *Recognitiones*, II, 8–12 (PG, 1, 1251–4). On Homeric allegory in the Simonite system, see H. Waltz, *Realenzyklopädie für protestantische Theologie*, XVIII, Leipzig, 1906, p. 361.

[4] Pseudo-Clement, *Homilia*, II, 25 (PG, 2, 93 B): Παμμήτωρ καὶ σοφία. Cf. also W. H. Roscher, *Mythol. Lexikon*, I, col. 9171.

[5] *Elenchus*, VI, 19, 1 (GCS, III, p. 145, ll. 6–10).

is formed in his mother's womb. The book of Exodus, on the other hand, really reveals after the manner of a great myth the tragic destiny of all that are born of woman and hurled into this dark world of sense, there to fight their way through blood and bitterness into the promised land which is the home of their souls. Their leader on this journey is Moses, the Logos, who with his staff and his power turns all that is bitter into sweetness, even as Hermes gave moly to homeward-faring Odysseus. Let us listen to the principal passage in this Gnostic biblical *Odyssey*:

"The title of the second book of Moses is Exodus. All that are born must pass through the Red Sea—by Red Sea he means blood—and come to the desert where they must drink bitter water, for bitter is the water beyond the Red Sea and this indicates our life of toil and bitterness. Yet transformed by Moses, that is by the Logos, this bitterness is made sweet. That this is so is proved by the poet's words which we hear on every hand:

> 'the root was
> Black, and the flow'r milk-white, and the high gods moly have named it.
> Hard, forsooth, is its digging to mortal men, but the gods can Do all things.'

"What was then said by pagans is, for those who have ears to hear, sufficient to enable them to know all things. Only he who tasted of this fruit was not turned by Circe into a beast; nay, through the power of this plant he could even restore his companions, who had been turned into beasts, to their own original nature and form them anew. This man who was beloved of the poisoner was by means of this milk-white divine flower proved true."[1]

If you reflect on what was said earlier about Homeric allegory among the Greeks, it should not be too difficult to discern behind these rather wild and fanciful edifices of Simonian Gnosis the

[1] *Elenchus*, VI, 15, 3-16, 2 (GCS, III, p. 141, l. 16-p. 142, l. 5).

late Platonic interpretation of our myth, for the basic premise of the whole system is the assumption that all things came into being through the δύναμις μεγάλη, the great primal power, as from some Heraclitan fire, and that all things must return to that fire after the birth of infinitely manifold aeons. But all this takes place within the human soul, "in that place where the root of all things is to be found".

"This place", says Hippolytus in his further exposition, "is according to Simon, man himself, begotten of blood, and in him dwells the infinite power which is the root of all things—ή ρίζα τῶν ὅλων."[1] It is in line with this general train of thought that the Exodus should, like the *Odyssey*, be simply a drama of the human soul. As to the root moly, this springs from the root of the "all" and the way shown by Hermes-Moses-Logos is the way of release, the homecoming and discovery of the spiritual spark of fire—we are reminded here of the moly mysticism of Maximus of Tyre—, the refashioning out of the beast he has become, of man, the divine, into his original form.

Clement, the Catholic gnostic, and Simon, the Gnostic who achieves his own redemption, Clement for whom moly is the Gospel of the Christian Church, Simon for whom it is the inner spark of fire—here are the two great classical antitypes that symbolize the tremendous struggle which in the third century was finally decided in favour of the Church.

In the fourth century there came into being an entirely new form of supernatural soul-therapy. It was monasticism. A veritable army fled into the desert in order to fight their way out of this demoniacally dark world into the realm of heavenly light. In the words of Boethius they felt they were "between mud and the stars"[2] and they sought by the leading of an angelic life to save their humanity and safeguard themselves from being turned into beasts. This βίος ἀγγελικός, this angelic life of theirs was to be the closest possible imitation of the Logos who was the *Angelos* in person.

We possess an engaging illustration of the manner in which

---

[1] *Ibid.*, 9, 4 (GCS, III, p. 136, ll. 18–21).
[2] *Philosophiae Consolatio*, IV, 4, 29 (CSEL, 67, p. 92, l. 9).

moribund paganism reacted to the flourishing of this vigorous new religion which had found in monasticism a fresh expression of its vitality. The pagan poet Rutilius Namatianus is sailing past a small island close to Pisa, on which a friend of his who had become a Christian had "buried himself alive". Rutilius now begins to grumble at the Church, this new Circe, this "sect" which has robbed him of his friend and turned him into a beast, even as Circe had turned the companions of Odysseus:

> *Num, rogo, deterior Circaeis secta venenis?*
> *Tunc mutabantur corpora, nunc animi.*

(Is not, I ask, this sect more evil than all the poisons of
    Circe?
Once it was bodies that were changed, now it is men's
    souls.)[1]

Perhaps this friend, when he read these words on his new Aeaea, thanked the Logos for lifting the evil spell from the world, and took into his hands the new moly of the Logos' heavenly message.

Yet to gain a true appreciation of the spiritual change that had taken place when monasticism was born, we should really have to study at no inconsiderable length the profound theological ideas and spiritual techniques that we find described in the monastic writings of antiquity. Here I can do little more than give a sketch of these things. Actually we could learn much, simply by reading that profound chapter of Origen[2] in which he seeks to show that the beasts are, so to speak, visible symbols, embodiments of human passions, that the animal kingdom still lies, as it were, under the dominion of the Satanic powers as an unredeemed part of creation and meanwhile serves as a mirror for unredeemed daemonic forces that lie dormant and threatening within the human soul. Contrariwise, it is one of the chief pieces of ancient monastic wisdom that the true gnostic who has overcome the beast within himself by the angel, not only acquires spiritual power over

[1] *De Reditu suo*, 525f. (Baehrens, *Poetae Latini Minores*, V, p. 23).
[2] *Contra Celsum*, IV, 93 (GCS, I, pp. 366f.). Cf. incidentally Plato, *Phaedo*, 81 E and 82 A; Clement of Alexandria, *Protrepticus*, I, 4 (GCS, I, p. 5, ll. 6ff.).

demons, but also possesses an ability to transfigure and change the nature of beast and plant. He becomes, in fact, like a beam sent out ahead of the redemption that is to come, the redemption of all creation.[1]

And this brings me to my final example from Christian antiquity of the theology that was developed round the Homeric myth. In this case our debt is to Boethius and to his twilight song of the *Consolations of Philosophy*, in the clear Christian glow of which Homer and Plato stand transfigured. Since all that is, is good—so Philosophy instructs her captive friend—everything that is evil ceases, in a perfectly real sense, to be. The wicked man continues to appear human, but only to the fleshly eye; in reality he has become a beast; for the soul, having been born out of God, is fashioned to become divine; if it falls short of this, it turns into a beast; there is no "no man's land" in the realm of the soul. Boethius condenses all this into a classical sentence which like a fine seed-corn carries within itself the germinal power of a thousand years of Greek and Christian spirituality: "*Ita fit, ut qui, probitate deserta, homo esse desierit, cum in divinam condicionem transire non possit, vertatur in beluam*—So it is that he who leaves virtue aside and so ceases to be a man, such a one, because he cannot enter into the divine state, is turned into a beast."[2]

And here Boethius takes up the lyre to sing one of those lovely songs of his which interrupt his prose much as the chorus interrupts the spoken dialogue in a Greek play. There rises before his mind Homer's immortal story of Odysseus, Hermes and the bewitched companions turned into beasts. The poem[3] opens with a description of the island over which Helios' daughter, mighty in magic, sits enthroned, and shows us the different kinds of beasts into which her poisons had caused men to be changed. Odysseus alone, the

---

[1] Cf. J. Bernhardt, *Heilige und Tiere* (Saints and Animals), Munich, 1937, a book that contains a mass of ancient Christian evidence "for the mysterious sympathy between holy people and animals, between what is highest and lowest in the domain of the soul" (Preface). Cf. also R. Reitzenstein, *Hellenistische Wundererzählungen* (Hellenistic Miracle Tales), Berlin, 1906.

[2] IV, 3, 25 (CSEL, 67, p. 87, ll. 17–19). This is preceded by a detailed description of various animals that are considered to stand in special relation with human passions—a sketch of a kind of psychic zoology.

[3] IV, 3, *Metrum*, "*Vela Neritii ducis*" (CSEL, 67, pp. 87f.).

man proved by suffering, escapes this fate—thanks to the gift of
Hermes:

> *Sed licet variis malis*
> *Numen Arcadis alitis*
> *Obsitum miserans ducem*
> *Peste solverit hospitis . . .*

(But though the divine mind of the winged Arcadian god took
compassion on the chieftain weighed down with so many sufferings and set him free of the poisons of his hostess . . .)

Surely those words, "*Numen miserans Arcadis alitis*", the divine
mind that pities, are a most touching farewell to the Greek god,
and we leave him in the act of setting free from "the poisons of his
hostess", a man who is both a sufferer and a leader. We know of
what the merciful gift consisted; it was the soul-healing flower
moly.

Boethius never expressly mentions the Hermetic herb, but the
interpretation of the myth which now follows shows us what he
sees symbolized in moly. Odysseus' comrades have become victims
of the poison of Circe. Even now they are feeding on acorns "and
nothing remains to them that is incorrupt". How wonderfully
he describes the spiritual effects of this poisoning:

> *Haec venena potentius*
> *Detrahunt hominem sibi*
> *Dira quae penitus meant,*
> *Nec nocentia corpori*
> *Mentis vulnere saeviunt.*

(This dread poison is even more powerful
To tear a man's own self out of him
That penetrates to the depths of his being.
Nor does poison for the body
Rage more terribly than this wound of the mind.)

Only one physic is effective against it—moly, the ascent of the
good man to those heights of the divine to which his innermost
nature is destined. Odysseus only is able, through the help of

Hermes, to withstand what is bestial; this is to interpreted in the sense that only the spirit that has conquered the bestial within himself is the victor: *Sola mens stabilis super monstra.* And so Boethius breaks into the paean of victory for the divine man against whom the magic herbs of Circe have no effect because the power of the Logos is supreme within the citadel of his soul:

> *O levem nimium manum*
> *Nec potentia gramina,*
> *Membra quae valeant licet*
> *Corda vertere non valent.*
> *Intus est hominum vigor*
> *Arce conditus abdita.*

> (O thou hand that art too feeble
> O ye herbs that are powerless
> Ye can change men's bodies
> But their hearts ye cannot change
> The strength of a man lies within
> Safe in his inner citadel.)

We must read right to the end of the *Consolations of Philosophy* if we are to form a conception of the manner in which Boethius pursues this theme of the upward rising of the good man under guidance from the Logos. Once again he calls in review before us all the patient sufferers of antiquity who rise upward to that love which is the cause of all things. "For nothing endures for ever, unless it re-direct once more its love and flow back to that cause which gave it being."

> *Quia non aliter durare queant*
> *Nisi converso rursus amore*
> *Refluant causae quae dedit esse.*[1]

But the ascent is difficult "and Odysseus wept".[2] Only he who is possessed of courage and so can overcome the things that pertain to earth and darkness, can hope to succeed in it. The immortal fourth book of the *Consolatio* sings antiquity's Christian farewell to the Homeric myth and it furnishes an end to this profound

[1] IV, 6, *Metrum*, verses 46-8 (CSEL, 67, p. 104).
[2] IV, 7, *Metrum*, verse 8 (CSEL, 67, p. 105).

theology of man's journey "from mud to the stars" with a challenge to man's spiritual courage:

"Follow then, ye brave men, where the steep path of good example leads you. Why do ye like cowards show your naked backs. Conquered earth gives you the stars."[1]

The story of moly symbolism in the Middle Ages and after makes rather a pitiful epilogue to all this, and when we set it beside the lyrical ecstasy with which the subject inspired antiquity, we may think rather poorly of it. For all that, I think I should reproduce its main outlines here so that you may see just how the black root and the white flower of this Hermetic herb found its way into the mysterious dens of the alchemists.

Naturally enough we encounter moly, and certain residual vestiges of the symbolism that surrounded it, wherever, thanks to tradition or a revived interest, the knowledge of Homer's *Odyssey* is still alive. First there are the Byzantines who had acquired a reasonably good acquaintance with the subject from Eustathius. There is, for instance, that improving and exceedingly dull writer John Tzetzes. The wiles of Circe, he insists, very much after the moralizing fashion of the Stoics, are the arts of the courtesan, but thanks to moly, Odysseus does not succumb to them, because the plant in his hand is endowed with counter-magic. "And taking up the moly he escaped from the whore's tricks of Circe."[2] To this Byzantine writer moly is nothing but just another magic herb and he mentions it in the same breath with "fleabane, buckthorn, ivy and a thousand other magical antidotes". Only once does he rise to a loftier view—when he speaks of moly as the symbol of wisdom.[3] Nicephorus Gregoras on the other hand simply says, "Hermes gave him moly. This is a herb which can be used as an antidote to magic."[4] Alas, the

[1] IV, 7, *Metrum*, verses 32–5 (CSEL, 67, p. 106): "*superata tellus sidera donat*"; this is the essence of the Platonic-Christian idea of the ascent of the soul.

[2] *Allegoriae in Odysseam*, X, verses 30–2 (ed. P. Matranga, *Anecdota Graeca*, I, Rome, 1850, p. 280).

[3] *Ibid.*, verses 113f. (Matranga, I, p. 283). Tzetzes also publishes the ancient allegories on moly in the *Scholia* on Lycophron, 679 (ed. Müller, II, Leipzig, 1811, p. 735).

[4] *Narratio Errorum Ulyssis* (Matranga, II, p. 528, ll. 2–7).

soul-healing plant seems to have got dried up in these Byzantine herbaria.

There is a change when we get to the humanists. The Greek Christophorus Contoleonti wrote a *Prothesis* to the *Odyssey* in which he sought to establish that Homer in his poems had tried to teach "the best kind of life – ἄριστος βίος". The superhuman misfortunes of the Ithacan were meant as a picture of the human soul, and showed that man could only overcome such dangers as those encountered by Odysseus from Circe, by the divine power of the heavenly light.[1] The humanists north of the Alps were soon affected by the Homeric enthusiasms of their Italian friends and when Simon Lemnius published the first Latin translation of the *Odyssey* in Basle, he prefaced it with a spirited poem, in which he treats the voyages of Odysseus as an allegory on human life. Here is part of the poem in translation; we can detect in it faint echoes of the ancient interpretations.

> Then he came to Circe's coasts
> Where he saw his companions shamefully transformed into swine.
> But the cunning moly defeated the Titanic monsters
> And at the bidding of the hero they were turned back into men.
> True that Circe had bewitched the bodies of his companions,
> Yet over Odysseus, and him alone, she had no power;
> For moly is wisdom which conquers all dangers
> If the sword and victorious courage be united to it.[2]

And now even earnest professors of Scripture become bitten with a desire to parade their classical erudition. The Jesuit, Benedict Pereira, for instance, contrives to smuggle the herb moly into his commentary on Genesis. In a lofty disputation about the tree of life in Paradise, he enumerates all the instances to be found in the literature of antiquity of plants that are supposed to produce spiritual healing—and, like the philosopher Justin, he asserts that the Greeks had got their facts from the books of Moses. The

---

[1] *Prothesis in Odysseam* (Matranga, II, pp. 504f.).

[2] *Odysseae Homeri libri XXIV, nuper a Simone Lemnio Emporico Rheto Curiensi heroico Latino carmine facti*, Basiliae, 1549, apud Oporinum, p. 34* of the introductory poem to the Connétable de Montmorency.

most wonderful of all these herbs, he insists, is Hermes' moly: "*Eodem spectat moly herba laudatissima Homero, homines ad iuventutem revocans, cuius vires Plinius multis verbis describit*—In the same class is moly, a herb greatly praised by Homer; it has the power to restore youth and its efficacy was described at great length by Pliny."[1]

So we come to a most charming book, which to some extent brings us into the spiritual neighbourhood of the alchemists whose day had also now returned. It is the first German translation of the *Odyssey*, the work of the good Simon Schaidenreisser, published in Augsburg in 1537. There the hero Ulysses appears as the embodiment of all human virtues. But his power comes to him from Mercury, no longer the ancient god but a star. The moly of his propitious horoscope enables him to overcome all dangers and temptations. I will let Schaidenreisser speak for himself in his own sixteenth-century German:

"*Ulysses ist von wein, wollust, lieb, von wind, Fortunen, mörwundern und von den Göttern selbst unüberwunden geblieben, vermittels des hailwertigsten krauts Moly (das ist die Weisheit), welche dem edlen blut und theuren Ulyssi anfenklich von oben herab, von dem gnadenreichen kunstmilten Planeten oder gestirn Mercurio durch mitwürckung Minervae eingegossen und eingepflantzt ware. . . . Moly das ist die weissheit; durch das kraut Moly verstehen wir die mannheit und tugent Ulyssis, die er von Mercurio empfangen und damit alle gefärligkeiten, auch verfürischen reitzungen der wollust obgesiegt hat, wie Tyrius Maximus schreibt.*"[2]

The above passage has been quoted at some length for the benefit of such readers as have an acquaintance with the German tongue. The chief interest of its content is that moly has become not a mere antidote of the poisons of Circe but the chief source of the hero's success in surmounting all his other difficulties, perils

---

[1] *Commentariorum et Disputationum in Genesim, Tomi IV*, Mayence, 1612, No. 79, p. 109.

[2] *Odyssea: Das seind die allerzierlichsten und lustigsten vier und zwantzig bücher des eltisten kunstreichsten Vatters aller poeten Homeri von der zehen jährigen irrfart des weltweisen griechischen fürstens Ulissis. Übersetzt von Simon Schaidenreisser* (These are the most graceful and merry four and twenty volumes of the oldest and most cunning father of all poets Homer concerning the ten-year wanderings of the worldly-wise Greek duke Ulysses, translated by Simon Schaidenreisser), Augsburg, 1537, p. 2* of the Preface.

and temptations. This is not surprising since moly is wisdom. It is the gift of Mercury who is no longer a god, however, but has become a planet. We thus pass from magic proper to the field of astrology and from there the distance to the herb gardens of the alchemists is not very great, nor is it remarkable that we should come across moly in that locality. Moly simply suffered the same fate as its own god Hermes and all the other figures and symbols who, being exiled from the sunlit realms of the conscious mind, lived on—and not so ineffectually at that—in the enchanted groves of "the kingly art".

In the true literature of alchemy moly becomes the symbol of that highly prized and eagerly desired end-product of all such "chemistry"—the philosopher's stone, the tincture of mercury. Stolcius in a Latin verse in his *Viridarium Chymicum* speaks of moly growing in the garden of Hermes next to other magic plants:

Hinc Hyacinthus adest, Vitis, Lunaria, Moly.[1]

The juxtaposition of moly and lunaria is noteworthy. There will be more to say on the subject when we come to examine the symbolism of mandragora.

We can learn more of the significance of moly for the alchemist from Michael Maier's *Septimana Philosophica*.[2] In this work the Queen of Sheba has a conversation with Solomon—an expert herbalist among his other attainments—concerning the secrets of the plants that pertain to the alchemist's art, a conversation which she starts with the engaging opening gambit: "For long I have had in my nostrils the scent of the herb moly which became so celebrated thanks to the poets of old. Does this moly perhaps possess a special 'chymical' property?" To which Solomon replies:

"This plant is entirely 'chymical'. It is said that Odysseus used it to protect himself against the poisons of Circe and the perilous

---

[1] Daniel Stolcius de Stolcenberg, *Viridarium Chymicum*, Frankfurt, 1624, Plate XXX. Cf. on this J. Read, *Prelude to Chemistry. An Outline of Alchemy, its Literature and Relationships*, London, 1939, p. 259.

[2] Michael Maier(us), *Septimana Philosophica, qua Aenigmata Aureola de omni Naturae Genere a Salomone Israelitarum sapientissimo Rege . . . enodantur* (The Philosophic Week in which the Golden Mysteries of all the Orders of Nature are unravelled by Solomon the most Wise King of the Jews), Frankfurt, 1620, pp. 126f.

singing of the Sirens. It is also related that Mercury himself found
it and that it is an effective antidote to all poisons. It grows plenti-
fully on Mount Cyllene in Arcadia, which is Mercury's birth-
place, whence he is often named Cyllenius. We ourselves however
understand by mercury a certain metal or mineral and by moly
the sulphur that is released from mercury and prevents the artifex,
who here enacts the part of Odysseus, from lending his ears or
his mind to other formulae and other sophistical and misleading
advice."

It is highly interesting to note the manner in which the ancient
myth is applied here to a process that is at one and the same time
both "chymical" and psychological. The moly of the chemical
process that has been successfully concluded is also the symbol of
that inner certainty experienced by the adept in virtue of which
he becomes a master, a man who is no longer dependent on any
mere formula at all. The inner process has succeeded and Odysseus
is saved by the power of the white flower of Hermes. In the case
of other alchemist's treatises we may therefore also think of moly
when there is mention of the white flower or the "gold-flower".[1]
For instance, in the treatise *Der kleine Bauer* (The Little Peasant),
it is expressly stated that "the one little flower can take all shapes
and loves all planets. . . . This saying may be understood as follows:
Mercury, i.e. the white flower, can be used and applied to the
tincture of all planets."[2] Hermes and his soul-healing plant have at
last become one; both are a symbol of that spiritual return to
perfection and to the beginning, which the alchemist projects
into his "chymical" activity.

Alongside moly, a feature that we frequently encounter in the
literature of alchemy is the phoenix, and the two symbols have
what is virtually an identical meaning. The phoenix, rising from
its ashes into the light, is well known both in pagan and Christian
mythology. It is the mysterious symbol of the delivered soul, of

[1] Cf. C. G. Jung, *Psychology and Alchemy*, English edition, London, 1953, p. 75, note 30.
[2] *Ein philosophischer und chemischer Traktat, genannt Der kleine Bauer . . . Von der Materia
und Erkenntnus des einigen und wahren subjecti universalis magni et illius praeparatione* (A
Philosophical and Chemical Tract called The Little Peasant concerning the Substance and
Knowledge of the one and true Great Universal Subject and its Preparation), Strasbourg,
1618, p. 215.

that birth into light which is the consummation of the ascent out of the dark chaos. Its significance is thus identical with that of the black root and white flower of moly. It is to the light that Mercury leads us—thus Prudentius had sung. It is from his own ashes that the phoenix rises towards it, even as moly's blossom rises from the black root. It was the process that Simonian Gnosis had spoken of as "reforming, transforming and refashioning into our own original nature". The liberated soul rises out of the world of matter into the spiritual; "from mud to the stars"—so went the journey of Boethius. By the power of the Hermetic flower the soul is changed from a beast to an angel, it finds its way back to that which God had purposed it to be when he created it, it takes once more the shape of that innermost man that dwells "deep in the fortress of its inmost being". If a man is possessed of moly, no poison can rob him of his "heart", said Boethius, and here for the last time we catch the echo of Homer's immortal verse that is now made to refer to the very ultimate in human perfection:

But thou bearest within thy breast a heart charmed and secure.
Truly thou art that agile-minded Odysseus
Of whom the god of the golden wand hath always spoken to
    me.[1]

If therefore, as Boethius says, the physic of Circe robs a man of his own true self, we may surely say that the physic of Hermes restores a man to his eternal I, and this, in the final analysis, is what the various practices of alchemy were seeking to achieve. All men are searching for the white flower of salvation.

I could here say more of the manner in which the pedagogy of the humanists who were contemporaries of the alchemists attempted the symbolic interpretation of moly, but Finsler's fine book on *Homer in the Modern Age from Dante to Goethe*[2] has told us about that. Let me therefore end my account of this lofty subject with a smile, and leave the final word to Roger Ascham, who declares that the best way of instilling a taste for Latin and the classics into young Englishmen is a journey to Italy and Rome.

[1] *Odyssey*, X, 329-31.
[2] *Homer in der Neuzeit von Dante bis Goethe*, Leipzig-Berlin, 1912, pp. 269, 281, 384f.

This, however, the anxious pedagogue declares, may prove a perilous venture all too like the voyages of Odysseus. Many a young Englishman, he alleges, had returned home with ruined morals, for the traveller might well find himself in the position where "some Circes shall make him of a plaine English man, a right Italian", and it had, alas, all too often proved true that "*Inglese italianato è un diabolo incarnato.*" From such a fate our young Englishman must at all costs be protected and the best antidote is nothing other than:

"That swete herbe Moly with the blake roote and white floore, [which is] given unto hym by Mercurie, to avoide all inchantmentes of Circes. Wherby the Divine Poete Homer ment covertlie (as wise and Godly men do iudge) that love of honestie and hatred of ill, which David more plainly doth call the feare of God: the onely remedie agaynst the inchantementes of sinne. The true medecine . . . is, in Homere, the herbe Moly, with the blacke roote, and white flooer, sower at the first, but sweete in the end . . . the divine Poete . . . sayth plainlie that this medicine against sinne and vanitie, is not found out by man, but given and taught by God."[1]

Thus, Roger Ascham with his *Odyssey* in one hand and his Psalter in the other—and the good schoolmaster is surely right; for that concluding sentence of his once again expresses the truth of which Plato was aware and which it was the crowning achievement of spiritual therapy, both pagan and Christian, to grasp and preserve in the symbolism of moly, for that symbolism does no more than restate the fact that man can only be made whole by something that is greater than himself, something that comes down to meet him from above, even as Hermes came with his soul-healing flower, and for the moly of true psychotherapy the words of that "sweet and divine" verse of Homer still hold true:

Hard, forsooth, is its digging to mortal men, but the gods can
Do all things.

[1] Roger Ascham, *The Scholemaster or plaine and perfite way of teachyng children, to understand, write, and speake, the Latin tong . . .*, London, 1570, ff. 24ᵛ-25ᵛ. (In Arber, *English Reprints*, 23, London, 1870, pp. 71-8.)

2 MANDRAGORA: THE EVERLASTING
ROOT OF MAN

Moly, the herb of Hermes, guide of souls, has led us upward to the very summits of Greek and Christian achievement in the therapy of souls, and we have followed the Logos in our journey 'twixt mud and the stars. We have now to study the symbolism connected with yet another flower, and that study will plunge us downward again into the very depths of the earth. Indeed the black root of mandragora, buried deep in Mother Gaia is the very antitype of the bright flower from Hermes' Cyllene. Mandragora is Circe's poison, it luxuriates in Hecate's magic garden, and no Greek could think of it without something of a shudder, a shudder we seem to feel in the Orphic song of the Argonauts when it tells of the loathsome herbs in the grove of the nocturnal goddess:

"Polium, mandragora, and pale dittany and crocus with sickly sweet scent."[1]

The magic voyage on which we are now embarking in our quest for mandragora, leads us to the fairy isle of Hypnos, the island of darkly rising dreams of which Lucian tells, "where nothing but tall poppies riot and mandragora blooms, where silent butterflies flit about, the only birds on the island".[2] The ancient symbolism connected with this plant will take us into the eerie depths of the dark, as we watch men digging from the earth in a grisly magic rite the black root that has a monstrous headless human form, to use it for the overcoming of all that is of the light within the human soul. And yet it is from the depths of this very darkness that Christian symbolism raises mandragora to heights that are sublime.

At first then mandragora—it will for the moment be more convenient to use the Latin name—is moly's antitype but at the end of this story of symbolism, a symbolism that pictures the healing of souls, all is unity: from the dark and earthy root an

[1] *Orph. Argonaut.*, 922f. (G. Hermann, Leipzig, 1805, p. 170). Cf. J. H. Dierbach, *Flora Mythologica*, Frankfurt, 1833, pp. 194f.
[2] *Verae Historiae*, II, 33 (Reitz, II, p. 128).

everlasting flower of light breaks forth. The Logos conquers. For
though the ancients once called mandragora morion, which means
the root of folly and of confusion in the soul,[1] though they saw in
it the essential "herb of Circe", the poisonous love charm and the
physic that turned men into beasts,[2] nevertheless this headless,
earthy growth ends by being crowned with the head of the
Logos, with wisdom that transfigures to all eternity, it thus becomes the symbol of an earth that has become heaven.

I shall arrange my superabundant material in the same fashion as
that pertaining to moly, in three groups. First I shall examine the
views held by antiquity about mandragora's botanical and medical
characteristics. Then I shall deal with the symbolism and magic
that paganism evolved in this connexion, and this will give me a
sort of plan which I can use in describing the Christian symbolism
that grew up around the plant, and it is of course this last to which
I attach the greatest importance; for it is a far richer thing than the
symbolism of moly and its theological ideas are much more profound, while the final apocalyptic vision of mandragora in which
this symbolism culminates, shows with a unique mingling of
clarity and loveliness all that can be read into the story of this
soul-healing flower.

I

Unlike that of moly the botanical identity of mandragora has
never been in any sort of doubt.[3] It grows all over the East, and

[1] Dioscurides, *De Materia Medica*, IV, 75, 7 (Wellmann, II, p. 233), μώριον; Pliny,
Nat. Hist., XXV, 147 (Mayhoff, IV, p. 164); *Corp. Gloss. Lat.*, III, 569 (Goetz): *moron,
id est mandragora*; Dioscurides Langobardus, IV, 72 (ed. H. Stadler, p. 42, ll. 11f.):
"Morion grows in shady hollows, it drives men mad and induces deep sleep."

[2] This will be discussed later in greater detail. D. W. Triller, *Moly Homericum*, p. 15,
holds that mandragora was the special poison of Circe and for this reason calls moly
"*celebratissimum remedium anticircaeum*", p. 22.

[3] In dealing with the botanical and magical properties of the mandrake reference has
been made to the following works: J. Schmidel, *Dissertatio de Mandragora*, Leipzig, 1671;
C. Brewster Randolph, "The Mandragora of the Ancients in Folk-lore and Medicine", in
Proceedings of the American Academy of Arts and Sciences, 40 (1905), pp. 487–537; *Verhand-
lungen der Berliner Gesellschaft für Anthropologie, Ethnologie und Urgeschichte*, October 17
1891 = *Zeitschrift für Ethnologie*, 23 (1891), pp. (726–46); contributors include F. von
Luschan, P. Ascherson and R. Beyer; article "Mandragora", in *Realenzyklopädie*, XIV
(1928), col. 1028–37 (Steier); H. Bächtold-Stäubli, *Handwörterbuch des deutschen Aber-
glaubens* (Manual of German Superstition), I, Berlin-Leipzig, 1927, col. 312–24. These
works provide an adequate guide to the rest of the extensive literature on this subject.

this includes the actual soil of Greece. The name, however, is not Greek and has about it the savour of a more primitive age. The actual word *mandragora* comes from that vanished world of which the Greeks were originally invaders. It may be of Carian origin or possibly derived from the Persian *mardum-giâ* which means "man-plant", and it may thus have the same origin as the Cappadocian moly. We cannot be certain. Yet we can already see that there was something mysterious about this plant, and that the Greeks took over its name from those who, though conquered by them, were to be their masters in matters of religion even as they learned from the same masters to follow with stumbling speech the dark cult of Gaia the Mother Earth, nor is it strange that they should have regarded the plant with awe, for mandragora is poisonous.

There is an indication of this in the first reference to mandragora which we find in Theophrastus, for though the plant described by him is not really mandragora at all, it is nevertheless a poisonous one—deadly nightshade with its black fruits and narcotic effect.[1] The unknown rhizotomist, however, who is the author of Theophrastus' ninth book falls into no such error.[2] He is a man of the people and knows his popular herb lore. He knows his mandragora and we shall encounter him again when he describes the magic rites that accompany the digging of this plant. From the days of Dioscurides onward, however, there has never been the slightest doubt concerning mandragora's identity or as to how it should be classified.[3]

Actually we must distinguish between three different kinds. There is the male or white mandragora which is also called morion or spring mandragora. Its root is thick, black on the outside, but white inside, its leaves spread out immediately above the ground and from the circle which they form there grow heavily scented blossoms which ripen into berries of a yellowish colour; these, if eaten, have a soporific effect. The female or black mandragora also has a black root, often divided into two or three branches; it is "black outside with a thick skin and is white within".

---

[1] *Hist. Plant.*, VI, 2, 9 (Wimmer, I, p. 162). But see the correct description in *Caus. Plant.*, VI, 4, 5 (Wimmer, II, p. 210).

[2] Pseudo-Theophrastus, *Hist. Plant.*, IX, 8, 8; 9, 1 (Wimmer, I, p. 240).

[3] *De Materia Medica*, IV, 75 (Wellmann, II, pp. 233-7).

The Romans, Dioscurides adds, call it *mala canina* or *mala terrestria*, which means "dog apples" or "earth apples". The third kind is really morion proper, or fool's herb, and Dioscurides had never actually been able to find a specimen. All three kinds are known to the modern botanist under the names of *Mandragora officinarum* Linné, *Mandragora autumnalis* Spreng and *Mandragora microcarpa* respectively. Pliny gives the same classification, though he is guilty of one or two inexactitudes,[1] and he is followed by the botanists of later antiquity, though of the latter we need only concern ourselves with the two Pseudo-Dioscurides,[2] since it is from these writers that the Church Fathers derived much of their information. We keep on coming across references to Pliny's statement about the two principal kinds of mandragora: "*candidus qui mas, niger qui femina existimatur*–the white which is accounted male, and the black female". Up to the Middle Ages nothing much more seems to have been known about the botanical properties of the root beyond what can be found in Dioscurides, though the plant's magical penumbra had by then been considerably extended —but more of that later.

With the triumph of Christianity the botanist's interest in mandragora was further enhanced by yet another factor, for the plant in question, already so well known to the pagans, was now rediscovered in the sacred books of the Old Testament. In Genesis 30. 14–16 we are told how Reuben went into the fields at the time of the wheat harvest and found *dūdā'īm* which he brought to his mother Leah. Leah is then induced to part with the *dūdā'īm* to her sister Rachel who hopes thereby to regain the love of her husband. The Septuagint renders the Hebrew word as οἱ μανδραγόραι and there seems to be no reason for questioning the botanical correctness of the translation.[3] The *dūdā'īm* are spring man-

---

[1] *Nat. Hist.*, XXV, 147–50 (Mayhoff, IV, pp. 164f.); *ibid.*, I, 25, 94 (I, p. 85, ll. 4f.).

[2] Pseudo-Dioscurides, *De Herbis Femininis*, 15 (ed. H. F. Kästner, in *Hermes*, 31, 1896, pp. 599f.); Dioscurides Langobardus, IV, 71–2 (ed. H. Stadler, *Romanische Forschungen*, 11, 1901, pp. 40–2).

[3] From the exegetical literature on the mandrake use has been made of the following: Livinus Lemnius, *Herbarum atque Arborum quae in Bibliis passim obviae sunt*, Antwerp, 1566, chap. 2: "De Natura et Conditione Mandragorae"; J. G. Wetzstein, "Über die Dûdâ'îm im Hohenlied 7, 14" (On the Dūdā'īm in the Song of Songs), in F. Delitzsch, *Biblischer Commentar über die poetischen Bücher des Alten Testaments*, vol. IV, "Hoheslied und Kohelet", Leipzig, 1875, pp. 439–45; H. B. Tristram, *The Natural History of the Bible*, London,

dragoras, for at the time of the wheat harvest—in late spring
that is to say—these plants are in full fruit; their greenish white
leaves and the small fruit that resembles a little bright golden
apple and exudes a heavy scent, have often been described by
visitors to Palestine. I shall have something to say later about the
magic power to induce love which their fruits were supposed to
possess.

The same plant is mentioned again in Song of Songs 7. 13,
where the bride describes the vernal brightness of nature and says:
"The *dūdā'īm* breathe forth their scent", which in the Greek is
rendered: "*αἱ μανδραγόραι ἔδωκαν ὀσμήν*". From these two brief,
almost casual references, from words which normally would be as
quickly forgotten as a whiff of the scent of mandragora itself, there
has sprung a whole world of symbolism—or perhaps I might more
aptly say that, thanks to the two Scripture texts, the mysterious
world of ancient mandragora magic contrived to force its way into
Christian symbolism and was there transformed. That is why the
allegory of mandragora is so much richer than that of moly. Two
relatively unimportant Scripture texts sufficed to create an entirely
new and most wonderful thing, fashioning it from a blend of
ancient whispered folk-tales and Christian faith.

Perhaps we can also now understand the purely botanical interest
of the Church Fathers in the biblical plant mandragora—the
mandrake as I will now call it—the most engaging example of
this being found in Augustine.[1] In his pagan surroundings
Augustine had heard many of the stories that went the rounds
about the magic power of this root, and being engaged in the
interpretation of Genesis during his controversy with Faustus,
the Manichean, he was faced with the aforesaid passage in
chapter 30. "I have heard", he says, "a lot of gossip to the effect
that these little apples have a magic effect on the fruitfulness of
women", and obviously he feels called upon to investigate the

1898 (9th edition), pp. 466ff.; L. Fonck, *Streifzüge durch die biblische Flora* (Excursions
among the Biblical Flora), Freiburg, 1900, pp. 132ff.; J. Frazer, "Jacob and the Mandrakes", in *Proceedings of the British Academy*, 8 (1917), pp. 346ff.; J. Löw, *Die Flora der
Juden*, Leipzig-Vienna, III, 1924, pp. 363f.

[1] *Contra Faustum Manichaeum*, XXII, 56 (CSEL, 25, pp. 651f.), repeated word for word
in Isidore of Seville, *Quaest. in Vetus Test.*, 25, 19f. (PL, 83, 262 BC).

matter. He contrives to get hold of a genuine mandrake root, paying, like many another in those days, a not inconsiderable sum of money to some travelling herbalist. "*Rara enim est*–it is rare," he sighs, and no doubt the purchase had noticeably lightened his purse. He then tells us how he examined the thing, "without any of the far-fetched ideas of herb lore, with nothing else in fact than an ordinary man's sense of taste and smell and an ordinary man's eyes". He actually bit into his precious root; and the result— "*Proinde rem comperi pulchram et suave olentem, sapore autem insipido*–I found it a pleasing thing and pleasant to smell, but with an insipid flavour." For a man such as Augustine this was enough to trigger off a whole series of symbolic ideas with which I shall deal at a later stage. Other Fathers also discuss the botanical aspects of the mandrake—Ambrose[1] and Basil[2] for instance—and, following them, a whole host of others concerned with the exegesis of the Song of Songs and Genesis. They are all children of their own Graeco-Roman age.

We can deal with the question of the mandrake's medical uses as briefly as we have done with that of its botanical classification. All the relevant texts have long since been collated, and all the appropriate explanations have been duly put forward.[3] For an understanding of mandrake symbolism, however, it is necessary that two such uses should in particular be stressed. The various preparations and specifics derived from the root and fruit of the mandrake were used, among other things, to excite love, and also —this is perhaps the most important—as a narcotic during certain types of illness and during operations.

Let me deal first with the mandrake as an aphrodisiac. We find it stated in so early a writer as Pseudo-Theophrastus that the root

---

[1] *Exameron*, III, 9, 39 (CSEL, 32, 1, p. 85, ll. 18 ff.). Ambrose here justifies the existence of poisonous herbs and maintains that this does not contradict the goodness of the Creator and in support of his argument points to the existence of wicked angels (p. 84, l. 15).

[2] *Hexaemeron*, II, 4 (PG, 29, 101 D). Previously Basil had enumerated the various herbal poisons (101 B); cf. also, on this, the Latin adaptation of Basil by Eustathius (PL, 53, 913 AC); Ephraem, *In Genesim*, 30 (*Opera Syriace-Latine*, I, Rome, 1737, p. 84); Isidore, *Etymol.*, XVII, 9, 30 (PL, 82, 627 BC); here the mandrake is compared to the *mala Matiana*, a species of apple that derived its name from Matius, a friend of Augustus; cf. Pliny, *Nat. Hist.*, XV, 14, 15 (Mayhoff, II, p. 527, l. 12).

[3] In great detail in Brewster Randolph, *op. cit.* The original texts are in the appendix of this work.

can be used πρὸς φίλτρα[1] and Dioscurides seems almost to empha-
size the propriety of the name "Root of Circe" when he says, "It
would appear that this root is a means of exciting love."[2] Even
though, as Steier points out,[3] the evidence for this quality in the
root is scarce in the literature of antiquity, the two references here
quoted being the only relevant ones known, we must nevertheless assume that the popular belief in the mandrake's efficacy as
an aphrodisiac was very much alive.[4] Did not Aphrodite bear the
name Mandragoritis[5] and are we not told in relatively late Christian
times that "*Mandragora . . . circeon dixerunt; huius radicem ad amorem
multi dant*—They call it Circe's plant and many administer its root
in order to foster love"?[6]

The fact is that in Greece matters stood very much as they did
in the Semitic East, where to the present day the belief still
obtains—it is a belief belonging to a sort of borderland between
magic and medicine—that aphrodisiacs can be brewed from the
fruits of the mandrake and from its black root.[7]

This was the kind of talk that Augustine had heard, and the
symbolism with which I shall deal later on will have plenty to
tell us about it.

As I have already indicated, however, it was the narcotic use of
the mandrake that throughout the whole of antiquity was by far
the most important. The juice of the root distilled in wine could
make men mad, it was said, if given in sufficiently large doses, and
could even be lethal; in moderate doses, it could be used as a cure
for insomnia; it was also said to give relief to those suffering from

---

[1] *Hist. Plant.*, IX, 9, 1 (Wimmer, I, p. 240). The same conclusion is to be drawn from
the magical instruction that is given here, according to which the rhizotomist's assistant
must shout, as hard as he can, erotic ejaculations while the digging is in process.

[2] *De Materia Medica*, IV, 75 (Wellmann, II, p. 233, ll. 12 f.); Pliny, *Hist. Nat.*, XXV,
147 (Mayhoff, IV, p. 164, l. 12): "*Mandragoram alii Circaeum vocant*".

[3] *Realenzyklopädie*, XIV, col. 1031, ll. 9 f.

[4] For instance apothecaries (*pigmentarii*) are legally prohibited from irresponsibly supplying aphrodisiacs made of mandragora. See Marcianus in *Digests*, 48, 8, 3: *Ut pigmentarii, si
cui temere mandragoram dederint, poena teneantur* (Mommsen, II, p. 819, ll. 28–30).

[5] Hesychius, *Lexicon* under "*Mandragoritis*" (ed. M. Schmidt, II, Jena, 1861, p. 69).
See also *Realenzyklopädie*, I, col. 2678; XIV, col. 1038.

[6] Dioscurides Langobardus, IV, 71 (Stadler, p. 40, ll. 14 f.).

[7] Concerning the use of mandragora for erotic purposes in the Near East, see F. von
Luschan, *op. cit.*, pp. 726 ff.; there are six illustrations of the "female" mandrake from
Damascus, Constantinople and Antioch.

nausea and to check the tendency to vomit; it could—so it was
alleged further—be used as a narcotic in painful operations.¹ Even
the smell of the fruit was stated to have a soporific effect and
physicians are said to have recommended placing these mandrake
"apples" under the pillow in cases of chronic sleeplessness.² It was
also considered useful in calming anxiety states.³

What people were obviously most impressed by, however, was
the effectiveness of mandrake juice as a narcotic during operations.
After a strong dose the patient is said to have remained insensible
for three or four hours. Morion was particularly effective in this
respect.⁴ The mandrake in fact was regarded—to quote Suidas—as
a "hypnotic fruit that brings oblivion".⁵ A saying has come down
to us, the substance of which can be traced back to Pliny (XXV,
150) and Dioscurides (IV, 75, 7), though I believe the actual form
of words occurs first in Pseudo-Dioscurides. This saying was
copied by Isidore and from thence was repeated right through the
Middle Ages: "*Praeterea cortix radicis eius . . . his bibendum datur
quorum corpus propter curam secandum est, ut hac potione soporati
dolorem secturae non sentiant*–Then, they give the peel of its root
as a drink to those whose bodies are about to be cut for surgical
reasons, so that, being lulled to sleep by this potion, they feel no
pain"⁶—thus Pseudo-Dioscurides. Isidore repeats this almost word
for word: "*Cuius cortex vino mistus, ad bibendum datur iis quorum
corpus propter curam secandum est, ut soporati dolorem non sentiant.*"⁷

¹ The original sources in *Realenzyklopädie*, XIV, col. 1033, and Randolph, *op. cit.*, pp. 516ff.
² Celsus, *Libri VIII de Medicina*, III, 18, 12 (*Corp. Med. Latin.*, I, p. 125, l. 1). Cf. also
Macrobius, *Sat.*, VII, 6, 7 (Eyssenhardt, II, p. 419, ll. 29f.).
³ Marcellus, *De Medicamentis*, VIII, 8, 12 (*Corp. Med. Latin.*, V, p. 54, l. 24); XX, 143
(p. 168, l. 23). See also Caelius Aurelianus, *Acutarum sive Celerum Passionum*, II, 4, 20
(Amann); Quintus Serenus Sammonicus, *Liber Medicinalis*, 54, verse 989 (*Poetae Lat.
Minores*, III, p. 153).
⁴ This is already to be found in Dioscurides, IV, 75, 7, but the Langobardic Dioscurides
can still write about mandragora: "If a man drink thereof, he becomes mad or falls
asleep, and remains lying for three or four hours without moving in whatever posture his
body had assumed after he had fallen down. The surgeons of the East make use of this"
(Stadler, p. 42, ll. 11–21).
⁵ *Lexicon*, 136 (*Lexicographi Graeci*, III, p. 317, ed. A. Adler); cf. also Hesychius, *Lex.*
(II, p. 69): οἰνικὸν καὶ ὑπνοτικόν. In Persian pharmacy mandragora also plays an
important part as a narcotic. See J. Berendes, *Die Pharmazie bei den alten Culturvölkern*
(Pharmacy in Ancient Cultures), I, Halle, 1892, pp. 43; 222f.
⁶ Pseudo-Dioscurides, *De Herbis Femininis*, 15 (ed. Kästner, in *Hermes*, 31, 1896, p. 600).
⁷ *Etymol.*, XVII, 9, 30 (PL, 82, 627 C).

In this form we find the thing in the commentary on the Song of Songs which was accepted as the leading authority throughout the Middle Ages, and was always ascribed to the leading theologian of the day, whether he was Cassiodorus or Thomas Aquinas; actually it was probably written by Haymo of Halberstadt.[1] Bruno of Asti was still to copy it verbatim,[2] and Brewster Randolph does this eleventh-century exegete too much honour when he speaks of him as one of the last persons to provide evidence of mandrake narcosis.[3]

So far as the symbolism that was to develop is concerned, the mandrake's most important botanical characteristic is the resemblance of its root to the human form. It has been correctly observed that we must not postulate for antiquity any such elaborate superstitions as those which subsequently surrounded the mandrake among the Germanic peoples.[4] But even the Greeks were aware of the root's strange semi-human shape, and if we are right in believing that the pre-Greek name mandragora has some connexion with the Persian *mardum-giâ* or "man-plant", then it is surely not too bold an inference to seek the ultimate origin of all that men have believed about the mandrake at that point where the people who were to be the Greeks branched off from our common parent stem. When Dioscurides calls the mandrake ἀνθρωπόμορφος,[5] "human-shaped", he claims to be using a term that goes back to Pythagoras and Pythagorean in such a context as this means something very old indeed, something that derives from time immemorial and goes back to the very beginnings of our race. Surely it was in this way that people must always have talked of the potent root. Surely Columella too is uttering old peasant lore when in his poem on gardens he speaks of the mandrakes rioting in his own, and tells how from the root that looks like the half of a man there springs a "herb of madness":

[1] Pseudo-Cassiodorus, *Expositio in Canticum*, 7, 13 (PL, 70, 1099 B); Haymo (PL, 117, 349 BC); Pseudo-Thomas Aquinas (Parma edition, XIV, Parma, 1863, p. 382).

[2] *Expositio in Cant.*, 7 (PL, 164, 1281 C).

[3] Randolph, *op. cit.*, pp. 515 and 534f.

[4] Thus von Steier, *Realenzyklopädie*, XIV, col. 1036, ll. 10f., in opposition to G. Hopf, "Zwei uralte Pflanzenorakel" (Two Ancient Plant Oracles), in *Kosmos*, 4 (1907), p. 244.

[5] *De Materia Medica*, IV, 75 (Wellmann, II, p. 234, l. 12).

Quamvis semihominis vesano gramine foeta
Mandragorae pariat flores . . .[1]

The old Latin glossary which has preserved for us so much of
the old popular speech and along with it so much of the old popular thought, has this to say about the mandrake: "*Mandragora:*
herba quae odorem habet grandem qui hominem extra mentem facit, et est
eius radix in similitudine corporis humani—Mandragora is a plant with
a very strong smell which drives men mad, and its root is shaped
in the likeness of a man."[2] Incidentally such notions were also
current in the Semitic East. Wetzstein tells us that in the case of
the two scriptural texts that I have mentioned, the Syrian translators rendered the word "dūdā'im" as *jebrûaḥ* which means "It
(only) needs life." This is equivalent to saying that the root is so
like a human body that it only needs to have a soul breathed into
it to become a small human being.[3] The Arabs have preserved this
tradition, as we can see from Avicenna,[4] and even today the Turks
call the mandrake *adam-kökü* which means "man-root".[5] The
Church Fathers knew of these things from the ordinary folk, and
I shall show later that it was just such thoughts as these that sparked
off some of the most exquisite of the symbolic ideas that they
developed round the mandrake. For there was an indestructible
quality about these fancies. The Pythagorean ἀνθρωπόμορφος from
Dioscurides turns up again in Isidore, who even renders the word
in the original Greek and so once more the thing is passed on to
survive throughout the Middle Ages: "*Hanc mandragoram poetae*
ἀνθρωπόμορφον appellant, quod habeat radicem formam hominis
simulantem—The poets describe it in this fashion because its root
resembles the human form."[6]

---

[1] *Res Rust.*, X, 19f., "Carmen de Cultu Hortorum" (Lundström, p. 5).

[2] *Corp. Glos. Lat.*, III (Goetz), 585.

[3] *Exkurs über die Dûdâ'im Hoheslied*, 7. 14 ("Essay on the Dūdā'im in Song of Songs, 7. 14"), p. 441.

[4] *Libri quinque Canonis* (Arabic), I, Rome, 1593, p. 187, 19, quoted by P. de Lagarde, *Gesammelte Abhandlungen*, p. 67. Cf. Richardson's *Persian Lexicon* quoted by Wetzstein, *loc. cit.*, where it is said that the Persians referred to the Mandrake as "the man-plant [*merdumgiâ*], on account of the strong resemblance of the root to the human figure".

[5] According to a statement by F. von Luschan, *loc. cit.*, p. 728.

[6] *Etymol.*, XVII, 9, 30 (PL, 82, 627 B).

2

The mandrake—and I think that somehow this must have been apparent to you while I was discussing its medical and botanical characteristics—is essentially a magic plant. Its root, which in so eerie a fashion resembles the human form, is embedded deep in the dark earth, and whosoever would have its mighty powers serve him comes within the magic circle of those demons within whose power it lies.[1] From the beginning of human history men have felt that supersensual forces were at work in any plant capable of exciting them, numbing them, curing them or poisoning them. The spirits of the stars, the demons of the nether parts of the earth, permit their influence, as it were, to "foam up" in certain plants, and puny man, standing midway between Gaia and Uranus, cannot hope to master the powers lying dormant within the roots thereof without magic—and mortal peril. He must turn in prayer to Mother Earth who will only after such supplication give him the plant that he needs, and by means of words and acts, which will only be effective if they are the "right" ones, he must conjure the demons who are sympathetically inclined towards the plant in question. The plant that is lifted in such circumstances as these must thereafter be prevented from touching the earth, so that its powers are not dissipated but remain gathered together within itself.

It is only at night and by the faint light of the moon that the true rhizotomist will go about his work. In a few immortal lines Ovid has preserved for us something of the moonlit horror of such digging. It is when he describes Medea searching for the herbs that will give eternal youth, praying, as she does so, to the stars, howling to Hecate and whispering to Mother Earth:

> *"Nox" ait "arcanis fidissima, quaeque divinis*
> *Aurea cum Luna succeditis ignibus astra,*
> *Tuque, triceps Hecate, quae coeptis conscia nostris*

[1] Cf. for what follows T. Hopfner, "Mageia", *Realenzyklopädie*, XIV, col. 319ff.; A. Abt, *Die Apologie des Apuleius von Madaura und die antike Zauberei* (The Apologia of Apuleius of Madaura and Ancient Witchcraft), Giessen, 1908, pp. 87ff. For the continuance of herb-magic into the Christian Middle Ages, see (in addition to Abt, pp. 91f.) especially A. Franz, *Die kirchlichen Benediktionen im Mittelalter* (Ecclesiastical Benedictions in the Middle Ages), I, Freiburg, 1909, pp. 393ff.

> *Adiutrixque venis cantusque artisque magorum,*
> *Quaeque magos, Tellus, pollentibus instruis herbis,*
> *Auraeque et venti montesque amnesque lacusque,*
> *Dique omnes nemorum, dique omnes noctis adeste."*

(Night that knowest all secrets, ye golden stars
That with Selene follow the heat of the day;
Thou, Hecate the three headed one, who knowing
    what I am about,
Helpest the murmured word and cunning magic;
And thou, earth that givest to witches the herbs of
    the night;
Ye winds and breezes and ye mountains and ponds,
Gods of the grove, hasten hither. O help me, ye
    gods of the night.)[1]

In the search for the mandrake root magic spells and ceremonies played just such a part as Ovid indicates, and were, indeed, matters of the highest importance. Once more it is the rhizotomist of the ninth book of Theophrastus who tells us what magic practices popular Greek belief held to be essential when the mandrake was to be dug.[2] Once the mandrake had been found, three circles must be drawn around it with an iron sword. Then the digger must turn westwards and in that position remove the root from the ground. During these proceedings an assistant must dance around the plant and murmur anything in the way of *erotica* that happens to come into his mind. The most important thing here is the looking towards the west while the plant is being dug, τέμνειν δὲ πρὸς ἑσπέραν βλέποντα.

Pliny has meticulously copied all this: "*Efossuri cavent contrarium ventum, et tribus circulis ante gladio circumscribunt, postea fodiunt ad occasum spectantes* – Those about to dig make sure there is no contrary wind; they first draw three circles round the place with a

---

[1] *Metamorphoses*, VII, 192–8.
[2] *Hist. Plant.*, IX, 8, 8 (Wimmer, I, p. 240). The author states, however (IX, 8, 5—p. 239, ll. 6f.), that we are here concerned with magical practices which were only indulged in by the rhizotomists and drug pedlars in order to enhance the value of their wares and increase their own importance, in order, so to speak to make a tragedy (ἐπιτραγῳδοῦντες) out of their root-gathering activities. This word is certainly a happy one that might well be applied to the medical charlatan in all ages.

sword, and when they dig out the plant, they face the west."[1] It is clear from this that popular belief held the mandrake to be a chthonic plant, coming within the dominion of the demons of darkness, for these evil spirits dwell in the West and by looking towards the west you prevented them from harming you.[2] Were not offerings to the dead and also curses directed towards the west? And did not the Cappadocians throw the moly into a dark place where the sun never shone? One must be careful about the wind. Otherwise the scent of the plant, while yet undug, could carry the evil influence of its demon along with it.

It is, however, possible that this practice of turning to the west may have a different explanation. It may be that the root-gatherer wished to make sure that the powers of the dark spirits which he believed to be present within the root, were not unfavourable, and so looked westward as one asking the spirits' permission. Only then could he lift the root without harm to himself. That the act had some such significance is suggested by Pliny's account of the magical practices that accompanied the digging of the Christmas rose. In this case the root-gatherer turns eastward in the direction where the good spirits are to be found to whom this plant is peculiar, and his prayer is just such a request for permission to dig: "*Dein qui succisurus est, ortum spectat et precatur, ut id liceat sibi concedentibus diis facere*–Then he who is about to dig out the plant turns to the east and prays that it may be accounted lawful for him to do this and that the gods may grant him permission."[3]

We are led further into the real inwardness of mandrake magic when we realize which of all the spirits that dwelt in the West was

---

[1] *Nat. Hist.*, XXV, 148 (Mayhoff, IV, p. 164, ll. 19–21).

[2] Cf. C. A. Lobeck, *Aglaophamus, sive de Theologiae mysticae Graecorum Causis*, II, Königsberg, 1829, pp. 915, 930; F. J. Dölger, *Die Sonne der Gerechtigkeit und der Schwarze*, pp. 80f.; T. Hopfner, *Offenbarungszauber*, I, pp. 45, 81 f.; on mandrake magic outside the area of Greek culture, see E. Brugsch, "Die Alraune als altägyptische Zauberplanze" (The Mandrake as an Ancient Egyptian Magic Plant), in *Zeitschrift für ägyptische Sprache*, 29 (1891), pp. 31 ff., and for a contrary view, F. Heide, *Tidsskrift for historisk botanik*, 1 (1918), pp. 8 ff. See also *Realenzyklopädie*, XIV, col. 1032, ll. 8–28. On customs connected with the mandrake in the Far East, see A. Eckardt, "Ginseng, die Wunderwurzel des Ostens" (Ginseng, the Wonder-root of the East), in *Festschrift für Wilhelm Schmidt*, Vienna, 1928, pp. 220 ff. Illustrations showing the Egyptian Nofretete with a mandrake, and a Chinese ginseng root in the special number of *Ciba-Zeitschrift* entitled "Die Arznei und ihre Zubereitung" (Medicine and its Preparation), June 18 1942, pp. 15 and 21.

[3] *Nat. Hist.*, XXV, 50 (Mayhoff, IV, p. 132, ll. 18f.). See also F. J. Dölger, *Sol Salutis*, p. 56.

especially sympathetic to the mandrake. There is no question that this was Hecate, the gruesome mistress of all ghosts and of all the demons of the dead. There is no definite evidence that the root-gatherer when turning westwards to pray was actually praying to Hecate; but there are so many grounds for supposing this that the magical connexion between Hecate and the mandrake can no longer be in doubt.

Hecate is in truth the dark foil of the bright Hermes.[1] Both are "guides of souls", but Hecate is νεοτέρων πρύτανις, mistress of the nether world,[2] and in her train there cower the spectres of the dead and the restless souls of murdered men who haunt graves and crossroads. Eusebius calls her "Ruler of all wicked demons".[3] She is "the black one", equal in rank with Persephone, who holds the power of the keys of Hades.[4] Out of the depths where she dwells she sends men unquiet sleep and oppressive dreams, she is the author of epilepsy and madness. In the practices of magic, Hecate is accounted the demon of love-madness and is treated as the equal of Aphrodite.[5] In a later tradition she became the mother of Circe and Medea, the two arch-witches of Greek mythology. In her garden grow the mandrakes and these are plants that induce love, give sleep and also death by poisoning and madness. Naturally enough men would not dig this root without securing themselves against the eerie power that, thanks to Hecate, dwelt within it.

But now for the actual proof. Hecate is surrounded by the

---

[1] Cf. sources quoted in A. Abt, *op. cit.*, pp. 126–30, *Realenzyklopädie*, VII, col. 2769–82.

[2] *Schol. Theocr.*, II, 12 (ed. C. Wendel, p. 272, l. 5). See also Apuleius, *Apologia*, 31 (Helm, p. 37, l. 20): "*manum potens Trivia*"; *Realenzyklopädie*, VII, col. 2773 f. This finds its most eloquent expression in the conjuration of Hecate which has been preserved in Hippolytus, *Elenchus*, IV, 35, 5 (GCS, III, p. 62):

> Come thou subterranean, Hellish and Heavenly Bombo,
> Goddess of the road, of the three roads, thou beacon of the night,
> Enemy of the light, friend of the night, faithful companion
> That delightest in the barking of dogs and streaming blood,
> That wanderest over corpses and over the graves of the dead
> Thirsting for blood, a horror to mortal men.

[3] *Praep. Evangelica*, IV, 22 (PG, 21, 304 C).

[4] Virgil, *Aen.* VI, 247 ff. See also E. Norden, *Aeneis*, Book VI, Leipzig, 1916, pp. 64 and 204; *Paris Magic Papyri*, 1403; F. J. Dölger, *Sol Salutis*, p. 347.

[5] *Paris Magic Papyri*, 2557; W. H. Roscher, *Selene und Verwandtes*, p. 83.

barking dogs of the nether world and often appears herself in the form of a dog-spectre; trembling warlocks address her as "black dog",[1] and indeed it behoves those who invoke her, first to make sure of her name, for only if she is named correctly are men safe against her malice.[2] But this brings us to the most important feature of the whole of this mandrake magic, which is that the root must be taken out of the earth with the help of a black dog. The magic lore decrees this, and this is a matter with which I shall deal at some length; for here we are at the very root of a most ancient super-stition—of that magic of the mandrake and the black dog which was at one time spread all over Western Christendom.[3]

For the man of the Graeco-Roman world the dog was essen-tially a chthonic beast; he was, one might say, the earthly embodi-ment of the demonic. Hecate was ruler of dogs,[4] and demons appeared in canine form. Even the Byzantine age could produce a piece of magic writing, the *Testament of Solomon*, which tells of an evil spirit appearing in the form of a loudly barking dog. This spirit had been conjured up by Solomon through the power of his magic ring, a ring that had a piece of mandrake concealed beneath its gem.[5] Here is a prose translation of some verses of Synesius which show us very vividly how people in Graeco-Roman times, even when they had become Christians, felt that this dark

---

[1] *Paris Magic Papyri*, 1432 ff. Cf. *Realenzyklopädie*, VII, col. 2776, ll. 40 ff.

[2] Cf. Pliny, *Nat. Hist.*, XXX, 18, which refers to a statement of Apion the grammarian according to which the root of the plant Cynocephalia or Dog's Head is *"divina et contra omnia veneficia"*, though the lifting thereof is dangerous to life: *"Si tota erueretur, statim eum qui eruisset mori."* The danger can however be averted if one knows the correct magical practice.

[3] See E. von Lippmann, "Alraun und schwarzer Hund" (The Mandrake and the Black Dog), in *Abhandlungen und Vorträge zur Geschichte der Naturwissenschaften*, I, Leipzig, 1906, pp. 190 ff.

[4] On the dog as a chthonic beast of Hecate, see Hopfner, *Offenbarungszauber*, I, pp. 112 f.; *Realenzyklopädie*, VIII, col. 2577 ff. The verses of Theocritus, II, 10 ff., in which the sorceress whispers in the lonely moonlit night are well known:

Up then, Selene and give me good light, thou silent goddess.
To thee now I sing, and to thee also, Hecate that dost live
   below ground
That dost frighten away whimpering dogs when thou dost walk
Over the graves of the dead and over the dark blood-stream.
Hail to thee, Hecate, goddess of horror.

[5] *Testamentum Salomonis*, concerning which see Hopfner, *Offenbarungszauber*, I, pp. 160 f. (PG, 122, 1330 f.).

submerged part of the soul was threatened by the hounds of Hecate and saw in this a symbol of the devil:

"Let the sinuous trend of serpents sink beneath the earth, and that winged serpent also, the demon of matter, he who clouds the soul, rejoicing in images and urging on his brood of whelps against my supplication. Do thou, O Father, O Blessed One, keep away from my soul these soul-devouring hounds, from my prayer, from my life, from my works."[1]

With these soul-devouring hounds we have arrived at the polar opposite of the "soul-healing flower". To the rather gruesome magical practices which we have already noted and to the accompaniment of which men possessed themselves of the mandrake and sought to become masters of its powers, we must now add this additional magic that was concerned with dogs. Pseudo-Apuleius gives a very detailed account of the way in which the mandrake must be dug, and, as a kind of justification for these precautionary practices, reminds us that the root of the mandrake "has great power and is able to bring healing".[2] We are told that this plant can be found at night—and night is the only time when it may be dug—because it shines like a lamp. The proper course, we are further instructed, is to dig away the earth from about the root, and when the said root has been freed from the earth around it but is still held fast within the earth's domain, a black dog must be tied to it by a new cord; the dog can then fully uproot it. "*Quia tantam fertur ipsa herba habere divinitatem, ut qui eam evellet, eodem momento canem decipiat.*" So runs the barbarous Latin of this addition to the *Herbarius* which we can translate: "It is said that this root has so divine a character that it kills the dog in the moment when the latter tears it up."[3] However, if one cannot get hold of a dog,

---

[1] "*Ψυχοβόϱους κύνας*", Hymn III, verses 86–98 (PG, 66, 1595). The English translation is by Augustine Fitzgerald, *The Essays and Hymns of Synesius of Cyrene*, Oxford, 1930.

[2] *Herbarius*, 131 (*Corp. Med. Lat.*, IV, p. 222, l. 2): "*quia magna est visio et beneficia eius*" though the correct reading must surely be "*vis*" and not "*visio*". Note the reading of the St Gall MS., "*magna est virtus et beneficia eius*".

[3] *Ibid.*, p. 222, "*quia tantum fertur ipsa herba habere divinitatem, ut qui eam evellet, eodem momento illum [canem] decipiat*". [Thus, the Latin text in both text and note as given by the author. The English translation also follows Fr Rahner's German one, but, no matter how "barbarous" the Latin, it surely could never mean this. We might tentatively translate:

we are then informed, a kind of machine (*manganum*) can be used by which a rod can be caused to jerk the root loose.

This account, however, is not the oldest we possess, though it is the first that explicitly associates this dog-sacrificing practice with the mandrake. There is yet another very strange tale in Josephus[1] which is well known in the literature of magic. Josephus describes a magical practice connected with the digging of a plant called "Baaras", and if we can show that this baaras of Josephus is really a mandrake, then this will be first-class evidence of the way in which the magic of the mandrake and the black dog developed. It would in that case become clear that this piece of magic had come from the East, and a new relevance would attach to the fact that the Persians called the mandrake *sag-kan* which means "dog-dug", no doubt this was so because here too a dog tore it out of the earth.[2] The text of Josephus is well worth quoting in full:

"In the valley which lies to the north of the town [Machairos] there is a place called Baaras and here there grows a root which also bears this name. Every evening it glows with a fire-red light. Yet when anyone draws near to pluck it out, it proves very difficult to grasp and draws away from your grasp, and it is impossible to gain power over it unless you pour menstrual blood or urine upon it. Even then, however, to touch the root directly brings instant death, unless it is carried in the hand so that the tip of the root points downwards. Nevertheless it is possible to gain possession of the root without any danger whatsoever if the following procedure is observed. First the earth must be dug up all around it, so that only a small part of it remains covered. Then a dog must be tied to it. When the dog then tries to follow the man who has thus tied him to the root, he naturally draws it quite easily out of the ground. In that moment however he dies, thus expiating the deed of him who was really responsible for the root's removal. One

"It is said that this plant has such a potent content of divinity that whoever will pluck it out deceives it (the dog)".—*Translator's note*.] The account ends with the praises "*Herbae mandragorae quantumcumque in media domo habeat, omnia mala expellit*—Whatever the quantity of the herb mandrake he may have in his house, it drives out all evils."

[1] *Bellum Iudaicum*, VII, 6, 3 (Niese, VI, pp. 450f.).

[2] Cf. P. de Lagarde, *Persische, armenische und indische Wörter im Syrischen* (Persian, Armenian and Indian Words in Syriac), No. 172=*Gesammelte Abhandlungen*, p. 67.

need now have no fear when touching it. The reason why this root is so much sought after, despite its dangerous character, is that it is possessed of certain quite unique properties; for it has the power of driving away, by its mere proximity, the so-called demons, which means the spirits of evil men who are dead and now enter the bodies of the living, sometimes even killing them."

Now is the baaras plant identical with the mandrake?[1] The mere fact that the baaras is credited with these demon-repelling powers inclines me towards an affirmative answer; also it is surely reasonable to suppose that we are here concerned with the same magic root with which, according to Josephus in the *Antiquities* the Jew Eleazar performed a feat in the presence of the Emperor Vespasian to be, that in this connexion is distinctly noteworthy: "He had concealed beneath his ring one of those roots that Solomon had once pointed out, and held the ring that contained this root to the nose of a man who was possessed. He let him smell the root and then drew out the evil spirit through the afflicted one's nostrils."[2] Now I shall shortly satisfy you that this root of Solomon's was nothing other than mandrake root. You will note that even the smell, of which the root-gatherer had to be so careful, becomes "apotropic" (a turner away of evil) once the root has been safely lifted and this is precisely what was supposed to happen, according to the above quoted excerpt, with the baaras root.

It must be remembered that all diseases, and particularly madness and epilepsy, had for the men of antiquity a demonic character and were regarded as a form of possession.[3] These roots are

[1] See for the interpretation P. Kohout, *Flavius Josephus' Jüdischer Krieg* (The Jewish War of Flavius Josephus), Linz, 1901, pp. 778ff.; P. Ascherson, *op. cit.*, p. 730, n. 3; T. Hopfner, *Offenbarungszauber*, I, p. 128.

[2] *Antiquitates Iudaicae*, VIII, 2, 5 (Niese, II, pp. 153f.). Cf. P. Ascherson, *op. cit.*, p. 732, which reproduces the engaging judgement of Johann Weyer in *Von Verzeuberungen* (On the Practice of Magic), Basle, 1565, p. 883, on Eleazar's mandrake magic: "*Hierzu können wir nicht anderst sagen, dass die drey alle zumal, Josephus nämlich als ein Jud, Vespasianus als ein Heyd und Eleazarus der Hebreer, von dem Teuffel gefatzet und umbgetrieben seyen worden*–On this we can only say that all three, Josephus the Jew, Vespasian the heathen and Eleazar the Hebrew were all seized and moved by the Devil."

[3] See F. J. Dölger, "Der Einfluss des Origenes auf die Beurteilung der Epilepsie und Mondsucht im christlichen Altertum" (The Influence of Origen on the Assessment of Epilepsy and Lunacy in Christian Antiquity), in *Antike und Christentum*, 4 (1934), pp. 95–109.

effective against such conditions because they have been magically snatched out of the control of the chthonic demons, whose powers lie packed in the extreme tips of the roots concerned and are neutralized when they are separated from the earth.

The identity of baaras becomes even clearer when we reflect on the fact that the plant is said to glow and then suddenly to disappear into darkness when the root-gatherer starts to search it out, so that the illusion would be created, as the different plants glow and are darkened again, that they are moving forward before him. Actually all this is a genuine natural phenomenon which has been made the subject of magical interpretation. The fact is that in Palestine glow-worms are very fond of settling on the lovely rosettes of leaves that are put forth by the spring mandrake, so that the plant really does look like a glowing lamp.[1] When anybody comes near it its light disappears but immediately one becomes aware of the light from another such luminous mandrake. Even today the Arabs in the Holy Land call the mandrake *sirag el-kotrub* or devil's lamp and another name for it, according to Arab lexicographers, is *glow-jebrûah* or Solomon's herb.[2]

Now we have seen earlier that the Aramaic *jebrûah* suggests a "man-like" plant, the mandrake, in fact. Further, according to Löw, the baaras of Josephus is simply a corruption of *jebrûah* which is certainly identical with the biblical *dūdā'îm*.[3] It is obvious that these scattered bits of evidence all point in one direction and even though Kohout[4] may be right when, in his commentary on Josephus, he points out that baaras is Hebrew for fire and that the plant is so named because it is luminous at night, this would not be an argument against me, since this quality of luminosity which

---

[1] According to Richardson's *Persian Lexicon* quoted by Wetzstein, *op. cit.*, p. 441, "The Arabians call it [the mandrake] the 'devil's candle' on account of its shining appearance in the night from the number of glow-worms which cover the leaves."

[2] Thus according to the Arabic botanical lexicon *Mâlâyesâ* quoted by Wetzstein, *op. cit.*, p. 442. Concerning the lexicon *Mâlâyesâ*, see also E. H. F. Meyer, *Geschichte der Botanik* (History of Botany), III, Königsberg, 1856, pp. 241 ff. This is why Pseudo-Apuleius (p. 222, ll. 3 f.), says of the mandrake, "*nocte tanquam lucerna sic lucet caput eius*". Diodorus of Tarsus says the same of the plant called *aglaophotis* in his lost work on destiny, namely that it flees from him who seeks it and glows at night. Cf. Photius, *Bibliotheca*, 223 (PG, 103, 853 B).

[3] J. Löw, *Die Flora der Juden* (Flora of the Jews), III, Vienna-Leipzig, 1924, p. 365.

[4] *Op. cit.*, p. 779, n. 180.

would then have been stressed would again lead us back to the mandrake.

There is, therefore, no reason to change my view that all that Josephus tells us of the magical rites surrounding the digging of the baaras root can safely be applied to the mandrake and that the mandrake was in fact the demonic root that grew upon the fields of Baaras on that sinister piece of ground close to the Wadi Zerqa Ma'in from which gush the hot springs of Callirhoe.[1]

The mandrake, the plant that glows at night is thus clearly a thing of Hades. Yet whosoever could become its master by means of the black dog was also master of all the demonic powers which dwelt within its root for just so long as it remained in contact with the earth. The dog however was condemned to die—a sacrifice to Hecate, the canine mistress of hell.

We are now in a position to understand the third text that has come down to us from antiquity and deals with this dog-magic that accompanied the drawing of the root. We find this text in Aelian's *Historia Animalium*[2] in which we hear of a plant called *cynospastus* and also *aglaophotis*. We are told that at night it shines like a star. Its root must be drawn out of the earth with the help of a dog and this too must be done at night. When the morning comes and Helios sees the root, then the dog must die, but it is incumbent on the root-gatherer to bury the dog "with unspeakable rites" at the exact spot where the root was found "since it was killed in place of the man". This plant, Aelian continues, is a physic against epilepsy—he calls this disease the sickness of Selene—and it grows in Eastern Arabia.

Now, are we not obviously here dealing once more with the mandrake? And is it not clear that this plant which is called "dog-snatched" and "shining with brightness" is the same as the shining baaras? The very mention of Eastern Arabia is a most eloquent indication here, for this is the region of the magic customs which Josephus describes, and once more it does look very much

---

[1] On the position of Baaras and this whole strange volcanic piece of country, see Jerome, *De Situ et Nominibus Loc. Hebr.* (PL, 23, 880 A); M. Hagen, *Atlas Biblicus*, Paris, 1907, col. 19; P. Kohout, *op. cit.*, pp. 779f.; F. M. Abel, *Géographie de la Palestine*, I, Paris, 1933, pp. 460f.

[2] Aelian, *Hist. Animal.*, XIV, 27 (Jacobs, pp. 328f.).

as though we were here concerned with magic practices that had come over from the East.

This view is confirmed by a passage in Pliny.[1] Pliny is speaking of the large number of magic books in circulation bearing the names of Pythagoras and Democritus which told of the most incredible things, and actually, Pythagoras was the guide in chief of all rhizotomists in the late Graeco-Roman world in which Democritus was accounted the great magician, his *Cheirokmeta* (things wrought by hand) which was a book about herbs, being known to everybody. Now both these men are declared to have been pupils of the Perso-Iranian magi—they had in Pliny's phrase "*consectati magos*".[2] Pliny knew perfectly well that these *Cheirokmeta* did no more than trade on popular credulity, but it so happens that he does refer to a passage that embodies a tradition coming from the Arabian East concerning the plant aglaophotis:

"What is it [he writes] that this Democritus, following a tradition of Pythagoras (who in his turn was an eager pupil of the magi), speaks of in his book as particularly remarkable? He states that in the marble quarries of Arabia towards the Persian side, there grows a plant named aglaophotis which is so called by admiring men because of its wonderful colour, and the magi use this plant when they wish to invoke the gods."

It is a pity that Pliny does not quote this remarkable book at greater length, but what he does quote is quite sufficient for our purpose, and it is obvious that the aglaophotis of Democritus is again nothing other than the brightly shining plant referred to by Aelian, the plant whose root must be drawn up by a dog, the plant which grows in Eastern Arabia "towards the Persian side".

Attempts have been made to identify the plant in question with the peony (*Paeonia officinalis*) for this flower is also called aglaophotis by Dioscurides[3] and is celebrated by the anonymous author of *De Herbis* in verse.[4] Be that as it may, the rhizotomists, who

---

[1] *Nat. Hist.*, XXIV, 160.

[2] *Ibid.* See also T. Hopfner, *Offenbarungszauber*, I, p. 117; *Realenzyklopädie*, V, col. 138.   [3] *De Materia Medica*, III, 147.

[4] *De Herbis*, cap. 11, verses 139 ff. Cf. E. H. F. Meyer, *Geschichte der Botanik*, II, pp. 336–40.

thought on essentially magical lines did not classify things in botanical categories but according to their supposed magical powers, and Hopfner[1] has shown beyond doubt that this name "aglaophotis" was given to more than one plant, possibly to any plant which because of its brightness was held to come under the influence of Hecate-Selene; its very quality of nocturnal brightness associated it with the demons of the moon and so with madness; our still surviving equation of madness with "lunacy" had its counterpart in the Greek tongue. Indeed we can see an example of this in the New Testament when it is said of the boy possessed by an evil spirit in Matthew 17. 14ff. that he σεληνιάζεται. The train of magical thought according to which a plant associated with the powers of the moon, having been withdrawn by one of Hecate's dogs from the power of their mistress, becomes itself a specific against "moon-sickness"[2] (including epilepsy) is not difficult to follow. Dioscurides calls the plant purely and simply σελήνιον.[3] Light is now also thrown on the use of "Solomon's root" in drawing an evil spirit out of a possessed person through the latter's nose.

To return for a moment to this question of the botanical identity of "Solomon's root": we have already noted the identity between jebrûah and the biblical dūdā'îm. However the Arabic lexicon Mâlâyesâ takes us yet further. "This species", it says, "is also called the Solomon plant, because King Solomon, following the tradition handed down from Hermes, made use of it in all his undertakings. Alexander the Great did the same. This is a noble plant and famed of old and its root which is in the image of two human beings embracing one another, was prized by kings and kept in their treasuries."[4] From this it is again clear that the piece of root

[1] Offenbarungszauber, I, p. 128.
[2] Concerning "moon-sickness", see W. H. Roscher, Selene und Verwandtes, pp. 68f., 167; including the matter supplied there (p. 185) by N. G. Politis; Realenzyklopädie für die protestantische Theologie und Kirche, XIII, pp. 343f.; H. Rahner, "Mysterium Lunae", in Zeitschrift für katholische Theologie, 64 (1940), p. 69; p. 121, n. 1a.
[3] See W. H. Roscher, Selene und Verwandtes, pp. 70f.; 109. Concerning the herb σεληνίτις in the magic papyri see Wessely's Index and A. Abt, op. cit., p. 91. The Romans seem to have regarded Etruria as being especially the land of magic herbs. Medea and Circe were reputed to have prepared their drugs in the caves near the town of Luna (see Strabo, V, 222, where it is referred to as Σελήνης πόλις). See also Realenzyklopädie, XIV, col. 320 (T. Hopfner).   [4] Quoted by Wetzstein, op. cit., p. 441.

in Solomon's ring which is also mentioned in the pseudepigraphic *Testament of Solomon*[1]—in reality a piece of magic literature—and which is there alleged to have formidable power over demons, was simply a piece of mandrake root.

The reference of the lexicon to the tradition of Hermes leads us to the Arabic *Trismegistos*; in the book *On the Pressing of Plants* the aglaophotis is designated as the plant of Selene and in other parts of the Arab Hermetic tradition this same moon-plant is referred to as the magic plant of Solomon.[2] Further, in another part of the lexicon there is a detailed description of the manner in which the *sirag el-kotrub* must be lifted. This must be done on a Monday, on the day of Selene that is to say, and before sunrise, and a black dog must do the lifting. We see quite plainly from this that the mandrake, like the aglaophotis, is a nocturnal moon-plant, and Wetzstein[3] must surely be right when he says that both the Semites of Asia Minor and the Greeks gained the relevant magical knowledge from the Persians, and if we find exactly the same magical ideas among the ancient Germanic peoples and have no valid ground for supposing that the Romans acted as intermediaries in this, then Wetzstein is surely right once again when he adds: "The Germanic belief in the magic powers of the mandrake probably came to Europe from its original Asian home together with our own people." Thus two streams of magical tradition which had been separated at an early stage, meet again in the Middle Ages. On the one hand we have the dog-magic imparted secretly from time immemorial by word of mouth, on the other the Greek tradition transmitted together with their own by the Arabs.

That is how the dividing-lines between mandrake and moly and lunaria tended to become indistinct botanically speaking, though even as this occurs the magician's eye sees in them all with

---

[1] PG, 122, 1317 A. Here we are only told that Solomon's magic ring was brought him by the Archangel Michael. We should however certainly think of a ring that had beneath the gem a piece of the root of "Solomon's plant".

[2] Cf. the Hermetic work, Περὶ βοτανῶν χυλήσεως, ed. G. Roether in the appendix to the edition of Lydos, *De Mensibus*, Leipzig-Darmstadt, 1827, pp. 313 ff. The Syriac *Hermes Trismegistos* (Ibn al Baithar), ed. Sontheimer, II, 14, pp. 606 f. More exact information further on. Cf. also E. H. F. Meyer, *Geschichte der Botanik*, II, pp. 340–8; T. Hopfner, *Offenbarungszauber*, I, p. 118; Ascherson, *op. cit.*, p. 731. [3] *Op. cit.*, p. 442, n. 1.

increasing clarity the embodiment of the *materia prima*, that chaos out of which all roots arise and into which all things must ultimately be resolved, and the more the alchemist enters into this matter the more all this holds true. The lunaria or berissa of the alchemists, the black moly root with which they concerned themselves and their practices when searching for the mandrake—all this flows together to form a single picture. Whether the berissa of the alchemists is derived from the "besasa" which we encountered in our study of moly symbolism or is an Arabic elaboration of Josephus' "baaras" is really immaterial. Moon-plant, lunaria, aglaophotis or the mandrake that glows at night—we may be concerned with any of these, for at this stage we are dealing simply with symbols, symbols with which certain ideas are associated. This explains why in an alchemist's treatise the *lapis*, the final goal of all magical effort, is described as being drawn up by a dog: *"Lapis per caudam canis ex suis sedibus evelli debet–*The 'stone' must be drawn out of its place by a dog's tail."[1]

This brings us to a feature of mandrake magic which played a considerable part in the Middle Ages but of which there is no evidence in the tradition of antiquity. When the black dog is pulling at the root, the root-gatherer must hold his ears, for when the mandrake is torn out of the earth, it utters a scream which it is death for men to hear. This reminds one of a very ancient fancy which we find mentioned in Proclus, namely that souls which are sunk too deeply in the material, utter a shrill cry ($\tau\rho\iota\sigma\mu\acute{o}\varsigma$) when they are parted from their bodies.[2] So far as the mandrake is concerned, however, we have no evidence of anything of this kind earlier than the Arab tradition. According to this last, a plant named *lûf* if torn out at the feast of Pentecost, utters a death-bringing cry.[3] This *lûf* is most certainly identical with that named *luffâh* by the Arabs—and this is none other than our mandrake.[4] It is evident that the Middle Ages got this story from the East-Arabian tradition, and thenceforward when root-gatherers are depicted lifting the mandrake we see them holding their ears so as not to imperil

[1] *Der kleine Bauer*, p. 259; cf. p. 220, n. 2.
[2] *In Rem Publicam Platonis* (ed. Kroll, I, Leipzig, 1899, p. 121, l. 19).
[3] Cf. J. Löw, *Aramäische Pflanzennamen*, Leipzig, 1881, p. 239.
[4] Wetzstein, *op. cit.*, p. 443.

their lives.[1] The secret teaching of the alchemists was very fond of dwelling on this. *"Das roth Männlein, das im Grund steckt, schreyt: iuva me et iuvabo te. Das ist eins rechten Alrauns Männleins geschrey und zuruffen: verschaff daz du die wurzel dem Hund an den schwantz bindest und dich alsbald davon machest*—The little red man in the ground cries: 'iuva me et iuvabo te' [help me and I will help thee]. That is the true cry of little man mandrake. See that thou bind the root to the dog's tail and be off quickly."

Even Shakespeare can still write the gruesome lines:

> . . . Shrieks like mandrakes' torn out of the earth,
> That living mortals, hearing them, run mad.[2]

3

It was necessary for us to plough our way through the various ideas of antiquity, botanical, medical and magical, about the mandrake in order to appreciate the heights to which this root, earthbound in every fibre, was elevated by Christian symbolism. In the end the mandrake too became a "soul-healing flower".

In Christian symbolism there was developed an idea which we have already recognized in the more ancient mandrake magic. We saw that as long as the root remains embedded in the dark earth, it is subject to the demons of Hecate, but that once the skilled rhizotomist comes to its aid and it ceases to be thus entrapped, it becomes health-giving and a warder off of demons,

---

[1] The oldest picture is the representation in the Vienna Dioscurides MS.; the goddess Heuresis is handing Dioscurides a mandrake root and holds the lead of the dead black dog. Illustration in P. Buberl, *Der Wiener Dioskurides und die Wiener Genesis*, Leipzig, 1937, Plate III. For other pictures, see J. F. Payne, *English Medicine in Anglo-Saxon Times*, London, 1904.

[2] *Romeo and Juliet*, act IV, scene 3. See also R. Sigismund, "Die Pflanze als Zaubermittel" (The Plant in Magic), in *Mitteilungen des botanischen Vereins für Thüringen*, 3 (1889), pp. 290 ff. For the subsequent history of the magic see Schmidel's book, Leipzig, 1671, where in para 53 the "Christian" form of this magic is described. The rhizotomist must pull the root out by means of a dog on a Friday before sunrise, having first made the sign of the cross three times over it and stopped his ears. Other information in W. Grimm, *Deutsche Mythologie* (German Mythology), II, pp. 1153 ff. We are now in a better position to understand Goethe's lines in the second part of *Faust*, 4979 f.:

> Der eine faselt von Alraunen,
> Der andre von dem schwarzen Hund.
> (The one babbles of mandrakes
> The other of a black dog.)

while in the hands of a competent physician its erstwhile poison becomes a physic that brings rest to the soul. All this is more explicitly developed in the symbolism of Christianity. The dark root which is our human nature becomes a source of health, because God himself, the eternal rhizotomist has come to its aid and has freed it from its entanglement with the dark powers. The poisonous root, made in the semblance of a man, but lacking a head, is crowned with eternal rest in Christ, the head of all.

Before we deal with the separate aspects of this symbolism, I must first show you how the Christian symbolism of antiquity applied the idea of the "root" to the human race and to its spiritual problems. Both the individual man or woman, and the whole family of Adam, from the point of view of their ultimate supernatural fate, can be compared, as Gregory the Great once said, to a root that spreads its tentacles in the ground:

"By this root we may understand the nature of man, that nature that is the essential part of him. Even as a root ages in the ground and gradually begins to die, so it is with man, who, according to the nature of his flesh, resolves himself at the last into ashes. The root becomes dust, and the beauty of man's body suffers corruption. But the fragrance of the living water causes the root to revive, and similarly the human body is recreated when the Holy Ghost descends. For all things return to that beauty for which they were destined at our creation, had we not sinned in Paradise."[1]

Adam is the root of our race and what was done in him was a prefiguration for all that sprang from him, in the bad and ultimately in the good sense of the words. "*Radix apostatica*" is what Augustine calls the father of mankind.[2] This refers, of course, to his original sin, but even apart from that Adam is a root belonging to the earth simply because he is created out of matter, out of the loam of the earth. According to the thought of antiquity all

[1] *Moralia in Iob*, XII, 5, 7 (PL, 75, 989f.).
[2] *Enchiridion*, 99 (PL, 40, 278 D).

living things come from the domain of the dark earth, from the life-engendering "warm and moist" elements. This, according to Plutarch's account, represented the "Chemia", or Chemmi, the "Black Land" of Egypt.[1] And so when the Christian of antiquity read in his Bible that Adam had been formed out of clay, he immediately thought of this black matter; Adam was "black" so far as his body was concerned, being formed of the same elements as the roots that are of the earth.[2]

This is entirely in harmony with a very ancient piece of teaching which played an important part right up to the Middle Ages. According to a very old tradition Adam was formed by God out of "red earth", from the clay of primal matter.[3] In ancient colour symbolism however, red and black have the same significance. Red is the colour of the material, of the Typhonic—"for Typhon, the Egyptians believe is of a red colour tending towards paleness", says Plutarch. Red is therefore the colour of the non-spiritual or anti-spiritual; red is the colour of death, and whatever is red must die.[4] Red is for this reason even the colour of evil itself. Indeed we still possess a prayer to Isis which some pious person composed. "O Isis, great one of the magic formulae! Free me from the hand

[1] *De Iside et Osiride*, 364 C.

[2] See *The Syrian Treasure Cave*, II, 7–12, where the forming of Adam out of the four original elements is described: P. Riessler, *Altjüdisches Schrifttum ausserhalb der Bibel* (Ancient Jewish Writing outside the Bible), Augsburg, 1928, p. 944. The manner in which people conceived of this primal element of the earth is clearly shown in the Slavic *Book of Enoch* which was closely connected with the ideas of the Essenes in the first century. In it (XXVI, 1), the Creator says: "I called out and said that some solid and visible thing should come forth out of the invisible; then Aruchas came forth, solid, heavy and black" (Riessler, *op. cit.*, p. 461).

[3] Thus first in Flavius Josephus, *Antiq. Iud.*, I, 1, 2 (Niese, I, p. 9, ll. 8–12): "Man was called Adam, for this word in Hebrew signifies 'red', for he was formed out of red, kneaded earth—for thus was the virginal and true earth created." This is later repeated by Jerome, *De Nom. Hebr.* (PL, 23, 773), and Isidore, *Etym.*, VII, 6, 4 (PL, 82, 275 A), and it was from them that the Middle Ages inherited it, e.g. Vincent of Beauvais, *Speculum Naturale*, XXIX, 2. See Rahner, *Zeitschrift für Aszese und Mystik*, 17 (1942), p. 74. How very much alive this conception remained, even in the sphere of alchemy, is proved by H. Kunrath, *Vom Hyleatischen, das ist Pri-Materialischen . . . Chaos* (Concerning the Hylic, i.e. the pre-Material Chaos), Frankfurt, 1708, p. 52, "Adamah, das ist *limo terrae rubrae*, der roten Erden/Laimb/Letten oder dicken Primaterialischen Schlamm, daraus Adams leib formieret war" (Adam means the lime of the red earth, loam or thick prime-material slime out of which Adam's body was formed).

[4] See J. von Duhn, "Rot und tot" (Red and Dead), in *Archiv für Religionswissenschaft*, 9 (1916), pp. 1 ff.; E. Rhode, *Psyche*, I (9th edition), p. 226; T. Hopfner, *Offenbarungszauber*, I, pp. 155 f.; F. J. Dölger, *Die Sonne der Gerechtigkeit*, p. 82.

of all wicked, evil and red things!"[1] When therefore the Christian
of those days spoke of Adam as being formed out of red earth, he
meant to convey that he was material and mortal—and ultimately
that he was subject to the demonic powers. To convey this he
might, however, equally well have said that Adam's bodily form
was black and indeed in the mosaics of the entrance of St Mark's in
Venice this essentially Graeco-Roman conception finds pictorial
expression. Adam is here represented as coming out of God's
hands completely black. He is ultimately represented as white and
beautiful like a classical statue, but only when the spirit of God is
breathed into him, his soul that is to say, which is here represented as a "Psyche" with butterfly wings.[2]

Now this last is precisely the transition that we were able to read
into the story of the "soul-healing flower" which, as you will remember, served as a kind of preparation for the Christian fulfilment. Black becomes brightness, the formless assumes beauty of
form, the earthy root is raised up on high. Translated into Christian terms, this means that God, the Redeemer, takes pity on the
root which, dark and demon-dominated, is caught in the deep
fastnesses of the earth, and that in the end of days, when all flesh is
glorified and all earthly, dark and sinful things are transfigured by
the light, this process in which the root is slowly raised from the
ground, will be completed. Under the symbol of the mandrake all
this is expressed in a prayer spoken by the Christian root-gatherer
after searching by night for the holy root that could cure
demoniac diseases; for it is not the root grown from out the
innocent earth that is in danger of the dark powers, but the
progeny of the apostate root, Adam.

*"Deus, qui hominem de limo terrae absque dolore fecisti, nunc terram
istam, quae nunquam transgressa est, iuxta me pono, ut etiam terra mea
pacem illam sentiat, sicut eam creasti."*

(O God who hast fashioned man out of clay without pain,
see, I lay beside me this piece of earth which has never sinned, so

[1] Thus in the *Papyrus Ebers*. Cf. A. Wiedemann, "Magie und Zauberei im alten
Ägypten" (Magic and Sorcery in Ancient Egypt), in *Der alte Orient*, VI (1905), p. 26.

[2] L. Troje, "Eine alte Schöpfungsdarstelluing in San Marco" (An Ancient Conception
of Creation in St Mark's), appendix to Reitzenstein's *Die Vorgeschichte der christlichen Taufe*,
Leipzig, 1929, pp. 317–27, with illustration.

that my own clay may at length come to know that peace in
which thou didst create it.)[1]

I hope in the pages that follow to describe this Christian mandrake symbolism in some detail and so to bring to life before
you a forgotten chapter of Christian history. I hope to acquaint
you more closely with a forgotten piece of what I might well call
pictorial theology and a forgotten conception of the healing of
souls. If I am to make my points successfully, however, I must ask
you to keep two things in mind: first, Christian theology's chief
interest in the mandrake has always centred on the two Bible texts
to which I have already drawn attention, namely Genesis 30. 14 ff.
and Song of Songs 7. 13; second, it never wholly forgot what the
old pagan world had thought and said about this subject.

I think it is quite proper that when dealing with this question of
biblical exegesis, I should arrange the enormous wealth of Patristic
material on which I can draw in an order roughly corresponding
to that which I observed when describing the root's supposed
medical and magical effects. I will therefore deal first with
the healing scent which the mandrake's berries exude in spring.
After that I shall touch on the Christian interpretation of the plant's
putative power to awaken love, and then, on the mystical interpretation placed on the narcotic powers of the drug distilled from
its root. Finally, I shall speak of the apocalyptic transformation of
the human-shaped root, of the bride Mandragora, in the heavenly
blossoming of the soul-healing flower.

As we saw, the people of antiquity believed that the very scent
of the mandrake berries could have powerful effects. That scent
could be healing if the mandrake had been lifted from the soil in
the prescribed fashion—it will be remembered that even during
the digging it was necessary to guard against a contrary wind—for
while the demonic powers still inhabited the root, that same scent
could be poisonous. When salutary the scent could, after the
fashion of a good physician, quieten the nerves, but for the Christian there was more than this involved. He read in the Song of
Songs: "The mandrakes breathe forth their scent", and for him this

---

[1] Hildegard, *Physica*, I, 56 (PL, 197, 1152 A). See also A. Franz, *Die kirchlichen Benediktionen*, I, p. 420.

springtime which the bride greets with such an ecstasy of song is the time of grace and the doors on which hangs a bunch of these heavily scented mandrake berries, are the doors of the Church. The Christian had now but to recall the words of Paul (II Cor. 2. 15–16) in which both grace and the work of the apostles are likened to "the good odour of Christ" and contrasted with "the odour of death" and his world of pictorial imagery relating to this matter was complete.

It is strange what varied changes of fortune a set of words can undergo. Just now we were standing by Augustine's side when he was examining the root and berries of a mandrake. He found, it will be remembered, that the berries had a sweet smell but that there was little taste in the root: "*Proinde rem comperi pulchram et suave olentem, sapore autem insipido*"[1] and in that very moment his mind gives birth to a symbol. "I think", he says, "that what such a mandrake berry really symbolizes is what we call a good name." The words were uttered on the spur of the moment, yet they were to live on and have a very considerable history—as was the comparison they expressed, for Isidore of Seville copied them word for word[2] and they thus became the heritage of the whole Middle Ages. From now on the mandrake stands for the good name, for the sweet savour of good example, of virtue and of the soul-healing physic of apostolic doctrine.

There is something touching in the way in which Hrabanus in his peaceful monastery at Fulda quietly reproduces Augustine's words without drawing attention to the circumstance that they are in point of fact Augustine's. "And what shall I say of the mandrake?" he writes. "Well, I have observed that it is a beautiful thing and has a sweet smell, but little taste, and that is why I regard such a mandrake berry as a symbol of a good name."[3] The learned Alcuin, court theologian to Charles the Great, amplifies the image still further. "The mandrake is compared to the virtues of the saints because of its manifold healing qualities. The doors on which it hangs are the holy doctors of the Church. They give

[1] *Contra Faustum Manichaeum*, XXII, 56 (CSEL, 25, p. 651, ll. 18f.).
[2] PL, 83, 262 BC.
[3] *Comment. in Genesim*, III, 17 (PL, 107, 600 CD); *Allegoriae in Scripturam* (PL, 112, 995 B).

forth a sweet odour at the doors, because spiritual men breathe forth far and wide the fragrance of their virtue."[1]

I could cite many similar examples.[2] Here, for instance, is Angelomus of Luxeuil re-echoing the thoughts of his master Alcuin: "Mandrakes because of their many medicinal uses are compared with the virtues of the saints which, like good physicians, cure souls of their sinful infirmities."[3] The mandrake then has a soul-healing fragrance and the time soon comes when even the virtue of the Blessed Virgin is compared to "the sweet-smelling physic of the mandrake".[4] Let me produce just one more illustration. It is the exquisite paraphrase of the Song of Songs, written half in German and half in Latin about the year 1060 by Williram von Ebersberg. Here the physic derived from the fragrant mandrake is made to convey the following symbolic meaning:

"Díe árzat uuúrze stínkent uíle dráho in únseren pórton. Odor virtutum an dén apostolis unte án íro successoribus dér lókket íro auditores, daz síe per eos veluti per portas îlen intrare ad vitam. Iro praedicatio díu íst ôuh quasi odor mandragorae, quae in radicibus suis similitudinem habet humani corporis, uuánte síe sínt omnibus omnia facti unte kúnnon compati et consimilari auditorum infirmitati."

(The medicinal root gives forth a strong scent upon our doors. The fragrance of the virtues in the apostles and their successors draws their hearers towards them, so that they hasten to enter into life through the apostles as through a door. Their preaching is similarly like the scent of the mandrake. This last shows in its root a similarity to the human form, for the apostles became all things to all men and can suffer in sympathy with them and adapt themselves to their infirmity.)[5]

So much for the mandrake's life-giving scent and the symbolism which grew up around it. We touch even deeper ground with

[1] *Compendium in Cant.*, 7 (PL, 100, 661 B).

[2] Thus Nilus of Ancyra in the *Procopius Catena* (PG, 87, 2, 1736 D). Among Latin writers, Pseudo-Gregorius (PL, 79, 538 B), Justus of Urgel (PL, 67, 989 B).

[3] *Enarrat. in Cant.*, 7 (PL, 115, 623 BC).

[4] Alanus of Lille, *Elucidatio in Cant.*, 7 (PL, 210, 103 AB).

[5] Williram, "Deutsche Paraphrase des Hohenliedes" (German Paraphrase of the Song of Songs), ed. J. Seemüller, *Quellen und Forschungen zur Sprachgeschichte der germanischen Völker*, XXVIII, Strasbourg, 1878, p. 58, ll. 1-21.

its second property that of a physic for love and for the fruitfulness of women. We saw earlier how widespread was this medico-magical belief both in the Graeco-Roman world and among Semitic peoples. That it survived right into the Christian era is, however, due to other causes than the obstinacy with which such opinions persist. The determining factor was the passage in Genesis alreadyalluded to, that most ancient piece of evidence for the mandrake's erotic powers.

We have already noted Augustine's scepticism in regard to this piece of folk-lore and his rather contemptuous reference to the belief that mandrake root, if mixed with their food, increased the fertility of women,[1] but though even in the Middle Ages Peter Comestor was still repeating these Augustinian doubts,[2] the ancient belief was too strong to succumb to them. When the man-shaped root is removed from the influence of the devil, we are told by Hildegard of Bingen, then it serves to regulate sexual attractions between man and wife.[3] Contrariwise, so long as the root is held fast in the earth, it is still within the power of diabolical Venus, as it was once in that of Hecate and Circe: "*Freitag das ist ein heilige zeit und frawen Venus im Hörselberg eigener tag, dô die alraunen wohnen* – Friday is a holy day and Mistress Venus' own day in the Hörselberg where the mandrakes live."[4] Mandrake continues for long to be both the symbol of female fertility and the means of achieving it. Even so late a writer as Conrad von Megenberg speaks of it in his *Book of Nature* as a means of facilitating childbirth: "*das zeucht die gepurt auz der muoter*".[5]

Christian symbolism fastened on to this tradition at an early stage. For instance Ambrose uses his knowledge of both botany and magic to build up his allegory. He begins by repeating the symbolic interpretation of the mandrake scent after the fashion with which we are already acquainted. He then continues: "Many make a distinction of sex in mandrakes and maintain that they are both male and female and that it is the female which has the

---

[1] *Contra Faustum*, XXII, 56 (CSEL, 25, p. 651, ll. 4f.).

[2] *Historia Schol. in Genesim*, 76 (PL, 198, 1117 A).

[3] *Physica*, I, 56 (PL, 197, 1151 BC).

[4] From an Erfurt MS., referred to by J. and W. Grimm, *Deutsches Wörterbuch*, I, Leipzig, 1854, p. 246.   [5] *Das Buch der Natur*, V, 48 (ed. F. Pfeiffer, Stuttgart, 1861, p. 407).

powerful scent. This signifies the heathen who at one time gave out an odour of corruption, since in the impotence of their un-belief they were, so to speak, unmanned, but now that they be-lieve in the coming of Christ, they are beginning to produce fruit with a sweet fragrance."¹ This is, of course, simply the botany of the good Pliny—but observe in what fashion this is formed into a garment for other truths! Ambrose is always ready for the chance of an allegory and the thought that is now aroused within him is that of the union, the loving embrace between God and man which is consummated in Christ and the Church—here is the male and female principle in its most perfect form.

But now Ambrose remembers the mandrake with which Rachel sought to regain her husband's love. "We read", he says, "that holy Rachel received a mandrake from her sister Leah . . . and Reuben, her first-born had brought his mother Leah one. But Leah with her streaming eyes is the image of the Synagogue who, because those eyes were weak, could not behold the grace of Christ, and so it came to pass that the fruit which the first-born, the Son of God, once offered to the Synagogue passed into the possession of the Church."² Thus the mandrake becomes the symbol of that new love between God and man of which the Church is the visible embodiment. Jerome in one of his letters gives us a similar interpretation. Rachel who till now had been childless represents the Church. Jacob's love is obtained by means of the fragrant mandrake.³

This perhaps is the place to say something of that allegory which was transmitted by the *Physiologus* and was the delight of Christians both in antiquity and in the Middle Ages. It is the story of the elephant who eats the mandrake and is consumed with love.⁴

---

¹ *Expositio in Psalm.* 118, *Sermo* 19, 24 (CSEL, 62, p. 434, ll. 11–16). Repeated verbatim in the Middle Ages in Werner, *Deflorationes Patrum* (PL, 157, 1152), and William of St Thierry in the commentary on the Song of Songs gathered from the writings of Ambrose (PL, 15, 1951 AB). ² *Ibid.*, ll. 17–23.

³ *Epist.*, 22, 21, 3 (CSEL, 54, p. 172, ll. 3–5). See also Procopius, *Comment. in Genesim*, 30 (PG, 87, 1, 439); Fulgentius Afer, *De Aetatibus Mundi*, 5 (Helm, p. 145, ll. 27ff.).

⁴ *Physiologus*, 43 (ed. F. Sbordone, Milan, 1936, pp. 128–33); F. Lauchert, *Geschichte des Physiologus* (History of the Physiologus), Strasbourg, 1889, pp. 271–3. See also M. Well-mann, "Der Physiologos, eine religionsgeschichtliche-naturwissenschaftliche Unter-suchung" (A Study from the point of view of Comparative Religion and Science), in *Philologus*, supplementary vol. XXII, 1, Leipzig, 1930.

The elephant is the symbol of wisdom, of quiet recollectedness, of chastity and frigidity.[1] "This animal", says the *Physiologus*, "is devoid of all appetite for sexual intercourse. When, however, he is concerned to produce progeny, he wanders in an easterly direction till he is quite close to Paradise. There grows the plant known as the mandrake."[2] The female eats of the plant first and then gives the male to eat "of that sweet-smelling plant".[3] As a result, both begin to burn with love, and the female receives the seed of new life.

These mythical happenings became the symbol of the events that occured in Paradise at the beginning of the human race. The real mandrake is the tree of knowledge, and the love that resulted from the tasting of it was the origin of mankind. The wicked Cain was born first, but at the end came Christ the νοερὸς ἐλέφας (literally, the intelligible, i.e. metaphorical or allegorical elephant) and all is once more put right and healed.

Wellmann's researches seem to have established the fact pretty clearly that the kernel of this allegory—we must of course disregard the Christian additions—is of Jewish-Syrian origin, and at this point Wellmann's findings join on very aptly to what I was saying a little while ago about Solomon's root. It is indeed the Hermetic tradition among the Syrians and Arabs that enables us to throw some light on *Physiologus'* allegory. "In this," says Wellmann, "the part played by the mandrake fruit rests upon Jewish superstition. The Syrian *Hermes Trismegistos*[4] tells us that King Solomon had this 'tree' planted in all his properties because of its beneficent and healing powers and that he carried a piece of it in his signet ring; through this he was able to work the miracle that all spirits were made subject to him. Also the blossoms make childbirth easier, so that women can bear children without great pain."[5] This Eastern tradition, with the background of which

---

[1] Cf. Pliny, *Nat. Hist.*, VIII, 5, 12. On the elephant and ivory as the Christian symbol of chastity, see Pseudo-Cassiodorus (PL, 70, 1087 B); Gregory (Paterius) (PL, 79, 524 B); Isidore (PL, 82, 436 B); Hrabanus (PL, 111, 464 CD). See also J. Baum, "Die Schaffhauser Elephanten" (The Schaffhausen Elephants), in *Neue Zürcher Zeitung*, May 21, 1944, No. 854 (23).

[2] Sbordone, p. 128, ll. 2–5.

[3] Thus in the Byzantine *Physiologus* (Sbordone, p. 168, l. 60).

[4] Ibn al Baithar (ed. Sontheimer, II, 14, 606f.).   [5] Wellmann, *op. cit.*, p. 41.

we became familiar when I dealt with the mandrake's magic properties, was appropriated by the Christian author of the *Physiologus* and given a theological reinterpretation. The mandrake grows close to Paradise, the place where once God fashioned Adam out of the same earth-element from which there grew the human-shaped mandrake root. Yet around this tree the serpent is coiled: the mandrake is poisonous and the partaking thereof decides a man's fate for he falls down out of his "angelic" life and is caught within the dark powers of the senses.

Speaking of *Physiologus'* allegory of the mandrake and the elephant, the Byzantine Michael Glykas can still write: "Clearly this is a symbol of our first parents, for before these had tasted of the fruit of the wood, the life they led was even as that of the angels, but when they had tasted it and the transgression had been committed, then Adam knew Eve as his wife, and Cain was born."[1] The whole Middle Ages took delight in this deep symbolism and its writers would often take this opportunity to air their magical and botanical erudition concerning the mandrake.[2] Indeed in an old German *Physiologus* manuscript there is a picture which shows the two elephants standing before the wonderful "tree"; the mandrake is represented as an upright torso, human in shape, and the life-giving flower grows out of it. The text which keeps alive for the Middle Ages the love allegory of the mandrake reads:

"*Sô sîn zît chumit, daz er chint wil giwinnen, sô nimit er sîn gimachide unte vert unze zuo dem paradîse. dâ vindit er eine wurze heizit mandragora.*"

(When his time comes and he wants to beget offspring, he takes his mate and journeys until he comes to paradise. There he finds a herb called mandrake.)[3]

We have seen that even as the mandrake can give forth both an odour of corruption and a fragrant scent of life, so also can it be

---

[1] *Biblios chronikè*, I (PG, 158, 120 B).

[2] Cf. Hugo de Folieto (Pseudo-Hugo of St Victor) (PL, 177, 72–4). The Anglo-Norman *Bestiaire* of Philippe de Thaun (ed. T. Wright), contains, in chap. 16, a detailed account of the botanical and magic features of the mandrake. The same is true of the *Bestiaire* of the cleric Guillaume. See also F. Lauchert, *op. cit.*, pp. 129 and 145.

[3] Text in Lauchert, *op. cit.*, p. 286.

the herb of life or of death, a symbol of both sensual love, the bringer of death, or of divine love, the restorer of life.

This dialectic of the magical which is here given new symbolic values becomes even more arresting when we study the mandrake in the allegorical interpretation of the plant's narcotic qualities. As we have seen, the juice of the mandrake root was the best means known to antiquity of inducing anaesthesia and sleep, and that is why Apuleius spoke of this drug as *"venenum sed somniferum mandragoram, illud gravedinis compertae famosum et morti simillimi soporis efficax*–mandragora which is a poison but a bringer of sleep and renowned for the numbness and death-like slumber it produces".[1] These words eloquently express the essentially dual nature of the mandrake. It is poison, yet it is a bringer of sleep; it quietens, yet such quiet is like the quiet of death. Frontinus expresses this in a famous story about the soldiers of Maharbal who drugged their enemies with mandrake wine, which *"inter venenum ac soporem media vis est*–is an agent half-way between poison and sleep".[2]

Here then is another source of much imaginative symbolism which has its beginnings right back in the days of antiquity, for even of old slothful, sleepy and excessively easy-going people were called mandrake drinkers. One need only recall the thunder of Demosthenes when he said to his Athenians: "You men, you are like people who have taken a draught of the mandrake."[3] Plato too has a passage in which he says that it would be well if when an incompetent person seizes the rudder of the ship of State, he could be made drunk with a draught of mandrake.[4] So the figure of speech was already known in Greek literature and that was natural enough, since the mandrake was already in use as a soporific and as a means of deadening pain in surgery.

The narcotic effects of the mandrake were a subject to which Christian preachers were extremely fond of referring. Actually it was Ambrose who was the author of the sentence that was repeated again and again all through the Middle Ages: *"Per mandra-*

[1] *Metamorph.* X, 11 (Helm, p. 245, ll. 1 f.).
[2] *Strategemata*, II, 5, 12 (Gundermann, p. 60, ll. 14 f.).
[3] (Pseudo- ?) Demosthenes, *Philipp.*, IV, 6 (Butcher, I, p. 131, ll. 27–9). See also Lucian, *Demosthenis Encomium*, 36 (Reitz, III, p. 517).
[4] *Repub.*, 488 C.

goram quoque somnus frequenter accersitur, ubi vigiliarum aegri affectan-tur incommodo-Sleep is often induced by means of the mandrake in cases where sick people are disturbed by wakefulness."[1]

Among Christian writers Clement of Alexandria is the first to use the simile in the manner which had almost become traditional among pagan writers. He is addressing himself to the heathen who resist the Logos or appear to understand nothing of his witness. "You foolish men," he cries in very nearly the same words as Demosthenes, "you are like people who have been lapping up mandragora or some other poison."[2] Here we see one feature of the mandrake being used in allegory, namely its poisonous quality; but this poison—as the Christian preachers put it—has been given us by God for our use and healing, and so it is easy to understand how the beneficent qualities of the mandrake's nar-cotic powers came also to play their part in Christian symbolism, and so served the cause of Christian truth.

Cyril of Alexandria speaks at one point of the medical use of the mandrake and tells how physicians employ it as a soporific. But herein, he continues, there is hidden the mystery of Christ. God who became man and descended into the midst of us like one descending into the depths of an abyss, became like unto one who has drunk of the mandrake and so has become numb: "Like one who sinks into a deep sleep, so did he come down amongst us to suffer annihilation and death, in order that he might rise again unto life."[3]

Loosely connected with this system of symbolism in which the properties of the mandrake are used to throw light on the person and story of Christ, is an extensive complex of ascetical ideas which forms one of the most interesting chapters in the history of the psychotherapy of the soul-healing flower; such ideas are in evi-dence both in antiquity and the Middle Ages. Even as Christ, like one who is poisoned, fell asleep in death and yet awoke to life as the wondrous root from the earth of Adam, so too the Christian

---

[1] *Exameron*, III, 9, 39 (CSEL, 32, 1, p. 85, ll. 18 f.). Cf. Basil, *Hexaemeron*, V, 4 (PG, 29, 101 D).

[2] *Protrepticus*, X, 103, 2 (GCS, I, p. 74, ll. 7 f.).

[3] *Glaphyra in Genesim*, IV, 11 (PG, 69, 220 A). Thus also Procopius, *In Genesim*, 30 (PG, 87, 1, 439).

who wishes to free himself from Adam's poisoning and numbness, must take the cup of mandrake in his hand. We encounter this piece of teaching first in Theodoret, though there is little doubt that Theodoret has taken the idea from Origen's lost commentary on Genesis. "Medical experts (ἰατρῶν παῖδες) tell us that the mandrake acts as a soporific but that, if taken in the right quantities, it is not poisonous. The Christian should follow the lesson contained in this: he must not kill himself, but he must fall asleep to sin, καθεύδειν ταῖς ἁμαρτίαις. And even as those who have drunk of the mandrake no longer feel the movements of their body, so should those who seek to cultivate virtue empty the cup and thus lull their passions into quiet sleep."[1]

This therapy of spiritual quiet continued to be taught by the Western theologians—and what psychologists some of them were! Bede is an excellent example. In his commentary on the Song of Songs, Bede quotes from Isidore and Ambrose the words with which we are already familiar about the narcotic effects of the mandrake and applies them to the sleeplessness of the soul, to that state of the soul which is the origin of all spiritual sickness, in which it is torn to pieces by a thousand worldly hopes and cares. Then this great spiritual expert goes on to say that such diseased psychic conditions tend chiefly to occur when a man is earnestly striving to free himself from the forces that are thus pulling him asunder and when, because of his previous habits, he is unable to achieve his liberation.

In the middle of the allegory that is woven round the mandrake there is one sentence that is eloquent of the most profound experience: "Plagued indeed is he by a most evil sleeplessness who seeks to free his soul from the cares and desires of this world but is hindered by the residue of his bad habits and so cannot attain that rest which he so ardently desires."[2] The physic for this malady is that blessed sleep which is vouchsafed by the true mandragora, which is the grace of God. It is the sleep of heavenly contemplation, that most exquisite draught, which cures all nausea and frees us from that inclination to vomit which life engenders. The

---

[1] *In Canticum*, IV, 11 (PG, 81, 197 CD). Cf. also Michael Psellos, *Comm. in Cant.* (PG, 122, 676 C).   [2] *Allegorica Expositio in Cant.*, 7 (PL, 91, 1203 f.).

Glossa ordinaria was later to preserve for all time the wisdom of this Anglo-Saxon monk in a sentence which in the Middle Ages was read by all who concerned themselves with the reference of the Song of Songs to the mandrake. "The mandrake [i.e. the grace of God] gives us that rest from all the disturbances of the world which removes all tendencies to vomit before God's word; it gives us that numbness which prevents us from feeling any pain when our vices are excised."[1]

It is the sweetness of heavenly contemplation which quietens men's souls and makes them free, it is that blessed sleep in which the soul closes its eyes and knows only God. Bruno of Asti has expressed all this with perhaps greater beauty than any other. It is, he says, the apostles who brought us the mandrake of eternal rest, that draught which causes us to forget all things and extinguishes all memory of our former sinful life;[2] but in this connexion it is also well worth reading the magical directions given by the great Hildegard of Bingen concerning the mandrake. How wonderfully she describes those spiritual states that can be relieved by the holy root after it has been baptized in water and freed from all demoniac influence. The mandrake is a cure for melancholy: "When a human creature is torn asunder in his innermost being, so that he continually goes about in sadness and unceasingly is full of grief, if constantly he feels a want in his heart and a pain—then let him take a mandrake that has been uprooted from the earth and has lain for a night and a day in a fountain of living water and let him lay this mandrake beside him in his bed, so that the root becomes warm from the heat of his body and then let him say as follows."[3] Here follows that prayer that comes from the very depths of the spirit, the prayer which I quoted above,[4] the prayer that expresses longing for that paradisial freedom in which before his first sin man was created by God.

Here we have the psychotherapeutic wisdom of the people of

[1] *Glossa ordinaria on Cant.*, 7, 13 (PL, 113, 1164 A), and *On Genesis*, 30, 14 (PL, 113, 157 AB).

[2] *Expositio in Genesim*, 30 (PL, 164, 211 A); *Expos. in Cant.*, 7 (PL, 164, 1281 C).

[3] *Physica*, I, 56 (PL, 197, 1152 A). See G. Killermann, *Naturwissen. Zeitschrift*, new series, 16 (1917), p. 141.

[4] See p. 250.

old who, under the image of the soporific mandrake draught, with which they were familiar from antiquity, concealed the profound insights that had been given them through their knowledge of souls.

Even before Hildegard's day, Williram had expressed this idea:

"*Also daz pomum mandragorae quod simile est malo terrae haustum in vino máchet díe slaffelôson dormire et requiescere, sámo tûont doctores eos, qui laborant strepitu mundanarum rerum . . . als ábo díu ûzzera rînta eiusdem pomi, in uuîne getrúnkeníu duálm máchet dén, díe man scál snîdan óder brénnan, sámo tûont doctores: mit sola superficie divini verbi geárzenont síe díe infirmos auditores unte máchent síe quodammodo insensibiles ad mundi mala toleranda.*"

(Even as the mandrake apple which resembles the earth apple [the reference is probably to 'sow bread'—*Cyclamen europaeum*] when taken in wine, makes sleepless persons sleep and rest, so do the teachers of those who suffer from the noise of worldly things also seek to do . . . and even as the outer rind of this apple, when drunk in wine, numbs those who must be cut or burned, so do the teachers also seek to do; for even with the mere outer rind of the divine word they heal their sick hearers after the manner of physicians and make them, as it were, insensible to all the evils of the world which they have to bear.)[1]

Thus the traditional narcotic of antiquity became a symbol of a state of psychic healing which Philo and Origen had already called νηφάλιος μέθη, and which Ambrose rendered in a descriptive phrase which the Latin world was never to forget, calling it *sobria ebrietas* or sober drunkenness,[2] the sober drunkenness of the spirit which is mystical contemplation and in which the soul descends into the inmost recesses of itself where God himself touches it and raises it up above its own level.

Here we encounter once again the same concept of theology and of spiritual medicine that we observed in the final stage of moly symbolism. To enter into God is for the soul to be freed

---

[1] *Deutsche Paraphrase des Hohenliedes*, 128 (Seemüller, p. 58, ll. 12–21).

[2] Cf. F. Lewy, *Sobria Ebrietas: Untersuchungen zur Geschichte der antiken Mystik* (Studies in the History of Ancient Mysticism), Giessen, 1928.

from the earthly world; what we experience is the painful dying away, the mystical τρισμός, or shriek of pain, of the black mandrake root which is ourself. But what was previously chthonic poison is now transformed into a health-giving gift, so that dying turns into life. The truth that is here again restated amounts to this: only when the soul can escape beyond itself, only when its root is freed, can it be made whole. In the idiom of Augustine, the mystic would say that only when the soul is wholly in God is it wholly in itself. A medieval mystic speaks as follows:

"The mandrake is a plant that brings such deep sleep that it makes it possible to cut people without their feeling any pain. The mandrake thus symbolizes contemplation. Contemplation permits man to sink into a slumber of such precious sweetness that he no longer feels the cuts inflicted on him by his earthly enemies and pays no more attention to worldly things; for the soul has now closed all its senses to external matters—and lies in the good sleep of its own inner being."[1]

Here we have been concerned with a condition of the individual, a blessed state of final perfection in which all dark roots are mystically lifted. Something analogous however takes place in the story of the whole progeny of Adam, in the development of the whole plant that is sprung from the apostate root, and it now remains for me to say something of the unfolding of that ultimate form of symbolism that is woven round the mandrake. It is the symbolism of that apocalyptic consummation which takes place when the divine rhizotomist finally lifts the human root from out of the earth and raises it into the light.

The subject-matter with which I now have to deal has an especially close connexion with that feature of the mandrake root which from the earliest times seemed both to the Greek and Oriental peoples to be particularly mysterious. The feature in question is the mandrake's likeness to the human form. The mandrake is "ἀνθρωπόμορφος" and, needless to say, this feature was not lost upon the Fathers of the Church. "*Hanc mandragoram poetae*

---

[1] Thomas Cisterciensis, *Comment. in Cant.*, XI (PL, 206, 759 D).

ἀνθρωπόμορφον appellant," writes Isidore citing verbatim from Dioscurides, *"quod habet radicem formam hominis simulantem*–Poets call the mandrake man-shaped because the shape of its root resembles that of a man."

The Carolingian Angelomus and the German Rupert of Deutz both cite the Greek word from Isidore.[1] Bede[2] speaks of *"mandragora habens radicem formam hominis imitantem"*, and Williram[3] and Bruno of Asti[4] write to the same effect, while Conrad von Megenberg, to whom the later Middle Ages and the alchemists owe such botanical wisdom as they possessed, remarks, *"Diû gleicht dem menschen, sam Avicenna spricht*–This is like man, as Avicenna says."[5] For all of these the mandrake is, before all else, the "human root".

Yet if we are truly to grasp the inwardness of the symbolism to which this aspect of the mandrake gave rise, we must once more hark back to the plant's supposed magical powers. This strange human-shaped root, which resembles a human body without a head was, it will be remembered, subject to the demonic powers for so long as it remained embedded in the earth. When they saw it, the people of antiquity thought of the ghosts of the dead who went about as headless demons, and it is relevant for me here to refer to the plant of the Egyptian Bes, for Bes too was an *ἀκέφαλος δαίμων*, a demon without a head, and this headlessness expressed for the ancient peoples the essential nature of the demon world, contrary to God and bereft of logos.[6] It is, therefore, not surprising to find in the *Testament of Solomon*, alongside the dog demon, "a demon who had the members of a human body but was headless".[7]

If, therefore, the mere sight of the mandrake's uncanny shape was sufficient to suggest to the ancients that it must have its origin in the dark subterranean kingdom of Hecate, we can well understand that it should have conjured up a related idea, in the

[1] Angelomus, *Enarrat. in Cant.*, 7 (PL, 115, 623 B); Rupert of Deutz, *Comment. in Cant.*, XI (PL, 168, 949 A).
[2] *Allegorica Expos. in Cant.*, 7 (PL, 91, 1203 A).
[3] Seemüller, p. 58, ll. 5f.
[4] *Expositio in Genesim*, 30 (PL, 164, 211 A).
[5] *Buch der Natur*, V, 48 (Pfeiffer, p. 406).
[6] Cf. T. Hopfner, *Offenbarungszauber*, II, pp. 90f.
[7] *Testamentum Salomonis* (PG, 122, 1329 B).

Christian mind, namely that this human-shaped root which came out of the dark earth was possessed of sinister and devilish powers, and that it must first be taken out of the ground and fashioned anew before it could act as a physic for souls. Had it not been formed out of the same earth from which was fashioned the flesh of sinful Adam?

The most illuminating utterance, illustrative of this train of thought is to be found in Hildegard of Bingen. The period to which her words belong is late, but their content is a very ancient mixture of magic and theology:

"Mandragora . . . de terra illa de qua Adam creatus est, dilatata est; homini aliquantulum assimilatur. Sed tamen herba haec et propter simi- litudinem hominis, suggestio diaboli huic plus quam aliis herbis adest et insidiatur. Unde etiam secundum desideria sua homo, sive bona sive mala sint, per eam suscitatur, sicut olim cum idolis fecit."

(The mandrake grew forth from the same earth out of which Adam was created and to some extent its shape resembles that of man. Such is this plant, and because of this likeness which it has to man, it is more amenable to the influence of the devil and his wiles than other plants. Thus also, a man can conjure up with it, according to his desires, either good or ill, as was once the case with idols.)[1]

Hence, according to Hildegard's directions, this human root must first be cleansed in spring water and so withdrawn from the demon's power, for it was believed that it would retain its diabolical power if such "baptism" were omitted or if only a crumb of earth were left adhering to it. So strong was this revived sense of the mandrake's essentially chthonic character.

Let us follow a little more closely the story of the symbolism that developed around this human root. The mandrake, as has already been made clear, is the image of the ever-increasing progeny of Adam that is embedded deep in the dark earth yet yearns for the light and strives to unfold the fragrant flower of eternal life from its headless root. Though such thought had been traditional and had originally derived from Origen, we encounter

[1] *Physica*, I, 56 (PL, 197, 1151 A).

this allegory for the first time in Philo of Carpasia and again it is the magic sentence in the Song of Songs, "The mandrakes breathe forth their fragrance", that causes the ideas to unfold. Philo puts the following interpretation on the words: "The roots of the mandrake lie deep under the earth and have the appearance of human bodies. They thus bear upon themselves the image of the dead. For the dead already sense the coming of the Lord Christ into Hades, and so they give forth the savour of their future resurrection."[1] Nilus of Ancyra gives a similar interpretation of the mandrake's scent in the Song of Songs—and Nilus' commentary, though we no longer possess the whole of it, most certainly drew on Origen and was the leading authority right into Byzantine times. Nilus says: "Thou couldst also interpret the word of Scripture as follows: the mandrakes are those who are to rise with Christ for they have a root in human form and signify with this man's dedication to death."[2]

It is, however, not only after death that the fragrance of the longing for eternal life proceeds out of the dark human root. No, even now while man is still rooted in the dark earth, the apocalyptic fragrance begins, the longing for the glory that is to come ascends to heaven. For Procopius of Gaza, however, the "man-shaped root deep under the earth signifies that those who die unto the world for Christ's sake breathe forth the sweet odour of their good works. It also signifies that the dead who sense the glorious coming of Christ let the fragrance of their resurrection mount upwards."[3]

We can see from the similarity of the ideas expressed that these writers draw on a common source. That source is the immortal Origen who speaks to us through them—and these ideas continued right into the days of Byzantine mysticism.

Matthew Cantacuzenus sees the matter a little differently. His commentary on the Song of Songs declares that the scented

---

[1] *Enarrat. in Cant.*, 217 (PG, 40, 136 B). In regard to sources, see W. Riedel, *Die Auslegung des Hohenliedes in der jüdischen Gemeinde und der griechischen Kirche* (The Interpretation of the Song of Songs among the Jewish Community and in the Greek Church), Leipzig, 1898, p. 77.

[2] Fragment of his commentary on the Song of Songs preserved in the *Catena* of Procopius (PG, 87, 2, 1737 A).

[3] *Comment. in Cant.*, 7 (PG, 87, 2, 1737 B).

9. Odysseus at the Mast
Fifth-century vase-painting from Vulci (British Museum)

10. Odysseus at the Mast of the Cross
Fourth-century Christian Sarcophagus (Rome, Museo delle
Terme)

11. Duke Ulysses at the Mast
From Herrad of Landsberg, *Hortus Deliciarum*

mandrakes first signified the Synagogue and then the Church that grew up among the Gentiles with its victorious martyrs. But this mystical story of the divine fragrance has an ending and this comes at the end of days. "For the Scripture, when it speaks of the mandrake, is also mindful of those who are waiting in Hades, for this plant with its man-shaped root is buried deep in the earth, and this signifies that the time will come when those who are now held fast in the depths of Hades will be led up into freedom by the Redeemer, by him who humbled himself unto death."[1]

When we turn to the symbolism with which Latin writers surrounded the mandrake, we immediately encounter a comparatively unknown author whose work even today does not receive the attention it deserves. I refer to the contemporary of Augustine, Aponius. He is the spiritual father of the interpretation of Song of Songs 7. 13 which held its own till the advent of the Middle Ages.

"The mandrake [so begins his exegesis] is a plant whose root resembles exactly the human form though it lacks a head . . . it sends forth its fragrance at the doors, which means at the very entrance, as it were, to the day of judgment, at the end of the world; it is then that it begins to send forth its scent. Now it seems to me that these mandrakes are the symbols of those heathen peoples who till now grew wild and lived all their life sunk deep in the earth; thanks to the law of nature they were like men endowed with reason, but they lacked the head of faith, by which I mean him who is the head of man, namely Christ."[2]

And now Aponius harks back to that magical practice of the root-gatherers about which we were told in Pseudo-Apuleius. It will be remembered that a black dog was not the only means used in removing the root from the earth. Another and more innocent thing was used, namely a machine (*manganum*) which was in effect a rod made to serve as a catapult. The essential point is that the root was not removed by the root-gatherer himself. So it will be at the end of days; the dark root, which is those peoples that are still far from Christ, will at the end be drawn forth from

[1] *Comment. in Cant.* (PG, 152, 1073 B).
[2] *Explanatio in Canticum,* XI (ed. H. Bottino and J. Martini, Rome, 1843, pp. 210f.).

the devilish realm of the earth; and they that will do this are the angels herding the whole human race in apocalyptic droves, and gathering the peoples from the ends of the earth so that their fate may provide us, who have been true to Christ, with a physic like that made from the mandrake's root. *"De suis sedibus evulsae [gentes] ab angelis, ad medicinam animae nostrae in nostris terminis adducuntur; sicut praedicta herba propter remedia corporum non ab homine, sed reflexo stirpe evelli de suis sedibus refertur*—The heathen will be torn from their abodes by the angels and brought where we are as a medicine for our souls; just as the plant of which we have heard which acts as a physic for our bodies is not uprooted from the earth by a man but by a catapulting rod." And even as a draught of the mandrake quietens a man and takes away his nausea and his desire to vomit, so will it be now; through the sufferings which, at the end of time, will tear the peoples from their homes, even those who are far from Christ will lose their loathing for the word of God; through being uprooted they will become their own soul-healing flower, and now, even as men desire a draught of the mandrake, they will long for the food which previously revolted them. *"Nunc angustiis coartatae cum magno desiderio in tribulatione et penuria vel captivitatis ergastulo requirunt cibos quos in deliciis et omnium rerum abundantia positae fastidiebant*—And now in the affliction of their final fears, amid tribulation and poverty or even in the close confinement of prison, they ask with burning desire for those foods which filled them with loathing when they were wantoning and lived in superfluity." Here we have the apocalyptic cure of souls, the reconsecration of the black mandrake into the heavenly flower. Aponius ends his instruction with the words:

"In the last days, before the gates of the end of the world, all peoples who live under heaven will be converted to the God of heaven, they will enter into the faith in Christ, and their faithful confession of him will be as the fragrance of the mandrake."

There were in the view of the early Middle Ages two sides to this apocalyptic conversion of all peoples at the end of days. There would be a conversion of the heathen, but to this was added another thing, namely a change of heart on the part of the surviving remainder of Israel which, after the victory over Antichrist, would penitently make its submission to Christ. Both these ideas found expression in the mandrake symbolism. Bede speaks of this, but only in very general terms: "This plant, the mandrake," he says, "is reputed to possess the shape of a man, having hands, feet and fingers, but it has no head; it lacks the head Christ who is the head of the Church."[1] The nations in the days before the glorious coming of Christ had what appeared to be a head, namely Antichrist. They were sprigs from the apostate root, the devil.

Here was a very ancient form of symbolism. We find it in Cassiodorus,[2] and the *Glossa ordinaria*[3] transmitted it to the Middle Ages. It is connected with a verse from Psalm 51: "God shall likewise destroy thee forever. He shall take thee up and pluck thee out of thy tent and take thee as a root out of the land of the living" (Ps. 51. 7). "This root", says Cassiodorus, "is Antichrist and his helpers the devils, and that is why we read that they will be taken up as a root out of the land of the living, because neither Antichrist, nor the devil, nor any of his company shall have any portion with the saints." To this there is now added the very ancient teaching that all these things will be fulfilled in the Jews—save only for that small remnant that, in the end of days and after the destruction of Antichrist, will be converted to Christ. For this was the interpretation placed on Isaiah 10. 22 and Romans 9. 27. We can already see the thing in Ambrose,[4] and Augustine has a famous chapter on it in the *Civitas Dei*.[5]

There is a close connexion between this conception of the last days and of what would happen therein, and the symbolism of the headless mandrake. When the phantom head of Antichrist has been cut off, heathen and Jew will be like headless roots, but in the fateful days before the coming of the Lord they will be converted and Christ will be the eternal head of the headless mandrake.

[1] *Comment. in Genesim*, 30 (PL, 91, 257 C).
[2] *Expositio in Psalterium*, 51, 7 (PL, 70, 375 B).
[3] PL, 113, 921 A.
[4] *De Iacob Patriarcha*, II, 3, 13 (CSEL, 32, 2, p. 40, ll. 15f.).
[5] *De Civitate Dei*, XX, 29 (CSEL, 40, 2, pp. 503–5).

The early Middle Ages, which had such a lively interest in the apocalyptic solution of the Jewish problem, worked out the final details of this symbolic theology. Wolbero of Cologne writes as follows:

"The mandrake is a sweet-smelling plant which is formed in the likeness of the human body but has no head. . . . If thou seekest a spiritual meaning in this, thou mightest well discern therein the conversion of the heathen . . . for the heathen were indeed possessed of the likeness of men, in that they had the natural powers of knowledge and were able to choose between good and evil; but because they were unable to recognize their Maker, the power of their knowledge was in some measure weakened by this, and because they did not recognize God, it was as if they lacked a head. Yet we can also regard the headless mandrake as signifying the Jewish nation which was indeed endowed with human reason and applied that reason to the observance of its laws, but was nevertheless headless, in so far as it would not accept the headship of Christ. Even so, in the end, the mandrake gives forth its fragrance, for what was unfruitful in unbelief now putteth forth shoots in the begetting of many sons of God."[1]

This is the teaching that is continually propounded throughout the Middle Ages. In the mystery plays that told of the victory of the Ecclesia over the perfidious Synagogue, in the superb figures of these two chief characters in this divine drama as we see them in our Gothic cathedrals—in and through all of these, this vivid and picturesque theology began to assume its ultimate shape. In the Tegernsee drama of Antichrist, the Synagogue, after the adversary has been overthrown, returns home to the Church to the singing of that same Psalm 51 which speaks of the adversary's uprooting. "As for me, I am as a green olive tree in the house of the Lord", cries Ecclesia in her joy as she folds her returning sister in her arms.[2]

Now, what is here made to come to life in folk poetry and folk imagery found expression in the theology of the time under the symbolism of the mandrake. "Mandrakes are plants which

---

[1] *Comment. in Cant.*, 7 (PL, 195, 1239f.).
[2] See H. Rahner, *Mater Ecclesia*, Einsiedeln, 1944, p. 21.

resemble the human body though they have no head, and they are a sign of the Jews who still lack the head which is Christ." Thus, Anselm of Laon,[1] while Philip of Harveng declares that the headless root is "the clever Jews, who for all their cleverness have gone astray and who will remain a mere stump of root so long as they do not possess Christ, the head of the faithful".[2] Even that commentary on the Song of Songs which is wrongly ascribed to the great Thomas Aquinas, though it is really from the pen of his pupil Aegidius Romanus, the commentary that in its day had so wide an influence, concludes the argument by saying:

"Note well that the mandrake is a herb whose root has limbs like a man, but it has no head. This signifies the Jews who are still without a head. But at the end of days when they receive the word and the fragrance of the Church, they will breathe the sweet odour of their longing, and their longing will be to unite themselves with Christ the head."[3]

This apocalyptic vision of the end of days has found a rather different but equally vivid expression in an Old High German piece of writing in which once again the mandrake has a part to play. This is the so-called *Trudperter Hohelied* (the Trudpert Song of Songs). In this Christ himself appears as the divine rhizotomist who lifts the screaming mandrake, which is mankind, out of the earth, so that he may endow it with the power of blossoming everlastingly and give it an undying fragrance. This he does by the power of his incarnation through which he himself descended into the dark kingdom in which our human roots are embedded. Then by an extraordinary boldness of metaphor Christ himself is at his final coming conceived as the mandrake who by the crying out of its mighty voice becomes a dispenser of everlasting life and death:

"*Die edelen wurzen die stinchent in unseren porten, dass ist furtrefec-líchen mandragora. der wurze ist gelîch ainis mennisken bilde, unde*

---

[1] *Enarrat. in Cant.*, 7 (PL, 162, 1222 D).

[2] *Comment. in Cant.*, VI, 31 (PL, 203, 473 D).

[3] Commentary *Sonet vox tua*, c. 7 (Thomas Aquinas, *Opera omnia*, XIV, Parma, 1863, p. 421); see also M. Grabmann, *Die echten Schriften des hl. Thomas von Aquin* (The Genuine Writings of St Thomas Aquinas), Münster, 1920, pp. 189–91.

haizet dûtisken alrûn. der ir stimme vernimet der mûz des todes sîn, so
man sie ûz zuchet . . . disiu wurze bezêchenot got, des pilde was christ.
in der erde was er aineme mennisken gelîch. er ist uns ain arzentum unde
ain phant des êwigen lîbes . . . sîn rinde daz ist der hailige gaist, daz ist
der tualm der slâfente machet alle die minâre des hailigen christes. sîn
stimme daz ist sîn gewalticlich urtaile, diu ertôtet alle sîne raizzâre."[1]

(The noble roots smell sweet upon our doors. That is the excellent mandragora. Its root has the likeness of a man and is called in
German Alraun. Whoever hears its voice when it is drawn out of
the earth, he belongs to death. . . . This root symbolizes God of
whom Christ was the image. On earth he was like a man. He is our
physic and a pledge of eternal life. . . . Its rind is the Holy Ghost
and he is the intoxicating drink who causes all who love Christ to
fall asleep. Its voice is his mighty judgment that slays all his
adversaries.)

And now we are prepared to scale the ultimate summits of mandrake symbolism, there to delight in that even more pregnant
imagery which has produced some of the most exquisite examples
of the miniaturist's craft and in which all the artistry of thought
that Christian and classical symbolism had accumulated around
the headless mandrake achieves its ultimate perfection. Honorius
Augustodunensis is here the central figure; it is he who can truly
claim to have conjured up this world of magic imagery, and he
did so in his commentary on the Song of Songs, a work that draws
generously both on Christian and classical tradition, yet nowhere
loses the mark of the author's unique and individual genius.[2] For
this inspired symbolist the Song of Songs is a revelation of the
last days; he seems to see Solomon's love poem as a drama in four
great acts, and the four chief characters are the four queens who
are led to Christ the bridegroom, when he appears in his glory,
from the four quarters of heaven.

Honorius is a true poet with all a true poet's visual imagination.
He is rightly credited with having conceived of the Song of Songs
as a strange and rather special kind of mystery play. Certainly his

[1] *Trudperter Hohelied,* 125, 11–30 (ed. H. Menhardt, in *Rheinische Beiträge zur germanischen Philologie,* vol. 22, Halle, 1934, pp. 263 f.).
[2] *Expositio in Cant.* (PL, 172, 347–496).

interpretation is unique. In the first act there comes from the east the first of the queens; she is Pharaoh's daughter, the symbol for all those who found their way to Christ before the law of the Old Covenant. From the south comes the second figure, the Queen of Babylon; she represents the multitude of people who found the faith under the Law and the Prophets. Then there comes to meet Christ from the west "Queen Sunamitis" personifying all pagans who have believed.

But the drama is not yet over, for now, after the overthrow of Antichrist, in the last few days before the coming of Christ, a strange thing comes to pass. From the north, from the region of demonic darkness where till now no sun had shone, there comes one who stands for "Eternal Israel"[1]—Queen Mandragora. She is solemnly escorted to Christ by the other three queens and their retinues—"Mandragora, our little sister who as yet has no breasts",[2] she stands for that little band who will still be converted before the doors of eternity close. The heathen and the Jews, who till now were under the power of Antichrist, are coming home to Christ, and the poor, headless, spectre-like root Mandragora is crowned with a head which is the head of Christ. But let us hear the story in Honorius' own words:

"After all the train of Sunamitis had been received into the hall of the king and had been admitted to the royal wedding, then with great pomp, a new bride, from the north, is led before the bridegroom. It is Mandragora who has no head. And the bridegroom sets upon her shoulders a golden head adorned with a crown and so she is led in to the wedding.

"For as Sunamitis departed from the royal city, she found Mandragora, the royal maid, lying in a ploughed field without a head. She was seized by a deep compassion and returned to the king whom she earnestly begged to go with her and succour the hapless one. So the king went into the ploughed field and found the unhappy one in pitiful nakedness, and he raised her up and clothed her and put a golden head upon her and led her to his bridal chamber.

---

[1] Honorius, *Sigillum B. Mariae*, 7 (PL, 172, 514 D).
[2] *Expositio in Cant.*, IV (PL, 172, 485 A).

"Now mandragora is a plant that is shaped in the likeness of a man without a head, and it is a figure of the great multitude of unbelievers who will live at the end of days, whose head is Antichrist, the head of all evil men. But Mandragora's head is cut off when Antichrist is killed. After his destruction the Synagogue sees the desire for conversion that moves these unbelievers who are without their head, Antichrist, but also lack the head, Christ, and it desires that these also should join it in faith in Christ and grow taller by a head, the head of Christ. Therefore it says, 'Come, my beloved, let us go into the fields and go through the hamlets. Already the mandrakes send forth their fragrance upon our doors.'

"Now the mandrake, as I have said, is a plant that is shaped like the body of a man without a head, and it is of use in the making of many physics, and we understand it as signifying the world of the heathen who are indeed possessed of human reason but had as yet not Christ as their head, although they had many salutary beliefs. Upon this world the bridegroom now places his golden head by making known to it in faith his Godhead (which is a greater thing than all else in the world, even as gold is a greater thing than all the other metals). So it is crowned with honour and glory and enters wedlock with him in the clear light of the vision of God. The mandrakes without a head are the heathen who lack Christ as their head after their head, which was Antichrist, has been cut off."[1]

This rich and imaginative symbolism to which Honorius makes a number of references elsewhere,[2] moved the miniaturists, who were subsequently to illustrate this commentary of the enigmatic Augustodunensis, to some of their most delightful achievements. We still possess and can still admire their work.[3] Above the fire-

[1] *Expositio in Cant.*, IV (PL. 172, 471 f.).

[2] Thus already in detailed fashion in the Prologue (PL, 172, 353 BC) and later several times (475 B, 477 BC); see also the anonymous author of a commentary on the Song of Songs conceived after the manner of Honorius (PL, 172, 539 D).

[3] For a catalogue of these miniatures from Vienna, Munich, Lambach and St Florian, see Endres, *Das St. Jakobsportal in Regensburg und Honorius Augustodunensis* (The St James Door in Regensburg and Honorius Augustodunensis [of Autun]), Kempten, 1903, pp. 32 ff. and K. Künstle, *Ikonographie der christlichen Kunst* (Iconography of Christian Art) Freiburg, 1928, p. 319. To this must be added a further miniature from St Paul in Carinthia (Wickhoff, III, p. 95, Figures 49 and 50).

breathing figure of Aquilo, the dragon of hell, we see as a lovely, naked beauty, Queen Mandragora, beside whom lies the severed head of Antichrist. The headless bride is being escorted in by the three other queens of the work of redemption who are already crowned and who are advancing, designated as *reginae* and accompanied by their trains of *adulescentulae*. King Christ, followed by the "king's friends", namely the apostles, crowns the bride with a head which these inspired artist-theologians have drawn in the likeness of his own. And now Mandragora can enter into the "clear vision of God"—since she has received divine eyes—, can enter the company of the queens and of the friends of Christ.[1] The Romanesque miniatures which depict this coronation, have in certain instances this superscription around them:

> *Cui caput imponit sponsam diademate comit,*
> *Aequat reginis sponsus, coniungit amicis.*

(On whom he sets a head, her he adorns with a crown
   as his bride,
As bridegroom makes her the equal of queens, and joins
   her to his friends.)

And now the summits of this symbolism have been scaled and we see to what heights the mandrake has been raised, the mandrake that was once a thing full of demonic powers and is now a soul-healing flower.

What was still to be said in the later Middle Ages[2] of the mandrake's nature and significance falls short of the levels of a theology that could still speak in pictures when it sought to express the inexpressible. Only a few specialists in classical and Patristic symbolism were again for a moment to catch the mandrake's enchanting scent. In the sixteenth century the Spaniard, Luis de

---

[1] The "friends" in Honorius and on the miniatures are the apostles and teachers, who stand as "fragrant mandrakes by the doors", that is to say beside the Ecclesia. This is already to be found in Williram and is expressed artistically on the St James door in Regensburg where the "teachers" are shown upon the doorway, and next to them a naked dwarf figure, our Mandragora. Cf. Endres, *op. cit.*, p. 64.

[2] Cf. for instance, Bartholomaeus Anglicus, *De Genuinis Rerum Proprietatibus*, XVII, 104 (ed. Frankfurt, 1601); Vincent of Beauvais, *Speculum Naturale*, X, 97 (Strasbourg edition, 1476), which is the most complete collection of ancient and Christian symbolic lore in the Middle Ages; K. Gessner, *Historia Plantarum*, Basle, 1541, pp. 94ff.

la Puente,[1] wrote a mystical and very profound commentary on the Song of Songs in which he seeks felicitously to apply the idea of the mandrake to the interior life. Its scent in spring, its healing power and its ability to excite love or a divine intoxication—all these things are connected, according to de la Puente, with the secrets of the contemplative life. For him the mandrake is the symbol of the heroic life that roots deep in the soul, of that ultimate secret of spiritual healing, which earth-bound man can only find if God himself lifts him out of the depths into his own light.

We may, perhaps, close this account of the symbolism surrounding the soul-healing flower, this story of Platonic and Christian psychotherapy, with some verses of that Platonist in cardinal's robes, John Henry Newman, verses that are formed with that sureness of touch that this ever human type of imagery always seems to inspire:

> O man, strange composite of heaven and earth!
> Majesty dwarfed to baseness! fragrant flower
> Running to poisonous seed! and seeming worth
> Cloaking corruption![2]

In all the imagery that has passed before our eyes in this story of the soul-healing flowers moly and mandragora, in all that has been said in pagan myth or Christian allegory, there lurk those eternal questions whose substance I have endeavoured to compress into the charged phrase "healing of souls". The black root and the white flower have been symbols since time immemorial of man's search for God. From the dim past of Homer to the days of Romanesque miniatures, from the quiet clarity of Plato to the dark bubbling world of the alchemists, from the searching of the Greek to the finding of the Christian, a single longing passes through the soul of man—to rise from darkness into light and salvation, from ashes into crystal, from formless matter into articulately fashioned and eternal stone, from root to gleaming flower. All is, to quote that anonymous alchemist, the author of

---

[1] *Expositio Moralis et Mystica in Canticum Canticorum*, II, Cologne, 1622, pp. 499 ff. Considerable erudition in the matter of symbolic sources is also possessed by Cornelius à Lapide, *Commentarius in Canticum*, VIII (ed. Paris, 1868), p. 202.

[2] J. H. Newman, *The Dream of Gerontius*, ll. 291–4.

Der kleine Bauer, "*eine eygentliche und vollkommene Idea und klarer Spiegel*—a true and perfect image and mirror of man's created nature, of his infirmity, of his redemption, of his cleansing and rebirth, of his death, corruption and resurrection, of the parting of his soul and body, of their return or reunion, of the welfare of both in unending, everlasting blessedness".[1]

[1] *Ein philosophischer und chemischer Traktat, genannt der Kleine Bauer* . . . *von der Materia und Erkenntnus des einzigen und wahren subjecti universalis magni et illius praeparatione* (A Philosophical and Chemical Tract entitled "The Little Peasant" . . . concerning the Substance and Knowledge of the one true *subjecti universalis magni,* etc.), Strasbourg, 1618. p. 118.

Part Three
HOLY HOMER

INTRODUCTION

AND now I come to the third part of my book, the part which will complete what I might call an essay in psychagogic science. In it our spirit will travel up to the heights towards which the ancients looked with poignant longing and which the Christian, with his mind fixed on the beatific vision, hopes joyfully to attain. As I proceed I shall, amongst other things, be making clear the real meaning and inwardness of Christian humanism, for Christian humanism reposes on the simple truth that the successful fashioning of this our earthly life, the fashioning of it into a life of true humane goodness and nobility, can only be achieved if we go beyond our present world and take our stand in the world to come; for only thus can we find and learn to love what is eternal in man. Only by relaxing his hold on created things can man hope to make their hidden worth his own. To find we must renounce, and it is only by the light that streams from the door which we only enter in death, that earthly things disclose their clear and truly lovely forms. That is why Odysseus, the eternal voyager, had first to sail to the dark doors of Persephone—and how strange that it should have been Circe herself who sent him thither—ere he was permitted to find the way to his sweet earthly home, for this story of Odysseus rests on an intimation, even though dim and fleeting, of that truth that is the foundation of Christian humanism, the humanism that is proof against all illusion; the truth is this: God has willed it that heaven is not to be the only thing that man should enjoy. Earth also, transfigured but still delectably tangible, earth with all its loveliness is also there, here and now, for his delight, "But we look for new heavens and a new earth in which justice dwelleth" (II Peter 3. 13).

The arduous way to these heights has already been made plain in the imagery of those Greek myths of which I have tried to expound the Christian interpretation. Man must rise from the Acherontic swamp to Christ Helios, he must rise from the darkness of his mother's womb, which is the baptismal pool, to that Platonic mystery of the cross which glitters in the night sky and heralds the coming day of light; he must rise from mud to the stars. This ascent is a true purgatory, a process of discernment and decision within the soul, for in man giant's blood does battle with the light of Helios and soul-eating dogs seek to destroy the human longing for the soul-healing flower to unfold. And now the final summits remain to be climbed, for from the mountain of purification the road leads to Paradise.

Before attempting to interpret the pictures evoked by Greek mythology in terms of Christian fulfilment, may I preface my remarks with the immortal lines from Dante's *Purgatorio* whose music perfectly expresses what my own halting words will seek to convey:

> *E canterò di quel secondo regno*
> *Ove l'umano spirito si purga*
> *E di salire al ciel diventa degno.*
> (I will sing of that other kingdom
> Where the human spirit is purged
> And made worthy to soar to heaven.)[1]

For this heavenward journey I will make so bold as to invite Homer to act as our poetic counsellor and guide and I shall seek to form two scenes from his *Odyssey* into a kind of covering or veil for the Christian interpretation of those hidden things of the next world by which the present one is already transfigured; for Homer is—to use a phrase of Plato—"one who under the concealing cloak of poetry has true knowledge of wisdom".[2] That is why I have given to this portion of my book the title "Holy Homer". Yet I do not wish this phrase to bear the somewhat nebulous significance of Goethe's well-known words in *Des Künstlers Morgenlied* (The Artist's Song at Morning):

> *Ich trete vor den Altar hin*
> *Und lese, wie sich's ziemt,*

---

[1] *Purgatorio*, I, 4–6.   [2] *Protagoras*, 316 D.

Andacht liturg'scher Lektion
Im heiligen Homer.
(I step before the altar
And read, as I fittingly should,
My devotion of a liturgical reading
In holy Homer.)

Not after that fashion should we call Homer holy. Rather should
my choice of words convey something of the humanistic insight
shown by the ageing Goethe when in 1814 he gave expression to a
vague feeling that there is some common ultimate depth where all
that is beautiful and true is somehow related to Christianity. "Let
a man accustom himself daily to read the Bible or Homer, or to
look at medallions or beautiful pictures, or to hear good music."[1]
Yet even that would not really satisfy me, for Goethe's "Bible or
Homer" might well be open to the imputation of implying the
kind of confusion of values which normally is characteristic of
the shallower types of mind. Certainly it does justice neither to the
unsurpassed majesty of the divine Word nor to the unique loveliness of the poetry of ancient Greece. Objections of a rather similar
kind were raised long ago by Hippolytus of Rome when he was
inveighing against the Gnostics: "They exalt their prophet
Homer", he said, "and in their presumption seek to make profane
writings the equals of Holy Scripture."[2] Were I to fall into an error
of that kind, I should come near to embarking on those ill-starred
attempts of a now moribund humanism that sought to bring
about a reconciliation between Homer and the Bible.[3] Or again I
might be held to share the pathetically simple view of those early
Christians of antiquity who insisted that their darling Homer had
achieved such profundity of wisdom from his perusal of the Old

---

[1] To Chancellor von Müller, May 30, 1814. See on this, O. Regenbogen, *Griechische Gegenwart. Zwei Vorträge über Goethes Griechentum* (The Presence of Greece. Two Lectures on Goethe's Hellenism), Leipzig, 1942, p. 11.

[2] *Elenchos*, V, 8, 1 (GCS, II, p. 89, ll. 7 f.).

[3] Amongst this strange literature I wish especially to refer to the following: Zacharius Bogan, *Homerus Hebraizon, sive Comparatio Homeri cum Scriptoribus sacris quoad Normam loquendi*, Oxford, 1658; G. Croesius, "Ομηρος ἑβραῖος, Dordrecht, 1704; F. B. Koester, *Erläuterungen der Hl. Schrift aus Homer* (Homer as a Source for the Interpretation of Holy Scripture), Kiel, 1833.

Testament. After all, had he not lived in the days of Saul and Samuel?[1]

Homer is holy for us in a much deeper sense than this. Guided by the genius of poetry, this blind singer touched with trembling hands the primal forms of truth, and for us this makes him the forerunner of the Word that appeared to us clothed in the flesh of man.[2] Homer is in Plato's words the pedagogue of all Hellas (τὴν Ἑλλάδα πεπαίδευκεν),[3] but it was the vocation of Hellas to be paganism's pedagogue and lead it to the Logos. Clement of Alexandria said as much when he said of Homer that he had a seer's gift of "striking home to the truth".[4] This hidden connexion between the poet's insight at its highest potential and the divine Word finds pictorial expression in the drawing that forms the frontispiece of this book, the drawing made by Raphael as a study for his Vatican Parnassus. That which blind Homer perceives while gazing into apparent nothingness, is seen by Dante, the Christian, with open eyes.[5] "This blindness that has sunk deep into his soul," says Goethe speaking of a Greek bust of the poet, "the seer's power that has turned inwards, has made the inner life grow

[1] We know principally from the *Address to the Hellenes* which dates from the second century and is wrongly attributed to Justin, that Christians believed that Homer had been in Egypt and had there read the writings of Moses and the prophets as at a later date Plato had done. See the *Address*, chap. 14 (Otto, *Corpus Apologetarum* III, 2, p. 58), chap. 24 (p. 82) and chap. 28 (p. 96, ll. 12–14): "We will endeavour to show that the poet has taken much from the divine history of the prophets into his work." Clement of Alexandria also declares that in certain passages Homer depends on Holy Scripture; cf. *Stromata*, V, 14, 99, 5 (GCS, II, p. 392); V, 14, 100, 5 (II, p. 393, ll. 4f.); according to Isidore of Seville, Homer lived in the time of Samuel and Saul and the medieval chronicles express the same view. Cf. PL, 83, 1029A.

[2] This is meant in the sense of Justin's statement, *Apologia*, II, 10 (Otto, I, p. 226): "Whatever the law-givers and thinkers have said and discovered that corresponds with truth, they have said and discovered by virtue of such slight portion of the Logos (κατὰ λόγου μέρος) as has been vouchsafed to them and that after much travail, labour and reflexion." Or, *Apologia*, II, 13 (Otto, I, pp. 236f.): "To be found to be a Christian— that is the goal of my prayer and my intensive struggle, not that the teachings of the poets and historians are alien to those of Christ, for each one of them has said things that are excellent according to the portion he had in what the Logos of God has scattered abroad in the form of seed, and in such measure as he had an eye for all that was related to this Logos."

[3] *Republic*, X, 606 E; see also W. Jaeger, *Paideia: Die Formung des griechischen Menschen* (The Education of the Greek), I, Berlin-Leipzig, 1936, pp. 63–88: "Homer als Erzieher" (Homer as Educator).

[4] *Stromata*, V, 14, 116, 1 (GCS, II, p. 404, ll. 15f.).

[5] Illustration taken from R. and E. Boehringer, *Homer: Bildwerke und Nachweise* (Homer: Illustrations and Confirmations), I, Tafelband, No. 119, Breslau, 1939.

stronger and stronger and it is this that makes perfect the father of poets."[1] Homer is what Dante calls him—"*poeta sovrano*", about whom is gathered the "lovely school" of poetic spirits; he is "the master of lofty song, who soars above all others like an eagle":

> *Di quel signor' dell'altissimo canto*
> *Che sovra gli altri com'aquila vola.*[2]

Among Christians all the great humanists have thus loved him, and thus do we deem him holy. "Sweet comfort and a physic to the soul," Gregory of Nazianzus calls him,[3] while Boethius at the beginning of his song to the sun declares that he "sings with a honey-sweet mouth".[4] Christians then could recognize Homer's greatness even as did that unidentified Greek poet who said of him:

> From time immemorial Homer's song has echoed down the
> ages and it will do so for all time to come.
> All the garlands of Olympia crown him.
> Long did nature meditate and create, and when she had created
> She rested and said "A Homer for the world".[5]

And so, let Homer guide us—Homer as the Christian interprets him. Let him lead us to "that other kingdom" where we can gain the knowledge that the lovely world of the humanities, which can also be one of the true homes of our spirit, can only be won and loved if we first dare to make the voyage to the gates of eternity, and boldly sail our ship past the tempting sirens. I will try and illustrate my point by examining two themes from the *Odyssey*, in each of which the myth is pregnant with meaning. They are those of the willow branch at the gateway of the next world and of Odysseus tied to the mast.

---

[1] See text in Regenbogen, *op. cit.*, pp. 13f.

[2] *Inferno*, IV, 95f.

[3] *Epistula*, 70, "To Eutropius" (PG, 37, 136 A).

[4] *Philosophiae Consolatio*, V, Metrum 2 (CSEL, 67, p. 110).

[5] Anonymous Greek author quoted from H. Rüdiger, *Griechische Gedichte mit Übertragungen deutscher Dichter* (Greek Poems with Translations by German Poets), Leipzig, 1936, pp. 12f.

VI

THE WILLOW BRANCH
OF THE NEXT WORLD

THE development of the symbolism with which I am here concerned is connected with just one word in Homer's *Odyssey*. In the tenth book the witch Circe enjoins Odysseus to go "to the house of Hades and to gruesome Persephone",[1] and the son of Laertes hears the words "with breaking heart"[2] for "never did any man reach Hades in his black ship".[3] But Circe using her demon knowledge, gives him precise directions and she describes the quiet, eerie shore at which the ship must anchor:

> But when thy ship has passed through the waters of the ocean
> And thou comest to a place where there is an untidy grove on
>   the shores of Persephone's kingdom.
> Where there are tall poplars and fruit-destroying willows—
> There make fast thy ship in the deep-swirling ocean
> And do thou thyself descend into the mouldering house
>   of Hades.[4]

I would like to concentrate on one line here whose long-drawn vowels themselves suggest the long shadows cast by the other world:

$$\mu\alpha\varkappa\varrho\alpha\acute{\iota}\ \tau'\ \alpha\ddot{\iota}\gamma\varepsilon\iota\varrho\iota\ \varkappa\alpha\grave{\iota}\ \grave{\iota}\tau\acute{\varepsilon}\alpha\iota\ \grave{\omega}\lambda\varepsilon\sigma\acute{\iota}\varkappa\alpha\varrho\pi\iota\iota.$$

(Lofty poplars grow there and fruit-destroying willows.)

This line concerning the ἰτέαι ὠλεσίκαρποι the "fruit-destroying" willows has behind it a long history of symbolic significance which till now has never been fully investigated. Even so erudite a scholar as Rüegg in his work *Jenseitsvorstellungen vor Dante* (Conceptions

---

[1] *Odyssey*, X, 491, 534; XI, 47. [2] X, 496.
[3] X, 502. [4] X, 508–12.

286

of the Next World before Dante) can say of the landscapes in the eleventh book: "The flat river bank with a few clumps of tall poplars and fruit-losing willows that overhang the water makes a picture of unique melancholy. What the poet could mean by 'fruit-losing' remains wrapped in mystery."[1]

It may well be, however, that the pagan and Christian interpreters of old may betray some knowledge of what Homer really meant by that curious phrase "fruit-destroying willows", or, to put the matter more precisely, the history of the symbolic interpretation of this line will show us what thoughts and mental images it aroused.

To understand the symbolism which Homer intended to suggest when he described the melancholy coast by the gates of Hades—or, at any rate, the symbolism his readers found in this description—, we must first visualize the situation in which the myth sets the seafaring Odysseus. He sails towards the north into the dark and distant land of the Cimmerians, where the gate of the next world opens to him. His voyage is like a dream in which the winds sent by heaven carry him forward; his progress is not due to any purposeful work of the oar. When he reaches this land, darkness sets in: "The sun sank and all the paths were darkened."[2] It is the right atmosphere for the offerings on behalf of the dead to "Hades, the mighty god and to terrible Persephone."

Yet this other-worldly darkness is illuminated by a strange light. Throughout all that now happens there runs unceasingly through his mind the thought of his return to Ithaca and home, and the ghost of Tiresias, the seer to whom Circe had especially directed him, rises from Hades to "speak to him unerring words".[3] But the seer's message from the realm of the dead is "sweet homecoming"[4] and the precious expectation of returning to the light of the sun and to the loveliness of life among men far from all the dangers of the threatful sea:

---

[1] A. Rüegg, *Die Jenseitsvorstellungen vor Dante und die übrigen literarischen Voraussetzungen der Divina Commedia* (Conceptions of the Next World before Dante and the other Literary Assumptions of the *Divina Commedia*), I, Einsiedeln, 1945, p. 27. See also P. von der Mühll "Zur Erfindung in der Nekyia der Odyssey" (Invention in the Nekyia of the *Odyssey*), in *Philologus*, 93 (1938).

[2] *Odyssey*, XI, 12.   [3] XI 96; 137.   [4] XI, 100.

And far away from the sea death shall come to thee, sweet
and gentle,
And shall reach thee when in happy old age thy strength
is failing,
And all about thee thou shalt leave thriving peoples.
These are unerring words.[1]

Thus darkness and light, life and death, meet at this outer border of human life, at the gateway to the next world.

It is a situation charged with contrasts. Before Odysseus lies the land of human shadows who quietly and in eerie fashion come swarming out of the mouth of the earth "cloaked in fog and mist, and Helios' rays never shed their light among them",[2] while behind him lies the land of life, the ship and the blue sea, friends and home, and Tiresias, like a true Greek, is only moved by this contrast to say:

Unhappy man why didst thou leave the light of the sun out
yonder
And come to see the sad homes of the dead?[3]

On the narrow strip of land that separates Helios and Hades there grow the tall poplars and the fruit-destroying willows, the trees of death and of life.

This placing of Odysseus in the region of tension between life and death, as it is described in the eleventh book of the *Odyssey*, has found clear artistic expression in the wonderful painting of the so-called Esquiline *Odyssey* landscapes which are now in the Vatican.[4] How fantastically the gates of the next world tower upwards, with a riot of willow branches growing round them. In front stretches the sea, made beautiful by the bright light of Helios, and upon it is the ship of Odysseus, "with shimmering sails"[5] and rocked gently by the waves. But beyond the gates is

---

[1] *Odyssey*, XI, 134-7.   [2] XI, 15f.   [3] XI, 93f.
[4] Illustration in K. Wörmann, *Die antiken Odysseelandschaften* (The Ancient *Odyssey* Landscapes), Munich, 1877. See also J. Gramm, *Die ideale Landschaft, ihre Entstehung und Entwicklung* (The Ideal Landscape, its Origin and Development), Freiburg, 1912, Tafelband, No. 11 b.
[5] *Odyssey*, X, 506.

darkness and the souls that come streaming up from the depths
are only visible because an evening glow from the earth plays
about them.

The qualities of "grandeur" and of the "heroic and mythically-
mysterious" have rightly been praised in this picture,[1] and there
can be no doubt that in the inspired brevity of his description of
this landscape before the gates of Hades, it was Homer's intention
to convey some profound mythical meaning. He may well have
done this quite unconsciously, of course, but he does it with the
unerring certainty of true poetic genius. The phrase about "fruit-
destroying willows" is a case in point. The words give the misleading impression of having been almost casually chosen. Behind
them, however, there lurks a hidden significance of which it fell
to the poet's successors to attempt an elucidation. Let us therefore
see what Greek and Christian symbolism have had to say of the
willows growing about the portals of Hades.

I GREEK SYMBOLISM AND THE WILLOW

Poplars and willows grew green and plentiful by the springs
and rivers of Greece, and were thus from time immemorial felt to
come within that magic influence adhering to any living water
that gushed from eternal Mother Earth. These trees are "water-
loving", the phrase used in the charming description of the spring
in the homeland of Odysseus, Ithaca. They are also sacred to the
nymphs, those daughters of the dark underworld which was felt
to be opening in every gap of the earth from which water came
forth.

"About it, standing in a circle, there was a grove of water-loving
poplars and the cool water flowed down from a rock, and above
it an altar to the nymphs had been erected."[2]

Yet the same trees also grow near graves; the elm, the willow
and the tamarisk lined the banks of the Scamander and for the ancients they were a symbol of mourning and death.[3] Thus around

[1] J. Gramm, *op. cit.*, text volume, p. 77.   [2] *Odyssey*, XVII, 208–11.
[3] *Iliad*, XXI, 349. Cf. on this E. Buchholz, *Homerische Realien* (Homeric Antiquities),
I, 2, Leipzig, 1873, pp. 239f.

the willow there is dimly present the same atmosphere of mystery that attaches to Mother Earth herself. It is a symbol of fresh and bubbling life, and also of the womb of death to which all things must return. For this reason the willow-tree is sacred to the great Mother Goddesses. Under the age-old willow in the Heraion in Samos Hera was born and Pausanias tells us that the willow was one of the three holiest trees in Greece.[1] The willow was not the only tree sacred to motherly Hera. The chaste-tree or agnus castus, which was taken to be a species of willow, was also sacred to her. In Sparta men honoured Artemis Lygodesma, a cultic image of the great succourer of childbirth adorned with branches of the lygos, yet another member of the willow family. The willow was in fact a kind of life-wand for Artemis Orthia.[2]

Now the simple folk had observed from the very earliest days of Greece that this lively plant of the brooks and streams throws off its blossoms before the fruit begins to grow, that it apparently does not propagate itself through seeding and fruit but only through the mysterious power producing suckers from its roots in the damp earth. Here was a starting-point for the dialectic of mythological growth, for this living tree is the murderer of its own fruit. Both life and death are at work in this tree that continually dies unto itself and is at the same time its own procreator. For all birth is already a dying within the root and all death is a return to the new life that continually streams forth from the moist realm of Mother Earth.

This alone gives us a deeper insight into the reason which moved Homer's poetic genius to place the willow on the borderland between death and life. We can also understand more clearly why he calls the willow "fruit-destroying", as though he were repeating a piece of popular folk-lore or a popular poetic fancy which would be intelligible to everybody.[3] We receive a further hint from what used to occur at a very ancient Greek feast. I refer to

---

[1] Pausanias, VII, 4, 4 (Hitzig, I, 2, p. 705); VIII, 23, 5 (III, 1, p. 45).

[2] *Athenaios*, XV, 12 (Kaibel, III, p. 485, ll. 5 ff.); Pausanias, III, 16, 11. On Artemis Lygodesma see also the material in Pauly-Wissowa, *Realenzyklopädie*, II (1895), col. 1393 and XIII (1927), col. 2286f. On the agnos see *Realenzyklopädie*, I (1894), col. 832–4.

[3] For more detailed references see H. Rahner, "Die Weide als Symbol der Keuschheit in der Antike und im Christentum" (The Willow as a Symbol of Chastity in Ancient and in Christian Times), in *Zeitschrift für katholische Theologie*, 56 (1932), pp. 231–53.

the Thesmophoria on which the myth of Demeter and Core was enacted. It was an event dedicated to the women of Greece and exclusively reserved for their sex. Now, what Diodorus tells us of the Thesmophoria in Syracuse is most certainly true of other parts of Greece, for the feast was common to all Greece. In it mysteries were celebrated in which the particulars recalled the practices of very ancient times (μιμούμενοι τὸν ἀρχαῖον βίον).[1] The mysteries dealt with the fertile field and the life-giving womb, with virginal life that springs upward from the ground, and with motherly child-bearing unto death.

During this feast it was the age-old custom for women to make themselves a kind of bed (στιβάς) out of willow branches strewed on the ground, on Mother Earth, and on these the women would rest during the festival. This custom, as is abundantly clear from textual evidence, was a dedication to chastity, for the willow, precisely because it was "fruit-destroying", was a symbol of sexual continence. As against this, it has been most plausibly contended that this could not possibly be the custom's actual origin; on the contrary, it is held that the bed of willow branches which rested upon the life-begetting earth and of which the green was sacred to the motherly goddesses, was originally looked upon as a means of sanctifying the womb and promoting fertility.

It was Fehrle who really took the lead in drawing attention to this change of significance, but the only explanation he could offer for it was that people had "forgotten" the original meaning of the practice.[2] This, however, seems to me too much like an attempt to interpret a mythological development by means of cold logic, and it appears to miss the element of paradox that figures with quite exceptional prominence in the symbolism of the fruit-destroying willow. For the willow is both these things; its dual character is essentially in accord with the use by the Greeks of the dual number when in Eleusis they spoke of Demeter and Core as τὼ θεώ. The willow is both mother and virgin, fruitful

---

[1] Diodorus, V, 4. See also M. P. Nilsson, *Griechische Feste* (Greek Festivals), Leipzig, 1906, pp. 315ff. Pauly-Wissowa, *Realenzyklopädie*, VI A, 1 (1936), col. 15–28 ("Thesmophorien").

[2] E. Fehrle, "Die kultische Keuschheit im Altertum" (Cultic Chastity in Antiquity) in *Religionsgeschichtliche Versuche und Vorarbeiten*, VI, 22, Giessen, 1910, pp. 141ff.

and chaste, living and dead.[1] The more it matures, the more quickly it discards its fruit, and when on the feast of Thesmophoria the women rested on their willow beds, they were expressing a desire to be both virgin and mother in one. Thus they lay, chaste and cut off from all intercourse with men—and the man who dared secretly to witness the mystery risked deprivation of his manhood[2]—yet they lay close to the womb of Mother Earth, thus sanctifying their own fruitfulness, the fruitfulness which in giving life also gave birth to death. The willow, therefore, is two things in one. It is "water-loving", and "fruit-destroying", it gives life after the manner of a mother, and at the same time dies to itself in chastity.

Let us follow this double symbolism a little more closely. I must admit that it is the second of the two qualities which the willow is held to signify, namely that of chastity, which comes more and more into prominence and no doubt this was due to Homer's own epithet "fruit-destroying". Yet it is clear that the other quality was never wholly forgotten. Homer may actually apply the word "water-loving" not so much to the willow as to the poplar, but it is to the willow that Theophrastus applies it. The willow to him is a true water plant (πάρυδρον ἡ ἰτέα), it is φίλυδρα or "water-loving".[3] What the ancients especially admired in it was its indestructible power of growth. Without the aid of man it continually bursts into new leaf. "*Nullis hominum cogentibus ipsae, sponte sua veniunt,*"[4] says Virgil. "Without human aid they grow up, by their own power." So familiar were both Roman and Greek with the willow's formidable power of growth that in the language of both, the tree's name was supposed to be derived from this quality. People connected the Latin *salix* with *salire*, to jump, and Festus on one occasion pokes fun at this popular etymology: "*Salicem ridicule interpretatur dictam, quod ea celeritate crescat, ut salire videatur*–People foolishly believe that the *salix* is so called because

---

[1] See C. G. Jung and K. Kerényi, *Einführung in das Wesen der Mythologie* (Introduction into the Nature of Mythology), Amsterdam-Leipzig, 1941, pp. 151f., 171, 200f.

[2] According to the account of Suidas, *Lexicon*, under Θεσμοφόρος and Σφάκτριαι (ed. Bernhardy, I, Halle, 1843, col. 1171; II, col. 996). See also the chorus in Aristophanes, *Thesmophoriazousae*, ll. 1150ff.

[3] *Hist. Plant.*, III, 1, 1 (Wimmer, p. 32, l. 10); III, 13, 7 (p. 51, l. 11).

[4] *Georgics*, II, ll. 10–13.

it grows so quickly that it seems to jump [*salire*]."[1] It was the
same with the Greeks; ἰτέα reminded them of the verbal adjective
ἰτός from ἰέναι, that is "to go", to which the *Etymologion Mega*
adds the remark, "because it shoots so quickly upwards".[2]

When, therefore, the ancients planted willows in or next to
their vineyards, as they were fond of doing, they were moved by
something other than the practical consideration of finding a good
support for their climbing vines: deep mythological beliefs lay behind this practice. It was hoped that the vital power of the willow
would communicate itself to the vine. Were not Demeter and
Dionysus close relations?[3] "Ἡ δ' ἄγνος ἀνθεῖ χὢ βότρυς πεπαίνεται
– When the chaste-tree blossoms the grapes will soon be ripe" ran
an old Attic peasant proverb, and in the popular mind this was
something more than a mere seasonal coincidence. There was here
a mysterious causal connexion. Plutarch in his table-talk ridicules
this habit of imputing a "mistaken" causality. But it is precisely
this that is so interesting in his account: the enlightened protest
still has a feeling for the argument of the Greek vintner who thinks
in terms of nature mythology.[4] The moment when the willow
blossoms, is the moment of its strongest life; it is also the moment
of its fruit-destroying death. It is at that moment that it can best
impart to the swelling grapes their mature sweetness. This proverb
therefore conceals the same dialectic as that of Homer. The fruit-
destroying chastity is in the blossoming, and it is this that gives it
its vitalizing power. "When the chaste-tree blossoms the grapes
will soon be ripe."

And now I should like to discuss the symbolism's second significance—that of chastity—in rather greater detail. It can be pretty
definitely proved that Homer's line in the *Odyssey* served to preserve and keep alive that same popular belief, but for which, of
course, the line itself would have had no meaning. A further argument in our favour is the fact that people most certainly identified

[1] Festus, *De Verborum Significatu* (Lindsay, p. 440, ll. 5f.).

[2] *Etymologion Mega*, 479, 27 (Gaisford, col. 1373).

[3] On the chthonic significance of the vine, see Artemidorus, *Oneirocritica*, V, 39: "In a
dream it signifies death; for because of its springing forth from the earth the vine is a
symbol of death, also it is robbed of its fruits at the moment of its greatest ripeness." Cf.
T. Hopfner, *Offenbarungszauber*, I, p. 133.

[4] *Quaestiones Convivales*, II, 7, 1 (Bernardakis, IV, p. 84, ll. 16ff.).

the tree called agnos (*Vitex agnus castus*) which we ourselves still call the chaste-tree, with the other two members of the willow family which they—botanically quite correctly—called *salix* (ἰτέα) and *populus* (αἴγειρος) and, no doubt they did so because their ear associated the name ἄγνος with ἁγνός – chaste, and ἄγονος – incapable of procreation.

Dioscurides illustrates the same train of thought. Summarizing the mixture of magic and plant-lore which the Greeks had woven around the agnos, he writes: "Agnos: some call it *agonos* or *amiktomiainos*, while the Romans name it *salix marina* or *piper agreste*. It is called 'agnos' because on the feast of Thesmophoria women who were zealous for their chastity laid it upon their beds, or because its seed, when taken in a drink, supposedly quiets the sexual passion."[1] He says something very similar about the leaves of the willow proper (*salix*): "Its leaves, when mixed with water, prevent all conception."[2]

It is into this world then that we must fit the Homeric line. Now it is remarkable how even Theophrastus, that most earnest naturalist, continually vacillates between the roles of an expert botanist and a retailer of purely mythical traditions. The Arcadians, he says, believe the willow to be fruitful, others, particularly the common folk, have a contrary opinion. He himself, he claims, had observed fruit upon the catkins. As against this, however, weight must be attached to Homer's myth-preserving line. One can only conclude that "the willow gets rid of its fruit, very quickly, before they are fully ripe, and so the poet is not far wrong when he calls this tree 'fruit-destroying'".[3]

But the more the late Greek plant-lore departs from the sober observation practised by Aristotle, the more powerfully there come to the surface the very ancient beliefs concerning the effectiveness of the willow as an aid to chastity, and almost always the line from Homer is cited in support of these views, as is also the custom obtaining at the feast of Thesmophoria. In the *Scholia* to the *Theriaca* of Nicander of Colophon we read: "There are many

---

[1] *De Materia Medica*, I, 103 (Wellmann, I, p. 95, ll. 12ff.).

[2] *Ibid.*, I, 104 (p. 96, ll. 17f.).

[3] *Hist. Plant.*, III, 1, 3 (Wimmer, I, p. 51). See also *Caus. Plant.*, II, 9, 14 (Wimmer, II, p. 66); IV, 4, 1 (II, p. 248).

blossoms on the lygus or agnus, the tree whose twigs women strew on their beds during the Thesmophoria. These are effective as a means of calming sexual passion. That is why the tree is called *agnos* because it is, as it were, 'childless' (*agonos*)."[1] This statement is most probably derived from the Alexandrine Apollodorus who, along with Crateuas, transmitted so much popular plant-lore to Dioscurides and Pliny; the last two, of course, constituted the chief source on which late antiquity and the Middle Ages were to draw. Let us for a moment look at some words of Pliny's to which many allusions were subsequently to be made:

"*Ocissime autem salix amittit semen, antequam omnino maturitatem sentiat, ob id dicta a Homero frugiperda. Secuta aetas scelere suo interpretata est hanc sententiam, quando semen salicis mulieri sterilitatis medicamentum esse constat.*"[2]

(Very quickly the willow loses its seeds before it has in any way attained maturity. That is why Homer calls it a destroyer of fruit. A later age interpreted this conceit in the light of its own crimes, when it became apparent that willow seed was a means of ensuring sterility.)

From the evidence that I have already adduced it is clear that we are here concerned with a kind of medical plant magic, a magical practice that uses the leaves or blossoms of a tree which hides lethal powers within itself. The willow is a chthonic growth, and sympathetically inclined towards Hades and Persephone; indeed for the ancients every "unfruitful" tree was sacred to the realm of the dead.[3] If one carefully collates the different pieces of source material one can really reconstruct the recipe or "prescription" quite accurately on which this "chastity draught of willow blossoms" was based: "Take willow blossoms, rub them into water and drink the mixture. This will subdue all amorous appetite and render women unfruitful."[4]

[1] Nicander, *Scholia on Theriaca*, 71 (ed. Schneider and Keil, p. 10, ll. 20ff.).
[2] *Nat. Hist.*, XVI, 26, 110 (Mayhoff, III, p. 29, ll. 1ff.). See also XXIV, 9, 37 (IV, p. 74, ll. 3f.), where there is a reference to the lygus and agnus and their use at the feast of Thesmophoria. [3] T. Hopfner, *Offenbarungszauber*, p. 133.
[4] Detailed references in H. Rahner, *Zeitschrift für katholische Theologie*, 56 (1932), p. 248.

Here then lies the "deadly" secret of the tree of Hades, of Homer's willow that stands at the gates of the next world. Aelian writes in his animal stories: "If any one rubs to pieces the fruit of the willow and drinks it, he will destroy the procreative power of his seed." In this, however, he continues, there lies hidden something "unspeakable", and it was this mystery of nature that Homer was seeking to express, or at any rate to hint at. "I think", he says, "that Homer called the willow 'fruit-destroying' in his poem by way of a dark hint, because he was on the track of the unspeakable things of nature – τὰ τῆς φύσεως ἀπόρρητα."[1]

Even the later ages of dying antiquity, when Christian trans-figuration had long caused Homer's willow wand to put forth new leaves, did not forget the awe felt by the Greek for the supposedly unfruitful tree, the tree of chastity that died unto itself. In the By-zantine *Geoponica* we read: "If the fruit of the willow is rubbed down to a powder and drunk, it makes human beings incapable of procreation, and that is why Homer says: 'There are elms and pop-lars and fruit-destroying willows.'"[2] Again the *Etymologion Mega* contains a statement about the agnus-tree in which pagan and Christian things are curiously mingled: "The agnus-tree has its name because it makes those who eat thereof childless (*agonos*), being itself an unfruitful tree. Or again, it may derive its name from chastity (ἁγνεία), for whosoever eats of this tree or prepares a drink from it or places its twigs upon his bed, is ensured of con-tinence (σωφροσύνη) and his lusts are quenched."[3]

There is indeed reason to believe that the age-old magic of the chaste bed of willow branches, such as those once prepared by the women of Greece, lasted well into Christian times. Certainly in this same Byzantine lexicon, when it deals with the lygos (which had once been used to adorn the image of Artemis Lygodesma), we can read the following words: "Some call the lygos 'agnos', for if anyone eats of its fruit his lust disappears. That is why priests strew twigs of this tree upon their beds for they believe that there is a natural power in them (δύναμις φυσική) that aids chastity."[4]

---

[1] *Hist. animal.*, IV, 23 (Hercher, p. 89, ll. 9ff.). See also IX, 26 (p. 227, ll. 27ff.).

[2] *Geoponica*, XI, 13 (Beckh, p. 334, ll. 1ff.). Note should be taken of the variant to *Odyssey*, X, 510: κλῆθροι elms (instead of the μαχραί–tall, which belongs to poplars).

[3] *Etymologion Mega*, XI, 49 (Gaisford, 29, 55f.).   [4] *Ibid.* (Gaisford, 1687, 50).

That this forgotten world still lives on is proved by the fact that the agnus is still designated as the chaste-tree. In German it is also called *Mönchspfeffer* or monk's pepper, a term with obvious implications, and to these hidden meanings Homer's line provides the key. The complications of nomenclature are still further increased by the resemblance between *agnos* and the Latin *agnus*, a lamb; the resulting confusion has passed into the German tongue, and the tree is still known in popular German speech by the alternative name of *Keuschlamm* (literally, "chaste lamb").

Eustathius, Bishop and Catholicos of Thessaly, provides another pregnant example of the lingering of the pagan belief into Christian times. His commentary on the *Odyssey* contains the following statement: "Willows are called 'fruit-destroying' because they get rid of their blossoms before any fruit can begin to grow, but also because those who drink a brew of willow blossoms, kill thereby the fruit of the womb or become incapable of procreation."[1] Thus the water-loving willow is also a plant that dies and is a bringer of death—it is life and death in one.

Homer's poetic image of the fruit-destroying willow contains a real truth clothed in the language of myth, a truth that is, as it were, hidden away within a bud. When the light causes the bud to open the tension that till now had been kept stable releases a dramatic conflict of opposites, a conflict that is only resolved in a higher unity of new-won life. One is tempted here to give ear to the voice of the Christian poet who wrote:

> *Mors et vita duello*
> *Conflixere mirando.*
> (Death and life here engaged
> In a wondrous conflict.)

The light which opened the Homeric bud, however, is the Christian interpretation of the allegory of the life-giving and yet

[1] *In Odysseam*, 1667, 20 (ed. Leipzig, 1825, p. 391). For how long this chastity magic connected with willow blossoms lived on can be shown by one out of many examples. In J. Hiebner von Schneebergk's *Mysterium Sigillorum, Herbarum et Lapidum* (Erfurt, 1651), pp. 68 f., we read: "Willows . . . lose their seed before it ripens; in this nature gives us to understand that the seed when used 'antipathetically', renders persons sterile and dispels all venereal desire (*alle venerischen Begierden*)".

death-bringing willow. In the Christian mystery the battle comes to an end and now the willow sprouts, not at the gates of Hades, but at the bright portals of heaven.

2 THE WILLOW IN CHRISTIAN SYMBOLISM

I want to paint for you the general background against which the Christian allegory of Homer's willow must be seen, an allegory, by the way, that never loses touch with the old pagan symbolism. If I am to succeed in this, however, I must first tell you in what form the story of Odysseus' journeying through the underworld continued to live on in Christian times, though I shall content myself with a few very general observations. Even back in late Hellenistic times the story of Odysseus' journey to the underworld was already being regarded as a parable, illustrating man's undying urge to learn the mysteries of the other world. Here, incidentally, we have something akin to that φρόνησις of Odysseus of which we heard something when moly symbolism was being discussed. "*Phronesis*", declares Heraclitus, "descends even into Hades, so that even the ultimate things of the next world shall not escape man's searching enquiry."[1]

For the Christian of antiquity the ultimate question in all that pertained to the next world was the resurrection of the body, and it was a question to which he applied his mind with real passion. The resurrection of the body, of course, implies the immortality of the soul and it is significant for the attitude which the Christian of these early days took up towards certain Greek conceptions that we often find him appealing to the authority of ancient Greek thought and fancy as proof of the validity of Christian ideas concerning the world to come. Thus we find him referring "to utterances of Empedocles, Pythagoras, Plato and Socrates", as was in point of fact done, for instance, by Justin.

On the occasion in question, Justin does not forget the eleventh book of the *Odyssey*, for "Homer's cave and Odysseus' journey to the next world in order to examine these things" are proof for him that the best among the Greeks had intimations of the truth. He concludes his apostrophe to the Greek world with the

[1] *Problemata Homerica*, 70 (ed. Bonnensis, Leipzig, 1910, p. 92).

words: "You could give us Christians the same credence that you give to these, for we believe in a God no less than they—indeed we do so to a still greater degree, for we even nurse the hope that our bodies, after we are dead and our remains have been laid in the earth, will one day belong to us again."[1]

It is in these prevailing hopes of a world to come, a world of the spirit and of bodies glorified, that we must seek the true origin of the interpretation placed by the Christians of that day on the willow-tree that grows before the gates of Hades. The willow, water-loving and yet fruit-destroying, which he knew so well from his *Odyssey*, became for the Hellenistic Christian the symbol of those Christian mysteries which only unfold the full abundance of their life after death, but nevertheless send forth their shoots even in this present world where men, both mystically and in fact, have still to die. Here life and death are still united as in a bud and mutually condition each other, but at the threshold of the next world and in the moment when the descent into the kingdom of the dead begins, the conflict is decided. Now it will be one thing or the other—death or life. The willow-tree that stands at this borderland of death, fruitless and yet living, is the mysterious symbol of this Christian dialectic.

Now, we can observe the same thing happening here that we saw taking place when the symbolism of Helios or the mandrake passed over to the world of Christian imagery. It is through the finding of a vaguely relevant passage in Holy Scripture that a channel is opened for the Hellenistic Christian—and usually a welcome one—through which the ideas of the old pagan culture can come in and mingle with Christian thought without any resulting distortion of the revealed word's essential meaning. It was the same with the lovely Greek symbolism of the willow-tree as it was in other cases I have noted. The Christian managed to find confirmatory texts in the Old Testament, texts which at the same time raised the whole matter to a more exalted plane. I want now to go through them and observe how the Church Fathers, both Greek and Roman, use them to play their exquisite game.

Let me begin with the directions given in the ancient Jewish law

[1] *Apologia*, I, 18 (Otto, I, pp. 58f.).

for the observance of the feast of tabernacles (Lev. 23. 33 ff.).[1] The feast begins on the fifteenth day of the seventh month (Tishri) and for seven days thanks are offered up for the harvest of fruit and wine. At the same time, while dwelling in their shelters of branches, the Jews recall their people's liberation from bondage in Egypt. On the eighth day this feast of the "ingathering" ends in a joyful celebration, and, as an expression of his joy, every pious Jew plucks himself a bunch of flowers (*lulab*).

The relevant key passage in respect of all this reads as follows:

"And ye shall take you on the first day the fruit of goodly trees, branches of palm trees and boughs of thick trees, and willows of the brook; and ye shall rejoice before the Lord your God seven days."[2]

Now it is very well worth noting that in the Alexandrine translation of the Bible, the words "willows of the brook" are rendered with a markedly extended meaning. The Greek reads: "Λήψεσθε ἑαυτοῖς ἰτέας καὶ ἄγνου κλάδους-Ye shall take you branches of willow and of the agnos-tree."[3] It is also significant that in the liturgical ritual of a later time branches of willow and agnos were carried in procession round the altar of sacrifice during the seven days of the festival. Further, in the old Latin translation of this passage the word *populus*, or poplar, has been substituted for agnos. And so it came about that the two trees which were by Homer especially connected with Persephone, came to be regarded as the scripturally indicated symbols of festive joy.

It was, moreover, natural for the Jewish mind to regard the "living water" of the brooks, which in that hot country only flowed in winter, as a precious symbol of life itself, and to love it accordingly. It was also natural enough that it should look upon the willow with its abundant foliage as typifying the ever-renewed process of blossoming and growth. It is with this thought in mind that we must seek to understand the second of the scriptural

---

[1] For the material relating to the history and Jewish symbolism of the feast of tabernacles, see H. Strack and P. Billerbeck, *Kommentar zum Neuen Testament aus Talmud und Midrasch* (Commentary on the New Testament from Talmud and Midrash), Munich, 1924, II, Excursus 5, pp. 774–812.

[2] Leviticus 23. 40.

[3] See H. Rahner, in *Zeitschrift für katholische Theologie*, 56 (1932), pp. 236f.

texts that is relevant to this enquiry into the development of symbolism.

The passage in question occurs in Isaiah. It is the text in which the prophet speaks of the coming Messianic kingdom, and of the outpouring of the living water of the Spirit, out of which new life would be begotten:

> I will pour water upon him that is thirsty
> And streams upon the dry ground.
> I will pour my spirit upon thy seed
> And blessings upon thine offspring.
> And they will spring up
> Like grass by the waters
> And as willows by the watercourses.[1]

Yet a second prophecy is relevant to this question of symbolism. Zechariah describes the Messianic kingdom of the last days as though it were a glorified feast of tabernacles:

"And it shall come to pass that everyone that is left of all the nations which came against Jerusalem shall go up from year to year to worship the King, the Lord of hosts, and to keep the feast of tabernacles."[2]

This passage caused the Church Fathers to assume that all that was written in the law concerning the use of willow branches during this feast would attain perfection in the spiritual world of the "new earth".

Yet the pious student of Scripture could still find two other passages that bore on this subject and it was through these that he was able to link up Christian thought and practice with the idea of the fruit-destroying willow of Homer, the idea that had been vaguely current among the Greeks since the beginning of history. In the book of Job these words are said concerning the monster Behemoth:

> He lieth under the lotus trees
> In the covert of the reed and the fen.
> The lotus trees cover him with their shadow;
> The willows of the brook compass him about.[3]

[1] Isaiah 44. 3–4.   [2] Zechariah 14. 16.   [3] Job 40. 21–2 (Hebr.); 40. 16–17 (Vulg.).

Now it proved to be a fact of some consequence that the Alexandrine translators rendered the words of the last line as: ". . . σὺν ῥαδάμνοις καὶ κλῶνες ἄγνου–[The trees cover him] with twigs and [so also do] shoots of the agnos-tree." This gave the whole passage a kind of chthonic and eerie sound, so much so that from the earliest days Behemoth and Leviathan were regarded as symbols of evil, of the devil and the yawning mouth of hell.

Here then we have this hellish creature compassed about "by the branches of the agnos-tree" and thus all doors were open to admit those Homeric intimations which were expressed by the poet's descriptions of the willow at the gates of Hades. Moreover, this more sombre conception of the willow could find support in yet another text—that which described the weeping of the children of Israel during the Babylonian exile:

> By the rivers of Babylon
> There we sat down, yea, we wept
> When we remembered Zion.
> Upon the willows in the midst thereof
> We hanged up our harps.[1]

I need hardly point out that all these words of Scripture about the willow by the watercourses are simply observations of nature. At best, as in the case of Isaiah and in the autumn harvest festival, they use the sprouting willow as a symbol of life. Nevertheless I want to show you that the Greek Christians developed a whole world of unique imagery out of these texts and that is something that would never have happened but for that other world of mythical beliefs for whose existence Homer's line is the principal testimony.

The willow is the symbol both of life and death, of the sprouting green and of "fruit-destroying" withering away, and at one time or another each of these elements, both bequeathed by ancient pagan fancy, was found by the Church Fathers, as they interpreted the Scriptures, to be the one that gave its real meaning to the text. Both serve as a garment for their thought when they seek to give their imaginative expression to the mysteries of the next world. Let us, therefore, begin our journey through this

[1] Psalm 137 (136). 2.

world of symbolism and proceed with it from the earliest times to
the Middle Ages, right up to that point of time in fact where, for
the Western mind, the last glimmer of that light has died away
with which Homer had once illuminated truth.

(i) The Water-loving Willow

The first evidence in the early Church of the symbolism of the
life-sprouting willow occurs in a penitential work written about
the year 150 by a Roman named Hermas under the title *The Shepherd*. For a long time this piece of writing was accorded a well-nigh
canonical status and its mystic-prophetical imagery, its similitudes
and visions exercised a very considerable influence. In the eighth
Similitude Hermas is shown in a kind of dream-vision how the
faithful, even though they have sinned, are given a final opportunity for repentance and so can be received again into the life-
giving fellowship of the Church represented, with a wealth of
development, as a green willow-tree. "The shepherd showed me
a great willow-tree which was like a protective roof for hill and
plain, and in the shadow of this willow came all men who are
called in the name of the Lord."[1] "A glorious angel" (ἄγγελος
ἔνδοξος) named Michael cuts off twigs from this willow and gives
one to each of the countless multitude though the tree suffers no
harm thereby. And immediately all are made to return their twig
which must be grafted anew on to the tree, and herein is shown
the nature of penance, for most of the Christians can only give
back a half-withered twig, but even these, by reason of the
unimpaired vitality of the tree, are caused to put forth fair new
foliage. Only the martyrs who have remained faithful to the end,
wave in their hands a branch which is described as having a most
strange character, and one that wholly surpasses the nature of the
willow: "At length they gave back their branches which were
green and covered with shoots and on the shoots there was something that had the appearance of fruit. And those who were in this
case, were exceedingly joyful and the angel was full of delight
because of them, and the shepherd also rejoiced."[2]

[1] *Similitudo*, VIII, 1, 1 (Funk, *Patres Apostolici*, I, p. 554, l. 32).
[2] VIII, 1, 18 (p. 558, ll. 12–17).

First of all it is clear that what is here described is a kind of mystical feast of tabernacles with its typical accompanying joy. Did not the law say, "Ye shall rejoice before the Lord" while waving the bunch of palms and willow branches? And indeed Hermas immediately continues: "And wreaths were brought that had the appearance of palm leaves and the angel put them upon the men who had shoots and young fruit upon the willow twigs they had brought."[1] We are soon told that these last are martyrs who, according to the Church's teaching, have by their blood won the right, alone among men, to enter immediately into the beatific vision: "But those were crowned who had wrestled with the devil and had thrown him to the ground."[2]

There is a deeper meaning to this allegory, though in order to grasp it, we must fall back on the old pagan conceptions of the "water-loving" and "fruitless" tree. Hermas is amazed at the unimpaired vitality of the world-overshadowing willow and turns to the shepherd with new questions: "Sir, how will the withered twigs be able to put forth shoots?" and the answer comes, "This tree is a willow and its nature is life-loving—καὶ φιλόζωον τὸ γένος."[3] This tree which is, so to speak, a cosmic willow is the symbol of the vital power that was implanted in the earth through God's becoming man. "This great tree which covers the hills and the plains, and indeed the whole earth . . . is the Son of God who is proclaimed to the very ends of the earth, and the peoples in its shadow are they who have heard his message and believed it."[4] All the twigs partake of its abundant vitalizing power and even those that are half withered begin to put forth leaves again, thanks to the power of this world-tree which shoots upwards out of eternal waters. "For God who hath planted this tree desires that all should live who have received its twigs, and I hope that these twigs, when they have received moisture and have drunk water, will have new life."[5]

One final point: The twigs of the martyrs which have never withered display a quality that goes beyond nature. They have shoots which resemble very young fruit. We do not understand

---

[1] *Similitudo*, VIII, 2, 1 (p. 558, ll. 18–21).   [2] VIII, 3, 6 (p. 562, ll. 16f.).
[3] VIII, 2, 7 (p. 560, ll. 8f.).   [4] VIII, 3, 2.   [5] VIII, 2, 9.

this last utterance unless we remember that the willow is "fruit-destroying". When, therefore, we are expressly told that the willow twigs of the faithful bear "fruit" this is intended to symbolize the fact that the martyrs, who are now so joyful, who have thrown the devil to the ground, have progressed beyond their own unfruitful human nature and so represent a kind of higher contradiction. They are the palm-crowned victors. But they are also "fruit-bearing willow branches" of the divine tree—and it is precisely this last divine dialectic that can only be understood in the light of the ancient pagan conception of the unfruitful willow.

And here we come to the point where the Christian idea that finds expression in the image of the "water-loving" willow can be connected quite closely with those mysteries which in the ancient Church were expressed under such symbols as "living water", the "floods out of the heart of Christ" and the "outpouring of the Spirit".[1] Thus the Christian could read in his Isaiah how, by the power of the spirit that is poured out like water, the faithful in the Messianic kingdom would shoot up "like willows by the waterbrooks" and to this Eusebius adds the following comment: "For the willow with its everlasting greenery and the youthful vigour of its growth, is a symbol of the abundance of that spring of spiritual water which gushes forth in the Church of the Logos."[2] This is conceived wholly in the spirit of Hermas. The heavenly and mysterious power of the stream of grace that has its origin in the other world, is already effective here below in the Church, which is the all-overshadowing willow-tree.

In the Latin West we find much the same ideas in Cassiodorus. Commenting on this same passage in Isaiah he says: "Willows are trees that grow by the banks of rivers and there put forth the freshest of green, and even if one continually keeps cutting away a part of the root and buries it in moist ground, it will immediately send down fresh roots. To these willows we should compare holy and faithful souls, who, as Isaiah says, 'shoot up like willows by the waterbrooks'."[3]

[1] Cf. H. Rahner, "Flumina de Ventre Christi", in *Biblica*, 22 (1941), pp. 269–302; 367–403.
[2] *Commentarius in Isaiam*, 44, 4 (PG, 24, 401 D). According to Jerome, Eusebius is wholly dependent on Origen. [3] *Expositio in Psalterium*, 136, 2 (PL, 70, 975 C).

The slender but firm branches of the willow are used to bind up the shoots of the vine, for the willow favours the neighbourhood of vineyards, and this too, according to Ambrose[1] and Arnobius,[2] has a significance for the hidden truths of Christianity, and it is like a last echo of that old folk belief in a relationship between the willow and the vine when Ambrose, in words that have a strangely Virgilian ring, speaks of the poplar and the willow and of the withes furnished by these, that have a sinewy life of their own, and serve for the binding up of the vines. "What other significance", he asks, "can there be in the poplar, that shady tree crowned with the victor's crown, what other significance in the pliant willow, so suited to the binding up of the vine, than that they should show forth the blessings of the bonds of Christ, the bonds of grace, the bonds of love?" The poplar and the willow—as once in Homer! The willow and the vine, the trees once sacred to Demeter and Dionysus! Now all are raised up into the transfiguration of a Christian mystery; the willow is the willow of grace that gushes forth from heavenly water, the vine is the vine of fiery love, and both are crowned with the victor's crown fashioned out of poplar twigs in a heavenly feast of tabernacles.

But the vitalizing power of the earthly willow-tree that roots in heavenly water is only a shadowy image that shows forth dimly the life that is to come. Conversely, the unquenchable life of the heavenly Church, of the unending feast of tabernacles, is the archetype—what Plato would have called the idea—of that which imitatively takes place here below, and it is to this ultimate reality that the deepest urges and longings of mankind are directed.

Even as Odysseus, before he could enjoy his "sweet homecoming" had first to journey to the dark land of the "fruit-destroying" willow, so does the Christian here below sit under the willows by the waters of Babylon and sing his home-sick song. "Yonder are willow-trees in the midst of streams," says Arnobius, "and men use them to bind up the fruitful vine", and yonder the Christian sings: "Oh, come into my heart Jerusalem our mother, that art sweet in thy chastity and pure in thy simplicity." Here

---

[1] *Exameron*, III, 13, 53 (CSEL, 32, p. 96, ll. 12–15).
[2] Arnobius Junior, *Commentarius in Psalmos*, 136 (PL, 53, 541 BC).

below this mystery of the life to come already begins to put forth its living shoots, and Jerome sees this truth hidden in the imagery of Isaiah's willow, though he writes as one wholly filled with the old idea of the "fruit-destroying" tree:

"I will pour forth my Spirit upon thy seed and my blessing upon thy offspring which will be born again of water and the Holy Ghost in baptism. In the Gospel our Lord promised this: 'Whosoever thirsteth let him come to me and drink', and immediately there is added: 'This he said of the Holy Ghost whom the faithful should receive.' And then the prophet compares those who have been born again in the baptismal font with newly-green plants and with the willow-tree that puts forth its shoots by the side of running water. For this willow-tree brings forth fruit and this is contrary to its accustomed nature, since ordinarily the willow is unfruitful and whosoever partakes of its seed and eats it is himself made unfruitful."[1]

Here we see very vividly how the Christian of antiquity caused the strange dialectic of the willow which was both "water-loving" and "fruit-destroying" to be resolved in the mystery of grace by which all nature is transcended. And what is mystically begun here below is perfected in the unending life of heaven. No longer do the willows grow at the gates of Hades or by the waters of Babylon; they cast their shadow over the everlasting tents of the heavenly feast of tabernacles.

There is a wonderful passage in Hilary in which he expounds the verse dealing with the willow in Psalm 137 (136). I quote it:

"All weep who feel they are captive in Babylon and sit by the waters. I say 'by the waters', for all work of the world and of our earthly bodies flows away like the water of streams. Nothing has firm substance in the everlasting flow; all is carried away, flows into nothing and hurries hence. . . . But these men do more than sit and weep; they have also hung up their harps upon the willow-trees. Now, the nature of the willow is this: even when it has withered, it will put on fresh green once a stream of water starts flowing

---

[1] *Comment. in Isaiam*, XII, 44 (PL, 24, 435 BC).

round it. Nay, a branch that has been cut off from the tree will send down roots if it is planted in moist earth. That is why the teaching authority of the prophet likens the holy and faithful to this tree. In the words of Isaiah: 'They shoot up like willows by the waterbrooks.' Even so, every man, be he never so withered in his sins and cut off from the root that once gave him life, puts forth new greenery when he is revived as by life-giving waters, by the word of God and by the mystery of baptism. Indeed, when the earthly feast of tabernacles was given to the Jews, their law bade them adorn their huts with branches of the water willow, for thus was to be prefigured the perfect joy of the tents of heaven."[1]

To this testimony of a Latin let me add that of a Christian Greek, for he brings home to us even more convincingly the deepest mystery in man's home-coming to heaven. This lies in the new life that is given his flesh and in the coming of a new earth, from which alone the God-given symbols of this still earthly world derive their beauty—and it is in this that we see, as I indicated earlier, the real essence of a world-transfiguring Christian humanism. It is Procopius of Gaza who describes the feast of joy in a world illuminated by Christ. He does so in the following words:

"The feast of tabernacles, however, signifies our ascent into heaven, the rising up even of our bodies to eternity, when, after a righteous and pious life, we assume the garment of immortality. This feast of the everlasting tabernacles is adorned by branches of trees that are always green. For grace is ever putting forth life. These branches grow up out of living water, for Christ eternally flows round the souls of the pious with his stream of water out of heaven. And as once in Jerusalem the whole people celebrated the feast, so will all who have lived piously celebrate with Christ in the everlasting tabernacles a feast that never ends."[2]

(ii) The Fruit-destroying Willow

The symbolism so far discussed is connected wholly with the generative vigour of the willow and its apparently inexhaustible

[1] *Tractatus in Psalmos*, 136, 6 (CSEL, 22, p. 727, l. 15–p. 728, l. 10).
[2] *Comment. in Leviticum* (PG, 87, 1, 778).

power of putting forth new foliage. It was connected, that is to say, with a quality apparent to the ordinary powers of observation of the Greek and Semitic peoples. This symbolism of the "water-loving willow" therefore needed no special effort of a specifically Greek imagination and no elaborate myth to call it into being.

The imagery of the "fruit-destroying" willow, however, whose Christian elaboration I shall now attempt to describe, presents rather a different problem. The idea that the willow is "unfruit-ful" and so a symbol of death—or of a chastity that dies unto it-self—the idea in fact that it is an "agnos" tree, is typically Greek. It represents an age-old mythologizing of nature, a process of which Homer's famous line merely happens to be the first piece of evidence we possess. Only Greek Christians, bent on positively canonizing their Homer, could have regarded it as an intimation, however vague, of biblical truth. Indeed this symbolism of the unfruitful willow does not really occur in Holy Scripture at all, and if people interpreted the references to the willow in Job 40. 22 and Psalm 136. 2 in a chthonic sense as signifying death or that death to self which is chastity, it was because the thought of Greece had suggested such ideas. And if such a writer as Methodius, that most Greek of all the ancient Christian symbolists, says, as he does on one occasion, "Throughout Holy Scripture the willow is a symbol of chastity",[1] then this is a highly temerarious re-evalua-tion of meaning by a man who was above all a Greek, it represents —indeed it is the classical case of this—the arbitrary introduction of something wholly Greek into the thought of the Bible, an "*eisegesis*", a reading into it of an alien substance. And so I begin the Christian history of this verse from the eleventh book of the *Odyssey* with an account of the development of the symbolism of the "unfruitful willow".

It was a most natural thing that a cultured Greek, reading in his Bible of the weeping willows of Babylon, should immediately have thought of those melancholy willows on the shores of dread Persephone's domain. If we wanted proof of this, we could find it in a paraphrase of Psalm 136 written in the middle of the fourth century by Apollinaris, Bishop of Laodicea. When Julian the

[1] *Symposium*, IV, 3 (GCS, p. 48, ll. 20f.).

Apostate forbad Christians to have anything to do with the
poetical works of Greece or to instruct their young people in them
in the schools, Apollinaris, an expert both on Homer and Pindar,
set himself the task of providing Christians with a poetry of their
own. He composed a history of the Hebrew people in twenty-four
cantos "as a substitute for the poetry of Homer – ἀντὶ τῆς Ὁμήρου
ποιήσεως"[1] and turned the Psalms of David into hexameters. The
Christians of Asia Minor greatly admired his works.

Now the verse of the Psalm about the willows of Babylon reads
like this:

μεσσόθι γὰρ ποταμῶν ὑπὲρ ὠλεσίκαρπον ἰτέαν
ἡμέτεραι φόρμιγγες ἀπηώρηντο λιγεῖαι.

(In between the rivers upon the fruit-destroying willows.
We hung our harps which had once sounded so sweetly.)[2]

Yet the fact that Apollinaris here refers to the willows of the
Bible as "fruit-destroying" is due to something more than a mere
flashback on the part of his classical erudition. Apollinaris knew
his Christian exegesis, particularly that of Alexandria, where
Origen was looked up to as the much admired leader, and so it
is in Alexandria that we may safely look for the origin of the
Christian symbolism of the unfruitful willow-tree. The interpretation follows two different paths, but in both the leading idea
is that of the willow as a chthonic, unfruitful and deadly tree.

Let us begin by following just one of these two paths. The willow is the symbol of the death of the soul, of spiritual sterility. The
Greek visualizes it as growing at the gates of Hades, the Christian
as the tree of Babylon. It is the tree whose branches cover
Behemoth.

The background for this interpretation is that rich world of
ideas which informed Origen and the *Civitas Dei* of Augustine
and lasted on till the days of Ignatius Loyola, the world that saw
in Babylon, the great harlot, the embodiment of diabolical power.[3]

[1] Sozomenos, *Ecclesiastical History*, V, 18 (PG, 67, 1269 BC).
[2] *Metaphrasis in Psalterium* (PG, 33, 1520 B).
[3] See on this F. Tournier, "Les 'Deux Cités' dans la littérature chrétienne", in *Etudes*,
123 (1910), pp. 644ff.; H. Rahner, *Zeitschrift für katholische Theologie*, 56 (1932), p. 234,
and *Zeitschrift für Aszese und Mystik*, 17 (1942), p. 75.

In the shadow of the willows by Babylon's devilish rivers there sit people whose portion is death, men who are unfruitful. "All those souls who sit in the shadows and in ignorance", says Origen, "have a spirit of unfruitfulness – λόγον ἄκαρπον,"[1] an expression which only really makes sense if in some degree we hear the voice of Homer behind it. From that point onwards we can trace through the centuries right down to the Middle Ages a tradition of interpretation that is masterly in its knowledge of souls. It gives us a perfect picture, when expounding the various passages in question, of the states of spiritual unfruitfulness, it is indeed an ascetic of spiritual sterility, of that hopeless closing up of the soul against the vitalizing power of the heavenly waters of grace.

It is Augustine who in this matter must claim the credit for the most telling formulations of phrase. Indeed it is he that has really made the symbol of the unfruitful willow unforgettable:

"Willows [he says] are unfruitful trees and in this passage of the Psalms [136. 2] they are spoken of as though there were nothing good to be said about them, though in other parts of Holy Scripture it is not so. But in this passage you are to understand that the willows typify unfruitful trees such as in fact grow in abundance by the waters of Babylon. The waters of Babylon wash them but they bear no fruit. These trees represent persons who are greedy, niggardly and unfruitful in all good works, citizens of Babylon and trees from the country round about, nourished by lusts after the transient earthly things that stream past them."[2]

Such people are inaccessible to the word of God and Augustine completes his train of thought by saying that the pious have hung their harps upon the willow because the spiritually unfruitful are men untouched by the muses, men who have no organ for the song of grace.

Prosper of Aquitaine writes in much the same sense: "The willows that are watered by the rivers of Babylon but still bring forth no fruit, are a symbol of those sterile souls that are only nourished by the lusts of this world and remain unfruitful in virtue. Into these

---

[1] *Selecta in Psalmos* 136. 2 (PG, 12, 1657 C).
[2] *Enarratio in Psalmum* 136, 6 (PL, 37, 1764 CD).

the seminal power of the divine word cannot penetrate; they are simply incapable of receiving the word of God."[1] The allegories of the Carolingian theologians and of those of the early Middle Ages developed a wealth of new ideas in perfecting this Augustinian symbol.[2] Perhaps the most noteworthy example of this is to be found in the *Mystical Allegories* of Richard of St Victor in which, under the image of the fruit-destroying willow, a whole "psychography" of spiritual sterility is worked out.[3] Even the essentially Greek memory of the offspring-destroying draught of willow blossoms finds a voice once more in the writings of Bruno of Würzburg: "The willow is an unfruitful tree and men say that whosoever prepares a drink or eats therefrom, is made incapable of procreation."[4]

To the Christian, however, this spiritual sterility is a profound mystery of evil; spiritual death is for him the work of him who "was a murderer from the beginning". It is this thought that made him put the interpretation already described on Behemoth who was compassed about by willows. Even so, however, it is difficult for us to see the thing with his eyes unless we also remember the awe with which the ancient world regarded the fruit-destroying willow which was for it the tree of Hades and of death. But, as we have already seen, what the Greek read in his Bible was that Behemoth was compassed about with branches of the agnos-tree and that meant that even the tree of chastity is sometimes within the devil's power. This explains such utterances as those of the Alexandrine Olympiodorus when he says: "Quite often those who have dedicated themselves to the ascetic discipline of chastity (ἀγνεία) fall under the power of the devilish Behemoth, as did the foolish virgins and as do those who on principle despise the married state."[5]

---

[1] *Psalmorum Expositio* 136. 2 (PL, 51, 391 A).

[2] Cf., for example, Haymo of Halberstadt (PL, 116, 658 C); Remigius of Autun (PL, 131, 799 B); Bruno of Cologne (PL, 152, 1357 A); Bruno of Segni (PL, 164, 685 C); Gerhoh of Reichersberg (PL, 194, 906 B).

[3] *Adnotationes Mysticae in Psalmos* (PL, 196, 361 ff.).

[4] *Expositio Psalmorum* (PL, 142, 492 D).

[5] *In beatum Iob* 40. 17 (PG, 93, 429 D). This remark shows very clearly how the Greek Church, even in this world of symbols, defended itself against a form of asceticism that was hostile to the body, against a Gnosis which looked upon marriage as the work of the devil. That is why even Methodius, who so consistently praises virginity, feels compelled

Gregory the Great, however, puts the following interpretation on the willow branches that covered Behemoth, and the Middle Ages were never to forget his words:

"If by the unfruitful willows the Psalmist had not intended to indicate the lives of sinners, he would never have been able to say, 'Upon the willows we have hung up our harps.' For we are told that willows grow in great numbers in the midst of Babylon and the reason for this is that all unfruitful people, being far from the love of our heavenly home, root in the confusion of this earthly world with all the power of their hearts. . . . Why then is it said of Behemoth that the willows of the river cast their shadow upon him? It is because those who only love this earthly life of death are deprived of all fruit and are the more attached to the devil because the flood of transient lusts streams about them. Excellently therefore is it said, 'The willows of the river compass him about', for the unfruitful, being all those who are in the bondage of love for this temporal life, surround the old enemy—while living in perverted lust—with most officious devotion."[1]

And so this part of the story of the Christian symbolism that was woven around the unfruitful willow really does end at the gates of Hades, if this term is used in a Christian sense. It ends in the maw of Behemoth and in the destruction of that fruit which the divinely planted willow-tree should have brought forth.[2]

Yet, as I said, there are really two stories of this Christian development of the symbolism hidden in Homer's line, and the second one which I now propose to tell, is a much happier one, for it leads us to that "sweet return to our heavenly home".

For the Christian knows of yet another kind of dying, he knows of a mystical descent into the deadly depths, and without this *catabasis* into the land where the fruit-destroying willows cast

in his symbolism of the chaste willow branch to adorn with the branches of the heavenly willow those who live in a wedlock that has been kept holy (οἱ πρὸς τὰς ἑαυτῶν ἀγνεύοντες γαμετάς), *Symposium*, IX, 4 (GCS, p. 119, ll. 17f.).

[1] *Moralia in Iob*, XXXIII, 5 (PL, 76, 676 B/D).

[2] On Behemoth-Leviathan as the symbol of the devil, of Hades and the mouth of Hell, see H. Rahner, "Das Meer der Welt" (The Sea of the World), in *Zeitschrift für katholische Theologie*, 66 (1942), pp. 107ff.

their shadows there is no mounting upward into the transfiguring light. The willow, the agnos and the poplar, these are the symbols of the life that dies unto self and all that the Greek had gathered from the mythical story of these trees, is now used as a cloak and an image for deep truths of the Christian life. The willow becomes the symbol of virginity, the "destroyer of fruits" becomes the personification of that mystical dying which, by renouncing the propagation of that earthly life which is dedicated to death, hopes to acquire a heavenly power of procreation. The chaste partake even now of the "angel-like" life, the βίος ἀγγελικός, the state in which the spirit is glorified and even the body acquires a translucent quality, the state which was so poignantly longed for by the Greek and to which all the intimations of Plato appeared to point. One need but read those lines of Gregory of Nazianzus in which, in the form of an Homeric hymn, he sings the praises of chastity, of the βίος ἀγνός. It is a life that is

εὔσκοπον, εὐδιόωσαν, εὔπτερον, ὑψικάρηνον,
κούφην, παμφανόωσαν, ἄνω χθονός, ἀστήρικτον
γαίης ἐν γυάλοισιν, ἐν ἄστει δ᾽ εὐρυθεμέθλῳ
οὐρανίῳ . . . .[1]

These verbal coinings are really almost untranslatable. The chaste life is "clear-sighted, recollected, soaring aloft, uplifted, airy, bright-shining, lifted above the earth and seeking no prop in the valleys thereof, having a place in the well-founded city of heaven". Yet the spirit cannot rise towards this life, unless a man dies to self and thus becomes in the deepest sense of the word "fruit-destroying". Thus it is that the agnos becomes the symbol of ἀγνεία, of chastity that dies to self and thus becomes eternally fruitful. Death and life unite. The dialectical tension revealed in the ancient myth bursts the bud and there appears the flower of Christian truth.

In examining this side of the development of Christian symbolism we again start with Origen. In the ninth homily on the Book of Exodus which deals with the allegory of the tabernacles, this

---

[1] "Encomium on Virginity" (*Carmina Moralia*, II, 1, verses 529-32) (PG, 37, 562).

Alexandrine preacher ends his sermon by glancing upward towards the heavenly feast of tabernacles. Willow and poplar—in Homer the trees that grew on the shores of Hades—are here the symbols of chastity's victory over the world and their branches are tied together with palm leaves that signify the ending of man's battle for his ultimate glory. Origen assumes that his Greek audience knows all about the "chaste willow" and says:

"In my view the following interpretation should be placed on the feast of tabernacles which was prescribed by the law. On one day of the year the whole people was to go out and live in huts, taking palm leaves and branches of the willow and the poplar and other green foliage. The palm is the symbol of victory in the war between the spirit and the flesh. The willow and the poplar, however, both according to their nature and their name, are trees of chastity. If the branches remain untouched, you will obtain the green and shady growth which is everlasting blessedness, and this will be when the Lord leads you on to the meadows that are by the waters of rest, through Jesus Christ our Lord."[1]

Here the longing of a man who is both Christian and Greek finds utterance as, under an imagery which is both Greek and biblical, he describes the mysteries of the world to come, the world to which man can only ascend "with an untouched willow branch" and after dying, leaving no posterity on earth, the death of virginity. Here we are at the peak of that Christian symbolism whose meaning can only be understood if we approach it with the mind of Greece. And nobody has handed down to us more profound examples of it than Methodius, Methodius who came from that same Philippi in Macedonia to which Paul addressed the most inspired of his epistles.

If we are to understand both the Christian and the Greek elements in Methodius' theology and to appreciate how he came to regard both Homer and Plato as something in the nature of saints, we must have some idea of the basic principles of his symbolic thought and of the nature of his special kind of Platonism, which

[1] *Homily on Exodus*, IX, 4 (GCS, VI, p. 244, ll. 11–20).

was a Platonism transfigured by Christianity. All that was said in the law before the Gospels were proclaimed, all that was said in such fragments of truth as the Greeks contrived to discover—all this is but a shadowy outline of the reality which came to us with Christ and the Church. But—and here we come to that peculiar Platonic illumination of his ideas—even the Church herself is only a shadow and an imprint (*typos*) of a final everlasting reality that is still to come and that is beyond all imagery. And this heavenly last thing, the naked reality, so to speak, is also the first thing and is indeed the beginning of all, from which in an ascending scale of reality, the shadows and images derive their form and towards which they are longingly directed. "For the law is the imprint and shadow (τύπος καὶ σκιά) of the image (εἰκών). But the image is the Gospel and this in its turn is the *typos* or imprint of the truth. So the men of old (οἱ παλαιότεροι) and the law of Scripture were made prophets for us and foretold the marks of the Church. But the Church also foretells the marks of the eternal things that are to come."[1]

Into this magnificently conceived philosophical plan we must now build in what Methodius, drawing on Homer and Plato, "the men of old", and on texts from the prophets and psalms, had to say concerning the symbolism of the willow-tree. The willow is the symbol of the βίος ἁγνός, of chastity, which in its turn is merely a prefiguration of the glorified life of the eternal things to come to which all our longing is directed.

Let us for a moment say something of this heavenly archetype. Methodius describes it in Platonic terms but with a feeling that is wholly Christian. Eternal life is a παρθενία, a virginally pure existence, it is "καθαρώτατον, καὶ φαιδρὸν καὶ ἀμιγὲς καὶ εὐλαβὲς καὶ εὐπρεπές – perfectly pure, shining, unalloyed, devout and comely". Whosoever enters upon this life is "irradiated by beauty and is free of all the surging and painful passions". He is στεῖρος καὶ ἄγονος (literally, unfruitful and non-procreative)[2] so far as these passions are concerned—and here already is the first indication of the contradiction inherent in the symbolism of the chaste willow-tree. The man who dies unto self enters eternal life. The "unfruitful one" becomes "water-loving"; for—once more in Platonic imagery—he "is no longer welded to the concupiscence after earthly bodies".[1]

It is to this sanctifying archetype that the chaste look up as they sit here below by the waters of Babylon. They look upward with a longing that is both Christian and Greek, and, when he speaks of this, Methodius' vocabulary becomes strictly Platonic: "Sharp of eye, with noble minds and lofty spirits, they gaze upward, to the promises made from above, they thirst for the heavenly place which is conaturally theirs–τὸν οὐράνιον καὶ σύμφυτον τόπον."[2]

And that brings us to what may be called the second stage—to the Church as an intermediary image, to that virginity which, lived here on earth, is both an intimation of its heavenly archetype and has itself been prefigured in the words and imagery of the ancients of Greece and of the prophets of the law. And it is here that Methodius comes in with his interpretation of the psalm that sings of the willows. What the biblical singer here declares is confirmed by the words of Homer and both point to the mystery of the virginal life, a mystery that takes place in the Church.

The psalm that speaks of the willows of Babylon is for Methodius "the joyous hymn of praise sung by souls that have returned home to everlasting security and now, together with Christ, wander through the heavens, for they managed to escape being engulfed in the material and fleshy waters".[3] The phrase "they wander through the heavens with Christ" (περιπολοῦσι τὸν οὐρανόν) is a memory of Plato's *Phaedrus* where it is written of the soul that it περιπολεῖ τὸν οὐρανόν, it wanders through the heavens in the divine dance of primal blessedness.[4] Thither the Christian soul has now returned, and from there it looks back on to the "shadows and images" of earthly virginity and the days when it sat by the waters of Babylon and had hanged its harp upon the willow-trees. Harps (*organa*) here signify our earthly bodies, and the waters of Babylon are "the waters of confusion that mingle

---

[1] *Symposium*, IV, 5 (p. 50, l. 24). Cf. Plato, *Timaeus*, 73 D; 85 E.
[2] IV. 5 (p. 51, ll. 1f.). Cf. Plato, *Axiochus*, 366 A; 370 D.
[3] IV, 2 (p. 47, ll. 15–18).
[4] *Phaedrus*, 246 B; 250 B.

our life with the flesh, as the waves thereof surge about it".[1] The willows, however, are symbols of that chastity to which these men have dedicated their lives. And as the waves of Babylonian temptation rage around them, they cry out to God: "Let not our harps fall to the ground, let them not be torn away from the tree of chastity by the waves of lust."[2]

The willow is therefore in this context also thought of in truly Greek fashion as φυτὸν τῆς ἀγνείας – a plant of chastity, and we can only understand the allegory if we remember everything that we have learned of the willow symbolism of the Greeks. True as ever to his all-embracing typology, Methodius holds that all these things are to be learned from the men of antiquity and from the words of the law, so he now comes forward with the main part of his willow allegory, in which Homer and the Bible are united:

"Throughout Holy Scripture the willow is treated as a symbol of chastity. For if the flower of the willow is rubbed and mixed with water and drunk, it extinguishes within us all the boiling and passionate lusts of the senses. Indeed this drink renders all desire for the procreation of children unfruitful and ineffective. This was already indicated by Homer in mysterious fashion (ὥσπερ δὴ καὶ Ὅμηρος ἐμήνυσε) when he called the willows 'fruit-destroying'.

"Isaiah says: 'The righteous grow like willows by the running water'; for the sprig of virginity only grows up great and glorious when the righteous disciple who guards it and lives it, wets it with the grace-laden waters of Christ and waters it with wisdom."[3]

Here wonderfully united are Homer and the prophets, the "fruit-destroying" and the "water-loving" willow. The dialectic of the Hellenic myth is resolved in Christian truth. The destroyer of fruit no longer grows at the gates of Hades but by the heavenly streams of Christ. Willow branches adorn the victorious souls— and I will let Methodius tell something of this at a later stage when the description of the heavenly feast of tabernacles brings us to the consummation of all he has to say under this head.

[1] *Symposium*, IV, 3 (p. 48, ll. 11-15).
[2] IV, 3 (p. 48, ll. 18-20).
[3] IV, 3 (p. 48, l. 20-p. 49, l. 9).

How delicately perceptive the mind of the Greek Christian was of the tension between contradictories that is found within the symbol of the willow can be shown by yet one other example, that of the fourth-century writer Hesychius; for this Jerusalem monk writes entirely in the spirit of Origen when he gives an interpretation of the feast of tabernacles which is both Hellenic and Christian:

"Take willow branches, it is written; this means, the branches of chastity and of a married love that is wholly pure; for the willow is a symbol of chastity, since it has no fruit. Thus also the continent who 'become eunuchs for the sake of the Kingdom of Heaven', have no visible fruit. And yet God says to them by the prophet: 'To the eunuchs I will give in my house and within my walls, a place, and a name better than sons and daughters: I will give them an everlasting name which shall never perish.'[1] And these branches we are to pluck by the waterbrooks, which means by the stream of life in this world; for our earthly life is like unto a waterbrook that continually hurries away, a brook that only flows in the winter of sadness and temptation. And yet this feast in the seventh month is also a symbol of what will happen at the end of time. It prefigures that festive joy that comes with faith in Christ and his passion. But dost thou not see that the figures of these Jews point to yet greater mysteries which are given to us? To live in tents is a spiritual reminder that we have been freed from the power of spiritual Egypt and the mystical Pharaoh. And whosoever has found among the leaves of the letter the ripe fruit of spiritual understanding must now long for the heavenly feast of rest and the life that is undivided."[2]

Here too then we have the same structure of the symbolic vision. That which is accomplished by the virginity of this world points forward to the fruitfulness of life in heaven. To die to the flesh in fruit-destroying chastity is to win the power of heavenly procreation. Death is life. Gregory of Nyssa somewhere in his writings shows profound insight and a truly Greek appetite for dialectic

---

[1] Isaiah 56. 5.   [2] *Comment. in Leviticum*, 6 (PG, 93, 1098 A–1100 B).

when he gives expression to this eschatological mystery of virginity, this dying unto self which is a winning of life, by declaring that this fruit-destroying renunciation which refrains from propagating the earthly chain of generation and from procreating unto death, creates something like a direct connexion between the quality of virginity and the last day on which all procreation will be at an end; the death of procreation is the beginning of life. "And so he who is fully continent lives only for God, for he brings forth no fruit unto death (οὐκέτι καρποφορῶν τῷ θανάτῳ). So far as lay in his power, he has already made an end to the life of his flesh, and there is no longer any intervening of time between himself and the coming day of the glorious advent of the Lord, since no chain of generations separates him from this day."[1]

Here we have the most profound theological speculations of a Christian concerning the willow, the tree whose fruit-destroying quality has now become the begetter of life. Death anticipates on life and so man can here and now celebrate the heavenly feast of tabernacles, of the tabernacles covered with willow branches. Longingly he looks upward to the kingdom of pure spirit; and the willows which stand at his graves and which he regards with the loving eye of the man of antiquity, now become for him the sweet symbols of that life which can only be won by dying. On the fifteenth day of the month of harvest joy for fruit and vine, when Selene stood at the fullness of her radiance, there was celebrated in the shadow of the law the feast of willow branches and in this the Christian saw the prefiguring image of his own eternal mystery. Jerome described this in his exegesis of the prophetic vision of Zechariah and here once again all the wisdom of Hellenic symbolism serves to help elucidate a Christian mystery:

"So long as we are in the stage of development [he writes], so long as we are on the road and in battle, we are indeed living in tents. Yet with all our strength we long to return home from these huts to our firmly founded native city, to the house of God. Who-

---

[1] *De Virginitate*, 13 (PG, 46, 381 A).

soever therefore lives in these earthly tents must celebrate the feast of tabernacles as it is prescribed, with branches of willow and poplar. These two are held by many to be the same kind of tree and the Greek name for this tree, namely agnos, shows its symbolic meaning. It is indeed a sign of chastity, for the physicians and those writers who have knowledge of plants, say that whoever drinks the blossoms of the willow or the agnos mixed in water, all heat of lust immediately cools within him, the artery of his desire dries up and he becomes incapable of procreating children. Let him, therefore, celebrate the feast of tabernacles protected by the branches of such trees as these. He leaves behind him the sixth month which is the symbol of his earthly life; in the seventh month let him give himself over to spiritual Sabbath rest, namely on the fifteenth day of that month, the day when Luna gives her full light and all darkness is dispelled by her clear beams."[1]

(iii) The Heavenly Willow

"When Luna gives her full light"—the mystery of the chaste willow branch leads the purified soul upward into those same realms of light into which, as we saw previously, it was led by the mystery of Selene and baptism. The ascent through the ravine where grow the fruit-destroying willows, through the dying which is chastity, was a *Purgatorio*, "where the spirit of man is made clean and pure and worthy to soar upward to heaven–*E di salire al ciel diventa degno*". Thus Dante sang. And in the *Paradiso* he lets the poet's soul soar into the mystic light of Luna, into the region of the eternal pearl:

> Th' eternal pearl within its chining depth
> Took us as water takes a ray of sunlight
> And yet though cloven sho'ed not any cleft.[2]

Let us ourselves now enter this region, let us set foot upon the meadow where in the light of the full moon the feast of the "ingathering" is being held, where the blessed are crowned with chaplets of willow branches and the mystery that surpasses all nature is perfected in those who are faithful unto the Lord; for the

[1] *Comment. in Zachariam*, XII, 44 (PL, 24, 435 BC).   [2] *Paradiso*, II, 34-6.

willows whose leaf-covered branches they joyfully wave, now bear eternal fruit: no longer by the rivers of Hades "where Pyriphlegeton rushes down into Acheron and with thunder the Stygian waters unite";[1] no longer by the waters of Babylon, but by the eternal river of God. Irretrievably the earthly contradictions are now resolved in unity. The fruit-destroyer puts forth leaves and fruit by the divine springs. The sweet return is accomplished to the fountains of home.

"Whosoever has spiritual understanding of Holy Writ [says Origen in a sermon], knows that it is written of the soul that is still caught in the eddies of this earthly life: 'By the waters of Babylon we sat down and wept and on the willows we have hung up our harps.' These waters of Babylon are here below and beside them we weep, homesick for heaven our true land, and we have indeed hung our harps upon willows, the willows of the law and of the divine mysteries. But it is written somewhere: 'All who have believed shall receive a crown of willow', and Isaiah says: 'They shall shoot up like willows by the waterbrooks.' Truly when God's great feast is come and our tabernacles are erected, then willow branches will be used to set them up."[2]

This will happen on that blessed never-ending day—Origen speaks of this in yet another sermon—, "when we arrive in Jerusalem, at the place of the 'vision of peace', to sojourn there for ever. Then will our harps no longer hang mute on the willow-trees of Babylon; we will take them in our hands and pluck their strings without ceasing, and there will no longer be a moment when we do not sing the praises of God".[3]

Methodius also looks upward to such a "feast of Christ" and, glancing back towards the time of earthly testing, he exclaims:

"Yet whosoever desires to reach this feast of tabernacles must pluck . . . the branches of the agnos-tree so that he can adorn his

[1] *Odyssey*, X, 513–15.
[2] *Homily on Ezechiel*, I, 5 (GCS, VIII, p. 330, l. 12 to p. 331, l. 2). The quotation introduced here "from some book" was—probably incorrectly—held to refer to Hermas, *Similitudo*, VIII, 2, 1.
[3] *Homily on Jeremiah*, II, 1 (GCS, VIII, p. 291, ll. 8–11).

tent with them. For the agnos-tree already embodies in its very name the virtue of ἁγνεία, the purity of the chaste. How then shall we enter into this feast of Christ if we cannot adorn our tents with the branches of that blessed divine-making tree, purity?"[1] "For in the new creation to which there is no end, no man shall partake of everlasting rest who is found without the adornment of agnos branches."[2]

Here once again all that the Greek could tell us of the symbolism of the willow is transfigured by a new light; it is the light that shines over to us from the new creation that is to come and is already visible in the hidden messages of nature, a nature itself not yet transformed. As Methodius says, all is "like the dim light of dawn, like the ghostly shadows cast by the resurrection that is to come".[3] And it is precisely here that we can trace the profound humanism of these Greeks and Christians. All the symbols of nature are for them the means of conveying, however dimly, something higher. They see here and now the humble products of this earthly world in the light of the coming "new creation" and this makes even the simplest thing to them a thing of mystery.

The nature of the agnos, the "blessed, deifying" tree is no exception here. Once after leaving Egypt the children of Israel had adorned their huts with willow. In the fulfilment of the mystery this means: "I also am going far from hence and am leaving the Egypt of this life. I go homeward to the resurrection . . . to the everlasting fulfilment of the feast of the resurrection, far beyond the heavens to the house of God himself where he celebrates a feast amid the sound of jubilation and echoing shouts of joy."[4]

For the Christian Greek, then, who so loves his fair world, the real inwardness of the Gospel message lay in this: that in the resurrection of the body a new earth would also be given to man. Nay more, as Paul so often says, the new aeon of life has already begun, since the First-born of the dead rose up to life. The miracle of the willow that becomes fruitful in dying has already happened,

---

[1] *Symposium*, IX, 4 (GCS, p. 118, l. 18 to p. 119, l. 10).
[2] IX, 5 (p. 119, l. 29 to p. 120, l. 1).
[3] IX, 1 (p. 114, ll. 5f.).
[4] IX, 5 (p. 120, ll. 10–26).

the earth is already secretly transfigured. There is a passage in Cyril of Alexandria in which the author reveals to us the fulfilment of the mystery of the willow branch; he does so in these words:

"The law enjoined through Moses that the feast of tabernacles should be kept on the fifteenth day of the seventh month, when all the fruits of the field have been brought home into the barns. And he commanded that palm leaves should be broken off and that the fairest fruits of the trees should be gathered, together with thick bushes, willow branches and shoots from the agnos-tree and he commanded also that men should drink out of the springs and should rejoice and jubilate; and all this because Israel once lived in tents when it was freed from its bondage to Egypt. All this, however, was but a prefiguration of the mystery that was to be fulfilled in Christ. We too have been set free, but ours is freedom from bondage to the devil and we are called unto freedom through Christ and are subject to him alone, for he is the king of all the world. No longer are we troubled by the serpentine coils of those fallen powers of long ago. What we now celebrate is the true feast of tabernacles, the feast of the day of the resurrection of Christ, for in him even now our human bodies really remain indestructibly alive, though they may first be subject to corruption and to death. For he is the resurrection, he is the life, he is the first-fruits of the dead, the earnest of those who have fallen asleep. He fills us with the spiritual ripeness of good fruit and already begins to harvest us like sheaves from the fields and to store us in his heavenly barns. There he will give to us, the victors over sin, the food of Paradise and heavenly joys. The fragrance of the Spirit will breathe about us, for we will bear in our hands the sweet and adorable fruit of the Gospel life, since our lives have been chaste and holy, and of all this the palm leaves and greenery that we carry are the symbol. Christ is the waterbrook of bliss wherewith we are watered by God the Father. He is the source of life and the flowing river of peace."[1]

Here also then, with the fragrance of the Greek spirit blowing about it, the mystery of the chaste willow branch leads us in the end

[1] *Comment. in Zachariam,* III (PG, 72, 265 D–268 AB).

to the waterbrook of eternity. As we have seen, the symbolism of the willow was a divided thing, though in Christ that division was resolved in unity. But that symbolism was never forgotten so long as there remained in the theology of dying antiquity and of the Middle Ages even a shadow of an understanding for the value of this imagery as a vehicle for the expression of divine truth. For centuries men continued to repeat the passage from the *Moralia* of Gregory the Great: "Willows are unfruitful and yet possess such vigour in the putting forth of foliage that they can hardly ever wither, even though they be torn up by the roots and thrown away",[1] and men loved to dwell upon the comforting doctrine of grace that lay concealed here.

In Isidore also Christians could find preserved the ancient tradition concerning the powers of the willow and the meaning of its name. "The willow", he writes, "derives its name (*salix*) from the fact that it shoots up (*saliat*) very quickly which means that it grows with great vigour. It is a tree with pliable branches that can be used for binding up the vine, and it is said that its seed, if drunk in water, has the effect of depriving those who drink it of the power of procreation, and of making women unfruitful."[2] Last faint echoes from the Hellenism of long ago! Early medieval theologians who took pleasure in symbolism still had an ear for the thing.[3] Hrabanus of Fulda[4] provides evidence of that, while Vincent of Beauvais[5] passes on to his successors words on which these ideas have left their imprint though the full meaning has already been largely lost.

Yet whenever a true symbolist who was also a really inspired theologian read of the "fruit-destroying" and "water-loving" willow, the ancient, ever fertile contradiction really caused ideas to flare up illuminating a Christian mystery of heaven. Rupert of Deutz somewhere describes the heavenly feast of tabernacles where

---

[1] *Moralia in Iob*, XXXIII, 5 (PL, 76, 676 A). Repeated verbatim in Garnerus (PL, 193, 336 D) and Hervaeus (PL, 181, 422 A).

[2] *Etymol.*, XVII, 7, 47 (PL, 82, 617 A).

[3] Cf. *Clavis Melitonis*, VII, 12 (ed. Pitra, *Spicilegium Solesmense*, II, p. 365); Pseudo-Hieronymus, *Breviarium in Psalmos* (PL, 26, 1304 BC); Bruno of Würzburg, *Expositio in Psalmos* (PL, 142, 493 A).

[4] *De Universo*, XIX, 6 (PL, 111, 519 CD).

[5] *Speculum Naturale*, XIII, 95 (Nuremberg edition, 1493).

all the saints surround Christ with bunches of greenery in their hands. Some deep instinct, however, moves him to apportion the willow branches to the children of Bethlehem, a happy throng that plays in the heavenly fields. Using the old play upon words of *salix* and *salire* and mindful of the ancient tradition of the "fruit-destroying" and "water-loving" willow, he paints within the compass of a single sentence a picture that is wholly exquisite. These heavenly children are *"salices non habentes fructum, et tamen per solam gratiam ad viriditatem salierunt aeternae patriae* – They are willows that have no fruit and yet by grace alone they leapt upwards to the green of their eternal homeland."[1] *"E di salire al ciel diventa digno"*—again how apt is Dante's phrase!

Let me add one more piece of imagery from the mystic circle that surrounds the heavenly willow. Then I shall have completed the story of the Homeric fruit-destroyer. The Christian interpretation—and resolution—of the contradiction, mythically shown forth in the willow, between death and life, had its most direct application to the virtue of chastity, the virtue whereby we die unto self and yet are endowed with a heavenly fruitfulness. Yet here we are dealing with nothing less than the Christian mystery of the Blessed Virgin herself, the mystery of the human mother out of whose virginity God was born.

In Mary there is fulfilled that truth which was concealed beneath the mythical imagery as in an unopened bud; her chaste unfruitfulness becomes the seed of divine fruit. In a medieval work in praise of Mary, a work once ascribed to Albertus Magnus, though in fact the author is Richard a Sancto Laurentio, there is a description of the nature of the willow which borrows largely from Isidore—which means that it uses words that ultimately derive from Festus, Pliny and Ambrose. "It is called *salix*," he writes, "because it jumps, that is to say it grows very quickly, and we are told that its seed, if drunk, produces infertility." This, the writer continues, was fulfilled in the Blessed Virgin, "for she elected virginity and so chose an unfruitful life, but as the willow loves to grow by the waterside, so did the Blessed Virgin flourish by the waters of grace and heavenly gifts. And even as the willow is a

---

[1] "De Trinitate et Operibus eius", *In Leviticum*, II, 37 (PL, 167, 827 B).

token of chastity, so was she also full of cool chastity, for her seed, which is the Son of God, by his message makes many unfruitful in the fruit of the flesh in that he calls them to a life of virginity."[1]

This brings us to the end of that story of Christian exegesis which has gradually wound itself around Homer's immortal line. "*Ὥσπερ Ὅμηρος ἐμήνυσε*—even as Homer had revealed, so has it been fulfilled", and the Christian of antiquity used the high privileges of his freedom and seized upon this imagery so that he might express by symbols a knowledge that could only come from God. Like the mysteries of sun and moon, like the mystery of the tree of life, the story of the willow branch also ends with the Great Mother, who gives light to the dark earth, who gives to the dead earth life, who gives fruit to the earth that was unfruitful. Moon and tree and willow branch—all the primal and simple things of this world hide mysteries within themselves of which the Christian alone has the key, for to him alone has God made man's nature transparent and understandable. The willow of the Homeric underworld has become the "blessed, deifying tree – *φυτὸν θεοποιὸν καὶ μακάριον*".

---

[1] *De Laudibus Mariae Virginis*, XII, 6, 27 (Albertus Magnus, *Opera Omnia*, XXXVI, p. 815, ed. Borgnet).

VII

ODYSSEUS AT THE MAST

AFTER his voyage to the willow-shadowed land of mystical dying, Odysseus makes ready to return at last to his home; for in his much-tried heart there now lives only the longing for his father's house, and right at the beginning of the epic Athene is made to say to Zeus: "But Odysseus longs only to see the smoke rise up from Ithaca."[1]

Here was a mythical image that was readily seized on by the Hellenic Christian when he thought of the voyage which is this earthly life and of the longing which consumed him for his heavenly homeland. Yet if this last was to be attained, the Christian knew that there could be no respite from his sailing, no lingering at any place on the way. He must not dally in the caressing arms of Calypso or at the Phaeacian feast, neither must he fall under Circe's magic or hearken to the Sirens. Not even the purely worldly good of his earthly home may hold him. Mindful of this —and with discernible echoes of Plato—Clement of Alexandria contrasts the attitude of Odysseus with that of the Christian: "Men attach themselves to this world as certain kinds of seaweed cling to the rocks by the seashore. They care little about life eternal, for like the ancient from Ithaca they do not hunger for the truth or for their heavenly homeland, but only for the smoke of their earthly homes."[2]

Yet the Christian could take a view of Odysseus that differed from this. He could see in the voyage of the Ithacan, in which so many perils and so many hardships were overcome, an intimation of his own voyage through life, a voyage beset with so many deadly perils and yet capable of such glorious accomplishment.

[1] *Odyssey*, I, 57 f.
[2] *Protrepticus*, IX, 9, 86, 2 (GCS, I, p. 64, ll. 27–31); cf. Plato, *Republic*, 611 D.

Odysseus leaves the dark, distant land of the Cimmerians to sail past the Sirens into his sweet native sunlight. So too the Christian: his goal is "the light that truly is" and this light is the Logos "that enlighteneth all men". For, says Clement with characteristic Greek pregnancy: "οὐδεὶς Κιμμέριος ἐν λόγῳ–So far as the Logos is concerned, there are no Cimmerians."[1] Nobody need stay within the dark gates of Hades, all are called into the sweet sunlight of home, to a new life and a speedy voyage of return: "Σπεύσωμεν εἰς σωτηρίαν, ἐπὶ τὴν παλιγγενεσίαν–Let us hurry towards salvation, towards our rebirth",[2] Clement calls to his fellow-Hellenes.

But between the darkness of Hades and the light of home lies the island of Sirens. Only those who sail past these seductive powers and leave them behind, are secure against destruction. Once more in myth-form life and death do battle, and dark daemonic powers succumb to the victory of light. These shadowy intimations of the Homeric myth served the Hellenic Christian as a source of imagery wherein one of his mysteries could find expression; it was the mystery of that necessary and cleansing peril by which the life of grace must be tried before "*di salire al ciel diventa digno*".

Now like that of moly and the fruit-destroying willow, this myth of Odysseus and the Sirens is charged with contradictions. Upon a "flowering seashore"[3] dwell the "divinely voiced Sirens"[4] who with "sweet songs"[5] tempt those who pass by on their journey home. They promise more than man can hope for, these weird all-knowing beings who are neither wholly human nor divine, and all that is deepest in human longing is expressed in these few lines from their bewitching song:

"None has yet passed by in any dark ship without hearkening to the sweet songs proceeding from our lips. Rich in joy and wiser in knowledge the voyager then fares homeward, for we know all things."[6]

Odysseus, who is man eternal, drinks this in through all the pores of his senses, for seemingly the secret of this fair song is a

---

[1] *Protrepticus*, IX, 9, 88, 2 (GCS, I, p. 65, ll. 26f.).   [2] *Ibid.* (p. 65, ll. 27f.).
[3] *Odyssey*, XII, 45, 159.   [4] XII, 158.   [5] XII, 187.   [6] XII, 186-90.

thing of light: "My heart longed to listen still."[1] Yet Odysseus is
a man forewarned and there is a profound meaning in the fact
that it was none other than "holy Circe"[2] who had given him
warning counsel. Odysseus knows full well that the seemingly
sweet and bright nature of the Sirens is a mystery of death and of
destruction. That the voyage to the Sirens' island should have
proceeded so smoothly seems, as we read of it, somehow, vaguely
ominous and there is a sort of quiet horror in those wonderful lines
in which the scene is described:

"Swiftly, and borne along by favourable winds, our well-
wrought ship approached the island of the Sirens, and then the
wind fell and there was perfect stillness on the waters. A daemon
put the waves to sleep."[3]

Sirens are creatures of death—and it was a daemon who put the
waves to sleep! He who would indeed attain his home must have
a God-given wisdom within himself and be able to discern
between darkness and light, he must be able to sense what is of
life and what of death. The tempting words of the Sirens are
"witches' songs" and the end thereof is "destruction".[4]

The real point of Homer's myth however is that Odysseus, the
initiated, the man instructed by Circe, sails by within reach of the
Sirens' temptations with full knowledge of his peril. Unlike his
companions whose ears have been stopped with wax, Odysseus
can hear the song, but being tied to the mast, he sustains the
ordeal. He instructs his companions in the vessel:

"so that, having full knowledge, we shall either go to our death
or escape death's doom".[5]

The real essence of the myth lies wrapped in the words, "having
full knowledge". Odysseus is here the embodiment of that ven-
turesomeness whose possession risks coming within an inch of the

---

[1] *Odyssey*, XII, 192 f. Cf. also XII, 52.   [2] XII, 155, 115.   [3] XII, 166–9.
[4] Cf. Circe's words, XII, 41–6: "Whosoever approached the Sirens unwitting and
heard their song, such a one never returned home. Nay, sweetly singing the Sirens have
bewitched him on the green shore. All around are the white bones of rotting men."
[5] XII, 156 f.

deadliest peril and still is saved. The senses of such a man are fully open to the Sirens' song and yet he does not follow where it bids; for he has himself put bonds upon his freedom. Following divine direction, he has had himself tied to the mast. He tells his companions:

> . . . ἀλλά με δεσμῷ
> δήσατ᾽ ἐν ἀργαλέῳ ὄφρ᾽ ἔμπεδον αὐτόθι μίμνω
> ὀρθὸν ἐν ἱστοπέδῃ, ἐκ δ᾽ αὐτοῦ πείρατ᾽ ἀνήφθω.[1]
> (Circe enjoined that I alone should listen to the
> voices, but bind me with firm bonds, so that I stay
> immovable and upright upon the socket of the
> mast, and make fast the ropes.)

It is primarily with these lines that Christian humanism concerned itself when giving the interpretation which it gave for a thousand years to the story of Odysseus and the Sirens.[2] No scene from Homer's immortal epic was as beloved as this one.

I am going to try and tell you along what lines the symbolism attaching to the episode of the *Odyssey* developed over the course of time, and here I shall follow—indeed I am almost compelled to do so—the fine tradition of the humanists of Switzerland. It was, it will be recalled, in Basle that the first Latin translation of the *Odyssey* appeared—I referred to that when dealing with the story of moly—and in the introduction to this work Lemnius of Chur exalts Homer as the great teacher of wisdom and treats the *Odyssey* as the perfect guide in the art of the good life.[3] It was in Basle that Erasmus published his *De Ratione Studii*, a book of cardinal importance for the whole of humanism, in which he insists on the value of a moral interpretation of Homer's poems,[4] while Zwingli in a charming little book uses Homer's own imagery to enjoin on the reader—wholly in the spirit of the great Basil—certain precautions in the study of ancient authors. "Yet in this we must have

[1] XII, 160–2.

[2] For the pagan and Christian references concerning this development of symbolism, see H. Rahner, "Odysseus am Mastbaum" (Odysseus at the Mast), in *Zeitschrift für katholische Theologie*, 65 (1941), pp. 123–52.

[3] *Odysseae Homeri libri XXIV, nuper a Simone Lemnio Emporico Rheto Curiensi heroico Latino carmine facti*, Basiliae, 1549. Introductory poem.

[4] *Opera Omnia*, Basle edition, I, pp. 520ff.

a care to preserve a heart that is armoured with faith and inno-
cence. . . . Of course, a spirit that is prepared in advance will be
able to pass all these things by, as Odysseus passed by the Sirens, if
from the very first he utters the warning to himself, 'Thou hearest
this in order to beware thereof, not in order to accept it.'"[1] And
Erasmus in his great edition—also published in Basle—of the works
of Jerome[2] utters a warning—very much in the spirit of Plato—
against the seductive power of Homer's verse, though in his *Adagia*
he cannot refrain from mingling ancient Hellenic wisdom with
the best things to be found in Patristic writing. In a sense I too am
doing this last and this part of my essay might well be entitled,
"Homer among the Fathers of the Church".

The truth is that the great spirits of the ancient Church claimed
a lofty freedom in this matter and did not hesitate to treat Holy
Homer as one of themselves. They could do this because it was
in the light of the Logos that they interpreted him. True, this "interpretation" of theirs, like the Homeric allegories of the Stoics and
of the Neoplatonists before them, often failed to appreciate the
mountain-spring freshness and Ionic directness of the poet. True,
that upon occasion, under the spell of Plato and also by reason of
their Christian convictions, they would utter suitable warnings
and objections. By and large, however, Homer remained for them
the wise teacher of the true art of living, the seer whose blind
eyes could discern in advance the message of the Logos that was to
come.

The *Odyssey* is, for Basil and for all the humanists of the
ancient Church, an ἀρετῆς ἔπαινος, a hymn to virtue.[3] That had
been the lesson which on his own showing had been learned by
Basil in the great school of Athens at a time when Greek spirit
had already begun its weary death, and that was the lesson the
youthful Church received from him. Before, therefore, we examine
in greater detail the Christian interpretation of the myth of Odysseus and the Sirens, let us, as it were, put ourselves in the mood by

---

[1] G. Finsler, W. Köhler, A. Rüegg, *Ulrich Zwingli: Eine Auswahl aus seinen Schriften*
(A Choice of his Writings), Zürich, 1918, p. 372.

[2] Basle, 1516-20, Introduction, f. Vᵛ; cf. G. Finsler, *Homer in der Neuzeit von Dante bis
Goethe*, pp. 377f.

[3] *Ad Adolescentes*, 4 (PG, 31, 572 B).

glancing for a moment at the reverent love with which the Fathers received the author of that story into their ranks.

The Homeric interpretation of the Church Fathers joins on without any perceptible break to the general method in use in Hellenistic times.[1] We all know that Plato, in his *Republic*, voiced the strongest criticism of Homer's theology and was particularly outraged by the questionable ethics of Odysseus' ruses. We all know that he condemned the Homeric epics as corrupters of youth and wanted them eliminated from the educational plan of his ideal State.[2] But in Hellenistic times there grew up an ever more vehement opposition to such views and attempts began to be made at a reconciliation between Homer and his detractor. Both the Stoa and the Neoplatonists built up an entire system of allegorical Homeric interpretation. By applying the concept of ὑπόνοια, the hidden meaning, that is to say, concealed beneath the actual word, it was sought to prove that, despite everything, Homer was still the wisest of men, the prophet of secret mysteries, the divinely illuminated seer.

Men insisted on believing that through the chorus of the Muses Homer led men to the vision of the supreme God whose nature can be perceived dimly, and then only in poetic ecstasy—just what Archelaus of Priene had represented in his marble apotheosis of Homer.[3] So declared all the various works that were dedicated to the elucidation of Homer's secrets—so declared Heraclitus in his Homeric allegories, the unknown author of the *Voyages of Odysseus*, Porphyry in his *Homeric Questions* and in the book of the *Cave of the Nymphs*—so said they all right up to Bishop Eustathius of Thessalonica, who made a kind of synthesis of this large and confused subject, bringing true Byzantine industry to bear on the task.

And now, the voices of the Church Fathers join in this chorus.

[1] See on this F. Wehrli, *Zur Geschichte der allegorischen Deutung Homers im Altertum* (History of the Allegorical Interpretation of Homer in Ancient Times), Basle, 1928; E. Wüst in *Realenzyklopädie*, XVII (1937), col. 1913 ff.

[2] *Republic*, 377 E, 598 D, 605 C; a full discussion of the attempts to reconcile Plato and Homer in W. Schmid and O. Stählin, *Geschichte der griechischen Literatur* (History of Greek Literature), I, 1, Munich, 1929, pp. 129 ff.

[3] Dated about 160 B.C. Illustration in E. Bethe, *Die griechische Dichtung* (Greek Poetry), Potsdam, 1929, p. 1.

True, at the beginning of Christian thought about this matter we hear a few sharp words of criticism uttered wholly in the spirit of Plato. Minucius Felix writes: "Most properly did Plato expel from the State which he constructed on paper that famous, belauded and crowned poet Homer."[1] To the Christian apologists of the second century Plato's pure doctrine of God seemed the culminating-point of the Greek spirit while the colourful world of Homer's gods was the very essence of heathenism. Thus even the broad-minded Justin insists that Plato had expelled Homer from his State because of the power of the Logos at work within him, because of the spirit of God which was already effective before the coming of Christ.[2] Grim Tertullian once calls Homer the "*dedecorator deorum*",[3] the poet who has "disadorned", that is to say exposed the nakedness of the heathen gods by turning them into creatures in all respects like men. Even Gregory of Nazianzus, true humanist though he was, feels constrained to protest to the emperor Julian against the excessive cult of Homeric allegory.[4]

Yet even for the less tolerant of Christian apologists Homer still remained the wise and ancient poet, the oldest of them all, the seer who had acquired his recondite knowledge from the Egyptians or even from the perusal of the ancient Hebrew books. Each one of them was too much of a Greek, or too good a student of the Greeks, wholly to violate his instinct for Homer's poetic grandeur. For Clement Homer is ποιητῶν πρεσβύτατος,[5] the most venerably ancient of the poets. Tertullian speaks of him as "*princeps poetarum, poetarum unda et omne aequor* – prince of poets the very billow and ocean of poetry",[6] and in speaking thus he is of course merely echoing the Roman poets with whom this metaphor—or something very like it—had long been a favourite in regard to Homer. One need only think of Ovid's "that from him as from an everlasting source the mouths of seers had been watered with Pierian streams":

---

[1] *Octavius*, 23, 2 (CSEL, 2, p. 32, ll. 25 f.).   [2] *Apologia*, II, 10 (Otto, I, p. 226).
[3] *Apologeticus*, XIV, 4 (CSEL, 69, p. 38, ll. 14 f.; *Ad Nationes*, I, 10 (PL, I, 575 A).
[4] *Oratio contra Iulianum*, I, 118 (PG, 35, 657 AB).
[5] *Stromata*, V, 1, 2, 2 (GCS, II, p. 326, l. 24).
[6] *Ad Nationes*, I, 10 (PL, I, 575 B).

> . . . *a quo ceu fonte perenni*
> *vatum Pieriis ora rigantur aquis.*[1]

The more openly the Church Fathers accepted the Neoplatonic principles of Homeric interpretation—and this attitude became more marked as the third century progressed—the more enthusiastic became their encomia on the prince of poets. Jerome says somewhere that the song of Homer, the blind and wise, is a proof that men can only create mature and imperishable works in old age and that such works are the inexpressibly sweet swan-song of a lofty spirit: "*Nescio quid cygneum et solito dulcius vicina morte cecinit.*"[2] Strange how the word "sweet" continually rises to the lips of the Latin Fathers when they speak of Homer, despite the fact that they no longer knew the loveliness of the original Greek and were only acquainted with the poet through inadequate translations. "*Dulcissime vanus* – most sweetly useless", Augustine calls his Homer in the charming recollections of his schooldays,[3] and we are already familiar with Boethius' phrase, "Homer's honey-streaming mouth."[4]

The fact is that the Fathers had a most perceptive sense for that which so impressed their pagan contemporary, Macrobius, in Homer, namely his "greatness and simplicity, the never-failing readiness of his speech and his quiet majesty – *magnitudinem et simplicitatem et praesentiam orationis et tacitam maiestatem*".[5] There is thus nothing ridiculous—rather is there something touching—in the words used by Jerome at the beginning of his biography of the monk Hilarion when he says that even a Homer would have envied him such material for the writing of a heroic life.[6]

In an equally famous passage of ancient Christian biography, namely in Sulpicius Severus' life of St Martin, the ghost of Homer is conjured up in words which appear to have become conventional at the time. Homer himself, he says, were he to rise from the grave, as the saying is, could not worthily write such a life as

---

[1] *Elegiarum*, V, 27f. See also Manilius, *Astronomica*, V, 8f.: "*Cuius ex ore profusos omnis posteritas latices in carmina duxit.*"

[2] *Epistola*, 52, 3 *ad Nepotianum* (CSEL, 54, p. 418, ll. 6f.).

[3] *Confessions*, I, 14 (CSEL, 33, p. 20, l. 17).

[4] *Philosophiae Consolatio*, V, 2, Metrum (CSEL, 67, p. 110).

[5] *Saturnalia*, V, 13.   [6] *Vita Hilarionis*, Prologue (PL. 23, 29 A).

this.[1] For Cassiodorus the *Odyssey* is "Homer's noble song",[2] and so it remains from now onwards. In the Carolingian theologians Homer—though always along with Virgil—is the most exalted among the poet-prophets the *"summus vatum"* or *"princeps vatum"*[3]—as he was later in Dante. And Raphael was surely right when in his sketch for the picture of Parnassus that was to be painted for the Vatican he put the Greek and the Christian next to each other, the one blind, the other sighted.

And now to the actual hero of the *Odyssey*. Here we find that the judgement of antiquity and of Christian writers followed the same lines as in their appreciations of Homer—and so we approach closer to the question of the symbolism surrounding the story of Odysseus and the Sirens.

Plato in his *Republic* refers ironically to Odysseus as σοφώτατος (the very wise man), and expresses indignation over his ruses and lusts, conduct designed to corrupt the morals of youth.[4]

In the Homeric allegories of later Hellenism all this has undergone a radical change. The figure of Odysseus has now become a kind of personification of the art of life, the embodiment of prudent courage and of indomitable fortitude in suffering. Neither Circe nor the Sirens can gain any hold over him. It is in this spirit Horace sang of him:

> . . . *aspera multa*
> *pertulit, adversis rerum immersabilis undis.*[5]
> (He endured many hardships and could
> not be drowned in the waves of adversity.)

For Seneca too Odysseus is the model for all who would master the perils of life, the man who is *"invictus laboribus, contemptor voluntatis, victor omnium terrarum* – unconquered by tribulation, contemptuous of pleasure and the gainer of the whole world".[6]

Christian comment on the figure of Odysseus undergoes almost

---

[1] *Vita Martini*, 26 (CSEL, I, p. 136, ll. 12f.).

[2] *Variarum*, I, 39 (PL, 69, 535 A).

[3] Cf. for example Gottschalk and Wigbord writing to Charlemagne (*Monumenta Germaniae Historica, Poetae Latini*, I, p. 97, l. 54); Sedulius Scottus (*Poetae Lat.*, III, p. 172, ll. 71f.); earlier we find Claudius Claudianus (*M.G.H., Auct. Antiquissimi*, X, p. 300, l. 13).

[4] *Republic*, 390 A.   [5] *Epistolarum*, I, 2, ll. 21f.   [6] *De Constantia Sapientis*, 2.

exactly the same transition. The anonymous author of the *Address to the Hellenes* indulges in much the same kind of mockery as Plato. The Homeric wax with which Odysseus stops the ears of his companions, is, this writer says, "a famous piece of roguery".[1] As we have already seen, Clement of Alexandria saw in Odysseus the prototype of those who only long for the smoke of earthly well-being; the "ancient from Ithaca" is the symbol of man's attachment to the things of this world. Methodius takes a similar view, oddly enough using the identical expression "ancient from Ithaca".[2]

But these few voices soon count for little against the chorus of praise for Odysseus when that figure came to be reinterpreted by later schools of thought. There is a passage in the writings of Clement that has considerable relevance here and is indeed of the utmost importance for the whole history of Christian humanism. In it the writer seeks to defend his own breadth and generosity of mind against the more narrow-minded Christians of the day and his conviction that Greek culture should in no wise be denied a place within the Christian scheme. The incident of Odysseus and the Sirens proves an apt text for his discourse. Certain kinds of petty and hypercritical Christians, he avers, are like the companions of Odysseus who stop their ears with wax in order not to succumb to the sweet peril of the Sirens. Odysseus had been a different kind of man. Knowingly and with his ears open, he had approached the Sirens' isle without yielding to its temptation.

"It seems to me [he writes], that most of those who subscribe to the name of Christian are like the companions of Odysseus; for they approach our doctrine (λόγος) without any sense for a high culture. It is not so much the Sirens that they sail past and put behind them as the rhythms and melodies (of the genius of Greece). They stop their ears by their rejection of learning (ἀμαθία) because they would never find their way home again once they had opened those ears to the wisdom of Greece (ἑλληνικοῖς μαθήμασιν). Yet he who seeks to choose what is serviceable in all that for the

---

[1] *Oratio ad Gentiles*, I (Otto, III, 2, p. 4).
[2] *De Autexusio*, I, 1-4 (GCS, pp. 145f.).

instruction of catechumens—especially since many of these are Greeks (for the earth is the Lord's and the fullness thereof)—should in no wise turn aside from the love of wisdom (φιλομαθία) like a beast without reason. On the contrary he should make a kind of beggar's collection (ἐρανιστέον)—and that on as liberal a scale as he can—of helpful thoughts (from the wisdom of the Greeks). All that we must guard against is that we should dally there and go no further instead of returning home again to the true philosophy."[1]

No one can read these words without feeling that Clement regards heroic Odysseus who "in full knowledge" approaches close to death, as a kind of symbol of that humanist liberalism and receptivity towards the wisdom of Greece which he was so eager to see Christians display, and since he can express this aspiration in terms of the Homeric myth, it is obvious that the epics of the "wisest of poets" provide him with just the kind of "helpful thoughts" to which he had referred.[2] This is a good example of the way in which in the great schools of Athens and Alexandria the later Church Fathers absorbed the Homeric allegories of the Neoplatonists. Basil can tell us something of this:

"I once knew a man [he writes] who had the faculty of really penetrating into the poet's mind. He held that the whole of the poems of Homer were nothing less than a single great hymn in praise of virtue. Thus, by his story of Odysseus among the Phaeacians, my interpreter of Homer declared, the poet seeks to say aloud to mankind, 'Ye men must strive after virtue which swims to land alongside the shipwrecked mariner and makes him who has been washed naked ashore more worthy of honour than the frivolous Phaeacians.'"[3]

---

[1] *Stromata*, VI, 11, 89, 1 (GCS, II, p. 476, ll. 14–25).

[2] Clement uses the pregnant word "ἐρανιστέον" to denote the "bringing together" of helpful thoughts or their "contribution". The word suggests the practice according to which a group of friends would arrange a feast, each friend making a contribution. Gregory of Nazianzus speaks of the "eranos of mutual goodness" (ἔρανος τῆς χρηστότητος) in which men should participate simply because they are men. *Oratio*, XIV, 6 (PG, 35, 864 D).

[3] *Ad Adolescentes*, 4 (PG, 31, 572 BC).

From that time forth Odysseus became the model and personification of wisdom, the "*sapiens Ithacus*", and we can even see this idea at work in a rather naïve piece of popular etymology; for some maintained that the name "Ulixes" was derived from the Greek ὅλων ξένος, which means "a stranger to all things", the theory being that he was so named because "true wisdom stands equally aloof from all the things of this world".[1] Even in the Middle Ages we find Honorius saying: "*Ulixes dicitur sapiens*", meaning, "Ulysses means simply the wise."[2]

We are now in a position to understand the meaning which, thanks to the development of ideas on the part of the Church Fathers, came to be attached to the myth of Odysseus and the Sirens,[3] and once again we shall find how comely a garment they made out of this story to clothe the mystery of the Christian's homeward journey into the light. In this they were assisted by the fact that the tale of the Sirens was something of which they could always assume a knowledge among their audience, for no Homeric myth was more popular. The seductive creatures themselves or a mariner tied to the mast were themes that could be seen on vases, on bowls, on earthenware lamps, cake moulds, gems and on the graves and sarcophagi of late Hellenic times.[4]

Recollections of the story indeed play an interesting part even in the profane thinking of the Church Fathers, in contexts that is to say, that have no kind of theological implication. Thus when Jerome is travelling to distant Bethlehem and passing through the Straits of Messina, the classroom memories of his youth return to him and he thinks of the Sirens and Charybdis. "There I stood", he writes, "and tarried for a moment at the shores of Scylla, the place

---

[1] Fulgentius, *Fabulae secundum Philosophiam moraliter expositae*, II, 8. See further *Realenzyklopädie*, XVII (1937), col. 1910, ll. 18–22.

[2] *Speculum Ecclesiae* (PL, 172, 857 A).

[3] See the present author's work, "Odysseus am Mastbaum" (Odysseus at the Mast) which contains a very complete collation of all the material bearing on the Christian interpretation of the myth of the Sirens. See also G. Weicker, *Der Seelenvogel in der alten Literatur und Kunst* (The Soul as a Bird in Ancient Literature and Art), Leipzig, 1902, pp. 83f.; R. Garucci, *Storia dell'arte cristiana* (History of Christian Art), I, Prato, 1872, pp. 258 ff.; J. Wilpert, *I sarcofagi cristiani antichi* (Ancient Christian Sarcophagi), Rome, 1929–35, pp. 14 ff. of the text.

[4] The most recent confrontation of all the examples in E. Wüst's article in *Realenzyklopädie*, XVII, col. 1974, ll. 60ff.

by which, as I had learned from the ancient fables, Odysseus had passed, that man of many wiles, where the Sirens sang their songs and the insatiable maw of Charybdis yawned."[1]

Even Origen makes use of the myth in his battle with Celsus the Platonist. Celsus had alleged that Christ's utterances had been altogether too much concerned with punishments to come. Mockingly Origen replied: "To flatter and say nothing but what is pleasant to hear is peculiar to the Sirens, and these are surrounded by heaps of dead men's bones."[2] Another reference is to be found in the correspondence between the Neoplatonist rhetorician Libanius and Bishop Basil, a correspondence conducted with true humanist courtesy, in which the myth was made the occasion of a graceful compliment. Libanius writes to the eloquent bishop that listening to him speak had always been an exciting experience and that he had always told his friends: "This man is superior to the daughters of Achelous, for he is as sweetly seductive as they, yet he is wholly harmless."[3] One also thinks of the Church Father Synesius, who on a sea voyage observed one of the rower slaves tied to the mast to prevent him from breaking into the wine jars in the hold. The scene calls up an amused memory of Odysseus tied to the mast.[4] These snapshots out of the ordinary lives of the humanist-trained Church Fathers show us how living a thing was this particular myth. That it should have been the starting-point of a whole luxuriant world of theological symbolism is really not too hard to understand.

Let us then accompany these Church Fathers on a voyage upon the high seas and sail out with them into the glorious blue waters of Greece, over which Paul too had passed in order to fetch the Hellenes home to Christ. Basil once described it in words that were to delight the widely travelled Alexander von Humboldt: "What a beauteous spectacle is presented by the white-foaming sea, when perfect silence encompasses it, when only a gentle wind ruffles its waves, when it shines dark purple or deep

---

[1] *Apologia adversus libros Rufini*, 22 (PL, 23, 473 B).

[2] *Adversus Celsum*, II, 76 (GCS, I, p. 198, l. 20).

[3] Libanius to Basil, preserved in the letters of Basil as *Epistula*, 354 (PG, 32, 1089 B). On the Sirens as daughters of Achelous, cf. G. Weicker, *Der Seelenvogel*, pp. 46f.

[4] *Epistula*, 32 (PG, 66, 1361 B).

blue."[1] The Roman Ambrose, too, could be moved by this as he preached to the Christians of Milan in his mellifluous Latin about "the glorious great ships whose white sails shine upon the blue waters, like doves which soar in the distance over the sea".[2]

Here and now we will speak of that voyage which is our life, the voyage which is the Christian's most glorious but most mortally perilous venture. After that I shall deal with "the temptations of the Sirens" which lure homeward-faring man to his destruction. Finally I shall speak of "the mast which is the cross" to which the everlasting Odysseus ties himself, coming face to face with death in full knowledge of his peril yet bound unto a freedom that ensures him a victorious return to the haven of eternal rest.

I THE VOYAGE OF LIFE

If we are to get the feel of the tension-laden dialectic that lies within the Christian interpretation of this story about Odysseus and the Sirens, and if we are to do this with the nerves and the senses of a Greek, we must first try and enter into the feelings of the man of antiquity concerning sea voyages as such; for to him they were at one and the same time a deadly peril and a challenge to his daring and to his zest for adventure.[3]

To go to sea, to embark upon the great deeps with a piece of wood of wholly contemptible size was to dice with death, to become a direct neighbour to Hades; this alone made it easy for the sea voyage to become a symbol of our journey through life which ends in the haven of death. "Tomorrow the terrible voyage will be over," says the Greek sailor in an epigram of Antiphilus, "yet hardly has he said the words ere the sea becomes a Hades and swallows him. Therefore never say 'tomorrow'."[4]

[1] *Hexaemeron*, IV, 6 (PG, 29, 92 B); A. von Humboldt, *Kosmos*, II, Stuttgart, 1857, p. 29.

[2] *Exameron*, IV, 6, 26 (CSEL, 32, 1, p. 133, ll. 14–17).

[3] Detailed references in H. Rahner, "Das Meer der Welt" (The Sea of the World), in *Zeitschrift für katholische Theologie*, 66 (1942), pp. 91 ff.; "Das Schiff aus Holz", *ibid.*, 66 (1942), pp. 206 ff. and 67 (1943), pp. 2 ff.

[4] *Epigram* 17 (*Anthologia Palatina*, VII, 630). Cf. K. Müller, *Die Epigramme des Antiphilos von Byzanz*, Berlin, 1935, pp. 68 f.

That man should ever have dared to set out upon the devilish sea on a hollowed-out piece of wood appeared to antiquity so incomprehensible that it visualized the beginnings of seafaring as having originated in some strange mythical event, in an atmosphere both horrific and vaguely supernatural. Both the tale of the Argonauts[1] and the Isis mysteries[2] set the beginnings of the seafarer's art back into the dawn of time when the gods were still close at hand. This deadly feat of daring appeared to be something in the nature of original sin, in the blessed days of man's beginning, it was felt, people remained safely on land.[3] "An evil thing is the sea," says Alciphron in his *Epistolae Piscatoriae*, "and seafaring a very madness of daring."[4] Now man cannot escape the consequences of that ancient and daring sin, he is compelled to gamble with death; "careless of his life and careless of his soul" he goes to sea. Thus, a fragment of the elegies of Solon;[5] while in the maxims of Secundus the Silent, that were widely quoted right up to the Middle Ages, we are asked: "What is a seafarer?" and told, "He is one who is only a guest upon the firm land of earth, a deserter of his native soil, a battler against storms, a gladiator of the sea. Ever uncertain of salvation, a neighbour of death, and yet the sea's lover – θανάτου γείτων, θαλάσσης ἐραστής."[6] Only the breadth of the planks of his vessel separates him from death. Juvenal too brings out all these ideas in one of his satires—the nearness to death, the hollowed piece of wood to which man entrusts himself, only removed from death by the breadth of four fingers or at most seven, if the planking is as thick as that:

> . . . *dolato*
> *confisus ligno, digitis a morte remotus*
> *quattuor aut septem, si sit latissima taeda.*[7]

---

[1] Cf. Manilius, *Astronomica*, V, 32–56.

[2] Hyginus, *Fabulae*, 277; *Anthologia Latina*, 743 (Riese, II, p. 215).

[3] Synesius on one occasion uses some verses of Aratus to describe this "Saturnian" age; *De Providentia*, II, 5 (PG, 66, 1273 AB). Other documentation in H. Rahner, *Zeitschrift für katholische Theologie*, 66 (1942), p. 91.

[4] *Epistolae Piscatoriae*, I, 3 (Schepers, pp. 4f.).

[5] *Anthologia Lyrica Graeca*, I, Leipzig, 1936, p. 26.

[6] *Sententiae*, 18 (Mullach, *Fragmenta Philosoph. Graec.*, I, p. 515). Cf. also *ibid.*, 17: the ship is "a house without foundations, an ever-open grave, a seafaring death".

[7] *Satires*, XII, 57–9. Cf. also *ibid.*, XIV, 288f.

Indeed a number of authors voice much the same sentiment, and we know from a saying of Anarchis how vividly the seafarer of those days felt the proximity of death. "Four fingers width should the planking be. By that much is the mariner removed from death."[1] "'Ολίγον διὰ ξύλον 'Αιδ' ἐρύκει," says Aratus. "He keeps Hades at bay by a thin piece of wood."[2] It is in much the same fashion that Gregory of Nazianzus describes the dreadful disaster experienced by him in youth, the shipwreck between Rhodes and Alexandria: this "naked sea" is the ruin of men, and the seafarer must always be ready for gruesome and "corpse-cold" death.[3]

Yet, as has been said, to cross the sea is also a most glorious feat of daring. "Immeasurably daring is he who for the first time crossed the faithless waves on frail wood"—so runs one of the choruses from Seneca's *Medea*:

> *Audax nimium qui freta prius*
> *rate tam fragili perfida rupit.*[4]

We can thus understand why Antiphilus calls man's first ship Τόλμα[5] (*Daring*), and Greek ship-names in general testify to this sense of peril and peril gloriously overcome *Salvation, Grace, Lightbringer, Victorious, Blessed* were some of the names he gave to his good ships—and also *Saviour, Providence, Help* and *Peace*.[6]

The invention of the ship is one of the very great achievements of the human spirit; it is something that seems, as it were, to have the character of divinity about it, and there is just a hint of this in some words of Posidonius, an echo of which is still to be heard in the writings of the Christian Nemesius: "Who can tell what high rank should be given to man? He crosses the sea, he penetrates

[1] In Diogenes Laertius I, 103 (Hicks, I, p. 108, ll. 1 f.).

[2] *Phainomena*, 298.

[3] *Carmina*, I, 2, 31, verses 1–4 (PG, 37, 910f.). Cf. also *Oratio*, XVIII, 31 (PG, 35, 1024f.); *Carmina*, II, 1, 1, verses 307–19 (PG, 37, 993f.); *Carmina*, II, 1, 11, verses 124–74 (PG, 37, 1037–41).

[4] *Medea*, 301f. Cf. also Horace, *Carmina*, I, 3, 25f. and the Paetus song of Propertius, *Eleg.*, III, 7, in which the same mood is expressed.

[5] *Epigram* 23 (*Anthologia Palatina*, IX, 29).

[6] See the names in F. Miltner, *Realenzyklopädie*, Supplement V (1931), col. 946.

the heavens with his thought and understands the movement of the stars."[1] He thus is the victor over death.

In the same exalted humanist mood of the true Greek Eusebius writes of the seaman's daring. "Alone of all the creatures of the earth", he cries, "man entrusts his life to a small piece of a wooden tree, guides his ship over the back of the sea, entrusts himself to the depths of the watery element, and looking up to heaven, to the helmsman of the world, thrusts back death who stands by his side."[2] Well then may the seaman be proud of his well-built ships which sail the seas that have now become his home. Well may he take pleasure in the mere sight of them, as does Seneca when he describes the *bona navis* in the marts of Ostia or Puteoli.[3] Gregory of Nazianzus conveys that same feeling of delight, and though already seeing the ship symbolically as the "ship of life", he can still be carried away by a typically Greek pride:

"Let not thy ship be painted in pleasing colours. Let no harlot's comeliness be carried on the strong back of the sea. Nay, a good ship should be firmly nailed and seaworthy and soundly fashioned by its builder. Only such a ship as this will truly cleave the waves."[4]

Life and death were truly united in the seagoing vessel of the Greeks and this made the ship peculiarly fitted to be the symbol of man's life—as was the sea itself over which it sailed. "The sea ruins one man," cries Gregory, "while another spreads his shining sails and as he passes over the water looks down smiling at this great grave of the shipwrecked."[5] A little Greek poem—a rather poignantly melancholy one—brings out the symbolism of ship and sea even more forcefully:

"Voyage of life, so full of danger! victims of the storms, we all too often suffer shipwreck in more pitiful fashion than the pilot

---

[1] *De Natura Hominis*, I, 75 (PG, 40, 533 A). Cf. on this W. Jaeger, *Nemesios von Emesa*, Berlin, 1914, p. 134.

[2] *Syrian Theophany*, I, 54 (GCS, Eusebius, III, 2, p. 66, ll. 25–31).

[3] *Epistula ad Lucilium*, 76, 13.

[4] *Carmina*, I, 2, 9, verses 141–4 (PG, 37, 678f.).

[5] *Carmina*, I, 2, 1, verses 684f. (PG, 37, 574 A); II, 1, 23 (PG, 37, 1282 A).

on the water. Tyche sits at the rudder and guides our frail craft, as our hazardous journey proceeds over the waves of the sea. This one has favourable winds, that one is buffeted by gales, but at length the haven of night receives the seafarer under the earth."[1]

Now the idea of this mortally perilous voyage which nevertheless led back to the haven of home, found a kind of visible embodiment for the men of antiquity, and even for the Christians of antiquity, in the homeward-faring Odysseus, who, between Hades and Ithaca, must submit to his proving at the Sirens' isle. The symbolic potentialities of this myth with whose Christian interpretation we are here primarily concerned, were already familiar to the later Greek allegorists. "Whosoever passes over this present life as upon a ship", says the anonymous author of the *Voyages of Odysseus*, "is surrounded by the Sirens of temptation."[2]

It is, however, the dialectical juxtaposition of death and life, of peril and victory that is the truly fruitful element for Christian symbolism and it was this element that was developed and turned into a means of conveying the hidden truths of the Church and of showing forth the action of grace upon the soul.

For the Fathers it was the Church itself that was the ship of life here below, which in immense peril and yet in victorious security traverses the sea of the world, nor could the ancient Christian conceive of a better symbol of the Church than one of those majestic ships which he could see in Alexandria, in Ostia or Ephesus, from one of which St Paul, landing at Puteoli after deadly danger sustained, brought the joyous tidings from the East.[3] No symbol was capable of conveying in a simpler or more convincing manner the fact that the Church finds herself between two eternal situations. She is even now, in the midst of the daemonic sea of the world, the only thing to which a man may cling and be certain of his salvation, and her ultimate entry into the haven of eternity is assured. At the same time, however, she is still in peril, she is still on her

[1] *Anthologia Palatina*, X, 65. See also Seneca, *Marcia*, 17, where life is symbolized by a sea voyage to Syracuse.
[2] *Epitomos Diegesis*, 12 (*Mythographi Graeci*, ed. Westermann, p. 352).
[3] He reached Puteoli in an Alexandrine ship dedicated to Castor and Pollux, Acts 28. 11-13.

uncompleted voyage, still committed to her daring venture, and her goal, the attainment of which she hopes for in trembling, is still beyond the waves—there where on the heavenly shore the moles stretch out like a mother's protecting arms. Death and life unite with one another in this nautical fortune of the Church.

Hippolytus was the first of the Fathers to express the symbolism of this idea with something like a painter's sureness of touch. As a ship leaves no trace upon the changing waters, so also the Church which traverses this world after the manner of a ship; for she has left behind her on the shore all hopes that she otherwise might have had, and has pledged her life in advance to the heavens.[1] And yet this same Church is already herself a kind of landing-place, a haven of salvation vouchsafed to us in advance, certain amid all uncertainties.[2] This was a thought that inspired Ambrose. "The Church", he writes, "is a haven of salvation and with out-stretched arms she calls imperilled seafarers into the bosom of her rest (*in gremium tranquillitatis*), for she shows herself as the landing-place in which we may put our trust."[3] He who boards this ship leaves all old customs and conventions, indulgences of habit and weak-willed inclinations behind him; he is in a spiritual sense what Secundus called the seaman—a "deserter from the land".

Clement has summarized this leaving behind of heathen things which the Christian must give up when he embarks on his home-ward voyage in a most meaningful phrase. He calls it the aban-donment of the συνήθεια, the old habits,[4] and it is precisely in this that the glorious risk-taking, the stubborn courage of the Christian Odysseus is to be found; for he seeks to win the new life by a mortally dangerous contempt of the old. "If in a sea voyage, the departure from our accustomed way has the effect of filling us with a peculiar seductive joy, even though it may bring about our destruction and is full of peril, should we not, in embarking upon our voyage through life, joyfully leave behind our old and cus-tomary godless ways so full of evil and passion, and turn towards

---

[1] *Fragment 3, on Proverbs 30. 19* (GCS, I, 2, p. 165).
[2] *De Benedictionibus Iacob*, 20 (*Texte und Untersuchungen*, 38), Leipzig, 1912, p. 35, ll. 11–18.
[3] *De Patriarchis*, 5, 27 (CSEL, 32, 2, p. 140, ll. 5–7).
[4] Cf. Rahner, *Zeitschrift für katholische Theologie*, 65 (1941), pp. 136f.

the truth?"[1] Danger there must be and the embarking in the ship
of the Church represents a decision by which life is reorientated;
it is a death, it is making death our neighbour. Without encounter-
ing waves and storms, says Origen,[2] the ship of the Church can
never reach the shore of its homeland. Shipwreck is always a
possibility, and the Fathers, taking their cue from a phrase of St
Paul's[3] and using all the vivid imagery which their own
experiences at sea had inspired, made shipwreck the subject
of a profoundly meaningful system of symbolism. Only he who
remains within the protective planks, within the maternal bosom
of that ship which is the Church, is certain of the issue. "Oh, thou
most beauteous danger," cries Basil of Seleucia, "that teachest us
where alone to let go the anchor of salvation! Thou stormy sea
on which alone we learn the meaning of faith!"[4]

Yet this ship of the Church, surrounded by so much mortal
peril, is also a fortunate ship. It is the very concept of life, of
victory, of safe arrival in harbour. Yes indeed; for even in the
dream symbolism current in extra-Christian circles, εὐπλοεῖν, to
make a good voyage, was a presage of good fortune to come, and
to dream of a ship with swelling sails was accounted a most
encouraging omen.[5] These νῆες οὐριοδρομοῦσαι mentioned by
Artemidorus remind us once again of Christian symbolism.

Christians, according to Clement, were fond of wearing a signet
ring with a ship engraved upon it voyaging to heaven and with
the Holy Spirit filling its sails.[6] That was their ship. "Εὔπλοια-
Good voyage!", was what the seamen of those days called to each
other. We find them upon an earthenware lamp in the form of the

---

[1] *Protrepticus*, X, 89, 2 (GCS, I, p. 66, ll. 12–15).

[2] *Commentary on Matthew*, 11 (GCS, X, p. 43, ll. 8f.).

[3] I Timothy 1. 19: "Some . . . have made shipwreck concerning the faith – περὶ τὴν
πίστιν ἐναυάγησαν."

[4] *Oratio*, 22 (PG, 85, 267 A; 269 A). Here is a description, in the almost Baroque style
that often marked late Greek rhetoric, of the good ship of the Church sailing through the
roaring waves with rattling sails and groaning ropes.

[5] Artemidorus, *Oneirocritica*, II, 23 (Hercher, pp. 115f.) and II, 68 (pp. 159f.). Note also
the rhetorical use of these symbols in Dion Chrysostom, *Oratio*, 63 (Budé, II, p. 184,
ll. 15–25).

[6] *Paedagogus*, III, 11, 59, 2 (GCS, I, p. 270, ll. 7f.). The MSS. here read either
οὐρανοδρομοῦσα–travelling towards heaven, or οὐριοδρομοῦσα–sailing with a
favourable wind.

holy ship of Isis[1] and yet this was only a rough anticipation of all that the Christian read into the voyage of the ship of the Church. The ancient prayers for a prosperous voyage continue to be uttered by him, but with new meaning, and in the works of the Fathers there are lofty and moving prayers for a prosperous voyage to eternity.[2]

Some allusion was already made to these things—or at any rate to something pretty directly connected with them—when the mystery of baptism was under discussion. On that occasion I tried to show how the rebirth out of the motherly womb of the Church was an anticipation of the "arrival in harbour", a returning homeward to the motherly womb of the everlasting port, and this in its turn is the Christian interpretation of a Greek concept encountered in Empedocles who imagined the immense dialectic of the world elements resolved in the final homecoming into the "perfect harbour of love".[3] Birth in baptism is also a homecoming into harbour and into the motherly womb of truth, "into the sure port of mild and kindly mother Church"[4]—or as Pseudo-Clement expresses it, "into the haven of peace, into the peaceful city of the great king".[5] But what is concealed in the mystery of baptism and what takes place there under mystical forms, will at the end of days become the final reality and then will be fully revealed whether our voyage in the ship of the Church spelt death or life, victory or ruin.

---

[1] Illustration in Haas-Leipoldt, *Bilderatlas zur Religionsgeschichte: Die Religionen in der Umwelt des Urchristentums* (Picture Atlas of the History of Religion: The Religions Surrounding Primitive Christianity), Leipzig, 1926, No. 119; W. Wittmann, *Das Isisbuch des Apuleius* (Apuleius' Book of Isis), Stuttgart, 1938, pp. 47f. Further material in F. G. Welcker, *Alte Denkmäler*, III: *Griechische Vasengemälde* (Ancient Monuments: Greek Vase Paintings), Göttingen, 1851, pp. 248–54; A. Alföldi, *A Festival of Isis in Rome under the Christian Emperors of the IVth Century* (Dissertationes Pannonicae, II, 7), Budapest, 1937, pp. 44–55.

[2] For an ancient *euploia* prayer see *Anthologia Palatina*, IX, 9; Christian prayers in Gregory of Nyssa (PG, 44, 1013 D; 1016 A); in Victricius of Rouen (PL, 20, 444 B). A *euploia* prayer of classical simplicity, still in use in the Roman liturgy, asks for a fair voyage for the ship of the Church: "*Exaudi nos, Domine Deus noster, et Ecclesiam tuam inter mundi turbines fluctuantem clementi gubernatione moderare, ut tranquillo cursu portum perpetuae securitatis inveniat*–Hear us, O Lord our God and guide thy Church, which is afloat among the storms of the world, with gentle helmsman's art, so that after a tranquil voyage she may make the port of everlasting safety."

[3] *Fragment* 98 (Diels, I, 3rd edition, p. 257).

[4] Vincent of Lerins, *Commonitorium*, 20 (PL, 50, 666 B).

[5] Pseudo-Clement, *Epistula ad Iacobum*, 13 (PG, 2, 49 A).

When they entered harbour the sailors of those days joyously adorned the bows of their ship with wreaths. Virgil has an allusion to the practice:

> *Cum iam portum tetigere carinae*
> *Puppibus et laeti nautae imposuere coronas.*[1]

The Church Fathers did not hesitate to seize on this practice and apply it to the return in triumph of their own great ship. How gloriously the joy of the ancient seafarers re-echoes in the words of Ambrose: "What more splendid thing can there be than a ship? If it does but make port, then there are no defeated. There are only wreaths for ships that make a landfall in safety. Then the palm waves in token of a prosperous journey. Victory is no more than the guerdon of return."[2] Paulinus of Nola, touching on the same theme, rises to superb heights of prose as he describes the arrival of the ship of the Church at the end of days:

> "*Christus quasi naves suarum onerarias opum deducat in portum salutis, victricibus fluctuum puppibus virides laetus imponat coronas.*"[3]

(May Christ bring them like vessels laden with his riches into the port of salvation, may he also joyfully place green garlands on these prows that have proved victors over the waves.)

Yet one more word about this homeward-faring ship, the ship that is in deadly peril yet most gloriously makes harbour. What has here been predicated of the Church can also apply to the individual soul. Here the symbolism of antiquity once more repeats the old pattern and says of "the little ship of the soul" much the same as it has said of the ship of the Church, using the same Greek imagery. The soul of the individual is also like the homeward-faring Odysseus. It too is in peril between Hades and Ithaca and desires with an immense longing to return to its home, to peace, to the haven, "to escape from the turbulence of the members of its body"—that is how we find the matter put in the life of Plotinus —"and with the strong breeze of the spirit to reach the sands of the peaceful shore".[4]

[1] *Georgics*, I, 303 f.
[2] *Exameron*, V, 11, 34 (CSEL, 32, 1, p. 168, ll. 11-14).
[3] *Epistola XXIII*, 30 (CSEL, 29, p. 187, ll. 23-5).
[4] Porphyry, *Vita Plotini*, 22.

The Christian gnostics phrase their aspirations in very similar terms, as we can see from Clement. "They save themselves from the surging waves of the world," he writes, "reach port and escape to safety; in the depths of their heart they hide unspeakable secrets."[1] Yet before this can be attained there must be the cleansing process of passing through mortal peril, for between Hades and Ithaca, between hell, which has been escaped in the birth that is baptism, and heaven which is not yet reached, there dwell the demons. If victory is to be achieved, two things are needed, a ship of wood and the wisdom of Odysseus.

"No one [so run the words of a Greek ascetic],[2] even in this world of visible things, can traverse the sea and pass over it by his own unaided strength; he needs for that a light and agile craft that is fashioned out of wood and can for this reason alone pass over the water. Similarly the soul cannot traverse of its own power the bitter sea of sin and the perilous abyss of the evil powers and passions."

These evil powers are symbolized by the Sirens and it is only the wood of the mast that can save the wise soul, if it is wise enough, like Odysseus, freely to consent to be bound to it.

This thought brings us sufficiently close to the Christian interpretation of the myth to see it in greater detail. The ship of the Church and the smaller vessel of the soul must pass through this ordeal of peril, and it is here that the decision is made for life or death. I will illustrate my meaning by a few examples. Actually, however, the full depth of the symbolism will not be apparent until we have gone more closely into the real character of the Sirens and the role played by the mystical mast of Odysseus' ship.

The Church and the soul are sea-voyagers to heaven who have severed all the links that bound them to the land. They have left behind them the συνήθεια, by which we understand, among other things, all the dark powers from which baptism has enabled them

---

[1] *Quis Dives Salvetur*, 36, 1 (GCS, III, p. 183, ll. 19–22).

[2] Pseudo-Macarius, *Homiliae Spirituales*, 44, 6 (PG, 34, 781 D).

to escape. Their going to God is—to quote Clement's pregnant phrase—a καλὸς κίνδυνος, a comely or honourable risk,[1] since it is the risk that the heavenly voyage must necessarily entail. For the demons whom they have left behind still threaten and these demons meet the Odysseus of the soul in the form of the Sirens. How vividly this thought was present to the Christian mind can be seen from the following words of Clement, words which he must be conceived as uttering to his faithful companions in the ship of the Church:

"Let us flee from our old way of life as from the Sirens of which the story tells! For it throttles a man, it leads him away from truth, it robs him of his very life. It is a snare, an abyss, a trap, a devouring pestilence. For it [the old way of life] is indeed an island of doom heaped full of dead men's bones. And upon it there sits the comely harlot, lust, delighting men with the music of this world and crying: 'Come hither, Odysseus, rich in fame, come, thou pride of the Achaeans, steer thy ship to the shore and hearken to the voice of a god.'[2]

"She praises thee, thou seafarer, she speaks of thy high repute; but let her feast on those who are already dead. A wind from heaven comes to thy aid! Sail past lust! Sail away from the songs. They will bring thee death."[3]

The Christian then, is a seafarer; he is indeed a heavenly Odysseus, and the supernatural power that helps him master the deadly peril of the Sirens is the *Pneuma* from heaven. Knowingly he approaches near to death, and knowingly he remains the victor. Later we shall see more clearly from what the mastering knowledge derives, for it is the knowledge of him who is tied to the mast but is still free, the knowledge of the "pneumatic" man who is filled with the Spirit.

In a not altogether dissimilar fashion the myth reappears in its

---

[1] *Protrepticus*, X, 93, 2 (GCS, I, pp. 68–71). Here the word is used in connexion with another set of images, namely military ones—it is "a glorious risk to desert from Satan in order to join the battle array of God". The sense however is the same as in the more nautical types of symbolism.

[2] *Odyssey*, XII, 184f.

[3] *Protrepticus*, XII, 12, 118, 1–4 (GCS, I, p. 83, ll. 8–24).

Christian form in the pages of Methodius, though here the reference to the Christian mystery which it clothes is more pointed:

"As the Greek myth tells us, the ancient of Ithaca desired to hear the voice of the Sirens, because it was of unbridled sweetness; but he passed Sicily by, tied to the mast, and had his companions' ears stopped with wax, not because he grudged their hearing these voices or because he found it a pleasure to be bound, but rather because the end and purpose of that song was death for all who heard it. I myself am no listener to such songs, nor do I desire to hear the Sirens' voices, for their singing is as a singing of death. Rather do I pray to receive an ear for a divine voice, and the more often I hear such a voice, the more mightily rises my longing to hear it anew. I will not be conquered by the unbridled lusts of that other kind of singing; let me rather be instructed in the divine mysteries. For I would attain my end which is not death but everlasting salvation."[1]

Here the dialectical opposites of life and death stand clearly and visibly over against one another. Songs of death and songs of the mysteries, ruin and salvation—and between them stands man who makes the decision, or rather, as is here already more clearly indicated, surrenders to the divine voice, as his sail is filled with the divine *Pneuma*. So we have the same situation that was treated of in the chapters on the healing of souls and, as there, the situation is expressed in scenes from mythology. The situation, of course, is that of man standing between heaven and hell, between mud and the stars, but now it is clothed in the nautical metaphors of the heavenly *Odyssey*, in the imagery so familiar to the Greeks of the voyage of life. Some Greek verses in the *Anthologia Palatina* which were written by a Christian, give to all this a highly dramatic expression:

> The foul fiend excites in us
> The loathsome flood of sensual lust.
> He whips the sea into a storm
> And the little ship which is our soul

---

[1] *De Autexusio*, I, 1–3 (GCS, p. 145, l. 3 to p. 146, l. 6).

Threatens to founder under the weight of waters
And to sink in the eddying waves.
O Christ, my rest,
That dost mightily command wind and waves,
Lead thou me to the sure haven
And drown the enemy of my soul.[1]

We see then once again that if the ship of the Church is to return victorious and decked with garlands to a safe haven, it must first sustain the ordeal of demonic peril. "We are sailing with all speed back to our homeland," cries Jerome, "and so we must turn deaf ears to the death-bringing songs of the Sirens as we pass them on our way."[2]

2 THE TEMPTATION OF THE SIRENS

The mythical dialectic that lies in the conception of life's journey as a sea voyage appears even more heavily charged when we examine the character of the Sirens. These creatures too are both of heaven and of hell. And the saving knowledge which enables Odysseus to approach close to death is his ability to distinguish between darkness and light, between the beauty and the ruin which these seductive spirits seem able to bring. Classical scholars have long since examined exhaustively the origin and successive reinterpretations of this most ancient Greek myth.[3] However, the manner of its survival into Christian times and the character it took on there, have as yet only been lightly touched upon. I propose, therefore, to describe the main lines of the interpretation to which it was subjected, and this will, incidentally, give us a deeper understanding of the mystery of Ulysses' mast with which I have later to deal.

The task is a necessary one, for even in the works of Christian archaeology—and I include here the monumental work of Wilpert on ancient Christian sarcophagi—what has been said concerning the myth of the Sirens is utterly insufficient for our present

---

[1] *Anthologia Palatina*, I, 14 (118).

[2] *Capitulationes libri Iosue, Praefatio* (PL, 28, 464 B).

[3] In addition to G. Weicker, *Der Seelenvogel*, see the more recent work of F. Zwicker, *Realenzyklopädie*, III A, 1 (1927), col. 288–308.

purpose; it does not at all enable us to understand the interesting way in which this myth came to be reinterpreted by Christian thought.

In Patristic literature the Sirens appear in a twofold form and this corresponds to the twofold form of the deadly peril which in his heavenward journey Odysseus must sustain; for the Sirens are symbols both of deadly lust and of deadly knowledge. But the well-nigh self-contradictory character of this attribute is no more than a continuation of something that had been alive in the Greek myth from the most ancient times. Without a knowledge of it, it would be impossible for us to understand the symbolism of the Fathers of the Church.

Etymologically the Greek Σειρῆνες means entanglers or binders, and the Sirens were originally—this was most certainly in pre-Grecian times—vampire-like creatures who lived on the blood of the dead. Thanks to the form given them by Homer, but even more to Hesiod and Alcman, and most of all to the burlesques of Attic comedy, these grisly bird-like spectres became, as it were, beautified and were given a somewhat milder character. But the original significance was never forgotten and Homer sings of piles of bones that lie heaped around them "white bones with the skin tightening upon them".[1] Tertullian can still speak of the Sirens' "bloody mouths"[2] and Hippolytus calls them "cruel and evil beasts".[3] Even into Hellenistic times they remained figures of the grave and decorated sarcophagi and burial vaults. Yet, thanks to this transfiguration by Homer, one feature of these essentially chthonic creatures comes more and more into prominence and it is a feature that scarcely accords with their original cruel form: it is that their "entangling" character begins to be interpreted in an erotic sense; a seductive quality is now ascribed to their singing and to their form. The Sirens turn into bewitchingly beautiful women, whose bird-like claws—which, incidentally Homer does not mention—are the only things left to indicate their true nature.

We are here faced by the intriguing circumstance that it is their

[1] *Odyssey*, XII, 46.
[2] *Apologeticus*, VII, 5 (CSEL, 69, p. 19, ll. 1f.).
[3] *Elenchus*, VII, 13, 1 (GCS, III, p. 190, l. 27).

power of enticement that makes the Sirens so deadly. Danger and enticement are part of the same thing, even as birdsong and claw are part of the bird. Though death-bringing, the Sirens are sweet. In Martial's words they are "the happy pain of seamen, their enchanting death, their cruel delight".[1] Even in Homer they are "filled with divinity" though their song is a witches' song. They are at one and the same time of heaven and of hell.

This dual nature of the Sirens is made particularly clear in Plato. These heavenly beings intone the music of the spheres in the world to come—a mythical image which found a noble echo in the piety of later antiquity.[2] The Sirens ultimately thus become angels who help the soul in its ascent to God. An eloquent fragment of Euripides has been preserved for us by Clement of Alexandria:

"And now golden wings are laid upon my back and the sweet soles of the Sirens. I rise up into the heights of the aether to become the companion of Zeus."[3]

Yet for Plato the Sirens are also the dark beings of the underworld, whom Pluto fetters to Hades "with sweet words".[4] What the ordinary Greek thought of the bewitching power of their song is made clear by the words of Alcibiades in the *Symposium*. He seeks to get away from the voice of Socrates, which lays bare the innermost depths of his soul, "by force, if necessary, holding his ears as before the Sirens".[5] One also thinks of the passage in the *Phaedrus* where Socrates compares the entrancing song of the cicadas to that of the Sirens and says: "Come, let us escape from their magic like sailors 'giving the Sirens a wide berth'."[6] And yet this song is also the song of Hades, the song of the dark beings whom Euripides called "the virgin daughters of the chthonic world".[7]

In the allegories of Hellenistic times, especially in Alexandria, it is the erotic element that tends to be particularly emphasized. This

---

[1] *Epigrams*, III, 64.

[2] *Republic*, 617 B. Cf. Plutarch, *Quaestiones Convivales*, IX, 14, 6; Macrobius, *In Somnium Scipionis*, II, 3, 1; cf. also *Realenzyklopädie*, III A, 1, col. 298, ll. 14–30.

[3] *Fragmentum incertum* 911; Clement, *Stromata*, IV, 26, 172, 1 (GCS, II, p. 324, ll. 19–24).

[4] *Cratylus*, 403 D.　　　[5] *Symposium*, 216 A.　　　[6] *Phaedrus*, 259 A.

[7] *Helen*, 168 f. Cf. also *Fragment* 777.

occurs in the context of that moralizing interpretation of Homer
with which we are already familiar. The Sirens turn into courtesans who tempt the incautious to their ruin with subtly exciting
songs. This is delightfully conveyed in the figure of a dancing
Siren from Memphis, and even better in a sarcophagus statue from
Hellenistic Egypt; in the latter the expression of the eyes which is
somehow both sophisticated and demure, is quite unmistakably
reminiscent of certain courtesans of the Rococo.[1] Heraclitus,
following this Alexandrian tradition simply treats the Sirens as
ἑταῖραι εὐπρεπεῖς – comely harlots,[2] and from then onwards this
was the conception that prevailed. The Neoplatonic allegories
simply turn the chthonic Sirens of *Cratylus* into symbols of
worldly desire and sensual pleasure, through which the spirit
remains fettered "by sweet words" to the Hades of the things of
earth.[3]

Yet from the earliest times the Sirens had also been thought of
as beings filled with divine knowledge, and for Christian thought
this became a feature of equal importance. This belief in the knowledge possessed by the Sirens, was, I repeat, very ancient, and
Homer is doing no more than recall a very old piece of folk-lore
when he makes the Sirens sing: "For we know all things; we
know what was suffered on the fields of Troy by the will of the
gods, both by the Trojans and the Danai, and all else that happens
upon the nourishing earth."[4] Whosoever hearkens to their song
is said to go forth "wiser in knowledge".

This aspect of the Sirens—we have here something conceived
in the true spirit of the fairy tale—was not forgotten in the centuries that followed. Ovid[5] speaks of the *"doctae sirenes"*, the
"knowing" or "learned" Sirens, and there is a reference to this in
Cicero who treats the subject allegorically.[6] In the later period of
antiquity people went so far as to apply the term "Siren" to a man
who had great learning or even an easy flow of words. Both

---

[1] Illustrations in Weicker, *Der Seelenvogel*, pp. 180f. Illustrations 90 and 91.
[2] *De Incredibilibus*, 14.
[3] Proclus, *Comment. in Platonis Cratylum*, 157; *In Rempubl.*, 34, 10.
[4] *Odyssey*, XII, 189–91.
[5] *Metamorph.*, V, 535.
[6] *De Finibus*, V, 49.

Homer and Pindar are referred to as Sirens and among the Byzantine humanists the expression was treated as a compliment.[1]

Sensual pleasure and knowledge—these are the Sirens' two gifts to the seafarer and both are mentioned in the song wherewith in Homer the Sirens seek to tempt their victims: "Rich in delight and wiser in knowledge he will depart." But both gifts bring death. The Christian who "in full knowledge" approaches near to death, knows that both pleasure and knowledge can be demonic.

Now when we examine the way in which Christian interpretation of the Siren symbolism developed, we find a process at work which we had already noted in the cases of the mandrake and the willow. The reason why the symbolism developed around these figures continued for so long a period of time to be a living influence was that, when reading the Scriptures in his own tongue, the Greek Christian could find certain words there which acted as entry ports through which the imagery of profane mythology merged with the Christian interpretation of the Bible.

The Alexandrine translators who produced the Septuagint found six places in the ancient Hebrew books where there was mention of mysterious beasts referred to as *tannîm* and *benôt ya'anâh*, terms which mean literally "jackals" or "hen ostriches". They render these words by the Greek Σειρῆνες (Sirens). What inspired this gross but most interesting mistranslation in the minds of these Hellenistic translators is a mystery which has hitherto remained unsolved. The result, however, is plain enough: for over a thousand years Greek Christians read the words "Sirens" in the passages concerned, and the association of ideas connected with these mythical beings, so universally familiar in the folk-lore of antiquity, was sufficiently strong to arouse in the Christian Greek much the same horror that these deadly creatures had inspired in pagan forerunners and contemporaries.

I propose to examine certain passages of Scripture, and in doing so to use a translation that follows the Greek wording which here differs sharply from the Latin one of Jerome; for with one exception all these passages in Jerome avoid the Greek mistranslation,

---

[1] Cf. *Anthologia Palatina*, IX, 184; XIV, 102; Synesius, *Epist.*, 138 (PG, 66, 1529 A); Manuel Philes, *Carmina*, XI, 1 (Martini, p. 21).

so that the Bible scarcely brought the Roman Christian into direct contact with the Siren myth at all.

In the Book of Job, the central character, utterly forsaken by God, utters his heart-breaking lament over his own spiritual loneliness:

> I am a brother to sirens
> and a companion of ostriches.
> My skin is black and falleth from me
> and my bones are burned with heat.[1]

Obviously sirens are here mysterious creatures of the desert, into which the man who had been forsaken by God feels himself to have been thrust. This is even clearer in the wonderful verses of Isaiah in which the eerie loneliness of Babylon is depicted after its conquest by the Medes:

> Now beasts make their homes there
> and an empty echo is heard in the houses.
> Sirens have their habitation there
> and demons dance.
> Ass-centaurs dwell there
> and hedgehogs breed in the halls.[2]

The last verse is retranslated by Jerome: "And howls answer each other through the halls and sirens dwell in the temples of pleasure—*Et sirenes in delubris voluptatis*". This is the only passage in which the Latin Christian heard of Sirens in his Bible, and Jerome promptly proceeds to give his own commentary on the passage in which he describes the demonic character of these beings, doing so wholly in the spirit of classical mythology: "By sweet and yet death-bringing song (*dulci et mortifero carmine*) they snatch the souls into the abyss so that with the raging of the ship-wreck they may be devoured by dogs and wolves."[3]

[1] Job, 30. 29–30: ἀδελφὸς γέγονα σειρήνων.
[2] Isaiah 13. 21, 22: καὶ ἀναπαύσονται ἐκεῖ σειρῆνες.
[3] *Comment. in Isaiam* (PL, 24, 216 B). By "wolves and dogs" Jerome here understands the dogs of Scylla, as indeed he later expressly declares (PL, 24, 432 C). Augustine also speaks in the same symbolic connexion of the dogs of the sea (PL, 39, 1885 CD). The allusion is always to "soul-devouring dogs" exactly as in the case of mandrake symbolism. For further references to the Christian symbolism of the dogs of Scylla, see H. Rahner, *Zeitschrift für katholische Theologie*, 66 (1942), p. 116.

In a very similar vein Isaiah describes deserted Edom:

> Thorns grow up in their cities
> and in their strong places.
> It will be a dwelling-place for sirens
> and a fold for ostriches.[1]

We have the same thing when Jeremiah says in the "Sword Song" concerning the Chaldeans of Babylon: "False images shall appear upon these islands and the daughters of the sirens shall dwell there",[2] or when Micah says of idolatrous Samaria: "She will mourn and lament and go about naked and without a garment and making a howling like the jackals and a mourning like the daughters of the sirens."[3] There is thus something particularly impressive for the Greek in the words of Isaiah when he breaks out into jubilation over the coming of the Messianic age when the terrible desert of the deserted of God will be caused to blossom anew from the stream of living water:

> Behold I will do a new thing;
> now it shall become visible:
> I will even make a way in the wilderness
> and rivers in the desert.
> Then shall the beasts of the field praise me
> the sirens and the daughters of the ostriches,
> because I give waters in the wilderness.[4]

Such were the siren symbols with which the Greek Christian could re-acquaint himself from his Bible, and there was little left here of the Sirens of Homer. The sirens of Holy Scripture are nocturnal, demonic bird figures that live in the desert, and it is interesting to note how such a writer as Cyril of Alexandria conceives the sirens to be a kind of night-owl, while the exegetes who follow him identify them with the kingfisher, halcyon, or again with owls, and this because of the latter's melancholy song.[5]

---

[1] Isaiah, 34. 13: καὶ ἔσται ἔπαυλις σειρήνων.
[2] Jeremiah, 50. 39 (LXX, 27. 39): θυγατέρες σειρήνων.
[3] Micah 1. 8: πένθος ὡς θυγατέρων σειρήνων. [4] Isaiah 43. 20.
[5] Cyril, *Comment. in Isaiam* (PG, 70, 908 D; 748 A; 364 D). Cf. also Olympiodorus, *In Beatum Job* (PG, 93, 317 D); Procopius of Gaza (PG, 87, 2, 2090 A; 2396 A); Theophylactus (PG, 126, 1064 C).

Yet there is still one connecting link with Homer: for the Biblical sirens are nocturnal and demonic beings, and it was held—wholly in the spirit of the original myth—that the purpose of Scripture was in this case to express the fact that these God-forsaken places had been delivered over to the power of the demons. "It is certain demons, loathsome and savage spirits" that live there, says Eusebius, and immediately he remembers the Greek myth: "For the Greeks say that the Sirens are sweet-singing but deceptive creatures."[1] And in another place: "With their lusts and with their demonic songs (ᾄσμασι δαιμονικοῖς) they lead men's souls astray, as is described in the works of the poets."[2] Even Cyril, who, as we saw, tends to prefer an objective interpretation as of a natural animal, is too much of a Greek wholly to escape from the memory of his poets. In his commentary on Micah he writes: "The Greeks and those who follow them give the name 'Siren' to spirits who are able to sing most sweetly and so, as by magic, get those who hear them into their power."[3] And he interprets the whole passage of Satan and his demon hosts. Such views were part of the exegetic tradition of Alexandria. Even Origen already treats the Sirens as πονηρὰ πνεύματα, or evil spirits, and expressly states that the "pagan myth" tells us of these things.[4]

Thus the Bible provided the classical conception of the Sirens with a means of survival into Christianity. Indeed the Bible and Homer may be said to unite in introducing into patristic theology this twofold figure of the Siren with her twin characteristics of seductiveness and knowledge.

Actually we encounter the idea of the all-knowing Siren at the very beginning of this Christian symbolism. The Sirens become the personification and embodiment of "knowledge", which means primarily the learning and wisdom of Greece, and what the Christian's attitude was to be to this was something about which he had, sooner or later, to make up his mind. We can now see how important for the whole history of Christian humanism was the

[1] *Comment. in Isaiam*, 13, 21 (PG, 24, 189 D).
[2] *Ibid.*, 43, 20 (PG, 24, 400 D).
[3] *Comment. in Michaeam*, 1, 10 (PG, 71, 653 D; 656 A).
[4] *Fragment* 96 "*on Lamentations*", 4, 3 (GCS, III, p. 270, ll. 9–14).

attitude of Clement—to which some reference has already been made—on the question of the right relation of faith and knowledge. You will recollect how he opposed Odysseus who "in full knowledge" sailed by close to the Sirens, to the more small-minded type of Christian in the Church. The true gnostic can quietly dally among the good things of Greece, being secure in the power of his faith. But he also possesses the power of discrimination, and Clement expresses this in the words of the ancient saying of Pythagoras: "One should account the Muses sweeter than the Sirens – *Μούσας Σειρήνων ἡδίους ἡγεῖσθαι.*"[1]

By this, he says, Pythagoras wishes to show us that knowledge should be sought after but not as a means of satisfying our sensual appetites. Of this Odysseus is the great example. Only few are strong enough for such freedom, "But it is sufficient that a single one should have sailed by past the Sirens."[2]

Somewhat later Theodoret in a sermon was also to make use of this saying of Pythagoras. In this he declared that the Sirens stood for pretty and glib speeches while the Muses represented the naked beauty of the truth – *γυμνὸν τῆς ἀληθείας κάλλος.*[3] Clement defends the "noble risk" of the faithful who, certain of their faith, dare to make from the poetry of Greece an *eranos* of helpful thoughts for those whom they are instructing in Christian doctrine. Yet this kind of thing tends to be confined to "Odysseus alone", that means to the exceptional few. "The majority are as frightened of Greek philosophy as children are frightened of bogies who, they think, will run away with them."[4]

However, such humanistic liberalism was far from universal, and Clement himself does not deny the danger involved when those who have not attained the necessary degree of Christian illumination hearken too assiduously to the Sirens of Greek wisdom, and the happy phrase about the "sweet soles of the Sirens" which he found in Euripides inspired him to say: "But I pray that the *Pneuma* of Christ may lend me wings for the flight to my

---

[1] *Stromata*, I, 10, 48, 6 (GCS, II, p. 32, ll. 8f.).
[2] *Ibid.*, (p. 32, l. 10): *Σειρῆνας δὲ παραπλεύσας εἷς ἀρκεῖ.*
[3] *Graecarum Affectionum Curatio, Oratio*, VIII, 1 (PG, 83, 1008 A).
[4] *Stromata*, VI, 10, 80, 5 (GCS, II, p. 472, ll. 1-3): *καθάπερ οἱ παῖδες τὰ μορμολυκεῖα.*

Jerusalem",[1] and he warned against the danger of tarrying wantonly and imprudently in the neighbourhood of danger, since this may impede our return to the homeland where the true wisdom alone is loved. The naked beauty of truth is attained only when one has passed beyond the domain of all Greek imagery.

Thus Christians started off by seeing in the Sirens that "know all things", a symbol of the danger that threatened the faith from the allurements of pagan wisdom. In the very century in which Clement wrote we find in the *Address to the Hellenes* a sort of blustering rejection of all that was Greek; it was a rejection of their smooth-tongued fables, it was a rejection *in toto* of all Greek "Sirens", and Plato and Aristotle were accounted as being among the latter. As a protection against these dangers the Christian needs a prudent and virtuous perspicacity, ἀγαθὴ φρόνησις. "No one who is capable of prudent discrimination will prefer the fine phrases of these two philosophers to the salvation of his soul. No, he will rather, like the mariners in the old story, stop his ears with wax and so escape from the sweet peril of the Sirens that threatens to ensnare him."[2]

Again, as late as the early sixth century we find Zacharias the rhetorician declaring that the Christian theologians sing less seductively than Plato and the other sages of Greece, "who imitate the Sirens of Homer with the sensual sweetness of their song and so enchant the ears of those who are willing to listen to them. I for my part can only accord high praise to that hero of Ithaca who thanks to his prudent discrimination overcame the Sirens' wiles."[3] These are strange words for so late an age. Yet even then men had not put such views wholly out of their minds and the last words of dying Neoplatonism still had the power of bewitching noble spirits. Small wonder then that, as we know not only from Basil but from Cyril writing in the fifth century, the Sirens should, above all else, have symbolized the culture of pagan Hellas.[4]

[1] *Stromata*, IV, 26, 172, 2 (GCS, II, p. 324, ll. 24f.).

[2] *Cohortatio ad Gentiles*, 36 (Otto, III, 2, pp. 116f.).

[3] *De Opificio Mundi* (PG, 85, 1037 A; 1073 B).

[4] Basil, *Ad Adulescentes*, 2 (PG, 31, 586 D; 569 A). *Epistulae*, I, 1 (PG, 32, 221 A); Cyril, *Comment. in Isaiam* (PG, 70, 908 A).

Now a further stage is to be noted in the development of the "knowledge-harbouring Sirens" as the *Odyssey*'s imagery begins to be applied to the purely internal problem of heresy. The earliest example is to be found in Hippolytus, and, as in the Clementine defence of humanism, Odysseus, who "in full knowledge approached close to death", is held up as the model of conduct. The prudent hero, tied of his own free choice to the mast —I shall dwell on this last aspect of the matter later—is the exemplar of the spiritually mature Christian who concerns himself with the doctrines of the heretics without endangering his soul, hearing but not following. But this is not for simpler souls, to whom Hippolytus gives the following advice:

"When men hear the doctrines of heretics which are like unto a sea whipped up by storms, they should sail past these rough waters and seek out the quiet haven. For this sea is full of wild beasts and not to be navigated—as is the Sicilian sea of which the legend tells that the mountain of the Sirens is to be found there. Odysseus sailed through it, as the Greek poets tell, dealing in most cunning fashion with these loathsome, cruel beasts. These Sirens indeed were beings filled with the most hideous savagery towards all who passed that way, though by the sweetness of their song they deceived the seafarers and tempted them by the enchantment of this singing to draw near. Since Odysseus knew this full well, he stopped the ears of his companions with wax. . . . My counsel then to those who would concern themselves with such doctrines is that, having regard to their weakness, they should stuff up their ears and in this fashion sail through the teachings of heretics."[1]

Only to the strong and the wise then is it vouchsafed to listen to the heretics without peril to the soul.

For the moment, however, I am merely concerned to point out that the idea of the Sirens is equated with false doctrine, and such equation was only possible because the Homeric image of the Sirens as "knowers of all things" was still alive in men's minds. It was thus not difficult to make the Siren the symbol of those who

[1] *Elenchus*, VII, 13, 1–3 (GCS, III, pp. 190f.).

attack the faith under the profession of esoteric knowledge or superior intellectual power.

For over a thousand years the notion of the heretical Siren remained popular, this being chiefly due to the work known as *Physiologus*,[1] and there is no doubt that Jerome is referring to this piece of writing which originated in Palestine, when, commenting on the passage in Micah already quoted, he says: "They will intone a song of mourning like the daughters of the sirens; for the songs of heretics can be sweet indeed and they deceive the peoples with pleasant sounds. No man can sail past their song unless he stops his ears and becomes like one deaf."[2]

The Christian then must survive the perils of false doctrine or he will never reach the haven of heaven; between Hades and Ithaca there lurk the demons, and, at bottom, it was this that was implied by their words when they spoke of the Greeks and other teachers of false doctrine as the dread all-knowing Sirens. For the Sirens are in fact symbols of Satan and his demon host; their song, as the *Address to the Hellenes* points out, is but an imitation of that first deceit of man which was perpetrated by the devil himself.[3] "Our opponent and adversary is the devil aided by his demons," says Methodius in the *Symposium*; "that is why we must rouse ourselves and soar upward, that is why we must flee the arts and temptations of their fair words, which have only outwardly the brilliance of virtue and wisdom—more so indeed than Homer's Sirens."[4]

All that the Greek Christian read in Holy Scripture of the terrible and demonically bewitched places where the Sirens dwelt became for him the essential image of diabolical power. It was that power that on his voyage through life whipped up the waves in the storms of heresy or smoothed the waters for the seductions of lust. Thus the myth became for the Christian an expression of

---

[1] *Physiologus*, 13 (Lauchert, pp. 245f.). The latest critical edition of the *Physiologus*, that of F. Sbordone, Florence-Milan, 1936, contains on pp. 51 ff., the most complete commentary to date, though somewhat confused in its arrangement, of the Church Fathers on the Siren myth.

[2] *Comment. in Michaeam*, I, 1 (PL, 25, 1158 C). The heresy of Jovinian is a "Siren's song": *Adv. Iovinianum*, I, 4 (PL, 23, 25 B).

[3] *Cohortatio*, 36 (Otto, III, 2, p. 118, ll. 3f.).

[4] *Symposium*, VIII, 1 (GCS, p. 81, ll. 16f.).

the belief he so passionately held, the belief that while he was on his journey to the port of eternity, he was in the throes of a decision, the issues of which were life or death. True, he sailed in the good ship of the Church, but a "shipwreck of the faith" was still possible, for the all-knowing Sirens still threatened. We can now understand a passage in the commentary on Isaiah by an anonymous Greek: "Whosoever, in the words of the apostle, hearkens to the fables of heretics with itching ears, must be looked upon as one caught by the Sirens, for he no longer has any thought of the return to his true homeland."[1]

As time goes on, however, the idea of the Siren as a seducer to lust begins to assume the ascendancy over the other image, that of the "all-knowing" Siren, and this is as true of Christian thought as of any other. Indeed the reason for this development was none other than the dependence of Patristic allegory on contemporary Hellenistic ideas of myth interpretation, which, particularly in Alexandria—as we have already seen—elaborated the theme of the "harlot-siren". Even in Clement, despite all her wisdom, the Siren is primarily a pretty little strumpet (πορνίδιον ὡραῖον), the symbol of delight (ἡδονή).[2] This is also true of Hippolytus, and it is interesting to note how, despite the stress he lays on the "all-knowing" Siren as the symbol of heresy, he directly combines with it this other idea. The Christian, because of his weakness, "should sail through the doctrines of heretics with his ears stuffed up, nor should he hearken to anything at all that, like the Siren's sweet song, could easily excite delight (ἡδονή)".[3] No doubt he wants to drive home by this that the heresies of that day, namely the doctrines of the Gnostics against whom Hippolytus' book the *Refutation of All Heresies* had been directed, were, among other things, a danger to morals. Thus in the figure of the Sirens the twin aspects of Greek Gnosticism were combined—its esoteric "knowledge" and the lax morality which made all things permissible to the illuminate.

It is not till the fourth century that the figure of the Siren assumes a meaning that is entirely unequivocal, and this corresponds

[1] Pseudo-Basil, *Commentary on Isaiah*, 276 (PG, 30, 604 C).
[2] *Protrepticus*, XII, 118, 2 (GCS, I, p. 83, l. 16).
[3] *Elenchus*, VII, 13, 3 (GCS, III, p. 191, l. 8).

to the changing circumstances and attitudes of the Church from the third century onward. The violent argument with pagan culture and the counter-attack against the Gnostic threat begin to come to an end. Instead, the Church is faced with the moral problem of worldliness and this becomes increasingly acute with the conversion of the masses. Of all this the change in the significance attached to the Siren myth is an excellent gauge. Now it is the Siren that entices with carnal desire against whom the anxious Fathers of the Church issue one warning after another. Here we must also note the manner in which the Biblical siren theme seems gradually to become more effectively present to men's minds as the intellectual life of antiquity ceases to be a living force.

Let us hearken for a moment to that great teacher of morals, Ambrose of Milan, as he unites Homer with the Bible in order to warn his flock of the sweet danger of the Sirens. Thus we find him on one occasion commenting to his congregation in church on the text of Psalm 43. 20, "Thou hast humbled us in the place of affliction". In the middle of his sermon his learned memory suddenly recalls the manner in which the Greek translator Aquilas had rendered the passage, "Thou hast humbled us in the place of the sirens". And Ambrose preaches on in a lively conversational sort of way with echoes of his classical learning continually becoming audible in his talk:

"Excellently does Aquilas' translation show us how the phrase 'place of affliction' should be interpreted, for he says, 'Thou hast humbled us in the place of the sirens. . . .' The Sirens, to which there are two or three references in Holy Scripture, are young maidens—so the pagan story tells—who tempted seafarers by the sweetness of their song—and the seafarers heard it gladly—to run their ship ashore on their coast. And the ancient tale has passed on to posterity that all who were enticed by the seductiveness of their voices suffered shipwreck upon the many rocks of that place.

"The meaning of this tale is this: the Sirens symbolize singing lust and flattery. Just so does the lust of the world (*saeculi voluptas*) delight us with flattering flesh in order to deceive us. Yet as, in the story, it was not the nature of the coast that was to blame for the ruin that occurred, but rather the sweetness of the song—for it was this that caused the rocks on the coast to be forgotten—, so also it is not the flesh as such that is the cause of our ruin, but the power by which the flesh is excited and disturbed."[1]

These words are of some importance for the development of our psychagogy and we have already encountered a similar line of thought in the symbolism of the chaste willow branch. It is not the world as such that is rejected—neither is the flesh, nor marriage, nor the culture of antiquity. All that is condemned is the deliberate misuse of these things, the moral indiscipline of a complete surrender to the things of this world. What Ambrose is endeavouring to say is that the Christian is like Odysseus, free and yet bound, who "in full knowledge" approaches close to death, being possessed of the power of "wise discrimination". What he must avoid is the ever present power in the things of this world to tempt us to our death. For those things are "sweet and deadly" and these are the words applied to them from now on when they are figured under the image of the Sirens.

In a letter to the young emperor Gratian, Ambrose recalls the relevant passage in Jeremiah and instructs the *Imperator* of the world, the lord of the *imperium*, of the Babylon of this world as follows:

"Jeremiah wrote of Babylon that the daughters of the sirens dwelt there. By this he sought to indicate that the temptations of Babylon, that is to say, of the confusion that marks this world, are like those temptations to lust of which the ancient myths had to tell. And we should note well that these temptations enmesh the spirits of young folk with sweet but death-bringing song (*dulcem sed mortiferam cantilenam*) as they pass the rock-infested shores of this earthly life."[2]

It is hardly surprising that the myth of the Sirens should have been a favourite topic of the monks, the despisers of this world.

---

[1] *Explanatio Psalmorum*, 43, 75 (CSEL, 64, p. 315, ll. 6-20).
[2] *De Fide ad Gratianum*, III, 1, 4 (PL, 16, 590 C).

Jerome, grim ascetic that he was, warns a noble lady who was his spiritual daughter, to regard all singing girls with their worldly songs as "death-bringing Sirens"[1] and to ban them from her palace. Treading all worldly pleasures beneath his feet he cries: "What have I to do with these pleasures that are soon ended? What have I to do with the sweet and death-bringing song of the Sirens—*cum hoc dulci et mortifero carmine Sirenarum?*"[2] Sidonius Apollinaris tells of a young man who, because of sexual temptations, stopped his ears with "Odyssean wax" and so escaped the "harlots' arts of the flattering Sirens".[3]

As the culture of antiquity begins to die, the mythical symbol pales into an abstract allegory of sensuality, as it does in Proclus' commentary on Plato, and this is as true of the Christian Fathers as of the rest. The Christian Neoplatonist Synesius remarks somewhere that he had asked wise men who understood the interpretation of myths, as to the meaning of the Sirens and had been told that they signified the lusts of the senses.[4] We see the same thing in the Latin West. There is no more a mythological story, all that is left is an allegory. Paulinus of Nola writes in one of his letters: "The beings which men once imagined and called the Sirens are in reality (*revera*) nothing else than the promptings of lust and the seductions of vice; their outward appearance is enticingly lovely, but it is poison to enjoy them; to do what they invite is ruin and the price of it death."[5]

And yet it is remarkable how even in this shadowy dimness of outline the Sirens go living on—actually for no less than another thousand years. No other creatures out of all that buried life of the Homeric epic are so much a part of the stock in trade of the bookish scholarship of late antiquity. They attained a new flicker of life in the monastic culture of Carolingian times, the culture that so dearly loved to go through classic motions, and of this last there is an enormous mass of evidence. More than that—the Sirens become the very personification of that creature so virtuously

---

[1] *Epistola* 54, 13 (CSEL, 54, p. 479, l. 6).
[2] *Epistola* 22, 18 (CSEL, 54, p. 167, ll. 10–12). See also *Epistola* 82, 5 (CSEL, 55, p. 112, ll. 8f.).
[3] *Epistola* 9, 6 (PL, 58, 620 C).   [4] *Epistola* 145 (PG, 66, 1541 A).
[5] *Epistola* 16, 7 (CSEL, 29, p. 121, ll. 18–22).

shunned by the monks—woman herself. In Leander of Seville[1] they are the ladies of the wicked world whose chatter the zealous nun should avoid, and a good monk from Clairvaux declares that "the song of the Sirens is the gossip of worldly women".[2] A monastic poet has put the whole matter very charmingly and not without wit, in some verses preserved in a Bernese codex. He complains that the memory of the Sirens disturbs him in his work of poetic creation:

> *Sirenae quoque dulces*
> *Blande dira sonantes*
> *Carmen carmine laedunt*
> *Cantu cantibus obstant.*[3]

(The gentle sirens
Pleasantly uttering dreadful things
Disturb my own song with theirs
And hinder my song with a song.)

At the very end of this story the myth of the Homeric Sirens comes yet again to life; it is as though Odysseus, the everlasting seafarer, could not die. The inexhaustible Honorius of Autun brings the myth back to the pulpit in a collection of model sermons, sermons written for the use and comfort of audiences that had come from afar and liked to have some edifying tale of the past interspersed between the eternal verities. And Honorius seems to have been ready enough to oblige them. "For it is fitting", he writes, "that we should also use for the edification of the Church any worthy thing that we have found in the books of the heathen." After which he proceeds as follows:

"The wise men of this world tell that upon an island in the sea there lived three Sirens, who, each in a different manner, made sweet music, the first with her voice, the second with a flute, the third with a lyre. Their appearance was that of women but they had wings and claws like birds. They attracted the attention of all ships that passed that way with the sweetness of their song, so that

---

[1] *Regula*, 1 (PL, 72, 881 D; 882 A).

[2] Pseudo-Bernard, *De Modo Bene Vivendi*, 57 (PL, 184, 1285 D). For the continuance of the Siren myth into the Middle Ages and modern times, see references in H. Rahner, *Zeitschrift für katholische Theologie*, 65 (1941), p. 142, notes 84 and 86.

[3] *Monumenta Germaniae Historica, Poetae Latini*, IV, p. 244, ll. 53–6.

the mariners fell asleep. Then the Sirens came and tore them to pieces and sank their ship in the depths of the sea.

"Once, however, a certain duke, named Ulysses, was constrained to pass that island. He commanded that he should be tied to the mast, but his companions' ears he had stopped with wax. Thus they escaped from this peril without hurt, and even drowned the Sirens in the depths. These, my beloved, are mystical images, even though they have been conceived by the enemies of Christ.

"The sea represents this earthly world, which is always being disturbed by the storms of tribulation. The island stands for the pleasures of this world, and the three Sirens who by their sweet music enchant the mariners and lull them to sleep are the three lusts which make the heart of man soft unto evil and lull us into the sleep of death."[1]

Here, a Carolingian, in simple-hearted fashion and after the manner of one telling a fairy-tale, relates the ancient myth to his Christians, and we shall see later how he concludes this edifying story of Duke Ulysses. Let us note, however, that here the same liberal spirit is still alive which was defended by Clement; Homer's stories are *"mystica"*, even though they have been written by Greeks, the enemies of Christ. Moved by such a spirit as this, and doubtless stimulated by Honorius himself, the nun Herrad of Landsberg includes the Siren myth in the charming pictures of her *Hortus Deliciarum*.[2]

Homer is still very much alive—for indeed Homer is immortal. It is like a beautiful and painful farewell to that lost world of blue seas, the blue seas on which Odysseus sailed, when in the high Middle Ages the great Pope Innocent spoke of the bitter flooding sea of the world and of the temptations of the Sirens who seductively delay us as we sail homeward to the port of Heaven: *"Mundus velut Sirena dulcis navigantes submergit*–The world, like a sweet Siren drowns mariners in the waters."[3]

But Odysseus remains the victor; for he has had himself bound

[1] *Speculum Ecclesiae* (Homily on Septuagesima) (PL, 172, 855 CD).

[2] *Hortus Deliciarum*, ed. Straub-Keller, Strasbourg, 1879–99, volume of illustrations, Plates 57 and 58; text-volume, pp. 43 f.

[3] *Sermo de Sanctis*, 22 (PL, 217, 555 CD); *Sermo de Communibus*, 6 (PL, 217, 617 C).

to the mast and so has saved his freedom. Only after he had been bound could he in full knowledge approach close to death. This is the decisive element in the myth. In the Christian mystery also the decision between life and death is made at the mast of the ship of the soul. For this mast is the cross and the Christian conquers by freely consenting to be bound to it.

3 THE MAST THAT IS THE CROSS

The story of Homeric interpretation, so rich in fancy, has many strange chapters, and among the latter is that on which we now embark; for in it I will endeavour to show how the drama of the myth finds its consummation in that supreme Christian decision which is represented by the cross. What the theory of *hyponoia*, both Hellenistic and Christian, has read into the story of Odysseus' inspired ruse, a story told with such glorious Ionic vividness and colour, is scarcely to be believed; and not everyone who loves the twelfth book of the *Odyssey* will follow it all with feelings of un-mixed pleasure. And yet we must remember that many of those who put these far-fetched interpretations on the beloved myth were Greeks.

The story told by Homer in such concrete terms gradually becomes dim and acquires a mystical vagueness, like a shape seen in the fading light of evening, so that all our straining eyes contrive to see is no more than the simple outlines of human nature, as it is now and as it has always been. Yet we must still admire the power and persistence of these images through the ages and ascribe this to some inherent dynamism of the work. There is no need for us to be more Greek than the Homeric interpreters of dying anti-quity whose true heirs are the Fathers of the Church. In any case, can we be so certain that even the Greeks of classical times did not read a deeper meaning into the myth which they so loved to illustrate on vases and amphorae, than that of the intriguing deeds of a bold seaman? Let us, therefore, boldly set about un-veiling the *mystica* of this mast upon Odysseus' ship.

If in the course of time Christians regarded the mast to which the immortal seafarer was bound, as a symbol of the cross, they were by no means guilty of any forced or arbitrary association of ideas, nor would their pagan predecessors or contemporaries who sailed those same Mediterranean waters in the same kind of ships, ever have accused them of that. The giant mast, crossed at right angles by the yard, of itself suggests the cross to which rightless or foreign criminals were nailed or tied. One could even read in Homer himself how Odysseus, aided by Calypso, had built his famous raft and erected mast and yard upon it:

"On it rose up the mast, crossed by the sail-yard."[1]

The Greek word itself ἐπίκριον which is used in this context indicates that the yard-arm was a piece of wood "fitted across".[2] Go and look at some of the ancient vases which illustrate this myth of Odysseus bound. Perhaps the most perfect example is the red-figure amphora from Vulci which is reproduced in Plate 9. The mast (ἱστός) and the yard-arm (κεραία) make a quite recognizable cross. That the ancients, when they saw a ship with its mast and yard, instinctively thought of a cross is shown in a passage from Festus when he speaks of the linen sailcloths reefed under the yard-arm, exactly as we see them in the Vulci amphora: "*Vela linea in crucem expansa*–The linen sails are stretched out crosswise."[3]

This is made even clearer in the dream book of Artemidorus, a Greek from Daldis in Asia Minor. To dream of a crucifixion, we are there told, means luck for the seafarer; "for both the cross and a ship are made of wood and nails, and the mast of a ship is like a cross".[4] How familiar this comparison was to the ancients is shown by the fact that the first Christian apologists assume a knowledge of it in their readers and feel no need for any explanation. "*Signum sane crucis naturaliter visimus in navi, cum velis tumentibus vehitur*", as Minucius Felix concisely observes: "We have no difficulty in seeing the sign of the cross in a ship when it moves across the water with bellying sails."[5] And in view of all this, it is easy to

---

[1] *Odyssey*, V, 253.

[2] Also in *Odyssey* V, 317, ἐπίκριον is the yard-arm, the piece of wood set crosswise on the ἵκριον. It is also worth noting that at a later stage the wood of the cross was designated by the word "ἵκριον", a relatively rare expression. Cf. Theodoret (PG, 80, 1308 C; 1756 B; PG, 83, 1012 A). Suidas, *Lexicon*, under "ἵκριον".

[3] *De Verborum Significatu* (ed. O. Müller, p. 310, l. 2).

[4] *Oneirocritica*, II, 5 (Hercher, p. 152, l. 6).

[5] *Octavius*, 29, 6–8 (CSEL, 2, p. 43, ll. 10–15).

understand how Tertullian often came to speak of "the cross of the yard-arm".[1] Justin too sees in the mast the symbol of the power that conquers storms at sea. It is, as it were, the ship's triumphant standard. "The sea cannot be crossed," he writes, "unless this sign of victory, which is the mast, remains unharmed upon the ship."[2] The sign of victory, as we know from the plentiful imagery of early Christianity, is the cross.

The symbolism which the Christians of antiquity used to describe their good ship, the Church, now becomes much easier to understand. The mystery of their certain salvation lies in the power of the mast, that is to say in the wood of the cross. I said something of this when I dealt with the "mystery of the cross". Now this leading idea becomes richer in its texture, as the figure of Odysseus tied to the mast inspires a new world of imagery.

I will only take a few examples from the vast treasury of thought on this subject, to which the Greek and Roman Fathers gave expression; but these few examples will serve to make the picture come alive. With a loving sense of detail Hippolytus describes the ship of the Church:

"The sea is the world [he writes] upon which the Church is tossed about as a ship is tossed by storms upon the deep, but still does not founder; for she has on board the tried helmsman Christ. Amidships she carries the sign of victory over death, for she carries the cross of the Lord; and the ladder that leads up to the yard-arm crossbar is the symbol of Christ's passion by which the faithful ascend homeward into heaven."[3]

Ambrose, who learned so much from Hippolytus, and who from his loving observation so admirably describes the ships on the seas of the Roman Empire, develops the picture still further:

"A prosperous voyage awaits those who in their ships embrace the cross as the mast they follow. They are secure and certain of

[1] *Adversus Marcionem*, III, 18 (CSEL, 47, p. 406, ll. 25 f.); *Ad Nationes*, I, 12 (CSEL, 20, p. 82, ll. 3 f.).
[2] *Apologia*, I, 55, 3 (Otto, I, p. 150, ll. 13 f.).
[3] *De Antichristo*, 59 (GCS, I, 2, pp. 39 f.). Cf. a further list of nautical symbols in H. Rahner, "Das Schiff aus Holz": Ship-catalogues in Patristic Literature, in *Zeitschrift für katholische Theologie*, 66 (1942), pp. 198–205.

salvation in the wood of the Lord. They do not suffer their vessel to stray without direction on the waters of the sea, but hurry homeward into the haven of salvation with their course set towards the fulfilment of grace."[1]

This theology of what might almost be called a positively Odyssean love of seafaring released in the Greek Fathers a veritable flood of imagery which they could apply to the Church. Their eyes seem almost bewitched by this mystery of the mast on which the yard-arm makes the cross complete.

"Here is something that we learn from sailors," says Gregory of Nyssa. "They call the piece of wood that crosses the mast and on which the sails are hung, the yard-arm. In it we can see as in a mirror the figure of the cross."[2] It sounds like the roar of the surf of the Ionian sea when the Greek Proclus speaks in the manner of an Asiatic rhetorician of the ship of the Church:

"High rise the waves, but the helmsman is from heaven. Raging the tempests blow, but the ship has the cross amidships. The storms battle furiously against one another, but the keel of the ship is divinely secure. The waters can never reach to heaven. The evil spirit of the wind is powerless against the Holy Spirit. And the ship can never become a wreck since it is steered by life itself."[3]

This indeed is the heavenly *euploia*, the certainty of salvation in the ship of the Church, and salvation is founded on the mast which is the cross. "By this ship we must understand the Church" —so an anonymous Latin writer interprets the mystery—"the Church which sails upon the waters of the world. Temptations which beat on it like whipped-up waves, and the powers of this world foaming around it, seek to hurl this ship upon the rocks. But never will it suffer shipwreck or founder, for before the mast, which is the cross, Christ stands erect."[4]

This image of the ship's mast which is the cross, persists till it finds expression in the simple language of the wise monks who

[1] *Explanatio Psalmorum*, 43, 17 (CSEL, 64, p. 355, ll. 8-16).
[2] *Oratio* 1, *on Christ's Resurrection* (PG, 46, 624 D; 625 A).
[3] *Oratio*, 27, 5 (PG, 65, 813 BC).
[4] Pseudo-Ambrose, *Sermo* 46, 4, 10 (PL, 17, 697 AB).

escaped into the desert from the flooding seas of the world. "We
too should do as the sailors whose ship is caught by a storm. When
we encounter a contrary wind, then we set up the cross to hold
our sails and so safely rescue our little ship from the storms of this
world."[1] Dreadful beasts, which in the myth and in its Christian
versions infest the evil sea, continue to threaten the mariners—
dragons, the barking dogs of Scylla and the bird-like Sirens. "But
whosoever would traverse this billowing ocean in which dwell
beasts without number, let him hold fast to the cross and never
leave it until he reach the longed-for haven of salvation."[2]
Venantius Fortunatus embodied the idea in verse for the Middle
Ages:

"O Christ, steer our souls through these stormy waves by the
cross which is our mast and our sail-bearing yard-arm, until thy
strong hand, after all the storms of the age, lets us ride at anchor
in the port of eternal life."[3]

And the Middle Ages which took such delight in imagery did
not forget the conceit. "The cross is the mast in the ship of the
Church", says the same Honorius who once explained the myth
of Odysseus to his faithful flock; "and because the Church is
guided by this piece of wood, her voyage through the gurgling
seas of this world is safe and calm until she joyfully sails into the
longed-for haven of eternity."[4]

In the eleventh century the *Ezzolied* repeats in German accents
what the Greek Fathers of the Church had said about the mystery
of the Church:

O Crux Salvatoris
dû unser segelgerte bist.
disiu werlt elliu ist daz meri,
himelrîche ist unser heimnot,
dâ sculen wir lenten, gote lob.[5]

[1] *De Vitis Patrum,* V, *Verba Seniorum,* 7, 18 (PL, 73, 896 D).
[2] Pseudo-Augustine, *Sermo* 247, 7 (PL, 39, 2204 A).
[3] *Miscellanea,* VIII, 6 (PL, 88, 276 C).
[4] *Speculum Ecclesiae* (PL, 172, 944 D); *Scala Caeli Maior,* 1 (PL, 172, 1230 C).
[5] *Ezzoleich,* Verses, 395–7; 405 f., in *Kleinere deutsche Gedichte des XI. und XII. Jahrhunderts* (Shorter German Poems of the Eleventh and Twelfth Centuries), ed. by A. Waag, Halle, 1916, pp. 15 f.

(O Cross of Our Saviour,
Thou art our sail-yard;
This world is the sea;
The heavenly kingdom is our home;
There we are to land, praise God.)

We have now tuned the instruments which will accompany the chorus intoned by the Christian interpreters of this myth, the myth of Odysseus tied to the mast. It is to the mystery of Christ crucified, to the saving secret of the "wood" that the Christian binds himself in order to reach his blessed home.

I must now connect up the argument with those ideas which, when dealing with the theme of temptation by the Sirens, I could not yet fully express. The companions of Odysseus are types of human weakness, and it was only a single man who sailed past the Sirens' isle with his ears open to hear, for by divine command this man had been tied to the mast. Let us listen for a little longer to Clement as he gives a Christian meaning to the symbolism of the myth:

"Sail past their music and leave it behind thee, for it will bring about thy death. But if thou wilt, thou canst be the victor over the powers of destruction; tied to the wood, thou art made free of perdition. Thy helmsman will be God's Logos and the Holy Pneuma will waft thee into the port of the heavens.

"Then wilt thou behold my God, wilt be initiated into the holy mysteries and wilt be suffered to enjoy that which is hidden in heaven, that which has been prepared for me, which neither ear hath heard nor the heart of man conceived."[1]

This is not only a profoundly Christian interpretation; it is one which, with all the delicate perceptiveness of the Greek mind, carefully preserves the essential elements of the original myth and its inherent dialectic. The temptation of the Sirens was to a freedom that released the lusts, only to end in bondage and ruin; the victorious freedom of Odysseus derived from the very fact that he was bound to the mast. This truth now becomes a truth in a

[1] *Protrepticus*, XII, 118, 4 (GCS, I, p. 83, ll. 24–30).

Christian context. Most felicitously Clement here plays upon the contrast προσδεδεμένος and λελυμένος; the victory lies in the bonds which are accepted in full freedom of choice. The goal is the mysteries of the heavenly homeland, in the harbour of heaven. It is quite clear from the theological idiom of the primitive Church that the word "wood" in Clement means the cross of the Lord.

There can be no doubt that in his interpretation of the myth Clement was repeating a theme which was already a favourite in the early Church; for Hippolytus follows the line of his thought exactly—and yet he almost certainly does so in complete independence of Clement. We are here at the beginning of the third century—, the period from which we date the earliest archaeological evidence of a Christian interpretation of the Siren myth, and Hippolytus' words form the classical commentary to this. The Christian has Odysseus tied to the mast carved in marble on his sarcophagus, thereby expressing the idea that whosoever holds firmly to the wood of the cross will make the port of salvation, that such a man is indeed one who has returned to his heavenly home, a victor who has bound himself to the standard of the cross. Hippolytus continues the passage to which I have already drawn your attention by distinguishing the "weak" from the strong spirit that overcomes the danger.

"Since Odysseus knew this, he stopped the ears of his companions with wax. As for himself, however, he made them bind him to the mast, and so sailed past the Sirens without being imperilled (ἀκινδύνως) and hearkened to their song. My counsel to those who concern themselves with such things [namely heresies] is either that having regard to their own weakness they sail through the teachings of heretics with stopped up ears and do not listen to things which, like the song of the Sirens, can easily excite to lust, or that, in faithful trust, they have themselves tied to the wood of Christ, so that even though they hear, they may not become confused, but remain standing upright (ἑστηκέναι ὀρθῶς) and rely on the power of that to which they have bound themselves."[1]

[1] *Elenchus*, VII, 13, 2, 3 (GCS, III, p. 191, ll. 3-11).

Two things are now made plainer. Hippolytus explicitly says that Odysseus' mast is the wood of Christ, and he also is quite obviously recalling Homer's line in which Odysseus is made to command his companions to bind him in such a fashion that he "stands firm upright upon the socket of the mast – ὀϱϑὸν ἐν ἱστοπέδῃ". This idea now becomes that of "standing upright in the faith" and especially the orthodox faith, persisting in the true doctrine, despite the seductive songs of the heretics and the lusts of the Gnostics.

I do not think we should be at fault in detecting the memory of Homer's lines in a poem of Gregory of Nazianzus who knew his Greek epics so well. He sings of the stormy voyage of life which can only attain its haven of rest through the power of the mast on which hangs the Crucified.

> Storm threatens the voyage of the soul,
> The blustering winds rage
> And my heart trembles. I cling more firmly to Christ.
> Yet I love him also when the billows have become
> 　　smooth and kindly:
> Christ is mine; for he is steadfast and true to those who
> 　　love him.[1]

Now, in the actual Greek the words for "steadfast to those who love him" are ὃς ἔμπεδός ἐστι ποϑεῦσιν which certainly is an echo of Homer where he tells how Odysseus directs that he should be bound fast ὄφϱ᾽ ἔμπεδον αὐτόϑι μίμνω – so that I may stand fast here. Christ is here the heavenly Odysseus, bound to the wood of the mast, and the same bold thought is expressed by a Latin preacher who says: "Since the Lord Christ suffered himself to be fastened to the wood of the cross, we can sail through the tempting dangers of this world with our ears stopped."[2] Thus Christ is the solitary wise being who, by being bound, has given us freedom— Christ or the Christlike Christian soul. It is not the Platonic mystics who are returning to the homeland of the spirit, says Augustine, though they look towards the blessed coasts with sharp eyes,

---

[1] *Carmina*, II, 1, 1, verses 582-5 (PG, 37, 566 A).
[2] Maximus of Turin, *Homily* 49, (PL, 57, 339 C).

but the humble Christian who clings to the mast of his ship, even though his own eyes are weak.[1] This being tied to the cross is complete freedom of the spirit. "With us there are no Sicilian Sirens and no Odyssean bonds, with us there is only perfect freedom from all bonds whatsoever, a free ear for all who may come." Thus, Methodius.[2] In much the same sense, Ambrose interprets the mythical bonds, pointing to Christian freedom which is so different and so much more free than the freely assumed bonds of Odysseus. "The Greek poet shows us how this wise man sailed past the song of the Sirens, because he was, as it were, fettered by the bonds of his prudence. So difficult was it before the coming of Christ, even to men of strong spirit, to avoid being entrapped by the seductions of outwardly pleasing lust."[3] Yet if Odysseus is implied here to fall short of the perfect model and to have been superseded by Christian wisdom, Ambrose still treats him in his sermons on the Gospel according to St Luke as the man in bonds who is the mythical prototype of the Christian who is a bondman unto freedom. His remarks are not without interest in this present context, for he first offers a courteous apology to his flock for bringing a heathen myth into a discourse from the pulpit. In mitigation of his supposed offence he explicitly refers to the Scripture texts which mention sirens and adds, "And even if the prophet had said nothing of this, no one would have a right to complain!"[4] After that he fairly lets his passion for Homer run away with him. All the myths of the *Odyssey* must here play their part so that Ambrose's audience may be "moved to enchanted admiration of heavenly things". Let us listen to the words of this ancient Christian encomium on Homer:

"If the lotus-eaters by the sweetness of their fruits could cause Ulysses to tarry, when this same Ulysses, as the story tells, had wandered about for ten years after the warfare around Troy and had for ten years been longing for his home—if the gardens of Alcinous could hold him back, if, finally, the Sirens were able to

[1] *De Trinitate*, IV, 15, 20 (PL, 42, 901 D; 902 A); *Tractatus in Ioannem*, II, 2, 3 (PL, 35, 1389f.).
[2] *De Autexusio*, I, 4 (GCS, p. 146, ll. 13-16).
[3] *De Fide ad Gratianum*, III, 1, 4 (PL, 16, 590 C).
[4] *Expositio in Lucam*, IV, 2 (CSEL, 32, 4, p. 139, ll. 14f.).

entangle his heart by their song and would by their temptations have caused him to suffer the infamous shipwreck of lust, had he not stopped the ears of his companions with wax against the sounds of the enchanting song—how much more ought not pious men to be enchanted by heavenly truth! For in heaven there is something more than the juice of sweet berries, there is the bread that came down from heaven. Not only are such things to be seen there as the green gardens of Alcinous—the mysteries of Christ can there be witnessed.

"We should not stop our ears, nay we should open them, in order that we may hear the voice of Christ. For he who hears that voice need fear no shipwreck. Such a man should not, like Ulysses, bind himself to the mast with physical bonds, rather should he with the bonds of the spirit fasten himself to the wood of the cross. Then he will not be cozened by the lures of lust nor will he risk setting the course of his life into the dangerous waters of desire.

"For the poet's fancy painted the picture in this wise: Certain maidens were said to have lived upon a rocky shore. They seduced the seafarers with the sweetness of their voices, so that, because of this delight to the ear, they altered the course of their vessels. Then these poor, beguiled men would find themselves in dangerous shallows by a treacherous shore, so that they suffered sad shipwreck and were devoured by the Sirens.

"All this is but the imagining of poets, having no substance in truth and being nothing but empty fable and smoke. The sea, the voices of the maidens, the coasts and the perilous waters—all these are but things of fancy. And yet what sea is more bottomless than this faithless world, this world so changeable, so full of deep pits, so threatened by unclean spirits? What else do these maidens signify but the enticements of enfeebling lust, which robs the deceived spirit of its strength and makes a woman of it? What signify those dangerous shallows but the reefs that threaten our salvation? For there is no hidden danger so great as that of worldly desire; while it flatters the senses, it breaks into the ship of life and shatters the power of the spirit, as it might be upon the rocks of the flesh."[1]

[1] *Expositio in Lucam*, IV, 2, 3 (p. 139, l. 16 – p. 141, l. 3).

This is unmistakable Ambrose. He is fond of moralizing, but always manages to do so with considerable grace. He weaves into his discourse recollections of his worldly studies and by the nimbleness of his thought contrives to make of the whole a vivid illustration of Christian truth. Yet the essential matter is his grasp of that one aspect of the Homeric myth, which had been apparent from the very beginning to those who interpreted it, namely that victory means being bound to the wood of the cross. The wood is the standard of triumph; here lies the mystery, the immeasurably vast thing concealed beneath simplicity. The Christians of the fourth century who caused the myth of Odysseus to be depicted on their sarcophagi, intended by this to proclaim symbolically the triumph of the cross. The marble coffin of the young Roman Aurelius Romanus which is here reproduced (Plate 10), provides excellent evidence of this.[1] There stands Odysseus at the mast with the great sail-yard making, together with the mast, a pattern in the form of a cross, the sign so reverenced by Christians. The Ithacan wears the tiara-shaped travelling hat which marks him as a travelling foreigner or seafarer—exactly as on the Hellenistic vase paintings. This conventional sign was, according to Pliny,[2] first used by the painter Nicomachus and a chance remark of Jerome shows how familiar it was to Christians. Jerome says that the Jewish high priest wore a tiara "of a kind similar to that which we see Odysseus wearing in paintings".[3] Odysseus is in fact the traveller *par excellence*, and this is why we see his figure on the coffins of men who have begun their voyage to the port of eternity. But the Christian who thus went to his death was one who had "knowledge", and his journey homeward is a victory, for he has bound himself to the wood of the cross. "O man, fear not the loudly roaring waves in the sea of this life," says a Greek sermon, "for the cross is the pattern of a strength which cannot be broken, so that thou mayest nail thy flesh to that unlimited reverence for the Crucified and so with great gain attain the port of rest."[4]

[1] Illustration in J. Wilpert, *I sarcofagi cristiani antichi*, Rome, 1929. Illustration vol. I, Plate XXIV, 7.

[2] *Nat. Hist.*, XXXV, 128. See also *Realenzyklopädie*, XVII (1936), col. 465, ll. 59ff.

[3] *Epistula* 64, 13 (CSEL, 54, p. 599, l. 12).

[4] Germanus of Constantinople, *Homily on the Cross* (PG, 98, 240 C).

With Augustine's friend Paulinus of Nola we reach the time when the original mythical narrative begins to turn into a mere pale allegory. The imagery with which he describes the ship of the Church is confusingly rich, and has indeed, lost the essential simplicity of a true symbol. But here too the myth once more forces itself into the light and the mystery of the mast is here viewed in conjunction with the image of the root of Jesse.

"In this ship the mast is formed by the shoot from the root of Jesse. This tree guides the four-oared vessel of our body. And if we may turn this ancient tale of the poet and apply it to the truth the prophet preaches, we must bind ourselves to this mast with the bonds of freedom and must stop the ears not of our body but of our heart, with faith, not with wax. Then we shall be armed against all the seductions of this world and will be able to sail past the rocks of lust as Odysseus sailed past those of the Sirens."[1]

The true reason why, despite descent into the artifices of a purely intellectual allegory, the myth with its Christian interpretation lived on right into the Middle Ages, is apparent from a sermon that was often read and copied. Maximus of Turin, an imitator of Ambrose and a close follower of his reasoning, was the author of a homily in honour of the Cross of Christ, and in this he exalts the mystery of the wood under the imagery of the Homeric myth. I propose to extract from the moving words of this sermon only those parts that have relevance to the interpretation of the figure of Odysseus bound.

"If, therefore, the story of this Ulysses tells that his binding to the mast made him secure against all danger, how much more loudly must I proclaim that which truly came to pass!—namely that in our own day the mast of the cross saved the whole human race from the danger of death. Since the Lord Christ suffered himself to be fastened to the wood of the cross, we too can sail through the tempting perils of the world with our ears stopped. We are no longer held back by hearkening to earthly things—and such

---

[1] *Epistula* XXIII, 30 (CSEL, 29, p. 186, ll. 19–26).

hearkening might well bring about our ruin—neither do we seek to change our course, set straight for the better life, so as to run on to the rocks of lust. For the mast, which is the cross, enables him who is bound to it, to reach his homeland in safety. Nay more, by its very shadow which gives them strength, it protects the companions who are gathered around it. That after many wanderings the cross really does lead us back to the house of our Father has been made known to us by the Lord himself; for while hanging on the wood of the cross he declared to the thief beside him: 'This day shalt thou be with me in Paradise.' Oh, this thief! Long had he been straying from his true course, long since had he suffered shipwreck and never would he have returned to Paradise, his home, from which the first man had once departed, had he not been bound to the mast of a cross.

"And so we see that the cross is like a mast in the ship of the Church. Amidst the pleasant but deadly shipwrecks of this world this ship alone suffers no harm. Whosoever in this ship suffers himself to be bound to the mast of the cross, need have no more fear of the sweetly flattering tempest of unchaste desire. For it was for this reason that Christ, the Lord, hung upon the cross: that he might save the entire human race from the shipwreck of the world."[1]

We have come to the end, which is also the climax, of this story of the development of the symbolism of Odysseus bound. For none had previously ventured so bold an interpretation as this fifth-century preacher's, none did so after him. Even as, in the poem which I quoted when discussing the mystery of the cross, Christ the crucified was "our Orpheus", so here the Redeemer on the cross is most truly "our Odysseus". And all whom he has saved, beginning with the crucified sinner, are the companions in the Homeric ship of the Church. This, however, can hardly have been possible save at a time when in the pious thoughts of the mass of the people, who had long become Christian, the myth itself had already begun to grow dim. Slowly the Middle Ages begin to rise as the world of Homer sinks into oblivion. Yet wherever a

[1] *Homilia* 49, *de Cruce Domini*, 1 (PL, 57, 339 f.).

later time began to tell of the story of Odysseus and the Sirens, whether in the *scriptoria* of Carolingian days or the pulpits of the early Middle Ages, there we find the same basic forms of theological thought still alive which emboldened the Christians of antiquity to represent Christian truth under the images of Homer's epics—there we find the faith-inspired longing for the "sweet return" to a homeland that is fairer than the land of the Greeks.[1] We can still discern in the Odysseus sermon of medieval Honorius the same lines of interpretation which the myth had received from the greatest among the Fathers.

"Ulysses denotes the wise man. Without peril he sailed past the Sirens; this means that the Christian folk who are the truly wise men, glide safely in the ship of the Church over the waves of this world. For through the fear of God they tie themselves to the mast of the ship which is the cross of Christ, and so they overcome every peril without suffering hurt. Victorious, they enter into the joys of the saints."[2]

In the last of Herrad of Landsberg's pictures of Odysseus, Duke Ulysses stands upright against the mast, where the form of the cross is again plainly discernible, while the Sirens plunge into the sea, exactly as on the vase painting of the fifth century B.C. The tradition has remained unchanged. "*Ad sanctorum gaudia*", says Honorius at the end of his sermon, and the same words appear on the marble sarcophagi in which Christians caused themselves to be laid for their journey as heavenly seafarers to the port of salvation. Odysseus at the cross-shaped mast and yard is a favourite theme in the adornment of these last resting places. When, in the catacombs, we find the vaults decorated with the picture of a ship that with swelling sails makes towards a great lighthouse—often with the words "*In pace*" scribbled beside it—; when the Christians of antiquity depicted the beloved ship of their Church—and their soul—upon gold goblets, upon gems and lamps, —they were thus seeking to express the belief of a generation, bound with the bonds of faith and for that very reason free. They were saying: "We are

[1] See for instance, Aldhelm, *Chartae*, 1 (*Mon. Germ. Hist., Auctores antiquiss.,* XV, p. 508, ll. 8 f.); Dungal Scottus, *Epistola* 6 (*Mon. Germ. Hist., Epistolae,* IV, p. 581, ll. 12 f.).
[2] *Speculum Ecclesiae* (PL, 172, 857 A).

sailing home".[1] From the shores of the next world which the bold voyagers have now reached, believing, dying and putting the present world behind them, they look back upon this earth—and lo! all is transfigured, all becomes a symbol of the truth which no visual image can express. The beloved blue sea of the Greek home-land, the glorious ships, the cross of the mast, the lighthouse in the harbour and the motherly arms of the protecting moles—all suddenly becomes transparent, revealing a truth which is infinitely more perfect and exalted. And with the unfettered freedom of men who have found the truth in Christ, the Greek Christians reach back to the golden treasuries of their Homer and consecrate the poet's myths in the Logos. As a lamp shines, so shines for them the Grecian light, but that light, as Clement says, has been kindled for them by the sun. All this is as the dim glow of dawn or like fantastic shadows—the words are those of Methodius. We are in fact dealing with symbols and prefigurations which challenge us to seek the truth which they contained, a truth clouded and disguised no longer. All that was true and lovely in the world of the Greek mind was spoken and created by God, the God who has now sent his Logos amongst men. And so yet once again we will let Clement recite to us the lofty words of Sophocles:

> Such is God's nature. That I know full well.
> For the wise his divine word is ever full of riddles
> Yet to the weak it teaches much with little.

All symbols are indistinct, says this same Clement, and this is so that our search may be at pains to penetrate the inner meaning of what is cryptic and obscure and so rise upward to where the truth is to be found.

The strength of Christian humanism lies in the following fact—and the symbolic interpretation of the story of Odysseus brings this home most effectively—: Only the man who is in touch with the eternal, who can see the earth as a thing reborn, can recognize it and love it in a manner that befits the true nature of a created being. Only by becoming detached from the world can man

[1] Cf. G. Stuhlfauth, "Das Schiff als Symbol der altchristlichen Kunst" (The Ship as Symbol in Ancient Christian Art), in *Rivista di Archeologia cristiana*, 19 (1942), pp. 111-41.

recognize and embrace the true humanistic values. He alone finds who renounces, and he alone has freedom who is bound. The clear and lovely forms of earthly things only stand revealed by the light that streams through that door which we enter only on our death.

Odysseus awakes in his native land which he has so longed to see, but does not recognize it, and it is Pallas Athene who reveals to him that he has reached his home:

> And delight coursed through the long-suffering Odysseus.
> Joyfully he received the knowledge that Pallas Athene
> spoke of the dear land of his fathers.[1]

Like the Odysseus of the myth, the Christian Odysseus feels a deep delight when he thinks of the homeland that will one day again be his and of its mysteries no man's heart has yet conceived. Yet by the light of eternity all is transfigured for him and he loves all the excellence of man because it is in God. And upon the sarcophagus where his dead body must lie he writes the words of Clement:

Τοῖς λιμέσι οὐρανῶν.

---

[1] *Odyssey*, XIII, 250-2.

EPILOGUE

THE spiritual trail we have followed has reached the summit. From the dark womb of the mysteries we have painfully ascended, by way of the healing of souls, to that sweet home-coming which in holy Homer's mythical scenes enabled us to see the goal which endowed all our upward climbing with divine meaning. Let us now strip the knowledge out of which the Christian interpretation of Greek myths was born, of the bright imagery which surrounded it, let us put aside all the learned references and texts which I had more or less of necessity to introduce, and let us try and touch this thing of which the longing of Greek and Christian humanists sought to lay hold—τὸ γυμνὸν τῆς ἀληθείας κάλλος – the naked beauty of truth.

We can discern three things that we have learnt and they correspond to the three stages of our ascent; all show us in what dire straits we barbarians of today are living, yet they also provide the physic that can aid our recovery.

The first of these pieces of knowledge came to us when we glanced at the mysteries. That which the pious genius of Hellas vaguely guessed at was, ere that genius was utterly dead, brought home by the Church into the light of that divine revelation of which she is the guardian. The Church was "heir to the glories that only slept with open eyes".

Without mystery all religion must wither into barren rationalism. The Church alone has retained the element of mystery: by her sacraments she has consecrated sun, moon, water, bread, wine and oil and also the love of the flesh, nor will it ever be permitted to her to cease teaching mankind that behind the veils of the visible the eternal secrets lie concealed, and that it is only through the word of God which lives on in the Church, that we can recognize the true meaning of earthly things.

Since the West has turned away from the custodian of mystery it has died of the utter sterility of its pure intellectualism. Only

387

those peoples will live on who have suffered themselves to be re-born out of the mysteries' motherly womb. It was the profound grasp of this truth that led Hugo von Hofmannsthal to say: "This wide horizon of the Catholic Church is the only truly magnificent legacy of the past that remains to us of the West. Nothing else is really big enough, and hardly anything else remains. I see the moment coming—indeed it is already here—when all our German humanism of the eighteenth and early nineteenth century will seem like a paradisial episode—but most certainly an episode."[1]

The second piece of knowledge was granted to us under the imagery of the soul-healing flower. The Greek was never wholly a man of this present world, nor was he ever nothing more than a lover of the marble beauty of the body. He knew something of the fundamental law of all true humanity, and Plato, the greatest of the Greeks, saw the truth more clearly than anybody, for he knew that the soul can only be made whole through the divine, since it proceeds from God and is a seeker after him. Never can it become itself from out of itself. It needs a divine message and divine help. For a wing of the spirit has been mysteriously broken, one of the horses that draw the chariot of the soul is demoniacally headed for the abyss—all this can be read in the *Phaedrus*.

The Christian message of the Logos came from heaven to men who already possessed these intimations. That message more than confirmed these intimations by that great wisdom that knew of the devil's work in the fall of man. Yet that glad message also declared that God had been made man and that at the end of days the human body would be made Godlike, and that the dark root of our race would receive thereby a head of divine brightness.

Thus any sublime contempt of the flesh as such was made impossible, and our earthly life was also saved from that yawning emptiness of meaning which is the fertile breeding-ground of all sicknesses of the soul.

Since the West no longer has faith in the divine message and is no longer receptive towards it, and since the man of pure intellect and uninhibited technical achievement has no one but himself to

---

[1] C. J. Burckhardt, *Erinnerungen an Hofmannsthal und Briefe des Dichters* (Reminiscences of Hofmannsthal and Letters of the Poet), Klosterberg Collection, Basle, 1944, pp. 79 f.

speak to, a suppurating disease has spread abroad in the realm of souls. All our intellectual reasoning and all our enlightenment will not get rid of those two facts which seem so unsubstantial and yet are so undeniably present and real—God and the devil. They ever return as devourers of our souls. Only faith can heal us, only a heavenly man is truly of this earth; all others are torso, or hollowed-out root. *Homo* only becomes human in God.

The third piece of knowledge derives its ripeness, like a goodly fruit, out of the two others. He who has been born again out of the mystery and has by faith ensured his salvation, has already returned to the port of eternity. There he already possesses his *statio tranquilla*, his peaceful and secure place. For his birth out of the mystery is in itself the arrival in harbour, and the long and painful process of healing which he must still undergo is, despite all its perils, a voyage of life that is already certain of its landfall; and here lies the wonderful certitude of the Christian which resolves all that is tragic in this uncertain life, for, in truth, all has already ended happily in a new beginning that has all the freshness of youth. And because this is so, the Christian can already gaze backwards as one of the blessed and can see all earthly things transfigured and love them as such. For all the things of this world that we really love, from the willow branch to the orb of the sun, from Homer to Plato, already belong to his "new earth". The whole of creation has become his mystery, and in his ship the history of the human mind has entered on its everlasting surety.

He who is bound to the wood is truly free. He commands the flowers and the stars, Hellas and the world with a Pauline gesture of possession. All things are yours but ye are Christ's and Christ is God's.

This quiet and secure embrace between Hellas and the Church is the most precious fruit of a true humanism. It withered in this West of ours from the moment when it no longer sought its home upon the shore of the world to come. Dante gave superb expression in his Ulisse[1] to this fateful fall of the West into sin. For here we no longer have the home-loving Odysseus of the last books of

---

[1] *Inferno*, XXVI, 55–142; cf. A. Rüegg, *Die Jenseitsvorstellungen von Dante*, II, pp. 108–17: Ulisse.

Homer's epic but an unhappy man whose spirit drives him out of the security of his father's home into the bold and godless venture of mastering the world by his own strength. His end was shipwreck on the magnet mountain which drew him magically towards itself. But the mountain which causes Ulisse to come to grief is also the mountain of Purgatory. Will the shipwrecked West master it and so once more become worthy "to soar upwards towards heaven"? Only, surely, when it has begun to pray with the words of the lofty prayer to the Logos which was written by Clement, the Greek and the Christian,[1] and with which I will conclude this book on Greek myths and Christian mystery:

"Grant, since we hearken to thy word, that we may perfect the likeness to thine image that is within ourselves. Grant that we may live our lives in peace. Let us return to thy city without shipwreck as we voyage through the waves of sin. Rather let us be carried through calm and friendly waters borne along by the breath of the Holy Spirit, the inexpressible Wisdom."

[1] *Paedagogus*, III, 12, 101, 1 (GCS, I, p. 291, ll. 1-6).

INDEX

391